Governance and Resistance in World Politics

Edited by David Armstrong
Theo Farrell and Bice Maiguashca

T0349605

CAMBRIDGE
UNIVERSITY PRESS

PUBLISHED BY THE PRESS SYNDICATE OF THE UNIVERSITY OF CAMBRIDGE
The Pitt Building, Trumpington Street, Cambridge, United Kingdom

CAMBRIDGE UNIVERSITY PRESS
The Edinburgh Building, Cambridge CB2 2RU, UK
40 West 20th Street, New York, NY 10011-4211, USA
477 Williamstown Road, Port Melbourne, VIC 3207, Australia
Ruiz de Alarcón 13, 28104 Madrid, Spain

First published 2003

Printed in the United Kingdom by Henry Ling Ltd at the
Dorset Press, Dorchester, Dorset

A catalogue record for this book is available from the British Library

ISBN 0 521 54699 0 Paperback

Governance and Resistance in World Politics

CONTENTS

David Armstrong is Professor of International Relations in the Department of Politics, University of Exeter.

James Brassett is a research student in the Department of Politics and International Studies at Warwick University.

David Campbell is Professor in the Department of Politics at the University of Newcastle.

Ian Clark is Professor in the Department of International Politics, University of Wales at Aberystwyth.

Alejandro Colás is Lecturer in International Relations at Birkbeck College, London.

Theo Farrell is Senior Lecturer in the Department of Politics, University of Exeter.

Richard Higgott is Professor and Director of the ESRC Centre for the Study of Globalisation and Regionalisation at the University of Warwick.

Michael Kenny is Reader in the Department of Politics at the University of Sheffield.

Bice Maiguashca is Lecturer in the Department of Politics, University of Exeter.

Marianne Marchand is in the Depto de Relaciones Internacionales e Historia Universidad de las Américas-Puebla, Mexico.

Fiona Robinson is Associate Professor in the Political Science Department at Carleton University, Canada.

Mark Rupert is Professor in the Maxwell School of Citizenship and Public Affairs, Syracuse University, US.

Karena Shaw is Assistant Professor in the School of Environmental Studies, University of Victoria, Canada.

FOREWORD

The first four years of the new century have been as multifaceted and unpredictable as any in the previous century. The turn of the 1990s, with the ending of the Cold War and the Gulf War of 1991, represented an extraordinary time of change, not least in terms of the public movements that served to ensure regime change across Eastern Europe, but most of the developments were focused on state behaviour. Since 2000 there has been a far more complex set of international trends, producing a situation with which the developing discipline of International Relations (IR) is struggling to cope.

Around the end of the old century, popular movements against globalisation began developing across the world with a rapidity and an insistence that caught many scholars by surprise. Disruptions of international meetings may have been the visible indicators, not least at the Group of Eight meeting in Genoa in 2001, but they hid a much wider criticism of globalisation. This was particularly significant in its sheer strength in many Third World states if frequently allied in a disorganised manner with diverse movements in the states of the Atlantic community.

Meanwhile, the United States elected a new administration that seemed in many ways to be the embodiment of traditional power politics, taking a singularly unilateralist stance on issues from arms control to climate change, while willing to work cooperatively when clearly in its own interests. A few months into the new Bush administration this approach appeared to be proving successful and it is in this context that the atrocities of 11 September 2001 had such a profound impact, pointing to an inherent vulnerability that was far beyond anything that had been seriously anticipated. The response involved violent regime change in Afghanistan and Iraq, a vigorous 'war on terror' and, indirectly, the temporary abeyance of the anti-globalisation movement.

Four years into the new century, critiques of globalisation have re-emerged with renewed strength, circumstances in Afghanistan and Iraq are deeply problematic, al-Qaeda and its affiliates remain active and transnational problems such as HIV/AIDS and climate change are coming to the fore. Even so, there is little unity of purpose between Western Europe and the United States in responding to these many issues and the end result is a degree of uncertainty that has direct implications for the major schools of study within IR.

This book approaches the problematic of transnational uncertainty from the standpoint of a potential dichotomy between the politics of governance and the politics of resistance. In doing so it brings together scholars from a range of traditions and, more importantly, disciplines, to focus on the manner in which International Relations can offer effective analysis rooted in a strong theoretical base.

In the early twentieth century IR developed through embracing and integrating the perspectives of established disciplines and applying them to a largely state-centred if violent world. In the early twenty-first century, many scholars and practitioners would argue that IR should remember that experience – that it should be more willing to utilise the perspectives and outlooks of diverse disciplines and scholarship if it is to respond to the current global condition with wisdom and even foresight. This book seeks to assist that process.

PAUL ROGERS
Chair, BISA, 2002-2004

Governance and resistance in world politics

Introduction

BICE MAIGUASHCA

Questions

For several decades after International Relations (IR) became a fully-fledged field of study at British and American universities, it worked with a relatively simple conceptualisation of 'politics' as such. In the international context, 'politics' involved an ongoing struggle for power among sovereign states, with war the worst-case outcome of this struggle. Power itself was defined essentially in terms of military and economic 'capabilities'. The fundamental structural condition of international anarchy meant that, in the absence of the kinds of constraints upon conflict that operate within states, only such crude mechanisms as a balance of power, or fragile institutions such as diplomacy or international law, served to impose some degree of order upon the system as a whole. While the Cold War brought an additional, ideological dimension to this struggle for power, in other respects it also simplified it by making it bipolar. Hence although much more was seen to be at stake in this contest than, for example, the nineteenth-century struggle for power in Europe, which gave the Cold War confrontation a zero-sum quality, the nature of the political processes at work was conceptualised in relatively straightforward terms. The 'high politics' of the global strategic contest between the superpowers not only transcended the 'low politics' of issues such as trade, they subsumed and gave a particular shape to numerous lesser conflicts in the Third World, which were frequently characterised as Cold War 'proxies'.

Although a few far-reaching critiques of such perspectives appeared in the 1980s including Richard K. Ashley's 'Poverty of Neorealism' and Robert Cox's 'Social Forces, States and World Orders: Beyond International Relations Theory', the more influential alternative viewpoints to the dominant realist paradigm that appeared in the 1970s and 1980s did relatively little to undermine the fundamental theoretical underpinning of the subject. Notwithstanding their divisions on a variety of different issues, the realists, pluralists and Marxists of the 1980s were arguably bound together by a tacit agreement regarding what constituted politics and the political and, thereby, the core subject matter of their discipline. So while realists defined politics exclusively in terms of the actions of the state, pluralists sought to open up its scope to include all those actors (whether they be NGOs, intergovernmental bodies or individuals) that influenced these state actions. Despite conceptualising the origins and functions of the state in very different terms, Marxists such as

Wallerstein also tended to see international relations as primarily a story of states and markets. Thus, in all cases, politics has been primarily conceptualised as originating from a conflict of *interests* and as involving the actions of states and those of their accomplices or opponents to resolve them under conditions of anarchy. Relatively little attention was paid at this point to developments in political and social theory or indeed to much else that was taking place outside the relatively small community of IR scholars.

The end of the Cold War, combined with the impact of the complex and multi-faceted phenomenon known as 'globalisation' brought about a wide range of fundamental changes in the nature of world politics. One superpower emerged supreme while increasing numbers of states were failing to measure up to the most basic attributes of statehood. Ethnic and religious conflicts (re)appeared that frequently cut across conventional territorial delineations. Similarly, a variety of threats and problems in areas like health, crime, terrorism, drugs, the environment and migration all displayed significant transnational features that made it difficult (if they did not render it absurd) for them to be considered purely within orthodox inter-state boundaries. A neoliberal economic orthodoxy (the Washington Consensus) appeared to be sweeping all before it as the world's major economic organisations sought to impose sweeping financial and political conditions on their clients. At the same time the rapidly growing global financial markets exercised an ever more powerful constraint on the freedom of national governments to pursue economic policies of their choice. National cultures, even in relatively powerful states such as France, were seen as threatened by an all-devouring global culture variously labelled 'modernity', 'capitalism', 'westernisation', or, most simply, 'Americanisation'. The major cities of the richest states came to be seen by some as 'world cities', detached to some degree from their home state and inhabited by some of the world's new nomadic tribes, who included some of the richest individuals (top management personnel from the major transnational corporations and the heads of criminal enterprises) and some of the poorest (asylum seekers, illegal migrants). All this was powered, enabled, speeded up and further complicated by a communications revolution which, amongst other consequences, made it virtually impossible for states to control their citizens' access to information.

Realism, it is true, made relatively few concessions towards accommodating the new world 'disorder' that appeared to be emerging from all these developments. Indeed, by adopting more rigorous rational choice methodologies and assuming more 'scientific' trappings such as greater quantification, its hegemonial position within the discipline, if anything, increased. Others, however, in Karena Shaw's words in this volume, found themselves '... feeling perplexed and anxious about the loss of a clear sense of what politics is, where it happens, what it is about, and what we need to know to understand and engage with it'. An increasing number of disciplinary 'outsiders' including critical theorists, postmodernists and feminists began calling into question the understandings of politics that underpinned most of the more influential theoretical perspectives. Mainstream IR, and in particular realism, was subjected to a barrage of criticisms regarding its reification of the state and state sovereignty, its undeveloped conception of power, its structural deter-minism, its ahistorical reading of state/society relations and its anaemic view of social and political agency. In contrast, these new theoretical contenders talked of 'global civil society', 'hegemony', 'contingency', 'discursive relations' and 'historical structures', as well as the potential power of 'social movements', 'counter-hegemonic blocs' and 'identity politics'. It seemed that an alternative conception of politics and the political was in the making with the shift from 'international relations' to 'world politics' in the mid-1990s. However, the potential of this challenge to prevailing conceptions of the political has yet to be fully realised. While mainstream IR has largely refused to engage with the so-called 'third debate', the new contenders have increasingly become embroiled in abstract discussions about epistemology and ethics, postponing yet again any explicit dialogue about what constitutes the political and politics in our field.

The objective of this Special Issue is to seek to provoke such a dialogue. It does so by suggesting that the contemporary era has given rise to two implicit, but under-theorised conceptions of politics in the field. The first can be conceptualised as the 'politics of governance' and is usually associated with an emerging set of structures and processes, ranging from formal institutions like the WTO or the proposed International Criminal Court to informal market mechanisms, all developing alongside and to some extent in harness with an increasingly directive role played by the major Western powers, especially the United States. Supporters of these processes see them as serving to bring some degree of order and regulation to international politics, particularly in the context of globalisation. In theoretical terms, global governance, conceived as a complex array of systemic constraints that shapes the actions of states, challenges the notion of international anarchy at the heart of realist formulations of international politics, and raises a number of questions about the authority and legitimacy of the state and international institutions, the role of norms and norm-making, the possibility of democratic accountability, the nature of power and the meaning of citizenship, to name but a few. Given this list, it is not surprising that the notion of 'global governance' and the issues connected with it have become a subject of interest for political theorists and sociologists as well as IR scholars.[1]

The second and far less theorised conception of politics in the field can be characterised as the 'politics of resistance'. If international governance is associated with a 'politics from above' and with order and the efficient maintenance and reproduction of a hegemonic system, the 'politics of resistance' is often character-ised as a 'politics from below' and as transformative in nature. More substantively, it is seen as comprising social movements, global civil society actors such as NGOs and, potentially, coalitions of Third World states. While this form of politics, until

---

[1] The journal *Global Governance* appeared in the 1990s in response to this interest, while a vast array of books and articles are concerned with the subject. Examples include Paul Diehl (ed.), *The Politics of Global Governance* (Boulder, CO: Lynne Rienner, 2000); J. Rosneau and O. Young (eds.), *Global Governance: Drawing Insights from the Environmental Experience* (Cambridge, MA: The MIT Press, 1997); U. Beck, J. Dryzek, A. Giddens and D. Held, *Democracy and Global Order* (Cambridge: Cambridge University Press, 1995); D. Held and A. McGrew (eds.), *Governing Globalization: Power, Authority and Global Governance* (Cambridge: Polity, 2002); V. Cable, *Globalization and Global Governance* (London: Royal Institute of International Affairs, 1999); A. Prakash and J. A. Hart (eds.), *Globalization and Governance* (London: Routledge, 1999); R. Falk, *On Humane Global Governance* (Cambridge: Polity, 1995); M. Hewson and T. J. Sinclair (eds.), *Approaches to Global Governance Theory* (Albany, NY: State University of New York, 1999), C. Thomas, *Global Governance, Development and Human Security* (London: Pluto Press, 2000).

recently, has been largely ignored in mainstream IR – despite the persistent efforts of some to put it on the agenda[2] – outside the discipline it has been a central pre-occupation of sociologists and certainly an important topic of conversation among some political theorists/scientists.[3]

The Editors invited scholars from different theoretical perspectives to engage in a dialogue about the potential relevance of these two characterisations of politics *for the study of international politics.* More specifically, we invited all contributors to address one or more of the following broad theoretical/empirical questions:

- How relevant and useful is this dichotomy? What are the strengths and weaknesses of this dual characterisation of politics? Is there a different, more helpful way of thinking about politics and the political in our current world order?
- What is the best way of characterising and/or theorising the 'politics of governance'? Who are the main actors? How do we conceptualise them? What are the normative imperatives, if any, guiding them? What forms of power are operating within these forms of politics?
- How can we characterise the 'politics of resistance'? Who are the main actors and how can we conceptualise them? What normative imperatives, if any, guide these actors? What forms of power are they resisting?
- What is the relationship between these two forms of politics? When does 'governance' generate resistance? How do power relations simultaneously maintain and subvert the social order? How can we distinguish between 'progressive' and 'regressive' forms of politics?
- Do these two different conceptions of politics require alternative methodological approaches? More specifically, what should the relationship be between meta-theory, social theory and substantive empirical research?

---

[2] R. Cox, *Production Power and World Order: Social Forces in the Making of World History* (New York: Columbia University Press, 1987); Barry Gills (ed.), *Globalisation and The Politics of Resistance* (London: Macmillan, 2002); S. Gill, *Power and Resistance in the New World Order* (London: Palgrave, 2003); Warren Magnusson, 'Social Movements and the Global City', *Millennium* 23: 3 (1994), pp. 621–46; M. Shaw (ed.), *Politics and Globalisation: Knowledge, Ethics and Agency* (London: Routledge, 1999); R.B.J. Walker, *One World/Many Worlds: Struggles for a Just World Peace* (Boulder, CO: Lynne Rienner, 1988); Walker, 'Social Movements/World Politics', *Millennium,* 23: 3 (1994), pp. 669–700; and Paul Wagner, *Environmental Activism and World Civic Politics* (Albany, NY: State University of New York Press, 1996).

[3] A sample includes Carl Boggs, *Social Movements and Political Power: Emerging Forms of Radicalism in the West* (Philadelphia, PA: Temple University Press, 1986); William Carroll (ed.), *Organising Dissent: Contemporary Social Movements in Theory and Practice* (Victoria, BC: Garamond Press); Manuel Castells, *The Power of Identity* (London: Blackwells, 1997); Nira Yuval Davis, *Gender and Nation* (London: Sage, 1997); Nancy Fraser, *Justice Interruptus: Critical Reflections on the 'PostSocialist' Condition* (London: Routledge, 1997); Pierre Hamel *et al.* (eds.), *Globalization and Social Movements* (London: Palgrave, 2001); Sandra Harding, 'Subjectivity, Experience and Knowledge: An Epistemology from/for a Rainbow Coalition Politics', in *Development and Change,* 23: 3 (1992), pp. 175–94; Margaret Keck and Kathryn Sikkink, *Activists Beyond Borders: Advocacy Networks in International Politics* (Ithaca, NY: Cornell University Press, 1998); E. Laclau and C. Mouffe, *Hegemony and Socialist Strategy: Towards a Radical Democratic Politics* (London: Verso, 1985); Alberto Melucci, *Nomads of the Present: Social Movements and Individual Needs in Contemporary Society* (London: Radius, 1989); Alan Scott, *Ideology and the New Social Movements* (London: Unwin Hyman, 1990); Sydney Tarrow, *The Power in Movement: Social Movements and Contentious Politics* (Cambridge: Cambridge Univesity Press, 1998) and Ellen Woods, *Democracy Against Capitalism* (Cambridge: Cambridge University Press, 1995).

Answers

Perhaps unsurprisingly, there was no consensus about the relevance or utility of the governance/resistance dichotomy as a theoretical starting point to think about world politics, although there was some agreement about the limitations of ascribing particular actors to each category. Beyond offering us insights into the strengths and weaknesses of this dual characterisation of world politics, our authors also raised, implicitly and explicitly, a number of other related questions that follow from any attempt to delineate a conception of the political in our field: How do we conceptualise the workings of power in either or both of these characterisations of politics? Is a 'politics of knowledge' discernible in the very process of analysing and attempting to understand international affairs? What is the relationship between ethics and politics?

In this section we shall review what our authors had to say about how best to characterise politics in our discipline and how helpful the governance/resistance distinction is in this effort. In the next we shall turn our attention to the themes of power, knowledge and ethics in an effort to develop a research agenda that draws on the insights of our contributors, but goes beyond the work presented here.

By far the most explicit and enthusiastic support for the governance/resistance dichotomy comes from Mark Rupert, who regards the 'wilful and continuing conceptual blindness' of mainstream IR to 'mutually constitutive relations of governance/resistance at work in the production of global politics' to be a major factor in the impoverishment of the former. Drawing on Gramsci, Rupert paints a provocative picture of a world divided along class lines with the 'politics of governance' referring to an 'historic bloc comprised of particular fractions of the capitalist class, state managers and international bureaucrats, journalists and mainstream labour leaders'. If governance represents class power and in particular the power of capitalists to control investment and direct the labour process, resistance involves the construction of intellectual and moral alliances between different social groupings seeking to challenge capitalism and the power of this hegemonic bloc. In this context, politics for Rupert must be understood in terms of a conflict between capitalists and labour and between two opposing imperatives – governance and resistance. Focusing his article on the conditions for the possibility of counter-hegemony, Rupert reminds us that a politics of resistance is not inevitable, but must be *built* on the terrain of popular 'common sense' and alternative normative visions. One potential site of this kind of progressive resistance politics for Rupert can be found in the so-called Global Justice Movement.

In sum, for Rupert we live in a world shaped by the spread of capitalism across the globe and the increasingly coercive, neo-imperialist policies of the US. Within this global power configuration, Rupert offers a clear unequivocal picture of who the protagonists of world politics are, the nature and location of the power that is being resisted and the normative and political stakes involved in this contest. In a discipline that places a high premium on 'objectivity', Rupert's explicit commitment to trying to 'enable a politics of solidarity' that can challenge the *status quo* is thought-provoking.

Also working within a broadly Marxian framework, Alejandro Colas focuses on the question of how to render global governance more democratic. For Colas, global governance is shaped by 'the capitalist drive to constantly and everywhere appropriate time – not just labour time, but care-time and recreational time too'. Like Rupert, Colas sees globalisation in terms of the spread of capitalism and the logic of governance and resistance as representing the conflicting interests of capital and labour. He insists, however, that we do not see this class conflict as a direct one. As he states, 'far from facing each other in a direct, unmediated form, capital and labour clash on the global plane through the mediation of various socio-political institutions'. The key player in this process of mediation is the modern territorial state and it is this institution that must be at the centre of any effective global democratic resistance. Critical of Negri and Holloway's conceptions of resistance as anti-sovereign, deterritorialised and unhierarchical, Colas argues that any resistance premised on uninterrupted movement and an ever open-ended process is destined toward debilitation and exhaustion. Indeed the only way to build a democratic politics of resistance, according to Colas, is to recognise two basic realities, that is, 'the continuing tenacity of the mediating structures of global capitalism and the accompanying power of political institutions of representation'. In other words, for Colas, the state is an essential ingredient for any meaningful conception of resistance; it not only commands the material resources necessary for the implementation of any democratic practices, it is also the main representative body of a political community. In this context, democratic resistance must be an internationalised struggle for state power.

Given his grounding of democratic resistance in the state, Colas finds himself most sympathetic with the models of cosmopolitan democracy put forward by Held among others. Although critical of Held's propensity to decouple the state from the modes of social reproduction within which it is embedded, he agrees with the need to recognise both that democracy requires some delimitation of the represented *demos* if it is to avoid the naïve anti-politics of the 'anti-globalisation' protesters, and that any democratic deliberation requires democratic implementation, that is, the administrative authority to make binding decisions. As Colas concludes, 'alternative forms of political authority … are unlikely to develop without first democratising existing political institutions across the world – primarily but exclusively nation-states'. Like Rupert, Colas's normative vision is shaped by a concern with democracy and the eventual 'subordination of capital to the collective needs of labour'. Unlike Rupert, however, Colas holds out little hope for movements such as the Global Justice Movement and prefers to support the efforts of those seeking to directly engage the state. Thus, refusing to move in what he sees as a utopian direction, Colas tries to show how transformative resistance can and must emerge from within our existing state system.

What both articles do is encourage us to think about governance and resistance in the context of capitalism – rather than anarchy or complex interdependence – and in terms of a conflict of interests between classes. Given the undeniable and universal impact of such contemporary developments in capitalism as the increase in both size and degree of detachment from political control of financial markets, they both offer powerful arguments for placing capitalism and its attendant problems at centre-stage in the analyses of world politics.

James Brassett and Richard Higgott also understand what they call the politics of 'contested globalisation' in the context of capitalism and more particularly the market orthodoxies of the Washington consensus. Rather than identifying those social forces that may *overturn* the capitalist system *in toto*, however, the central problem for these two authors is to find ways of 'humanising globalisation'. In their view this entails rejecting a strict separation between governance and resistance and understanding the former in terms of 'multilateral institutions *and* non-state actors that actively transcend territorial politics in an attempt to realise their interests at multiple levels'. In other words, governance must be seen as an exercise in political contestation and negotiation and therefore as susceptible to reform.

Having argued that globalisation has generated a new form of politics that brings both states and civil society actors into dialogue, they go on to develop a case for both a *pragmatic praxis* within the global polity and an *ethic of pragmatic reform*. In the case of the former they argue that 'within institutions of global economic governance, the relationship with civil society is clearly developing but it is a process of experimentation in which uncertainty is a characteristic of and for both parties. The reformist potential of civil society is contingent, fallible and experimental'. A pragmatic political praxis, therefore, must focus on achieving what *can be achieved,* recognising that whatever gains are made will be based on experimentation and will always be contingent and fallible. In terms of the latter, they tell us that an ethic of pragmatic reform requires us to think about 'feasible globalisations not utopian alternatives'. More substantively, it makes us address the question of who is included and excluded from our communities as well as encourages us to recognise sympathy as an important source of our ethical behaviour and social hope as that which unites a community.

In sum, Brassett and Higgott challenge us to, in Rorty's words, 'get rid of the conviction common to Plato and Marx that there must be large theoretical ways of finding out how to end injustice as opposed to small experimental ways'. Further-more, they move us away from the 'politics from below' as 'good' and the 'politics from above' as 'bad' dichotomy that is prevalent in some of the IR literature and thereby challenge us to rethink what we mean by so-called 'progressive politics'. Finally, they introduce the notions of sympathy and social hope to a discipline inured to the role of the sentimental in political life.

Like Brassett and Higgott, Ian Clark also questions the usefulness of the governance/resistance dichotomy. He reminds us, for example, that civil society, usually considered to be the site of resistance, is often selectively co-opted into systems of global governance and in fact can be seen as the 'shock troops of the Empire'. Furthermore, he points out that states can engage in a politics of resistance of their own with the current war on terrorism as one possible exemplar. As he states, 'there is no simple tug of war between governance and resistance, but instead a multifaceted interaction involving a complex array of actors. It is this that makes the insertion of legitimacy into the discussion so difficult and gives the lie to any crude notion that global governance suffers from a single legitimacy deficit, caused by the solitary fault line that runs between the reified representatives of governance, on the one hand, and those of resistance, on the other.'

And it is the problem of legitimacy that most concerns Clark. There are two forms of legitimacy that are relevant for him. The first can be characterised as the 'legitimacy of authority' and concerns questions about the conformity to and justifiability of prevailing rules and power relations expressed in the existing systems of rule. The issue at stake in this particular sphere of legitimacy is the need for effective democratic procedures. The second is the 'legitimacy of order' and concerns the broader normative principles that define membership within a political community and entitlement to participation. Who is included and excluded? Who has the right to have rights? The issue at stake here is the need for a moral consensus about the constitution of political community. In this way Clark separates out two logics of legitimacy, that of power and control pertaining to systems of rule and that of norms and principles pertaining to conceptions of rightful membership. The working out of both of these logics requires political bargains between states and non-state actors. Thus, for Clark, legitimacy as an ethical concept/practice must be seen as the *outgrowth* of a political process understood in terms of power, calculation and compromise. In this picture, the ethical moment emerges out of and follows the political one.

Clark's article resonates with Brassett's and Higgott's in at least two ways. First, like them, he sees the solution of legitimacy problems (of either kind) as likely to be the result of a bargaining process between states and non-state actors rather than some form of collective social struggle. In this way he disabuses us of the notion that resistance must somehow be seen as good/progressive and governance as bad/controlling. Second, like Brassett and Higgott, he refuses to see resistance as a separate ontological category of politics from governance and suggests instead that we think in terms of the 'politics of legitimacy' which in his view 'lies at the heart of contemporary global governance and the manifold evidences of resistances at the present time'. Finally, like Colas, Clark reminds us that both the theory and practice of the state as well as the question of political community cannot be ignored in discussions of democratising global governance. While Colas, however, appropriates the state as a site of resistance, Clark sees it as an essential actor in the construction of legitimate forms of global governance.

Along with Brassett and Higgott as well as Clark, Michael Kenny is concerned with issues relating to the legitimacy of the prevailing international order and with the inadequacies of individualist perspectives that accompany neoliberal economic thought. Like Clark, he rejects the cosmopolitanist claim that the emergence of global civil society *acts as a kind of legitimating agency* for global governance. As several others have noted, the NGOs at the heart of global civil society tend to be dominated by Western groups and may lack transparency and accountability. But he also disputes what he characterises as 'subalternist' approaches to global civil society, that is, the argument that anti-capitalist groups and social movements and the radical political activism they embrace represent an authentic counter to global capitalism and an emerging alternative conception of community. According to Kenny, neither perspective pays enough attention to the *power dynamics* that give associational life its shape and character, and to the *social relations* through which group identity and collective action are shaped.

He suggests instead that a rediscovery of liberal republican ideas and their application to global civil society has much to offer in terms of 'the importance of fostering forms of social interaction that are likely to promote some of the values – trust, reciprocity, self-respect and civility, most notably – congruent with a *democratically orientated* global society'. Instilling civil society (and through it the agencies of global governance) with the values of liberal republicanism will promote a stronger sense of obligation to other members of the global community and greater attentiveness to redressing global inequalities that prevent many from exercising their entitlements to various rights.

This liberal republican approach opens up three lines of inquiry according to Kenny. First it asks us to consider the various kinds of public space and deliberative interchange that have become established on a transnational basis. That is, like Clark and Colas, Kenny is concerned with the issue of political community. Unlike Clark, however, his conception of political community includes not only those formal institutions that have been incorporated into multilateral processes but also individual citizens and social groupings far away from the bastions of power. In other words, like Colas, Kenny is explicitly concerned with not only delineating power relations, but within this remit, specifying relations of *domination, inequality* and *injustice*. Second, he asks us to consider how politics plays a constitutive role in respect to human flourishing. Drawing on a neo-Aristotelian vision of politics, Kenny argues that his approach requires scholars and practitioners alike to ask whether 'international initiatives are likely to promote the autonomy and political capacity of the oppressed and subordinated peoples affected by them'. In this way the liberal republican perspective prioritises the moral ends towards which decisions are made and the values towards which they are directed. Finally, like Clark, he highlights the issue of legitimacy: have systems of global governance secured the consent of, and some kind of input from, the citizens they claim to represent? In contrast to Clark, who conceptualises legitimacy as a 'pragmatic meeting point between political effectiveness and the need for moral consensus', Kenny depicts legitimacy in terms of a moral challenge 'of designing and enforcing laws that simultaneously promote individual liberty, represent a range of social interests and offset the domination of some parties over others ...'. In this view, then, the question of legitimacy cannot be separated from either the question of power and domination, or the ethical imperative to overcome these relations.

Karena Shaw's article is a forceful reminder to those of us interested in addressing these questions of power and domination that we need to pay much more attention to the politics of knowledge production both in academia and in the context of political activism. More specifically, Shaw is interested in exploring how tracing the politics of knowledge in both these contexts can help us think differently about how to theorise the political, in general, and what constitutes progressive political activism, in particular. In the first two parts of her article, Shaw focuses on the politics of disciplinary knowledge and how the fields of anthropology and IR have in different ways reproduced very specific and limited understandings of their respective subject matters. In terms of IR she examines three texts on social movements in IR and illustrates how each frames activism in ways that conform to the conventional paradigmatic understandings of what politics is and should be. As she states, 'in the end, each book forwards a revised framework which reinforces disciplinary adequacy. None of them argues for more than an adaptation of the boundaries, an act of greater flexibility or inclusion'. In this way, Shaw attempts to illustrate how our discipline can limit the way we think about the political. In the third and fourth part of the article, Shaw redirects her attention to outlining an alternative way of thinking about knowledge production in the context of political activism. Drawing on feminist philosopher Sandra Harding, Shaw entreats us to be attentive to the strategic nature of politics and in particular to the strategic knowledge claims of activists. Knowledge production in this context – and indeed the politics that surrounds it – must be understood as explicitly situated and as 'grounded in a reading of a particular site of condition'. Once the strategic and situated nature of politics is acknowledged, then it is possible to see coalition-building within movements as a means of maintaining unity while respecting diversity.

Shaw's article stands apart from the other chapters discussed thus far to the extent that it explicitly asks us to interrogate the intended and unintended consequences of our knowledge claims and to query the purpose and audience of our knowledge production. Her concern with the relationship between knowledge and power, however, is not unique and, as we shall see, it is a theme that re-emerges in Robinson's and Marchand's feminist analyses of resistance politics. In addition to highlighting the question of knowledge production in both academia and political activism, Shaw directs our attention to forms of politics that are usually ignored or hidden from view because they are strategically mobile and contingent and therefore hard to pin down. And yet, according to Shaw, it is precisely by exploring these strategic moments that we can learn not only about the politics of others, but also about our own politics of knowledge production. Again, as we shall see, Robinson and Marchand agree.

While wanting to hold on to the tension between the logic of governance and resistance, Fiona Robinson takes issue with the common assumption that global civil society and in particular human rights activism is a form of resistance to globalisation. Indeed, for Robinson, 'while there is certainly potential for resistance and transformation inherent within both the idea of human rights and the organis-ations and strategies of global civil society, their current incarnations have not, as yet, moved beyond the dominant, broadly liberal framework'. In other words, global civil society and human rights NGOs are seen as representing a culture that is Western and universalist in orientation and thus part and parcel of the configuration of power relations that maintain global governance structures.

Despite this, however, Robinson wants to hold on to the idea of resistance politics and locates one important site of such activism in the discourses of non-Western women. She argues that all too often, however, women's activism is ignored in IR because it does not fit into the prevailing definition and practice of global civil society. The practices of locally based women's groups in developing countries are easy to ignore in a discipline preoccupied with a conception of politics that is grounded only in large, fixed, formal institutions located in the familiar terrain of the West. Making them even harder to see or take seriously is the fact that these movements are employing non-liberal, feminist discourses on human rights.

In this way, along with Shaw, Robinson conceptualises feminist human rights discourses as a form of 'strategic knowledge' generated within the context of women's activism. As such, it is contingent and highly sensitive to power relations. It reflects the experiences of those disadvantaged by prevailing practices and rather than seeking to generate universals it is grounded and context-specific. Drawing on Hutchings, Robinson argues that 'rights become strategic weapons in the construc-tion of a form of ethical life which is not absolutely and universally good, but which may be useful for many if not all women living in particular moments in time and space'. In addition to their strategic and context-specific nature, feminist renditions of human rights are different from liberal accounts for two other reasons. First, they are based on the recognition of relationships as a fundamental ontological feature of human social life and second, they are sceptical of the notion of a universal humanity and are instead committed to the recognition of difference and specificity.

Robinson's article plays an important role in drawing our attention to *discourse* as a site of power and resistance politics. Furthermore, like Shaw, she highlights the strategic dimensions of politics and demonstrates how the strategic knowledge of activists – in this case about human rights – provides an interesting place to start analysing the workings of power and the formulation of alternative visions. Finally and most obviously, Robinson reminds us that supposedly neutral and progressive discourses, such as those surrounding human rights, are gendered and thus can reflect rather than overturn power relations.

Also interested in the possibility of gendered resistances to globalisation, Marianne Marchand poses two questions: first, what does a gender *analysis* of the politics of resistance entail and second, what does a *gendered politics* of resistance involve? In terms of the first question Marchand suggests that a gender analysis of this resistance politics must locate it in the context of global restructuring understood as the renegotiation of the boundaries between private/public, national/international and state/society/market. More particularly, this restructuring process must be seen as taking place at three interconnected levels at which gender operates: the ideological, the social and the body. Furthermore, she points to the contextual and embedded nature of resistances and the need to conceptualise these efforts in terms of what she calls the 'politics of location' that reflects women's different experiences and diverse identities. All of these lines of inquiry in her view require relational thinking which is oriented to exploring the connections between the material circumstances in which women live, the self-understandings and perceptions that these women have and the political identities that are generated.

If gendered processes of global restructuring create the conditions for the emergence of resistance, it is not self-evident that this resistance must be gendered in nature. Indeed, Marchand asks what it means to characterise resistances as either feminine or masculine and draws on Butler to conceptualise these gendered acts of resistance as performatively produced. Thus, in terms of her second question regarding the nature of a gendered politics of resistance, she notes that while women have mobilised against globalisation *as* women, men have adopted a range of other political identities – for example as workers, environmentalists, campesinos and anarchists – around which to organise. In other words, women have built solidarities around a gender identity and have allowed their experiences as mothers and wives as well as workers to shape their protests and strategies. In this connection, Marchand redirects our attention from large-scale protests to locally based community politics as it is here that one can most easily see resistance to global restructuring.

Marchand's article resonates in a number of interesting ways with those of Robinson and Shaw. First, along with Robinson, Marchand tells us that any feminist understanding of resistance must begin its analysis by recognising gender as a crucial power relation that shapes current global restructuring processes. Furthermore, like Robinson and Shaw, she reminds us that our fascination with large-scale events may blind us to the importance of exploring the local, everyday coping strategies of those seeking to resist power relations. By paying attention to the discourses and practices of women in their communities, we transform them into political subjects and thereby into sources of knowledge about their lives and about the nature of resistance politics more generally. Finally, all three authors bring to light the strategic dimensions of politics and remind us that any effort to theorise resistance politics requires us to be more sensitive not only to the specific context in which activists wage their struggle but to the particular, contingent choices they make when engaging in this process.

Introducing a theme that is only touched on in a few of the articles (Rupert, Marchand and Shaw), Campbell brings culture as a terrain of politics to the forefront of his analysis of governance and resistance. For Campbell, cultural governance involves 'a set of historical practices of representation – involving the state but never fully controlled by the state – in which the struggle for the state's identity is located'. Clearly for Campbell identity is not a given but is performatively produced through repeated acts of representation. In this context, the state's efforts to represent itself as the expression of a collective identity must be understood as a contested process which is located, among other places, on the terrain of popular culture and which implicates the state, the news media, the film industry and documentary photojournalism. Taking the case of war coverage, Campbell demonstrates how the US government has increasingly sought to manage the media by, on the one hand, preventing certain reports and images of war from being televised and, on the other, producing its own pictorial narratives of what is allegedly going on. This struggle over the control of information and representation goes beyond the official media. The entertainment business, including Hollywood, has been recruited to the cause, producing and promoting films that show US military and intelligence forces in a positive light. Thus for Campbell, Der Derian's notion of the 'military-industrial-media-entertainment network', or MIME-NET, is a relevant conceptual starting point for thinking about cultural governance and a world where 'the Pentagon's suffocating restrictions on the press, the demise of news programmes in the face of entertainment alternatives, intimate relations between Hollywood and the national security establishment, and the conduct of military operations for their information outcomes and representational value in the struggle for strategic influence are the norm rather than the exception'.

Described in these terms, the power of MIME-NET appears all pervasive and perhaps even invincible. Nevertheless, according to Campbell, there is one branch of the media – documentary photography and photojournalism – that has disrupted prevailing practices of cultural governance and that can be seen as a form of pictorial resistance. This form of resistance, however, is not without its potential traps. As Campbell makes clear the relationship between representation and truth in the photographic image is no less ambiguous than it is in television. After all, pictures can be contrived, constructed and manipulated in the same way as news footage. Furthermore, photographic images of the poor, the colonised and the war ravaged can turn the subjects of these pictures into passive objects of curiosity and knowledge. The question for Campbell then is when can photojournalism become a form of resistance? Here he turns to the work of Don McCullin who thinks of his photography as a form of empathetic witnessing of the despair of others. For this photographer each picture taken represents an act of deeply felt emotion in which disgust at the violence and empathy for its victims intermingle. His purpose is not only to be an eyewitness to the suffering of others, but also to 'break the hearts and spirit of secure people' so that they might act.

Clearly, inspired by the intentions and work of McCullin, Campbell suggests that the still photograph can be seen as a potential site of resistance to the extent that it can engender a space for reflection and critical thought as well as build or reinforce moral positions. In this sense pictures serve as reminders of what we can do to each other in the name of 'the good' and force us to ask uncomfortable questions about who is responsible for the images that we witness.

Campbell's piece is original and thought-provoking for a number of reasons. First, in terms of the governance/resistance dichotomy Campbell's focus on *individual* photographers as representing sites of cultural resistance is markedly different from other contributors who tend to conceptualise resistance in collective terms. Furthermore, his depiction of photojournalists as the potential agents of pictorial resistance provides an interesting contrast to Rupert who chooses to locate journalists within the governance camp. In other words, tracing politics through the actions of individuals, rather than social groups, may require us to complicate our mental maps of who is and who is not on 'our side'. Second, the conception of resistance that Campbell elicits – although does not explicitly develop – clearly implicates our capacity to evoke and feel empathy for others. Like Brassett and Higgott, the politics of resistance depicted here is not solely dependent on the articulation of interests, but requires the engagement of feelings such as empathy, indignation, and sorrow. Where this similarity ends, however, is with Campbell's insistence that resistance also requires the posing of critical questions about the causes of injustice and the location of individual and collective responsibility for these wrong-doings. In this way, for Campbell, the politics of resistance seems to necessitate taking a stand for and against specific others. Finally, in terms of thinking about power, the chapter opens up two lines of inquiry that have been ignored in IR, that is, the power of visual imagery and its relationship to political agency and the power of empathy and its role in the politicisation of particular issues.

Departures

Having reviewed the various arguments of our authors in light of their distinctive contributions to an ongoing dialogue about how we might best think about politics in our field, in this last section of the Introduction we would like to tentatively open up new or alternative lines of inquiry that still need attention. In other words, we now move from discussing what has been said in this Special Issue to what has not. In this way, this concluding section serves both as a critical assessment of the state of the art and as an agenda for future research. We begin this critical evaluation by revisiting our own brief for the Special Issue and the central question that we posed to our contributors, namely, is governance and resistance a useful way of framing our discussions of world politics? We then move on to address three themes – power, knowledge and ethics – that underlie the different arguments made in this volume and that, in our view, are essential to any reconceptualisation of politics in our field.

Rethinking politics as governance and resistance

Before addressing the governance/resistance dichotomy, it may be useful at this point to go over what our contributors share in terms of their understandings of politics/ world politics, and what issues they disagree on. The first point of consensus seems to be that there are at least three vital ingredients to any act of politics; *conflict, power relations* and some form of *collective action*. Thus, although both Marchand and Campbell direct our attention to individualised strategies of resistance, as they too can have important political implications, all of our authors presume the importance of collective actors whether they are social movements, institutions or states. This leads us to the second apparent point of agreement, which is that politics is best understood as emerging within the context of *social relations* or what Kenny calls 'social interaction' and 'associational life'. To this extent our contributors share a distinctly British/European approach to the field which yields little ground to the more American tendency of separating international politics from political studies and the latter from social or cultural studies. Instead, in different ways, all our contributors suggest that any effort to make sense of world politics must go beyond the mere delineation of group interests and power differentials and engage with questions of cultural and political identity, with the role of our beliefs and values and the nature of our ethical relations with others. Third, all our authors accept that politics does not simply erupt onto the scene when structural conditions make it propitious for it to do so. Instead, political action is seen as having to be socially constructed and *built* through the practices of politicised actors whether they are social movements or states. And finally, whether they are talking about governance or resistance, all the contributors in this volume seem to take for granted the notion of a human subject who has the capacity to engage in self-reflexive, purposeful action in the name of certain interests, beliefs, values and feelings. This does not mean that every act is intended or that every consequence is foreseen. It simply reminds us that we often do act according to concrete motivations and that, therefore, *intentional action* must be taken into account when conceptualising politics.

Despite these shared starting points, there are a number of underlying tensions cutting across the different narratives of world politics elaborated on here. One fault line that clearly runs through the volume is the question of whether politics is better understood as a clash of *non-negotiable* interests in the context of relations of oppression or whether it can be seen as a bargaining exercise over *negotiable* interests. In other words, are we talking about a zero-sum game or one of compromise and reform? It is interesting to note here that the Marxists and feminists in this volume share a scepticism towards reformist approaches and prefer to speak of structural change or social transformation. Thus, while revolution may not be on the agenda for these authors, a complete overhaul of particular power relations certainly is.

A second, and closely related tension concerns how we think about what motivates us to act politically. Is politics primarily about safeguarding our *interests* as individuals or classes or is it equally about defending/promoting our values, beliefs, political identities and different ways of being? While realists, liberals and Marxists have tended to highlight the logic of the former, feminists, post-structuralists and Gramscian critical theorists have been more ready to recognise the imperative of the latter. The question of what propels us to engage in certain types of politics in turn begs a further question concerning the rational nature of political action. While our discipline has tended to assume that politics, or at least international politics, is a logical, cognitive game played by rational actors, sociology and political science have been mired in debate about the putative rationality of political action. Within these two disciplines, social movements, for example, have been variously upheld as the irrational expression of anomie, as the cultural embodiments of new identities and as the rational efforts of people to gain access to resources.[4]

Thirdly, if all our authors agree that power and politics go together, they have different ideas about the nature and function of these power relations and the role they play in shaping the dominant logic of politics. Clearly, for some, the fundamental imperative of politics is the maintenance of order and, thus, the management of conflict and the regulation of power relations. For others, however, this imperative is understood more in terms of contestation and social transformation and thus challenging and overturning power relations. So do we need to make a distinction between these two logics and if so, can we construct a theory of politics that can address both dynamics simultaneously or do we need separate theories? In this context can the notions of 'governance' and 'resistance' serve as heuristic devices to help us distinguish between these two logics? While there is no consensus on the usefulness of this particular conceptual framing, it is important to note that all the authors explicitly or implicitly acknowledged the existence of these two countervailing logics.

So how have our authors distinguished between them? As we have already seen, in terms of political agents, all our contributors agreed that no simple, clear-cut division could be made between the *actors* of governance and those of resistance. Kenny and Robinson, for instance, point out that civil society groups and NGOs are often complicit in the practices of governance. Clark rightly reminds us that states can also engage in a form of resistance politics and Colas goes even further to tell us that the state is essential to any democratic resistance. Indeed, only three contributors seem content to work within the frame of this dichotomy in terms of the *agents* of politics. While Rupert is straightforward and unapologetic about his characterisation of global governance as implicating 'particular fractions of the capitalist class, state managers and international bureaucrats, journalists and mainstream labor leaders', Brassett and Higgott also tend to link governance with the practices of the World Bank, IMF and WTO as well as organisations of private and non-state regulation and resistance with the activities of 'global civil society'.

Interestingly, however, while recognising this overlap between the agents of governance and resistance, with the exception of Clark, all our authors either explicitly or implicitly accept the framing of world politics along these broad lines.[5] Those

---

[4] For an overview of these different perspectives see Alan Scott, *Ideology and the New Social Movements* (London: Unwin Hyman, 1990).

[5] Even Clark, who explicitly questions the relevance of this dichotomy to the issue of legitimacy, accepts that politics involves both the assertion of and challenge to authority. In other words, as he himself makes clear, both institutional rule-making and conceptions of rightful membership, the two aspects of legitimacy that he focuses on, are subject to political contestation and resistance. For example, the efforts of states to develop rule-making procedures within multilateral institutions has met with opposition from both state and non-state actors such as the case of the NIEO of the early 1970s or current efforts of Third World states to get the WTO to make concessions on a variety of fronts. Furthermore, the construction of morally agreed conceptions of political community has also generated resistance from excluded groups (indigenous peoples' movements, feminist human rights activism, women's reproductive rights movements, gay and lesbian movements, animal liberation movements). Thus, while the language of 'governance' and 'resistance' and its associated literature may be problematic for Clark, it seems clear that the 'politics of legitimacy' as he terms it cannot be understood outside the context of power relations and forms of resistance against them.

focusing on the question of governance tend to associate it with the imperatives of management, rule-making and maintaining legitimate authority. More substantively, it is connected to promoting capitalist relations and market-based economic development (Robinson, Marchand, Rupert, Colas, Brassett and Higgott) or hegemonic state identities and foreign policy (Campbell). In other words, it is seen as representing the interests and values of the powerful whether that is cashed out in terms of capitalist elites (Rupert, Colas), gender hierarchies (Robinson, Marchand), dominant states (Clark, Brassett and Higgott, Campbell), knowledge producers (Shaw) or a combination of the above (Kenny, Robinson, Marchand).

Resistance, on the other hand, is seen as contesting and challenging this configuration of power relations. In some cases the goal of resistance is articulated in terms of 'democratizing global governance' (Colas and Clark). In other cases it is seen more in terms of the construction of an 'emancipatory politics' that can bring about social transformation and the end of relations of domination (Kenny, Robinson, Marchand, Rupert). In Campbell's case, pictorial resistance has begun its work if it opens up space for critical thought and encourages us to ask questions about who is responsible for the atrocious images it depicts.

If governance and resistance represent two moments or logics of the political, however, what is less clear is how our authors conceive of the relationship between them. According to Rupert the relationship between governance and resistance must be understood as dialectical. While not conceiving of it in dialectical terms, both Colas and Campbell agree that the link between governance and resistance is inherent and that they cannot be seen as discrete modes of action. But when Colas says, 'since capitalist social relations – like most power relations – are politically contested ...' one cannot help but wonder whether it is true that *most* power relations are in fact contested and, if so, which ones are not and why not. In other words, in a discipline oriented to the study of politics it seems that one line of inquiry we need to explore more systematically is when and under what conditions we choose to fight against particular power relations.[6] After all, we do not mount resistance against any and all forms of governance or, for that matter, all forms of oppression. So when does 'governance' slide into 'oppression' and public 'reluctance' into social 'resistance'?

The aim of this Special Issue was to open up a conversation about how we conceptualise politics in our field in general, and what we actually mean when we deploy the now much used terms 'politics of governance' and 'politics of resistance' in particular. While our contributors have made an important start in both critically appraising the relevance of these concepts and adding substance to them, we would argue that there is still a need for more dialogue about how best to think about governance, resistance and the relationship between them.

In terms of the 'politics of governance', while we agree that organisations and states can develop a logic of their own that is important to explore, we feel that it is important not to lose sight of the *role of the individuals* within them and the impact they can have in propelling social change. For this reason we would argue that more substantive research on the role of individual and group leadership within these

---

[6] For a very thought provoking answer to this question see David Campbell's 'Why Fight: Humanitarianism, Principles and Post-structuralism', *Millennium* 27: 3 (1998), pp. 497–522).

corporate entities needs to be done. Furthermore, as Brassett and Higgott correctly remind us, we should be aware that, while the imperative behind the 'politics of governance' may well be stability, social control and crisis management, social change and reform can and does come from 'above', so to speak.

If more work has to be done on what we mean by 'governance', a concept that has been in play for some time now, there is an even more compelling need to develop a theoretically coherent, empirically sustained understanding of the more recent notion of 'politics of resistance'. To this end, at least three areas of exploration appear relevant.

First, if the 'politics of resistance' is going to be equated with political activism and in particular social movements, then much more empirical work needs to be done on a range of movements that have emerged over the last half century. These include so-called 'newer' movements such as environmental movements as well as 'older' ones such as the labour movement and nationalist movements. In fact the most recent exemplar of the 'politics of resistance', the controversially named 'anti-globalisation movement', provides an interesting context in which to examine the intersections of both the 'old' and the 'new'. As we pursue this line of research, it may be helpful to keep in mind three things. Methodologically, we would do well to remember Shaw's gentle warnings about the limitations of a disciplinary framing of social movements and the blind spots it creates in terms of our thinking about what and where politics is and should be. Theoretically, we can learn from Rupert and Marchand who encourage us to see collective action as a political achievement which is temporary in nature and subject to continual challenge. For coalitions do not emerge, Phoenix-like, from the discontented masses, but are *built*, step by step, from the 'ground up'. As we trace these strategic steps, we need to follow Robinson and continually ask ourselves who is included and excluded within the discourses and practices of these coalitions. Finally, politically, it is important for us to remember that resistance comes in many forms and that we need to find ways of delineating between those we think of as 'progressive' (or what Walker once called 'critical movements') and those we designate as 'regressive'.[7] In order to do this we need to extend our study of movements from the usual suspects and include, for example: fascist and neo-Nazi movements in Europe and the UK, some nationalist and revolutionary movements in Eastern Europe, Asia and Africa, right-wing women's movements in India, some environmental groups in the US and Canada, and some evangelical movements such as the US Promise Keepers.[8] In the post-Cold War era, how can we distinguish between progressive and non-progressive movements; what political, epistemological or ethical criteria can we rely on? Clearly, comparative work among and between these types of movements in terms of their practices, discourses and normative/political agendas is required before we can be sure that our intuitions about what is progressive and what is not are correct. This kind of work is especially important given what can be seen as the xenophobic

---

[7] Walker, *One World/Many Worlds: Struggles for a Just World Peace* (Boulder, CO: Lynne Rienner, 1988).

[8] The Promise Keepers is a fervently Christian movement of men seeking to re-establish their dominant role within the family and as leaders of the faith. For information about the Promise Keepers, see their web site: <http://www.promisekeepers.org> as well as Stodghill, 'God of our Fathers' in *Time* Canadian edn. (6 October 1997), pp. 52–8.

frenzy of the post-September 11th world where the branding of whole religions as 'evil' and regressive, whether that be Islam or Christianity, is becoming increasingly acceptable.

In addition to exploring social movements in their own terms, a second area of study concerns the relationship between these movements and the state. While a number of social movements have actually sought to take over state power and have done so successfully, others have engaged the state more indirectly, but no less politically. Why and how these different strategies have come about, their implications for progressive politics and the effect they have had on our understanding of the political has yet to be explored in much depth in our discipline. There is certainly no agreement on these questions. While Colas is clear about the political necessity of channelling social and political resistance through the locus of the state, others such as Shaw, Marchand, Robinson and Campbell see potentially important sites of resistance elsewhere.

Thirdly, as Clark rightly points out, paying attention to the collective practices of states also offers us another avenue to explore when it comes to resistance. By shifting our focus exclusively from movements to institutional actors such as states, we bring into view the efforts of individual state leaders and their attempts to build alliances in order to resist certain global configurations of power. The recent failure of the WTO talks in Cancun could be seen in this light.[9]

Turning now to the relationship between 'governance' and 'resistance', as mentioned above, there is a tendency on the part of our contributors to assume, as Colas does, that there is a direct, inherent relationship between the two, that is, the former necessarily begets the latter. To be fair, a number of our authors including Colas, Kenny, Rupert and Robinson prefer to talk about 'relations of oppression' and 'domination' rather than power relations, and therefore clearly feel the need to specify in more concrete terms the kind of power relations that engender resistance. Despite the fact that none of our authors explain what they mean by these two notions, it does provide an interesting alternative starting point to think about the relationship between governance and resistance. By centralising 'oppression' and 'domination' as the problem, then whatever else they may mean by these terms, they are implicitly suggesting that resistance must be understood in terms of challenging relations of injustice and perceived moral wrongs. Thought of in this way, the politics of resistance must be understood, at least partly, as an ethical endeavour, a topic that we shall return to later. This in turn prompts us to question the conventional conception of the subject as an exclusively rational actor and to explore how our political behaviour may be motivated by forces other than the pursuit of rationally defined interests. While many of our contributors allude to this question

---

[9] Representing twenty-one developing countries and led by Brazil, China and India, the G21 became a powerful voice at Cancun pushing for OECD countries to reduce their subsidies to farmers. A second alliance of mainly African states tried to get the issue of subsidies for cotton trade on the agenda. Rather than accept the terms set to them, these states refused to negotiate when their concerns were not acknowledged in the draft text. The talks ended early when the Chairman of the meeting declared that no compromise was possible. For better or for worse, Third World states dug in their heels and resisted the pressure to play a game that they thought unfair from the start. See "The WTO Under Fire', *The Economist*, 20–26 September 2003 for a detailed description of the Cancun Meeting.

with Brassett, Higgott, Campbell and Robinson explicitly touching on our capacity for empathy, it would be interesting to see more work done on this question in IR.

Power and the politics of governance and resistance

According to all our contributors, power is an essential parameter of politics regardless of whether they conceptualise it in terms of resistance or governance. Despite this consensus, however, only a few of our contributors are explicit about what they mean by power and where they think it is located. For Colas and Rupert the location and nature of power is clear and unambiguous. Held in the hands of capitalists it emerges from the social relations of production and takes both a material and ideological form. Robinson adds another level of analysis to this picture by locating power at the discursive level. So while power can be wielded through guns as well as through taken-for-granted 'common sense' beliefs, it can also find expression in the language we use to talk about who we are and, in the case of Robinson's article, what rights we are entitled to.

In addition to these different forms or expressions of power, Robinson's and Marchand's exploration of gender as a power relation introduces a challenge to those who choose to locate it exclusively in either the realm of production relations or state interactions. Clearly, for these two feminist scholars, gender as a power relation must be understood as *sui generis* and cannot be made reducible to other power dynamics. At the same time, however, they remind us that gender relations are sustained by overlapping power relations of class, race and sexuality which also need to be analysed.

Two other authors who offer us interesting hints about the location and nature of power are Shaw and Campbell. While Shaw argues that the production of knowledge is itself a form of power that generates its own politics, Campbell evokes the notion of power through both the visual image and the feeling of empathy. Both have the potential capacity to make us think and act differently.

Despite these important insights, the question of what we mean by power in the context of theorising politics is still largely taken for granted in our discipline. This is not to say that we need *a* theory of power that can be inserted into our already made frames of world politics. It is to say that while both the notions of 'governance' and 'resistance' help us centralise the question of power relations, they offer us only a crude starting point to conceptualise these relations.

Perhaps a more concrete way of thinking about power is to treat it not as an abstract concept or as a substantive entity or thing, but as a socially constructed *relation* which is reproduced in different social realms (family/society/economy/ state); is expressed in different forms (material, discursive, ideological); and is centred around different 'nodal points' to borrow a term from Shaw (gender, race, class, sexuality).[10] Moreover, rather than deriving a notion of politics from pre-determined sites of power (such as production relations or the state), one could

---

[10] This term was originally coined by Laclau and Mouffe, in *Hegemony and Socialist Strategy: Towards a Radical Democratic Politics* (London: Verso, 1985).

begin by identifying sites of resistance, wherever they manifest themselves, and then from there try to uncover the power relations being challenged. In other words, it would involve tracing power relations from the point of their impact rather than their source. In this way, we would be required to open up the question of what constitutes power and reject a monological view of politics that defines the political exclusively in terms of a preconceived understanding of where power is located. Finally, any effort to conceptualise power within the context of governance and resistance would need to explore the way different expressions of power – be they material, discursive or ideological – operate to simultaneously *maintain* as well as *subvert* the social order. So, for example, in terms of the imperative of *governance* – as opposed to that of direct coercion or domination – the importance of ideological and discursive forms of power become particularly salient when trying to understand how order and stability are maintained and how the co-optation of potential resistance can take place. At the same time, as we have seen in Robinson's article, international legal discourses, such as those on human rights, can also provide powerful ideological and discursive resources to those seeking to resist co-optation.

In addition to mapping power according to the different social realms it inhabits, forms it takes and nodal points it represents, applying this framework of power to the politics of governance would also require us – as mentioned earlier – to distin-guish between practices of 'governance', on the one hand, and 'relations of domination' and 'oppression' on the other. While the former certainly involve and reproduce power relations, they are not necessarily experienced as oppressive in nature and in fact are often enacted on the basis of consensus. It is only in the case of the latter that this consensus breaks down and relations of governance are translated into unjust relations of oppression. On the whole, however, there has been little effort to make or explore this distinction in the IR literature on resistance movements. Indeed, the assumption seems to be that it is enough to simply identify power relations – or in the case of the globalisation literature, processes of globalisation – to explain the rise of resistance to them. Thus, the exercise of power, in and of itself, is understood to produce resistance politics. But an overview of history should remind us that our efforts to organise collectively into resistance movements are few and far between since we do not mount resistance against any and all forms of governance. We are then back to the questions: how do people distinguish between 'governance' and 'oppression' and under what conditions do they (choose to?) fight the latter?

In terms of the politics of resistance it is possible to engage in a similar kind of mapping exercise. What specific expressions of power – material, ideological and discursive – are these movements challenging? Where do they locate the origins of these forms of power – state/society/economy/domestic sphere – and how do they conceptualise the particular kind of power relation – gender, race, sexuality, class – they are resisting? The challenge facing any researcher interested in analytically mapping power, however, is to avoid falling into the trap of assigning primacy *a priori* to one expression of power or one social realm over another. Indeed, assessing the relative weight of one expression of power or social realm over another in the constitution of relations of oppression, in our view, can only be done in the light of concrete empirical analysis and cannot be determined theoretically.

Knowledge and the politics of governance and resistance

While most of our contributors acknowledge directly or indirectly the relevance of power and power relations in their discussions of politics, only Shaw focuses on the politics of knowledge production and explicitly draws our attention to the relationship between knowledge and power. Indeed, little has been said in our discipline about the role of knowledge claims in the construction of either the politics of governance or resistance. More specifically, we need to be more curious about the sources of our knowledge as well as the multiple strategies that we deploy to know each other. Furthermore, we need to ask for whom and for what purpose knowledge is being produced in both contexts and what the intended and unintended consequences are of this knowledge production. Who does it address and who is excluded?

In terms of governance, any exploration of knowledge production would need to investigate the role of international institutions and in particular the role of experts within them in defining the international agenda and setting the terms of debate. This study would also have to examine NGOs as 'knowledge makers' especially with regards to scientific issues. To what extent does the knowledge produced by NGOs corroborate or challenge the dominant knowledge paradigms? What sources are deemed acceptable for the construction of authoritative knowledge in this context? So, for example, within the context of the UN Working Group for Indigenous Peoples, although all representatives were allowed to speak, it was only those who made concise legal arguments, rather than emotional, personal or political state-ments, that were seen as contributing to the ongoing dialogue between states and indigenous peoples.[11] True knowledge about the situation of indigenous peoples and the options available to them had to be framed within an impartial, rational discourse.

In terms of resistance, remarkably little attention has been paid to the origins and construction of what Jennifer Milliken terms 'subjugated knowledges'.[12] Along with Shaw, we would suggest that one potentially fruitful place to begin one's inquiry into the nature and role of knowledge within the context of resistance is with those subjugated knowledges developed within the political practices of social movements. How and where are conventional wisdoms, posing as universal truths, being challenged? What constitutes knowledge and 'knowledge claims' in these move-ments? Again, what sources of knowledge do they draw on, how are these sources validated and how are their claims articulated? What role do knowledge claims play in constituting social movements *as movements*, that is, as both a politics of solidarity as well as a politics of difference?

When exploring the construction and role of knowledge in either the context of resistance or governance, we suggest that three things be kept in mind. First, as feminist philosopher Sandra Harding reminds us, we need to distinguish between two types of knowledge, that is, *scientific* and *social* knowledge and to be clear about

---

[11] Interview of Rodrigo Contreras, Executive of the World Council Indigenous Peoples, 1999.
[12] For an interesting discussion of this neglect on the part of postmodernist scholars, see Jennifer Milliken, 'The Study of Discourse in International Relations: A Critique of Research and Methods', *European Journal of International Relations*, 5: 2 (1999), pp. 225–54.

which we are addressing. While the two are interrelated in a number of ways – for example both are socially situated and constructed – each type of knowledge requires different rules of engagement. Thus, when addressing the question of social knowledge, as we are in IR, it is important to remember that understanding social reality requires us not only to know what we think of ourselves and the world, but also what others think of us and our beliefs.[13] In other words, social knowledge should be *self*-reflexive and open to revision in light of the views of *others* whether those others are fellow colleagues in the field or the subjects of our inquiry.

Second, we would argue that much of the debate between critical theorists and postmodernists over knowledge has been reduced to the question of reason and its alleged oppressive or emancipatory value. 'Knowing' in both narratives is solely a cognitive activity. As Lorraine Code has argued:

> The ideals of rationality and objectivity that have guided and inspired theorists of knowledge throughout the history of western philosophy have been constructed through excluding the attributes and experiences commonly associated with femaleness and underclass status: emotion, connection, practicality, sensitivity and idiosyncrasy.[14]

But, knowing the world around us may require, and often does involve, more than the effective functioning of our cerebral and cognitive capacities. Affective relations, based on empathy and compassion, bodily impulses such as our sensations, lived experiences and spiritual insight, are all mediums through which we can come to know about ourselves and imagine the reality of others. Exploring the origins and nature of knowledge claims in the context of varied political practices may give us good reason to question the privileged status of 'reason' in the knowledge/truth-making game as Campbell's interesting discussion of the interplay between empathetic witnessing, visual representation and truth suggests.

Conceptualising politics as a contestation over competing 'truths' – however those truths are derived – does not imply, however, that it should be understood solely as an epistemological conflict. As Shaw has argued, within the context of activism, knowledge claims are mobilised in specific contexts and for particular purposes. Thus, the specific 'truths' mobilised within a movement can be seen as a *means to an end* that in turn must be understood in the broader context of the movement's ethical goals and normative agenda. This requires us to think about the relationship between knowledge and ethics, on the one hand, and politics and ethics, on the other. While many so called postmodernists tend to be suspicious about the relationship between ethics and knowledge, suggesting instead a more natural collusion between power and knowledge, Marxists and critical theorists tend to take the connection for granted, assuming that 'correct knowledge' necessarily leads to progressive politics. Interestingly, while feminists such as Robinson and Marchand would not dispute the postmodernist insight that knowledge claims do implicate power relations, they also highlight the way the quest for knowledge can be understood as part of the pursuit of the 'good life'. Indeed, it seems that the construction of knowledge in the context of either the politics of resistance or

---

[13] Sandra Harding, 'Subjectivity, Experience and Knowledge: An Epistemology from/for Rainbow Coalition Politics' in *Development and Change,* 23: 3 (1992), p. 190.

[14] Sara Ruddick, 'Reason's Femininity: A Case for Connected Knowing' in N. Goldberger *et al.* (eds.), *Knowledge, Difference and Power* (Basic Books: New York, 1996), p. 248.

governance cannot be easily separated from the *ethical commitment* on the part of its participants to particular political ideals, whether they be the nurturing of solidarity, the emancipation of a particular constituency of people, or the transformation or maintenance of a political community.

Ethics and the politics of governance and resistance

The problem is that until recently there has been remarkably little work on the relationship between ethics and politics in the discipline, and the work that is being done is of a highly theoretical nature. In fact conventional accounts of justice in IR have tended to locate ethical life within the territorial state. In other words, they assume that the precondition for justice is a stable political community with a legitimate authority demarcated by territorial borders.[15] More recent attempts to open up the discipline to ethical considerations, such as Linklater's, have suggested the need and possibility of extending our moral universe beyond the territorial state to include the outsider, that is, the non-citizen.[16] What both approaches share, however, is a propensity to separate out ethics from politics and to assume that the question of ethics in international life can only be broached from the point of view of state boundaries and an already established political community. In other words, politics is the condition of possibility for ethics. But can politics and ethics be understood as separatable realms?

In this Special Issue many of our contributors explicitly recognise that the enactment of politics necessarily involves the articulation of a normative agenda which serves to guide the political aspirations and actions of those involved. For example, explicit in the work of Rupert, Kenny and Robinson and implicit in the work of Marchand is a view of social movements as fighting for an alternative vision of the 'good life'. For these authors then the politics of resistance involves the collective effort of a particular constituency of people to transform society as a whole according to their normative aspirations. In this way, movements go beyond representing the 'interests' of a lobby group and must be seen as setting forth a normative agenda for the broader community in which they live.[17]

While there is some conceptual space in IR to depict the politics of resistance as an ethically oriented labour, it is considerably harder to conceptualise the politics of governance in this way. After all, as we have seen, the 'politics of resistance' is generally associated with domestic, non-state forces, actors that, in IR, are allowed

---

[15] Richard Higgott, 'Contested Globalisation: The Changing Context and Normative Challenges', *Review of International Studies,* 26 (December 2000), p. 131.

[16] Andrew Linklater, *The Transformation of Political Community* (Cambridge: Polity Press, 1998).

[17] It is for this reason that discussions which characterise social movements as 'bypassing' the state, ultimately, miss the point. While some of today's social movements may not wish to take over the state *per se* or even participate in official governmental politics, they are all concerned with obtaining an acknowledgement that the issues around which they are mobilised are a matter of *public concern* and, even more importantly, *public responsibility*. Thus, to the extent that the state represents the legitimate political authority of a community, and, thereby, the 'public good', it is a critical interlocutor for social movements.

to have and act upon a moral point of view. The politics of governance, however, is generally associated with the actions of states or institutions, entities that have not traditionally been endowed with moral sensibilities. Although Brassett and Higgott challenge this view when they characterise governance as an ethical enterprise, they do so by making a *normative argument for* the enactment of a pragmatist ethics. Thus, they are motivated by the question of what *can be* and in this context entreat state leaders and IR scholars to adopt a more pragmatic ethical attitude.

One way forward might be to meld Clark's call for the 'working out of the politics of legitimacy' with the Brassett/Higgott emphasis on the 'experimentalism of the pragmatic ethic'. As Clark notes, the main agencies of global governance, through the political conditionality of their loans to the Third World, have in effect begun to articulate a new conception of the 'legitimate state' in terms of states' observance of various norms of 'good governance'. All too often, this has mainly been translated into pressures towards 'structural adjustment' of the recipients' economies, provoking what Higgott has elsewhere described as the 'politics of resentment' and the suspicion that what is really involved is the advancement of Western economic interests. 'Good' in the 'good governance' formula means, at best, economic efficiency rather than any notion of the morally right. Yet any definition of what 'good governance' entails must include qualities such as democracy, human rights observance, the rule of law, and transparency and accountability of public institutions. These are universal values but are also capable of being given culturally specific meanings in different national contexts. There is here the possibility of a broad, ethically grounded agenda around which both Western-dominated agencies of governance and poorer countries might coalesce, as in the African Union's New Partnership for African Development, which involved acceptance of good governance principles worked out in part with the Group of Seven. But rather than being operationalised through grand designs, it might be possible for the specifics of what would amount to a new 'politics of legitimacy' to be elaborated through piecemeal experimentation *via* the sympathetic engagement of NGOs, individuals and other elements of 'global civil society'.

Such an approach might, however, be open to the criticism that it amounted to little more than yet another variant of Western imperialism, because it would unavoidably have a strong 'top down' element through the agenda-setting activities and carrots and sticks of the global governance agencies. An alternative way of thinking about ethics in the context of international politics would be to move away from conventional IR categories, including the governance/resistance dichotomy, and take as one's starting point how we relate ethically to others. This shift would require us to be more curious about three lines of inquiry.

First, if we accept the view put forward by some of our contributors that the 'politics of resistance' must be seen as the collective enactment of a shared ethical commitment to end relations of injustice and bring about social change, then we need to rethink our view of the human subject as an inherently moral being, or at least as a subject capable of what could be termed a 'moral imagination' and a 'moral will'. Indeed, too little work has been done in IR on developing a conception of ourselves as *normative beings*. Whether we develop this notion in terms of 'moral will' and 'moral imagination', or in some other way, we need to get to grips with the fact that theories of world politics are inevitably theories about the way we, as human beings, live and want to live together. Second, we also need to develop a fuller account of ourselves as *social beings* and of the social bonds that tie us together. In other words, we need to reflect more explicitly on the nature of our subjectivity (and inter-subjectivity) and on the way in which our ethical aspirations are almost invariably other-oriented. In this connection, Kenny's article points us in the right direction. Third, and connected to the first two questions, is the need to formulate a conception of politics that sees it as one way in which we give expression to our ethical and social aspirations. Moreover, this insight must be seen as equally true of the politics of governance as it is of the politics of resistance. After all, while some may seek to change the world in which they live on ethical grounds, others may just as ardently seek to defend it according to their own normative visions. In this way, the 'politics of governance' and the 'politics of resistance' can be reconceptualised, at least in part, as a conflict over different, opposing 'moral imaginations' in which people choose to act, alone or in concert, in the name of particular norms, values and aspirations. These aspirations, in turn, concern not only their own lives and those close to them, but embrace a broader conception of humanity. As such, the 'politics of governance' is as normative an endeavour as the 'politics of resistance'.[18]

Conclusion

By means of a conclusion we would like to say one last word about the methodology required to undertake such a research programme. On the whole, the articles in this Special Issue have said little about the methodological requirements for the study of politics in our discipline. Indeed, until now, the question of methodology in general and method in particular has been more of a concern for our American colleagues seeking to construct models that can predict or, at the very least, explain state actions. But even if we are less interested in defending the 'scientific' credentials of our approaches, we still need to be more self-reflective about the way we study politics. After all, thinking about *how* we do what we do, can also help us clarify *what* it is we are trying to do. Without wanting to close off any avenues of discussion, we offer the following three observations.

First, given the dominance of the realist narrative in IR until relatively recently, it is not surprising that most of the efforts of 'critical' IR scholars have focused on clearing some theoretical space for alternative understandings of politics. To this extent we agree with those who claim that, while philosophy and political theory may not be able to resolve politics, it can certainly inform our discussions of it and even make room for new political possibilities. This interest in theory, however, has not been matched by an equal concern with exploring concrete political practices. In other words, rather than develop theory from practice, much of the theoretical discussion on IR's critical margins – but not all – has taken place at a safe distance from empirical research. But one cannot extrapolate a conception of politics solely

---

[18] For a discussion about the normative demands and implications of the 'politics of governance' see Richard Higgott, 'Contested Globalisation: The Changing Context and Normative Challenges', *Review of International Studies*. 26, Special Issue (December 2000).

from one's meta- or social-theoretical starting points. Quoting Laclau, Campbell states, 'the notion that there is a politics of ... depends upon the discreditable idea that one can chart a clear course from metaphysics to politics'.[19] We agree and would argue that rather than build theory from theory, we need to allow substantive empirical research, social theory and metatheory to inform each other.

In terms of substantive research, it is important that we engage in both a macro- and micro-analysis of politics. While the former requires us to locate the historical context and trace the structural outlines of a particular political event or pheno- menon, the latter directs our attention to the *specific practices* and *self-understandings* of the political actors we wish to understand. This, in turn, requires methods that allow us to explore, among other things, the strategic knowledge claims of not only movement activists, but also bureaucrats and leaders within governance institutions. While we do this, we must be humble enough to recognise that it is impossible for us to assess these practices and perceptions from a neutral, ungrounded point of view. As both Shaw and Robinson suggest, objectivity of this kind is elusive at best and disingenuous at worst. For this reason, we agree with Shaw when she insists that we need to pay attention to both the intended and unintended consequences of our knowledge production and that we see the work that we do as historically situated and contingently relevant.

Finally, we think that it is important to see these methodological imperatives in the broader context of our intellectual and political responsibility as academics. As we have seen in this Special Issue, most of our contributors explicitly recognise the political import of theorising and the imperative of constructing theories that reflect not only our political practices, but also our values and aspirations. Nonetheless, in the heat of academic debate and under the pressure of academic production, it is easy for us to forget that, while we may not agree on the best way to accomplish this, we do share a common cause: to articulate theories of politics that serve to remind us that we not only reproduce the world in which we live, but that we can also change it. It is in this context that the notions of 'politics of governance' and 'politics of resistance' may offer one of many possible ways forward.

---

[19] David Campbell, 'The Politics of Radical Interdependence: A Rejoinder to Daniel Warner', *Millennium*, 25: 1 (1996), p. 136.

Building the normative dimension(s) of a global polity

JAMES BRASSETT AND RICHARD HIGGOTT

Introduction

Globalisation is not what it used to be. Earlier debates over how to read the indicators of economic liberalisation and the impact of technological expansion have now been joined by the increasingly pressing need to explore the social, environmental and political aspects of global change. Earlier discussions emphasised a number of dichotomies within the international political economy – open/closed, state/market and so on. These have proved limited in their ability to inform explanations of change under conditions of globalisation. To these we must now add what we might call the 'governance from above', 'resistance from below' dichotomy as a popular metaphor for understanding order and change in international relations under conditions of globalisation. But this new binary axis is in many ways as unsatisfactory as those that went before. It too can obscure as much as it reveals in terms of understanding the normative possibilities of reforming globalisation. In this article we wish to suggest that there is perhaps a more useful way of thinking about politics and the changing contours of political life in the contemporary global order. This approach blurs the distinction between governance and resistance by emphasising an ethical take on globalisation.

Building on some innovations in social theory that have found their way into international relations scholarship we stress the need for a permanently reflexive relationship between meta-theory, social, political and economic theory and policy practice at the global level. The social science academy, especially the tradition of neoclassical economics, offers (both explicitly and implicitly) much more than mere scholastic meditation. As we have long known, it informs the practical horizons for the policy community. Academic understanding is not simply the depoliticised provision of technical mechanisms for governing (or not governing). It is itself a political act that casts massive shadows over policy.

Globalisation is not simply 'out there'. It is constructed through our understandings of communicative practices. A self-conscious promotion of theoretical innovation as a political act is not an exercise in reflection for its own sake. Any attempt to understand and explain the nature of social structures and processes must subsequently provide a normative justification for a chosen preferred approach. As a critique of rationalism, the identification of the epistemology of power (the major strength of postmodernism) is not, of itself, sufficient. It must be accompanied by a self-conscious normative intent if we are to build the ethical dimensions of globalisation. If, to borrow a phrase, globalisation is what we make of it, the content of 'what' and the group that is 'we' are ethical questions of direct policy relevance to the contemporary global political economy. This article seeks to draw together a redescription of globalisation as both an ethical and political question with the bones of a reformist way of considering how to socially re-embed its more technocratic and economistic elements.

Apart from the work of a few notable, though often politically marginal authors, this normative facet of globalisation has either been ignored, or worse still, assumed to be a commonly agreed objective. This was invariably the case amongst leading globalisers – that is, proponents of the continued liberalisation of the global economic order occupying positions of influence in either the public or the private policy domains – during the 1990s. But it was also often the case in the community of academic economists interested in globalisation, for whom there has been an unproblematic conflation of economic growth with human welfare on the one hand, and the subsequent marginalisation of any reflective normative theorising about issues of justice in the policy domain on the other. For a range of reasons, including the efforts of resistance-based political groups, the period since the late 1990s has seen a recognition of this lacuna in both the global policy community and the scholarly economic community.[1]

This under-representation of the normative dimension of globalisation throughout the 1990s was, with a few exceptions, as much a weakness of (international) political theory as it was a failure of neoliberal economic theory and policy practice to engage the ethical underpinnings of *economic* globalisation.[2] As currently constituted, the institutions of global economic governance, and the rationalist theories of liberal economy which underpin them, offer little in the way of substantive, ethically sophisticated, political agendas for *humanising* globalisation.[3] Similarly, as currently constituted, competing cosmopolitan theories of international relations or liberal political philosophies of justice, upscaled to the global level, exhibit too little an appreciation of the dynamic(s) of the market place to offer meaningful ways of addressing the political legitimacy deficit in the global economic order. It is only in the creation of a dialogue across the domains of economics, political theory and policy practice that meaningful mechanisms for reform are likely to emerge. The article therefore seeks to operationalise a conception of justice *via* a redescription of globalisation as an explicitly political and ethical issue.

Our first section adopts an analytical focus that takes account of the extant sociopolitical transformations associated with globalisation. It aspires to a better understanding of the preponderance of non-state actors and competing sites of

---

[1] For an analysis of the mood swing that is causing a major rethink about the normative dimensions of the globalisation project, see Richard Higgott, 'Contested Globalisation: the Changing Context and Normative Challenges', *Review of International Studies*, 26 (2000), pp. 131–53.

[2] But see the essays in Andrew Hurrell and Ngaire Woods (eds.), *Inequality, Globalisation and World Politics* (Oxford: Oxford University Press, 1999), and Thomas Pogge (ed.), *Global Justice* (Oxford: Blackwells, 2001). See also Chris Brown, *Sovereignty, Rights and Justice* (Cambridge: Polity Press, 2002).

[3] For an explanation of these limitations, see Richard Higgott, 'Taming Economics, Emboldening International Relations: The Theory and Practice of International Political Economy in an Era of Globalisation', Stephanie Lawson (ed.), *The New Agenda for International Relations: From Polarisation to Globalisation in World Politics* (Cambridge: Polity, 2002).

authority in the global system than can be captured by 'systemic' or 'international society' theorising. To that end the article makes a cursory delineation of the contours of what has been called elsewhere '*a global polity*' and outlines some of its central points of contest. By this we do not mean that there is a world government, or that politics is no longer inter- or intra-state focused. Rather it is observed that the extant global space provides for a different, and emerging form of politics that requires alternative theoretical elaboration.[4]

A return to ethical theory might allow us a different and (potentially) more constructive way of regarding the development of the global polity than is gleaned from economically rationalist accounts of globalisation on the one hand, or some of the more traditional veins of international theory on the other. In both its problematisation of the relationship between individuals/groups and institutions, and in its preoccupation with the question of community, ethical theory in international relations – be it cosmopolitan or communitarian – represents a conduit into the politics of the global polity. But, we argue, this utility as a conduit does not necessarily lead to a meaningful agenda for change.

Our second section therefore examines the difficulties of extracting a 'practical' ethic commensurate with a broad-based political reform of globalisation. The debate between cosmopolitanism and communitarianism itself highlights the problem of achieving a standard of justice in a world of different sociocultural particularities and realistic power structures that delimit the 'arc of possibilities'[5] open to practitioners. It is all very well to suggest ethical utopias, but quite another thing to find agreement on their content, or 'convince' the deep structures of political, social, economic, and psychological interests at work in the global polity of their desirability.

In its more predictive forms the communitarian position – as it is understood within IR – is found to equate ethics with power, since most of the 'stuff' of ethical politics is reduced to the relations *between,* rather than within, communities. This article proposes that the strength of the communitarian position has perpetuated a tradition of middle-way theorising in IR. *Pace* the English School and Neoliberal Institutionalism, much speculation on the normative dimension(s) of the global polity has been presaged upon the need to reconcile the competing claims of individuals (usually read as a universal given) and communities (usually read as states). Whilst laudable, such philosophical refinement, even in those most sophisticated of renderings provided by, say, Andrew Linklater,[6] may be more exemplary of the limitations of normative theorising for the global polity than the possibilities that could be *built*. Indeed, the very framing of this debate may itself act to constrict the possibilities for *engagement*. Foundationalist arguments may simply waste too much intellectual energy attempting to define '*what is*' in order to legitimise their arguments for '*what should be*'?

---

[4] For an elaboration of this line of argument, see Richard Higgott and Morten Ougaard, 'Beyond System and Society: Towards a Global Polity?' in Morten Ougaard and Richard Higgott (eds.), *A Global Polity* (London: Routledge, 2002).

[5] Jim George, 'Creating Globalisation: "Patriotic Internationalism" and Symbiotic Power Relations in the Post WW2 Era', Working Paper 66/01, University of Warwick: Centre for the Study of Globalisation and Regionalisation, January 2001.

[6] See his *Transformation of Political Community: The Ethical Foundations of the Post Westphalian Era* (Cambridge: Polity, 1998).

Thus, in the third section we suggest that the anti-foundationalist pragmatism of Richard Rorty offers a more interesting and practical philosophical question of '*what could be?*' In this we follow previous work in normative IR that notes the heuristic utility of the cosmopolitan-communitarian debate while suggesting its ultimately constraining nature. By applying Rorty's thought to the salient political issue of globalisation, this article seeks to contribute towards the work of those contemporary international theorists who have engaged Rortian pragmatism.[7] We draw on Rorty's work to make an argument in favour of a pragmatic praxis as a viable means of developing understanding(s) of, and the normative potential within, the global polity.

In the simple and under-theorised sentimentality of the Rortian ethic of redescription we find an imaginative springboard for launching a reformist agenda. Rortian pragmatism is advanced for its 'enabling qualities'. Firstly, it enables us to view our approach as both contingent and fallible, thus imploring us to *build* the normative agendas we support. Political praxis is central to such theory/practice. And secondly, it enables us to view our approaches as experimental. Rather than losing ourselves in some ethic that 'changes the world' we should instead focus our energies upon 'small' experimental approaches to issues like poverty, selfishness, technocratic ignorance, depoliticised economism, the achievement of 'voice' for those accustomed to going without it, and institutional reform. These agendas alone will not solve all problems, rather they offer a focus and a drive to realise the (more) normative dimension(s) that the global polity could potentially harbour.

By combining a *political* ontology of globalisation with an ethic of pragmatic reformism we raise the salience of the role of sympathy and hope in the everyday practices of the global polity. The propensity to elicit and actualise ethical values is a function of the reflexive interrelations of multiple actors (international organisations, states, NGOs, civil society, MNCs, financial market actors) operating at multiple levels (international, supra-territorial, regional, local, and through the media) within the global polity. There is no ethical end game to be realised: just a more ethically and politically aware *set of games* to be played. In section four we offer some initial and rudimentary suggestions about what pragmatic redescription in the global polity might mean.

Towards a global polity?

Globalisation is an often-used and radically underspecified term. It has been variously ascribed the characteristics of economic liberalisation, internationalisation, universalisation, Westernisation, and deterritorialisation.[8] Causal dynamics

---

[7] Chris Brown, *International Relations Theory: New Normative Approaches* (New York: Columbia University Press, 1992) and on Rorty: 'Universal Human Rights: A Critique', in Tim Dunne and Nicholas Wheeler (eds.), *Human Rights in Global Perspective* (Cambridge University Press, 1999), and Molly Cochran, *Normative Theory and International Relations* (Cambridge: Cambridge University Press, 1999).

[8] For the best introductory discussion, see Jan Aart Scholte, *Globalisation: A Critical Introduction* (London: Macmillan, 2000).

differ between perspectives but they all include some notion of heightened economic, communicative, and technological interconnection. Although elements of globalisation can be analytically separated and falsified, or not falsified, in this way, in this article we use a minimalist conception of globalisation as the creation of an extensively (though not uniformly) interconnected and *contested* global space. It is in the nature and extent of this interconnection and contest that globalisation provokes a number of questions that – *by their very nature* – serve to politicise the global space.

In the most popularly received and most criticised reading, globalisation heralds the dawn of a universal space in which the divisive influences of nationalism, ethnicity, and religion will be transcended by secular modern liberal democracy.[9] In its more economistic interpretations the thesis has been bound up with the growth of a global market for goods and services which, left unfettered, will break free from the shackles of state regulation. In the 1990s globalisation for many governments appeared to become a 'normalising discourse' of power that conditioned policy responses to the perception, if not always the reality, of global market integration.

As we now appreciate, this hyper-globalist view over-egged the ascendancy of the market and was too quick to write off the importance of the state both politically, and as Paul Krugman has recently noted, economically.[10] Such rhetorical depictions of the state as 'withering' or 'retreating'[11] prompted a sustained backlash from within a number of scholarly circles that sought to re-establish the importance of the state as the main actor in international relations.[12] Indeed much of the initially popular and populist debate over globalisation turned on a rationalist-driven 'states *vs.* markets' dichotomy. Such a seemingly zero-sum contest belied a capacity of the state to secure a more gradual transformation in state-market relations; or, a positive-sum diffusion of power amongst non-state actors operating in multiple sites of authority in the global system.

A subtler rendition of the relationship between states and markets sees it as a perpetual process of reconstruction of the mechanisms for sustaining capitalist accumulation in an era of global structural change. From this standpoint, we can accept the augmented power of the structures of global finance and production, whilst recognising that there is still no substitute for the state as the repository of sovereignty and rule-making and as provider of national security. But it is a state that is in a process of adaptation. States have been joined by a host of non-state actors operating at multiple sites of authority – both public and private – in the global policy process.[13]

---

[9] Quintessentially, see Francis Fukuyama, *The End of History and the Last Man* (Harmondsworth: Penguin, 1992).

[10] Paul Krugman, *The Return of Depression Economics* (London: The Allen Lane Press, 1999).

[11] See Kenichi Ohmae, *The End of the Nation State* (London: Harper Collins, 1995) and Susan Strange, *The Retreat of the State: The Diffusion of Power in the World Economy* (Cambridge: Cambridge University Press, 1996).

[12] For restatement of the strength of the state, see Paul Hirst and Grahame Thompson, 'Globalization – a Necessary Myth?' in David Held and Anthony McGrew, *The Global Transformations Reader: An Introduction to the Globalization Debate* (Cambridge Polity Press, 2000).

[13] See the essays in Claire Cutler, Virginia Haufler and Tony Porter (eds.), *Private Authority and International Affairs* (New York: SUNY Press, 1999) and Richard Higgott and Geoffrey Underhill and Andreas Bieler (eds.), *Non-State Actors and Authority in the Global System* (London: Routledge, 2000).

A diffusion of power and influence through international organisations like the IMF, World Bank, WTO, EU, and BIS, as well as the growing salience of private and voluntary regulatory bodies has meant a complex expansion, no matter that it is contested terrain, of the public sphere. There has, in short, been a 'globalisation of political life'. Three elements underwrite the claim for the emergence of the nascent 'global polity':[14]

1. Most obviously, there is a growing political interconnectedness. This is a pheno-menon recognised several decades ago,[15] but interconnectedness in a global polity, as opposed to traditional understandings of the international system or society, is not only between states, but also supra-, sub- and non-state actors.
2. There is a vast and interlocking network of global regulation and sites of decision-making where policies of a (quasi-) global nature are made. We include in this category the (international) institutions of global governance: the IMF, World Bank, WTO, the UN agencies as well as the growing (if underexposed) salience of organisations of private and non-state regulation in areas such as credit rating and industry standards setting. That ratings agencies like Moodys and Standard and Poors can strongly influence the economic fortunes of states is surely a political relation as much as an economic one.[16]
3. A more difficult dimension of this process to capture, but no less important for that, is the growing sense of 'community' that appears to be developing beyond the confines of the state. As Robertson would have it, globality is defined in the context of a consciousness '. . . of the world as a single place'. [17] This is not to suggest the emergence of a common set of global values, rather to indicate the growth of thinking about 'the world' as an identifiable sense of place or space where different values can legitimately contest one another. A quintessential fact of international political life has been the multiplication of global gatherings that argue over the validity of a multiple array of global principles and practices.[18]

It could even be argued that the contestable efficacy or legitimacy of these institutions is itself a salient feature in the politics of the global polity. Even if states and non-state actors are in disagreement about the norms and principles that are emerging, in practice, by the very fact that they contest the nature of these principles and practices in global assemblies and other instances of global public space, it has the consequence (unintended as it may be) of furthering the development of a global

---

[14] The discussion in this section draws on Higgott and Ougaard, *Global Polity*.
[15] See Robert O Keohane and Joseph Nye, *Power and Interdependence* (Boston, MA: Little Brown, 1977).
[16] See T. J. Sinclair, 'Passing Judgement: Credit Rating Processes as Regulatory Mechanism of Governance in the Emerging World Order', *Review of International Political Economy*, 1: (1994), pp. 133–49.
[17] Roland Robertson, *Globalisation, Social Theory and Global Culture* (London: Sage, 1992), p. 132.
[18] These can range from meetings of small non-governmental organisations (NGOs) and Global Social Movements (GSMs), through to the UN conference system. Gatherings at the global level cover issues as diverse as gender, development, environment, welfare, cities, security to the Davos gatherings of the rich and powerful of the private (and public) sector policymaking world and their counterpart gatherings such as the Porto Allegro World Social Forum.

polity. On this view we might be able to understand realist or mercantilist positions regarding globalisation *for what they are* – that is, coherent attempts to contest the political meaning, and therefore social outcomes, of decision-making within the global polity.

Governance, resistance and the possibilities for reform

To refine the analytical focus, we wish to talk about something more than traditional state-centred understandings of world politics, as 'systemic' or 'societal' on the one hand (still the principal mode of reasoning in international relations scholarship along a Waltzian structuralist–international society/English School spectrum) but as something less than a single complex of enforceable societal relationships on the other. Greater attention has to be paid to the changes in the quality and quantity of global structural change. Financial interconnections over recent decades have had a profound effect upon the capacity of states to pursue national welfare options. This is not simply to privilege structure at the expense of agency. States remain important actors in world politics. But they have been joined by a host of non-state actors that actively 'transcend' territorial politics in an attempt to realise their interests at multiple levels, including the institutions of supra-territorial governance. To this extent they are the players in the polity. Agents that would have once focused most of their attention on attempting to influence the policy process within national polities now channel more energy than in the past towards securing influence beyond the boundaries of the state.

   Most notably, there have been a number of significant points of resistance to globalisation that have contested the free-market fundamentalism of the 1990s Washington Consensus (WC) and ushered in a period of more socially aware governance. For brevity's sake we term this the era of the Post-Washington Consensus (PWC).[19] Some key events and features of this era include the failure of MAI, the financial crises in Latin America, East Asia and Eastern Europe, the semi-institutionalisation of the anti-globalisation movement from Seattle on and, perhaps most importantly, the growing belief that globalisation is at least correlated with, if not proven to be causally related to, vast income differentials at the global level. These have been focal points for the critical activities of an ever-burgeoning global civil society. By contesting globalisation and the market orthodoxies of the earlier 'Washington Consensus' era through active public engagement, these events have brought to the public sphere a metapolitics of instititutional legitimacy in which the procedures of the global governance are subjected to greater public scrutiny than at any time since their inception in the Bretton Woods era. Whether this process is itself legitimate – according to the efficiency models of governance popular amongst the policy communities that inhabit the corridors of the IMF, World Bank, and WTO – or not, is itself contested.

---

[19] We are aware of the contentious and clichéd status of the terms 'Washington and post-Washington consensus'. We use them to capture the changing international mood at the end of the twentieth century.

The important point for this article is that this growing public engagement, through non-state actor pressure, has had an impact. Governance is not merely resisted: interaction has on a number of occasions led to reform. A mood swing in the global governance agenda has led to an increased concentration on a more socially aware rhetoric of economic globalisation. In turn this has gone some way towards a recognition that globalisation has to be *politically* socialised, legitimised and democratised if the wider gains of the *economic* liberalisation process are not also to be lost to its major beneficiaries. But we are at the beginning, not the end, of this process of political deliberation. With neither agreement on the scope of the global polity, nor the institutions of global governance strong enough to administer to it, the global polity remains nascent and contested.

By reflecting such dynamics, we aim to demonstrate the inherent interrelationship, and normative value, of political contest, governance and reform. Importantly for this article, the growing salience of new actors in the formulation of public policy renders governance as a process more akin to 'political negotiation' – weak and inhibited as it may be – rather than merely 'efficient administration'. It is this latter view – governance as efficient administration – that roughly approximates the position of many in the policy community influential over the shape and course of globalisation. After the exposure of the institutions of the Washington consensus to the failures of the late 1990s and the resultant contest over the substantive content of future policy, 'governance' was a term that gained prevalence in the scholar *cum* policy community. In the recent public policy literature, governance refers to '. . . . the development of governing styles in which boundaries between and within public and private sectors have become blurred'.[20] But this definition neither notes the way globalisation has also blurred the domestic-international divide as material fact, nor the longer term historical development of systems of emerging international norms and regimes (both public and private) that represent the elements of a framework of 'governance without government' under globalisation.[21]

In this way, the *hosting metaphor* of the global polity allows us to situate the politics of 'contested globalisation' within the context of broader debates over governance within International Relations.[22] Understanding of, and attention to, the importance of normative questions of governance and state practice as exercises in accountability and democratic enhancement must catch up with our understanding of governance as exercises in effectiveness and efficiency. In this way 'politics', as opposed to 'efficiency', comes to occupy a more significant place in the discourse of globalisation than much of the contemporary literature reflects. More importantly for this article, with the introduction of politics as an explicitly normative concern, the global polity is rendered susceptible to ethical scrutiny and questions of legitimacy and justice, in a manner not possible under the hegemony of a neoliberal economic orthodoxy of the Washington consensus era.

---

[20] Gerry Stoker, 'Governance as Theory: Five Propositions', *International Social Science Journal*, 155 (1999), p. 17.

[21] See the pioneering essays in Ernst Otto Czempiel and James N. Rosenau, *Governance without Government: Order and Change in World Politics* (Cambridge: Cambridge University Press, 1992).

[22] See Higgott, 'Contested Globalisation', pp. 131–53.

The ethical dimension(s) of the global polity

In the reading we advance here, and we recognise that it might not be the only reading, the debate between cosmopolitans and communitarians can usefully help theorise the global polity for two reasons. Firstly, the status of individuals *vis à vis* states and other institutions is understood as a core point of ethical debate. Whether we accept the cosmopolitan view that man *qua* man is the ontological site for ethical deliberation on the one hand, or the communitarian riposte on the other that an acultural, ahistorical notion of individuality is simply untenable, it is clear that the rise of supraterritorial relations within the global polity goes to the heart of some profound philosophical questions. That the two debates should be combined appears self-evident.

Secondly, in the tensions between universalism and particularism, which the debate exposes, we can find illustrations of the kind of questions that can and should be posed of international organisations, states, capital markets, civil society, and MNCs. In the transnational spread of capitalist arrangements we discern a number of contests over market structure, regulation standards, credit agreements, and social welfare that are increasingly resolved within institutions of global governance. Whether we regard this as an opportunity (as yet unrealised) to institute universal standards for the global polity, or as an example of the putative particularist domination of the world through the ascendancy of the Anglo-Saxon model of capitalism, this contest will determine the way we frame the ethical dimension(s) of the global polity. This section offers a generalised account of cosmopolitanism and contrasts it with a communitarian perspective, before engaging the 'thinner' cosmopolitanism of Andrew Linklater.

Cosmopolitanism

Cosmopolitanism takes the view that social institutions should be justifiable on the basis that they meet the 'basic rights' of individuals in respect of universal standards of justice, liberty and equality. Although this position is not *presaged* upon the interdependence of the world economy and resultant liberal optimism that accompanied the naïve language of early 1990s globalisation,[23] it nevertheless attempts to construct notions of justice that draw upon and go some way towards constructing such an ideal. To the extent that human equality is a basic cosmopolitan world-view, the globalisation of technological and communicative linkages can be seen as a facilitator of cosmopolitan ethics. Although it is a large step from 'one world economy' to a 'community of mankind', cosmopolitans could highlight the ethical potentials of globalisation. Certainly when taken in the context of the end of the

---

[23] At its most naïve, this language contended that 'two meta trends – fundamental technological change and a new ethos of openness – will transform our world into the beginnings of a global civilisation, a new civilisation of civilisations, that will blossom through the coming century', Peter Schwarz and Peter Leyden, 'The Long Boom: A History of the Future', *Wired*, July 1997, p. 116.

Cold War and the genuine spread of 'freedoms' from ideological domination and militarism, there is some credence to this view.

More substantively, there is a raft of political changes concomitant with globalisation that could bring confidence to cosmopolitan positions. The division of the world into states is one manifestation of how reason can, in effect, 'globalise'. Norms of representation and the chance of peaceful stability amongst states represent an institutional medium for achieving universal standards. Add to that the growing auspices of international governance institutions and the global polity could be described as displaying what some have called 'embedded cosmopolitanism'.[24] The burgeoning membership of bodies like the IMF, the WBG and the WTO certainly creates the administrative capacity for a universal constituency. Indeed, if such overtly market-oriented institutions could coordinate their policies with the appropriate departments of the UN, as envisaged in the turn of the century UNDP initiatives on governance and global public goods, and the UN's Global Compact with the private sector to promote human rights and raise labour and environmental standards,[25] then an ethical cosmopolitan order could be considered a nascent reality.

However, as critics of cosmopolitanism would argue, the use of the word 'if' is crucial to this discussion. Indeed, the burden of political efficacy has been a central concern for late twentieth-century cosmopolitan theorists. One response has been to attach philosophical justification to extant changes associated with economic globalisation. In *Political Theory and International Relations* (1979), for example, Charles Beitz argued that interdependence in the global polity undermines the assumption common amongst political theorists – and John Rawls in particular – that states are self-sufficient entities which represent the sole site of political and ethical discourse.[26] From the perspective of the global polity outlined in our first section, this is an observation we would accept intuitively, at least. Certainly it opens the possibility for meaningful dialogue between political theory and IR. However, Beitz's development of this point serves rather to illustrate the institutional and political problems that cosmopolitanism must face when applied at the global level. He suggests that such extant trends in the international political economy could point to a 'global scheme of social co-operation.[27] On this view, a case can be made for viewing individuals as the prime foundation of justice and elicit the possibility of global redistributive justice. This is strong stuff. By locating moral value in the individual, Beitz questions the empirical and ethical autonomy of states and therefore challenges the fundamental assumptions of both political theory and IR. Yet we feel that the argument is undermined on two counts, one institutional, one empirical.

---

[24] See Toni Erskine, '"Citizen of Nowhere" or "Point Where Circles Intersect"? Impartialist and embedded cosmopolitans', *Review of International Studies*, 28 (2002), pp. 457–78.

[25] See Inge Kaul Isabell Grunberg and Marc A. Stern (eds.), *Global Public Goods: International Cooperation in the 21st Century* (New York: Oxford University Press for the UNDP and John G. Ruggie).

[26] Charles Beitz, *Political Theory and International Relations* (Princeton, NJ: University Press, 1979). Much of Beitz's discussion is set up as a critique of the bounded nature of justice in John Rawls' *A Theory of Justice* (Oxford: Oxford University Press, 1971). For the purposes of this article we concentrate on the side of Beitz's argument which focuses on economic interdependence.

[27] Ibid., p. 149.

Firstly, although Beitz undermines the empirical and ethical strength of states by founding justice in the person of the individual, he concedes that states – as the central players in the global polity – will remain the primary mechanism for implementing any kind of redistributive justice at the global level. As Molly Cochran judges, on this view: 'international distributive justice applies only derivatively to states and principally to persons in the founding principles for the establishment of just social arrangements'.[28] This appears to be a compromise argument that surely creates more problems than it solves. How one justifies the foundation of policy in the ethical value of individuals and then persuades (different) states to administer it, is a question that illustrates, rather than solves, the complexity of institutional arrangements in the global polity.

Secondly, by attaching universalist arguments for distributive justice to empirical rather than abstract criteria Beitz opens himself to empirical refutation. While interdependence has grown in the absolute, in certain parts of the world it remains very slight, even non-existent. If justice pertains to those areas with a higher level of interdependence because that represents a scheme for cooperative venture what becomes of those isolated areas less integrated into the global polity? Followed through to its logical conclusion, Beitz's argument would find a stronger case for redistributive justice in Europe than it would in sub-Saharan Africa.[29] This counter-intuitive point presses the need for a more nuanced appreciation of globalisation than simply a phenomenon of increased interdependence.

Further interpretations of the cosmopolitan tradition have taken this tack. David Held and Anthony McGrew have investigated the potential of the institutions of global governance for representation and accountability.[30] This brand of cosmopolitan democracy seeks to highlight the deficits between the major sites of power and the dispossessed in the global polity. They propose a democratisation along a scale of institutional form ranging from representative houses in the UN, the increased representation of small states in international bodies and, in a form of subsidiarity, the devolution of public policy to the lowest practicable level. Indeed, Held's notion of 'double democratisation', both within states and across borders, represents one of the most 'practical' agendas for institutionalising cosmopolitan justice in the global polity.[31]

Community and the global polity

Although we might note the 'forward looking' qualities of cosmopolitanism, both in its ability to open debate on how we justify social arrangements and its attempt to

---

[28] Molly Cochran, *Normative Theory and International Relations: A Pragmatic Approach* (Cambridge University Press, 1998), p. 28.

[29] See Chris Brown, *International Relations Theory: New Normative Approaches*, p. 176.

[30] See David Held, *Democracy and the Global Order: From the Modern State to Cosmopolitan Governance* (Cambridge: Polity, 1995), and Held and Anthony McGrew, *Global Transformations: Politics, Economics and Culture* (Cambridge: Polity, 1999).

[31] For a defence of this position against some of the more commonly expressed criticisms from within IR, see Barry Buzan and David Held, 'Realism versus Cosmopolitanism', *Review of International Studies*, 24:3 (1998), p. 390.

attach such a theory to extant social changes in the global polity, there are deep philosophical problems with such an account. Regardless of the complex institutional arrangements required to administer the kind of moral inclusion and redistributive justice which cosmopolitan theorists envisage, there are fundamental questions over the ontological primacy attributed to individuals and the resultant universalism it posits. From a communitarian perspective such universalism is rendered an inaccurate depiction of reality, or worse, one that could hasten a form of imperialism through ignorance to the social mores of different cultures.

A more critical reading of globalisation might highlight several different factors not given great consideration in the more optimistic (essentially economistic) liberal readings of cosmopolitanism. Whilst globalisation has been related to the transnational spread of communications and social relations through politico-economic contact, the idealistic view that this will result in some form of cultural homogeneity is severely questioned by the resurgence of religious, nationalist and ethnic politics in the post-Cold War world. Whilst we might forgo the alarmist proto-realist cultural determinism of authors like Samuel Huntington, it seems fair to recognise the remarkable proliferation of identity-based politics that challenge the 'Mc-World' of mainstream liberal discourse.[32] Indeed many Southern and critical European schools of thought have challenged the liberal discourse of socioeconomic governance in the global polity as instances of Western (or more specifically, American) imperialism. In doing this they necessarily highlight the relevance of community and communitarian values in the global polity.

The communitarian tradition seeks to locate its ethical framework within the 'polis' as opposed to some external foundation. Against the universalism of cosmopolitanism, communitarians assert the particular 'truths' of different cultures and belief systems. Against the privileging of the individual over society they seek to understand the individual as the product of contingent social relations of a community. More fundamentally, communitarian thinkers locate moral value in the very social relations and the institutions they produce. Thus the modern values of liberty, equality and justice are not understood as abstract standards against which institutions, like the state or market, can be judged. Rather ethics are seen as constituted within those very institutions.

The 'social embeddedness' of market relations provides us with an example of how cultural differences emerge within the global polity.[33] Production structures, organisational norms, and credit standards are all areas of human interaction. The social norms of such interaction are born of particular cultural understandings of reality prevalent in a given community. For example, in a communitarian analysis of the Asian financial crisis the IMF, rather than instituting a value-free universal standard of best economic practice, would be seen to be following a far more particularist line. If we view the IMF doctrines of transparency and accountability

---

[32] Samuel Huntington, *The Clash of Civilizations and the Remaking of World Order* (London: Touchstone, 1998), and Benjamin Barber, *Jihad vs. McWorld* (New York: Ballantine Books, 1996).

[33] The theme of social embeddedness in economic relations is well elaborated by the economic historians and sociologists. See for instance Karl Polanyi, *The Great Transformation* (Boston, MA: Beacon Press (1944), and Mark Granovetter, 'Economic Action and Social Embeddedness', in *American Journal of Sociology*, 91 (1985), pp. 481–510.

as 'Western' values presaged upon the cultural dominance of the 'Anglo-Saxon' model of capitalism, then the recommendations for the break up of Asian financial and production frameworks becomes less a simple search for economic efficiency and also (or more) a case of breaking the cultural norms of South East Asian economic actors. On such a view we might further question whether Western economic actors receive (unfair) competitive advantages from these new arrangements?[34]

In ethical philosophy, this idea of social embeddedness receives its most influential and complicated rendering in the quasi-mythological 'ethical state' of Hegelian thought. For Hegel the person is someone who is encumbered by social relations whilst able to realise freedom within them. The (ethical) state provides the context in which individuality and rules can be internalised so they are no longer regarded as constraints. As Chris Brown states: 'The state provides the element of unity necessary if the individual is to overcome the separateness inherent in civil society.'[35]

By extrapolation, the communitarian dimension(s) of the global polity raise a number of questions for institutions with a transnational influence. A strong communitarian position sees the state as the sole arbiter of ethical value. This view sits well with the realist assertion that international cooperation will, at all times, be limited and transient depending upon the interests of (powerful) states.[36] On weaker readings this view has underpinned many of the English School pronouncements upon the extent and limitations of international society.[37] Robert Gilpin has taken the communitarian perspective to infer the importance of 'groups'.[38] Thus his rational choice political economy of international relations sets out to understand, if not develop, the ethical value, of nations, classes and elites.[39] More reflexive sociological positions highlight the complexity of community-based interaction in which the global polity has born witness to a proliferation of nations, ethno-nations and transworld national diasporas. In addition there has been a growth of non-territorial communities such as managerial class allegiances, women's movements, lesbian and gay solidarities, racial groups, religious groups/identities and a spread of global youth culture.[40] In this complex web the emphasis is less upon the exclusivity of community in its demarcation of inside/outside binaries, but rather upon its capacity for penetration and hybridisation.

Despite the strengths of the communitarian ethical perspective for theorising the normative dimensions of the global polity, significant questions are evoked. For instance, Hegelian notions of the 'ethical state' might elicit acceptance for acts of

[34] For a discussion along these lines see Richard Higgott, 'The Asian Economic Crisis: A Study in the Politics of Resentment', *New Political Economy*, 3:3 (1998) and Linda Weiss, 'State Power and the Asian Crisis', *New Political Economy*, 4:3 (1999), pp. 317–42.
[35] Chris Brown, *International Relations Theory: New Normative Approaches* (New York: Columbia University Press, 1992), pp. 62–3.
[36] See for instance Kenneth Waltz, *Theory of International Politics* (New York: McGraw-Hill, 1979).
[37] Hedley Bull, *The Anarchical Society: A Study of Order in World Politics* (Basingstoke: Macmillan, 1977), remains the definitive statement on the English School position.
[38] Robert Gilpin, 'The Richness of the Tradition of Political Realism', in R.O. Keohane (ed.), *Neo-Realism and its Critics* (New York: Columbia University Press, 1986).
[39] Gilpin, R., *The Political Economy of International Relations* (Princeton, NJ: Princeton University Press, 1987).
[40] This sociological position is best reflected in the work of Jan Aart Scholte, *Globalization: A Critical Introduction* (Basingstoke: Macmillan, 2000).

violence and infringements of 'justice' in the name of the 'greater project' of the state. Hegelian method could be criticised for licensing a form of cultural relativism that ignores the capacity of the state to do harm. Further, if we accept the worth of social mores then moral judgement is made equivalent to power, since much of the 'stuff' of ethical politics will be understood as functional *between,* rather than within, communities. On this basis, the development of justice in the global polity is beholden to those communities that have the power and the will to act. Thus much of the ethical agenda of the global polity can become tied to the (lack of) interest shown by the USA.

We would argue that these critiques are more than a question of taste. There is an overwhelming theoretical flaw in the *predictive* nature of many communitarian perspectives which delimit ethical deliberation to some reified conception of the 'art of the possible'. We would argue that there are, in fact, few straightforward conclusions to be drawn from the 'situatedness' of social experience, except that life is contingent. Despite its obvious qualities, communitarianism should caution against the danger of deriving an *'ought'* from an *'is'*. But, it is in the tension between cosmopolitan ideals and the communitarian 'art of the possible' that much normative international theorising has been conducted. The next section looks at a recent significant attempt to develop a 'thinner' cosmopolitanism as a middle way in this tension between cosmopolitan and communitarian ethics.

Transcending the 'art of the possible'? Linklater and the 'art of synthesis'

In the debate between cosmopolitans and communitarians we have what appears to be an intractable impasse inhibiting our ability to theorise the normative dimensions of the global polity.[41] Against the trans-historical standard of 'justice as fairness', located in the universal rights of the individual, communitarians posit the social contingency of individual liberty. From this, two dangers arise. Firstly, the global polity might become conceived of as a 'zero-sum' ethical world in which we privilege either the individual (risking imperialism) or the community (risking despotism). Secondly, when framed in this way, the debate pre-favours a form of ethical compromise in which we strive for justice on individual and community lines whilst constantly qualifying that agenda with the realist(ic) 'art of the possible'. This wide acceptance of the fine balance between order and justice in international society has for too long led us to privilege the ethical limits of the global polity rather than search for its ethical possibilities. An attempt to transcend this conundrum can be found in the work of Andrew Linklater.

A cosmopolitan in orientation, Linklater employs Hegelian method to argue his case for reconstructing normative approaches to the social world.[42] Echoing the

---

[41] On the nature and implications of this impasse for International Relations, see Molly Cochran, *Normative Theory and International Relations* (Cambridge: Cambridge University Press, 1999).

[42] See Andrew Linklater, *The Transformation of Political Community: Ethical Foundations of the Post-Westphalian Era* (Oxford: Polity, 1998). See also his earlier work, *Men and Citizens in the Theory of International Relations* (London: Macmillan, 1990).

intentions of Anthony Giddens to take seriously the limitations of social enquiry posited by the delegitimation of Marxism and the assault of postmodernism, Linklater extracts the core qualities of enlightenment thought and seeks to reapply them to a post-Westphalian system.[43] Whilst strongly supportive of his attempt to reconstruct both the theory and practice of international relations we have three concerns. Firstly, our approach is sceptical of a notion of progress in human history that allows for the evolution of rationality in society through dialectical process. Secondly, we question the quasi-deterministic interpretation of *praxeological* development employed in Linklater's work. That humans can reflect on their surroundings and change them does not infer a capacity to know how to resolve their problems. And thirdly, we are critical of the employment of Habermasian 'discourse ethics' in Linklater's recent work. Habermas's notion of an 'ideal speech situation' is neither realistic nor does it resolve the dilemma that sooner or later a modernist framework must judge moral problems and risk undermining one or other concern against its own standard of truth.[44] On our reading of Linklater, we see discourse ethics as concerned with 'right' not 'good', with procedure not content.

Accepting the constitutive properties of society for the individual, Linklater posits that social theory must contend with three central questions: the sociological question of community binaries of inclusion/exclusion, the normative question of achieving some cosmopolitan ideal of liberty and equality, and the praxeological question of how humans reflect upon and change their circumstances through time to achieve such ends.[45] Thus Linklater's method rejects the more commonly understood rendering of the state as the final and ultimate source of 'actual reason' and looks to uncover the process by which reason has actualised itself in the past and will actualise itself in the future. He goes beyond the justice potentials of non-intervention and mutual recognition highlighted by the English School and seeks to illustrate how the development of citizenship rights in states has affected modern conceptions of justice in international affairs. By focusing on the potential of the conception of citizenship as a sign of a more inclusionary form of politics, Linklater asserts that the modern state has set in train a dialectical process that turns against itself. As he notes:

In modern times, it presses the anti-exclusionary dynamic in the evolution of modern citizenship further by considering its ramifications for the domain of world politics. The anti-exclusionary dynamic is a trend of lowering the barriers which prevent excluded groups, such as subordinate classes, racial and national minorities, and women from enjoying the social and political rights monopolised by more powerful groups. To press this further is to recognise that the nation state is one of the few bastions of exclusion which has not had its rights and claims against the rest of the world seriously questioned.[46]

---

[43] Anthony Giddens, *A Contemporary Critique of Historical Materialism: The Nation-State and Violence* (London: Polity, 1985).

[44] We do not deal explicitly with Habermas' notion of an 'ideal speech situation' in this article. Briefly, the model rests on the assumption that reason is written into the discursive practices of society through language. Thus an objective standard of 'good' can be achieved through the rational development of clear communication. See *The Theory Of Communicative Action*, vol. 1: *Reason And The Rationalization Of Society* (London: Heinemann, 1984).

[45] Andrew Linklater, 'The Question of the Next Stage in International Relations Theory: A Critical Theoretical Point of View', *Millenium: Journal of International Studies*, 21 (1992), pp. 77–98.

[46] Ibid., p. 93.

For Linklater, it is this dialectic, between reason already actualised and the ability of individuals and states to further actualise reason that will provoke the shift towards a post-Westphalian system. In this way the global polity might realise a greater level of moral inclusion. On the way, new forms of community that are national, subnational, regional or transnational will rise and fall with their own sociological inclusion/exclusion binaries. But, Linklater echoes some common cosmopolitan arguments by noting two factors in contemporary global politics that will support progress towards a moral community of humankind.

Firstly, there has been a growth in the scope and recognition of human rights in international law. The end of the Cold War has witnessed a profusion of both rhetorical and substantial humanitarian activities by states and non-state actors. Even if there is broad disagreement as to the shape and content of these rights, in practice they have served as a useful point of focus for people and groups seeking emancipation. And secondly, Linklater points to a global recognition of the require-ment to meet the negative impacts of material inequality, environmental degradation, and the growing incidence of transnational harm: the evolving 'communities of fate' within global politics. He argues that the institutions of global governance, which monitor such communities, must address the democratic deficit in their operations via reform and greater engagement with civil society.[47] As Molly Cochran surmises, these trends

... are a sign that we are moving beyond the men versus citizens moral dichotomy and that now our task is to envision new political forms which can further these developments.[48]

The final part of this transformation in moral and political community is to be found in Linklater's call for the development of Habermasian discourse ethics through a reconstruction of the idea of the state as a bounded moral community. He favours an open dialogue about the structure of society and politics as a means of achieving discourse ethics, but contends that this 'cannot be completed by a number of separate experiments in democratic participation within independent sovereign states', since sovereignty 'restricts the capacity of outsiders to participate in the discourse to consider issues which concern them.'[49] When combined with questions of the communities of fate created by various incidents of transnational harm like global warming, 'casino' capitalism, and the exploitation of poor working standards, this could prove quite a powerful argument for a form of cosmopolitan social democracy *via* multi-level governance institutions.

While we find merit in Linklater's attempt to reconstruct social theory to reclaim the emancipatory potential of the enlightenment, it seems to overstate the capacity for political engagement in modern states. It is arguable that the widespread realisation of citizenship rights in Western countries has to some extent tranquillised rather than radicalised the forces of popular emancipation within society. More critically, those politicised activities which cosmopolitans can point to are most

---

[47] See Linklater, A, 'The Evolving Spheres of International Justice', *International Affairs*, 75:3 (1999), pp. 473–82.

[48] Cochran, *Normative Theory*, p. 90.

[49] Andrew Linklater, 'The Achievements of Critical Theory', in Smith Booth and Zalewski (eds.), *International Theory: Positivism and Beyond* (Cambridge: Cambridge University Press, 1996), p. 294, cit. Cochran, *Normative Theory*, p. 91.

evident in the rich, northern, white, male, sections of the global polity. This poses a distinctive question to the content of any radical democracy associated with the ideal speech situation or discourse ethic: what is the requisite level of critical reflectivity required for 'enjoying' this situation? The principle of opening demo-cratic conversation does not deal with the question of those people/groups who may refuse, or are unable, to join the dialogue.

Developing from this point, there is a sense in which discourse ethics might fudge the issue of political judgement. On one interpretation, it seems to underestimate the fact that at some point, even within overlapping and diffuse moral political communities, some form of judgement will have to be made. In Robert Jackson's words:

It is not a solution merely to argue for recognition and respect for the 'other' and his, her or their inclusion in the sphere of equality and entitlement. For inclusion only postpones the unresolved problem of determining which facet of the others' conduct ought to be recognised and respected and which not . . . Exclusion and inclusion ultimately is not about class, sex, race, caste, nationality, and other sociological categories; *it is about human conduct.*[50]

It is this human conduct and, more particularly our ability to influence it that is the central issue in developing any normative agenda for the global polity.

Richard Rorty and an ethic of pragmatic reform?

We have suggested that the foundationalist positions reviewed thus far limit our capacity to theorise the normative dimension(s) of the global polity to the philosophical questions of 'what is?' – the nature of man, or the global polity – and then 'what should be?' Perhaps a more interesting/practical ethical question, derived from the philosophical pragmatism of Richard Rorty, might be to ask '*what could be?*'[51] We would argue that the universal individual of the cosmopolitan and the particular social mores of the communitarian are not sacrosanct truths that can or should dictate the way we think about ethics under conditions of globalisation. This is not to deny the importance of ethical or theoretical discourse. Rather it is intended to humble theory. On this view we could continue to support the aim of political reconstruction through a post-national public sphere alluded to in Linklater's work. But, as the attempt to solve some of the extant social problems we encounter in a *more effective way*, rather than as the continuance of some application of *timeless wisdom*.

Digging deep into Rorty, we draw out three interrelated facets of this position: contingency, fallibility and experimentalism, that can be elaborated to both establish the pragmatic ethic and demonstrate the implicit necessity for those political and practical aspects of ethical theorising highlighted in this article.

---

[50] Robert Jackson, 'Pluralism In International Political Theory', *Review of International Studies* (April 1992), p. 274. Emphasis added.
[51] Richard Rorty, 'Human Rights, Rationality and Sentimentality', in *Truth and Progress: Philosophical Papers* (Cambridge: Cambridge University Press, 1998), p. 170.

Contingency

Whereas the contingent nature of knowledge/ethics has created major tensions for the philosophers considered above, the pragmatic tradition of American philosophy has had no such insecurities. Rather than becoming transfixed by the nihilistic implications of cultural relativism, pragmatism seeks to identify and elaborate the *useful* aspects of contingent knowledge. As in MacIntyre's summary of Dewey's position:

> We only acquired whatever knowledge we have now because we had certain purposes, and the point of that knowledge is inseparable from our future purposes. All reason is practical reason . . . [T]o characterise something as good is to say that it will satisfy us in our purposes.[52]

Richard Rorty takes up this theme to attack correspondence theories of truth and seeks to colour as romantic fallacy the very idea that the human mind is a separable entity that can mirror nature. It is fallacy that simply wastes our intellectual energy.[53] The *practical* worth of philosophy is a recurrent concern of Rortian pragmatism and his scepticism is closely rivalled by the belief that in dispensing with truth we might develop a more useful contribution to political life. From this perspective, it can be argued that both cosmopolitans and communitarians, in their search for an onto-logical subject, undermine their own position by ignoring the contingency that they both, in some way, seek to engage. This is more than an abstract philosophical critique. It holds, we will argue, implications for the mindset we employ to theorise the normative dimension(s) of the global polity.

By stripping the foundation away from ethical debate, pragmatism tranquillises the impasse between the universal and the particular. Rorty echoes communitarian thought in believing that there is no Archimedean frame of reference outside the community. Practices and knowledge are constructed through interaction within a situated community. But Rorty does not infer a set of logical propositions based on the exclusivity of communal value systems. Instead he argues, '. . . the main lesson of both human history and anthropology is our extraordinary malleability.'[54] Thus community values are in a state of constant development and revision. Our ability to promote a belief is in no way constrained by contingency since all individuals and all cultures, to some extent at least, seek to universalise their particular view of the world in exchanges with others and it is through such exchanges that universal positions become amended.[55] For Rorty, linguistic tools have their purposes and so can be retired when that purpose is done, while other projects and other tools rise to supersede them. Rorty calls this a 'change of vocabularies'. In this regard, the adherence to a particular conceptual approach represents more a set of choices than a set of discoveries.[56]

Moreover, by emphasising malleability, pragmatism challenges the communitarian 'predictive' qualities emphasised in political realism. If communal value systems are

---

[52] Cited in Brown, *International Relations Theory*, p. 207.
[53] Richard Rorty, *Philosophy and the Mirror of Nature* (Oxford: Blackwell, 1980).
[54] Rorty, 'Human Rights, Rationality and Sentimentality', p. 169.
[55] Thanks to Owen Parker for his advice on this point.
[56] For a discussion, see Simon Blackburn, 'Richard Rorty: A Portrait', *Prospect* (April 2003), pp. 56–60.

in a condition of perpetual constitution through interaction then the 'art of the possible' could be regarded as a fairly myopic interpretation of the nature of contingency. Indeed when combined with themes of reflexive interpenetration and hybridisation we might argue that pragmatism can bring strength to cosmopolitan ideals by drawing a global map of moral communities that can be manipulated. Simply, if we want to universalise an ideal then that will surely involve a process of ethically 'lobbying' different communities to behave in certain ways. There is no concept of truth here, rather, ethics as an ideology.

Rorty has made some statements about how this kind of ethic could be related to international affairs. For example, he makes the argument that the theory and practical development of human rights in the international sphere does not rest upon the growing realisation of some ahistorical, transcultural truth about what constitutes human rights and how to implement them. Rather, he highlights the growth of a 'human rights culture' in the post-Holocaust world. Human rights need only cohere with our *beliefs* to gain massive support and practical application. Indeed, its success for Rorty owes 'nothing to increased moral knowledge, and everything to hearing sad and sentimental stories.'[57]

The implications of such a mode of ethical reasoning for developing a normative agenda for the reform of the global economy are important and as yet barely articulated within the scholarly *cum* policy community concerned with such questions. We only need to look to the sentimental underpinning of concepts such as social welfare, just distribution, voice, representation, and indeed politicisation of the economic realm to realise just how much theoretical space could be found in this brand of pragmatism. Perhaps it is time for the community of scholars working in these policy areas to engage in Rortian experimentation. To the extent that it is fallible, this potential is, of course, problematic. We discuss the fallibility before we discuss the experimentalism.

Fallibility

Accepting the social contingency of knowledge, Rorty (unlike most communitarians) does not extrapolate a set of common principles that can be applied to all communities. Instead, he emphasises that contingency implies *no* frame of reference outside the community. The rhetorical style employed repeatedly uses words like 'we', 'western liberals', and perhaps most famously Rorty's quip that he himself is nothing but a 'post-modern bourgeois liberal'.[58]

The ethical dimension of pragmatism is thus heavily imbued with a sense of irony, or 'fallibility'. When Rorty celebrates the 'liberal ironist' as someone who thinks 'cruelty is the worst thing we do', this (wet) optimism is qualified by the fact that liberal ironists must face '. . . up to the contingency of . . . [their] . . . own most

---

[57] Richard Rorty, 'Human Rights, Rationality and Sentimentality', in Rorty, *Truth and Progress: Philosophical Papers*, vol. 3 (Cambridge: Cambridge University Press, 1998), p. 169.
[58] See for instance Richard Rorty, 'Postmodernist Bourgois Liberalism', in *Objectivity, Relativism and Truth: Philosophical Papers*, vol. 1 (Cambridge: Cambridge University Press, 1991), pp. 197–202.

central beliefs and desires'.[59] This is because they believe that the contingency of knowledge means that there can be nothing but 'circular' justifications for political values. Although they might sympathise with the cosmopolitan urge to realise human dignity in a moral community of mankind, the liberal ironist cannot ignore the contingent construction of terms like 'dignity' and 'morality'. In essence, such words are always the discursive elements of social communication that represent the 'final vocabulary' of socially constituted individuals.[60] Our final vocabulary might include words like 'justice' 'liberty', 'equality' or indeed 'community' or 'nation' but the meaning which others and ourselves attribute to them is relative. For Rorty, the self-doubt and circularity of knowledge leads to an ethic of *redescription*.

Accepting that beliefs are fallible, and any justification of them is in the final analysis an essentially circular act, pragmatism seeks to redescribe our final vocabularies. In the case of the individual this ethic might lead to attempts to realise personal freedoms of sexuality or creative interest. In the case of the community Rorty seeks to extend solidarity by expanding the 'we' group within which ethical deliberation takes place. In this he makes the simple observation that it is much easier to feel sympathy for people who are in some sense 'one of us'. Whilst we might follow Linklater and note an evolving 'thin community' of mankind that recognises collective fate and some form of global identity, it is but one amongst many instances of 'we-ness' along other community lines (race, nation, area, sex, class, and common history.) Reading back we could attribute to Marxism the redescription of class as a form of fraternal sympathy. Thus the real strength of international socialism may have been as a sentimental metaphor about togetherness in the face of hardship rather than any positivistic law of capital labour relations. As Rorty surmises, solidarity

. . . is to be achieved not by inquiry, but imagination, the imaginative ability to see strange people as fellow sufferers. Solidarity is not discovered by reflection, but created. . . . [It] is a matter of detailed description of what unfamiliar people are like and of redescription of what we ourselves are like.[61]

At root this kind of view is, of course, intensely relativistic and has led to one of the central criticisms of Rorty: his complacency towards institutions. If there is an inherent tension in the desire of individuals to redescribe their own vocabularies and the kind of social vocabularies that bind social collectivities then this form of fallibility must, in some way, destabilise institutions like the state, the market, education, the military, and psychological care in the community. This poses a question of central importance to any attempt to understand the political processes inherent in the search for a global polity. How does one choose between a radical resistance that ultimately obliterates institutions of governance and the maintenance and reform of those very institutions? For Rorty, this is not an irreconcilable problem.

At one level, he argues that institutions are not bound by foundational philosophy but by the 'social hope' that unites community. He cites the decline of religious faith

---

[59] Richard Rorty, *Contingency, Irony and Solidarity* (Cambridge: Cambridge University Press, 1989), p. xv, cit. Molly Cochran, *Normative Theory*, p. 149.
[60] Ibid., p. 79.
[61] Ibid., xvi.

in Europe that left modern institutions unaffected, judging that the new secular vocabularies were able to replace 'hope of heaven' with the 'hope of better social outcomes'.[62] On this view, the Keynesian welfare state may have owed less to any socioeconomic truth, and more to its ability to bind European communities with the 'social hope' that they could leave behind the collective human suffering of World War II and fend off the new challenge of communism. At another level, Rorty concedes that the irony he celebrates could destabilise institutions. He therefore invokes a public/private split. Whilst the public rhetoric of his liberal utopia may remain historicist and nominalist – 'where public doubts are met not by Socratic requests for definitions and principles, but by Deweyan requests for concrete alternatives and programmes' – irony is a quality that he deems to be an 'inherently private matter'.[63] On this view, solidarity must fulfil the (difficult) dual function of being both a critical, and a stabilising force.[64] For example, the liberal values of individual freedom that catalysed civil rights groups in 1960s America presented a radical critique of US liberalism which have in turn reinforced liberalism's own legitimacy.

But Rorty's attempt to shore up Western institutions against the possibility of radical individualism nevertheless exhibits a complacency, or lack of interest not unfamiliar in most philosophical discourse, to issues of the international or global. The task for the twentieth century is to ask whether the ethic of redescription can be extended to the supraterritorial level. For example, on a minor reinterpretation we might propose that the construction of solidarity amongst communities interacting within the major international institutions such as the IMF, WBG, WTO, and the EU, could generate a pragmatic resolve to find more useful ways of talking about the world. Might not the introduction of Rortian 'irony' into the discourse of technocratic governance at the global level invoke a sense of doubt over the 'efficacy' of depoliticised economism of the type exhibited under the umbrella of the Washington consensus?

At an illustrative level, is it not possible to see the discourse of the post-Washington Consensus, or what Harvard economist, Dani Rodrik, calls the 'augmented Washington consensus' in this light? In more general terms might it not prompt us to 'redescribe' the institutions of the global polity? In times of crisis, with no obvious way forward other than regime collapse, might the adoption of the Rortian irony provide mitigation of the bad-tempered discourse between the globaphiles and globaphobes that is currently polarising and paralysing meaningful policy change in the global economy? These are important questions for future research in international relations and the study of the role of the institutions of governance in the operation of the global political economy in particular.

Experimentalism

Pragmatism takes the contingency and fallibility of ethics to infer the demise of grand frameworks like cosmopolitanism and communitarianism. In their stead,

[62] Richard Rorty, *Contingency, Irony and Solidarity*, pp. 85–6.
[63] Ibid., p. 87.
[64] Molly Cochran, *Normative Theory*, p. 150.

Rorty advocates the development of moral imagination to redescribe our final vocabularies. Although intended to restrict pragmatism to reform *within* liberal democratic states, we suggest that with a minor reinterpretation, such an ethic could be productively applied at a number of levels in the global polity. It is through experimentalism that we feel pragmatism affords its most practical application. After reviewing Rorty's critique of Marxism we will set out the parameters for engaging a pragmatic praxis within the global polity. As Rorty noted in the wake of the fall of Communism in Russia and Eastern Europe:

> I would hope that we have reached a time at which we can finally get rid of the conviction common to Plato and Marx that there *must* be large theoretical ways of finding out how to end injustice, as opposed to *small experimental ways*.[65]

He exhorts us to dispense with grand theoretical terms like 'anti-capitalist struggle' and instead substitute something banal and un-theoretical like 'the struggle against avoidable human misery'.[66] Critical politics could be supplemented by an ethical concern for notions like 'sympathy for human lives' and an agenda to create 'social hope' through the *construction* of solidarity, or we-ness, on issues relating to poverty, disease, famine, lack of representation, social alienation, or sociopolitical instability as a result of an utterly rigid financial architecture? In short, reformist or trans-formational politics could better concern itself with a sympathetic repetition of the words *we can* in the face of human suffering.

The experimentalism of this approach is twofold. Firstly, due to the contingency and fallibility of knowledge, a capacity to regard our agendas as potentially flawed in both motivation and outcome is vital. The experience of Communism in the USSR would illustrate the drawback of denying the possibility of failure. Secondly, perhaps more powerfully, the ability to regard such contingent social constructions as sympathy and solidarity as the bedrock of pragmatism brings a *perpetual* quality to reformism. It is a quality that is notably lacking on the agenda of international relations, of both the scholar and practitioner alike. Simply, the contingency of reform requires an ability to continually experiment with ways of understanding and creating sympathy and solidarity. The experimentalism of the pragmatic ethic means that human suffering is an ever-changing facet of reality, which requires innovative agendas for articulating and effecting responses. It is a perpetual reflex that requires greater elaboration in the global polity.

Thus we have in pragmatism an ethical agenda which points to many avenues. Accepting contingency, we might reinvigorate our belief in universalising a particular viewpoint on the basis that it might solve some of 'our' problems in a more effective way. The questions of who is 'we' and what is 'effective' are deemed as matters for ironic redescription. Thus at a certain point 'we' in Britain might convince ourselves of the 'effectiveness' of European level financial coordination *via* membership of the Euro and thus create a new 'we' for ethical deliberation. In doing so we will open both our institutions and understandings of solidarity to change through redescription.

---

[65] Richard Rorty, 'The End of Leninism: Havel and Social Hope', in *Truth and Progress: Philosophical Papers*, vol. 2 (Cambridge: Cambridge University Press), p. 228.
[66] Ibid., p. 229.

Reading global politics in this way, a pragmatic ethic opens itself to more institutional questions than even Rorty envisages. This is no major challenge to pragmatism. Rorty, an American bourgeois liberal, is used to the effectiveness and exclusivity of US political structures. (Although he would probably not have expected the degree of exclusivity and imperialness of the American structures in the early years of the twenty-first century). For European social democrats, concerned with the possibilities of reconstructing welfare systems through European and global institutions for example, the pragmatic ethic can be adapted. Accepting the experimentalism of pragmatism, reformist politics are exhorted to have sympathy for human lives and find innovative agendas for both describing and rescribing those lives.

Pragmatic redescription in the global polity: some early thoughts

Can pragmatic redescription provide something more than just a principled wish list? At the very least it is a question worth further investigation. Here we can do no more than suggest alternative ways of thinking and acting. We start by noting that the development of a contingent fallible ethic of redescription should be a project for both scholars and practitioners alike. The scholarly study of globalisation and an emerging global polity must develop a *critical problem-solving* purpose that takes us beyond Robert Cox's once useful, but now inhibiting, distinction between international relations scholarship as either *critical theory* or *problem-solving*.[67] By interpreting and redescribing discursive practices employed within the global polity (to date mostly the work of economists), philosophers and theorists of international relations should play a greater role in the development of the knowledge and power structures they contingently observe but have of late done little to affect.[68] Throughout the twentieth century, political philosophers and international relations scholars ceded the policy ground to the economists in the domains of global economic governance. In the twenty-first century they must battle the economists for the role of pragmatic redescribers. Let us remember Keynes' famous quote about the power of ideas *in full*:

The ideas of economists *and political philosophers,* both when they are right and when they are wrong, are more powerful than is commonly understood. Indeed, the world is ruled by little else.[69] (Emphasis added).

A pragmatic political praxis could be developed through 'acts of redescription' in the global polity. But it is not enough to endlessly theorise what the global polity *is,* we should also ask *what could it be?*[70] Is there, within the global polity, space for

---

[67]   R. W. Cox, 'Social Forces, States and World Orders: Beyond International Relations Theory', in Robert O. Keohane (ed.), *Neorealism and Its Critics* (New York: Columbia University Press, 1986), pp. 204–54.
[68]   This situation, and some of the reasons for it, is discussed in Higgott, 'Taming Economics'.
[69]   John Maynard Keynes, *The General Theory of Employment, Interest and Money* (London: 1936), p. 383.
[70]   One of the aims of producing the collection of essays on the 'global polity' (Higgott and Ougaard, *Global Polity*) was to provide an alternative hosting metaphor to the other popular metaphors of international scholarship like the 'anarchical society', 'international system' or a 'community of mankind'.

developing new understandings of 'we-ness'? We would not, of course, wish to over-state this idea. We are a long way from the kind of bottom-up dialogic potentials that Habermas and Linklater advance. Instead the pragmatic ethic of contingent fallible *reform* must be focused upon achieving what *can be achieved*. In the context of the global polity, for example, the issue is to what extent the real potential of the international institutions for promoting global welfare can be achieved by acts of pragmatic redescription supporting incremental change in rhetorical agendas. Emphasis on the human dimension of markets (as social constructs) that has crept into recent policy initiatives associated with the post-Washington and augmented Washington consensus and debates over the delivery of global public goods, could be elaborated and reinforced by scholarly deliberation on their content and meaning.[71]

At another level, those academics that have 'discovered' the vanguard potential in global civil society for reconstructing democratic activity and elaborating social concerns should check the fallibility of their interest.[72] Although civil society activists have undoubtedly made progress towards opening up a space in which to be heard within the recent discussion on globalisation, the content and democratic credentials of that voice are not viewed as unambiguously acceptable or beneficial in all quarters. 'Uncivil' society also abounds and some elements of the media are hostile on all occasions. Within the institutions of global economic governance, the relationship with civil society is clearly developing,[73] but it is a process of experimentation in which uncertainty is a characteristic of, and for, both parties. The reformist potential of civil society is contingent, fallible, and experimental. If an agenda of *re*globalisation, according to principles of social welfare, is to supplant the current agenda of anti-globalisation protest a discourse of pragmatism must gain ground. Support for pragmatic reformism can be found in strange quarters. See for example, the calls by George Soros for a new fund at the IMF for Special Drawing Rights for developing countries.[74]

'Feasible globalisations', not utopian alternatives, are required. Dani Rodrik, in one very interesting exercise in Rortian pragmatic redescription (although Rodrik, as an impeccably trained economist, would probably not recognise it as such) argues for a reform of the global market-governance nexus. The political trilemma of the global economy, he says, is the incompatibility of the continued existence of the nation state (to ensure self-determination), the development of democratic politics beyond the state (to ensure that public policy is accountable) and the continuing

---

[71] See Dani Rodrik, 'After Neoliberalism, What?' *After Neoliberalism: Economic Policies that Work for the Poor*, Conference sponsored by the New Rules of Global Finance Coalition, Washington DC, 23–24 May 2002, pp. 11–20, and Inge Kaul, Pedor Conceicao, Katell Le Goulven and Ronald Mendoza, *Providing Global Public Goods: Managing Globalisation* (New York: Oxford University Press for the UNDP, 2003).

[72] See Robert Cox, 'The Global Political Economy and Social Choice ', in Robert W. Cox with Timothy J. Sinclair (eds.), *Approaches to World Order* (Cambridge: Cambridge University Press, 1996).

[73] See a report prepared by Jan Art Scholte for the Ford Foundation, *Democratising the Global Economy: The Role of Civil Society* (Warwick University: Centre for the Study of Globalisation and Regionalisation, 2003), and Jan Aart Scholte and Albrecht Schnabel (eds.), *Civil Society and Global Finance* (London: Routledge, 2001).

[74] See George Soros, *On Globalisation* (New York: Rowman and Littlefield, 2002). For a discussion of this and other initiatives, see the Richard Higgott and Paolo Robbotti, *Reshaping Globalisation: Multilateral Dialogues and New Policy Initiatives* (Budapest: Central European University, 2002).

economic integration of the global economy to enhance living standards.[75] At best we can secure two of these three goals, never all of them, and global markets (economic integration) without global governance are unsustainable.

The current neoliberal agenda (as reflected, for example, in US strategy in the Doha round of multilateral trade negotiations with its emphasis on the continuing elimination of barriers to trade and capital movements) reflects an aggressive drive for enhanced (deep) global economic integration. But such integration sits at odds with the residual strength of nation states and the clamour for democratic politics. It thus remains neither feasible nor desirable, says Rodrik, to continue towards global economic integration greater than is compatible with the desires of nation states and the expansion of democratic accountability. Thus we need to think, more pragmatically, of what can be achieved. For Rodrik, the alternative is:

> . . . a renewed Bretton Woods Compromise: preserving some limits on integration, as built into original Bretton Woods arrangements, along with some more global rules to handle the integration that can be achieved. Those who would make different choices – towards tighter economic integration – must face up to the corollary: either tighter world government or less democracy.[76]

In an era when who wins and who loses are becoming increasingly important yardsticks for judging the fairness of competing models of economic organisation we might need to '. . . scale down our ambitions with respect to global economic integration . . . [and] . . . do a better job of writing the rules for a thinner version of globalization'.[77] Why is Rodrik's argument an important exercise in Rortian redescription? Four reasons:

1. The argument is not self-evident within the community of neoclassical economists from which Rodrik emanates. Rather, he assumes that markets are embedded in a non-market social institutional context. To readers of literature influenced by Karl Polanyi or John Ruggie over the last twenty years this may not seem particularly dramatic. In the context of the post-1990s neoliberal economic orthodoxy, it is transformative.
2. Rodrik accepts the reality of a wide divergence of both functions and form in the nature of capitalist institutional economic organisation. Again, there is a large body of continental European (social-democratic) and Asian (developmental statist) literature on the institutional arrangements of capitalist economic organisation. It is the extent to which Rodrik's position runs counter to much Anglo-American economic orthodoxy on the legitimacy of alternative forms of institutional economic organisation that makes for an important redescription.
3. His argument eschews the essentialist teleological logic of the neoliberal view of globalisation, one in which full global economic integration is the ultimate goal.
4. In an era when traditional restrictions on trade and investment (such as tariffs) are much less salient than in the second half of the twentieth century, juris-

---

[75] Dani Rodrik, 'Feasible Globalisations',
    <http://ksghome.harvard.edu/~.drodrik.academic.ksg/papers.html>
[76] Ibid., p. 1.
[77] Ibid., p. 2.

dictional and regulatory instruments emanating from state actors are the major constraints on deep integration. Attempts to remove these inhibitors (part of the WTO agenda) can only be justifiable, argues Rodrik, if one ignores the important sociopolitical and cultural functions that such institutions perform. The dismissal of the importance of these functions has been central to neoliberal economic thinking in the heyday of globalisation that dominated the closing quarter of the twentieth century. Hence Rodrik's assertion of their virtue, and the need to tread carefully in their dismantling, represents a departure from orthodox thinking about the management of globalisation.

In turning away from these key elements of neoliberal economic orthodoxy, yet without resisting the essential importance of market activity and structures, Rodrik is engaged in a major exercise in what we have chosen to call Rortian pragmatic redescription. Such an approach to trying to develop an ethic of globalisation is not found amongst either the globalisation boosters or much of the anti-globalisation movement that generate more heat than light in current discussions about how we might either manage or change the contemporary global economic order.

Finally, an ethical agenda must provide social hope. The construction of 'we-ness' cannot look backwards and find some transhistorical, transcultural 'proof' of human community or equality. Instead a pragmatic ethic must look forward to finding a 'we' that can talk more usefully about issues of transnational interdependence. If, for example, we are to universalise a belief in a reconstruction of systems of welfare that are analogous to an earlier Keynesian ethic, then an innovative redescription of the global polity – as a collection of human beings that share a capacity to suffer and an ability to mitigate that suffering – is required.

Conclusion

In this article we have offered but one way of trying to carve out some space for ethical thinking beyond the borders of the modern state in an era of globalisation. Like Rorty, who we think does himself a disservice in his self-description as a 'postmodern bourgeois liberal' our views are very much reformist. Two quotes, extracted from Chris Brown's delightfully cheeky last chapter to his *Sovereignty, Rights and Justice* volume, capture a key essence of this article. Citing the banner at the London 2001 May Day Rally – 'Replace capitalism with something nicer' – Brown hopes it is meant to be humorous. [78] So do we. It reflects the total lack of a positive agenda for change, rather than a negative agenda of mere resistance, that infuses much of the anti-globalisation movement. Again citing Rorty, '. . . [if] you still long for total revolution, for the Radical Other on a world historical scale, the events of 1989 show that you are out of luck'.[79]

A strategy of redescription, as part of a reformist strategy, assumes that the reform of capitalism has to be possible. We suspect it will not please observers on

---

[78] Brown, *International Relations Theory*, p. 237.
[79] Ibid., p. 239.

either end of the globalisation–anti-globalisation continuum. But, we would argue –
current problems in the global economy (indeed the global order in general)
notwithstanding – that there is nothing to suggest that the market economy is likely
to disappear in a hurry. Other world ideologies are not lining up to replace it.
Reform has to be the order of the day. The ethical redescription of globalisation
needs to be a starting point for that process. Philosophers, theorists and practitioners of IR must join economists as key players in this process in the first decade
of the twenty-first century in a way that they were not in the closing decade of the
twentieth.

Cultural governance and pictorial resistance: reflections on the imaging of war

DAVID CAMPBELL

Introduction

If we assume that the state has no ontological status apart from the many and varied practices that bring it into being, then the state is an artefact of a continual process of reproduction that performatively constitutes its identity. The inscription of boundaries, the articulation of coherence, and the identification of threats to its sense of self can be located in and driven by the official discourses of government. But they can equally be located in and driven by the cultural discourses of the community, and represented in sites as 'unofficial' as art, film and literature. While such cultural locations are often taken to be the sites of resistance to practices of government, their oppositional character is neither intrinsic nor guaranteed. Indeed, states have often engaged in or benefited from practices of cultural governance. As Michael Shapiro argues, cultural governance involves support for diverse genres of expression to constitute and legitimise practices of sovereignty, while restricting or preventing those representations that challenge sovereignty.[1] In this sense, cultural governance is a set of historical practices of representation – involving the state but never fully controlled by the state – in which the struggle for the state's identity is located.

In this article, I focus on some issues concerning the visual media's representation of recent wars as a means of exploring cultural governance in the contemporary period. Focusing on elements of the news media, film and documentary photography, this article explores how these diverse genres have contributed to the expression of collective identity. Arguing from a position in which governance and resistance are understood to be intrinsically related practices rather than discrete modes of acting, this article also explores the pictorial challenges to common understandings that underpin the collective identities enabled by cultural governance.[2] The story begins with a film.

[1] Michael J. Shapiro, *Methods and Nations: Cultural Governance and the Indigenous Subject* (New York: Routledge, 2004), especially chs. 4–6.
[2] For an argument about the theoretical interdependence of governance (power) and resistance, see David Campbell, 'Why Fight: Humanitarianism, Principles and Poststructuralism', *Millennium: Journal of International Studies*, 27:3 (1998), pp. 497–521.

A film fable

Long before the United States, Britain and Australia invaded Iraq, before the attack on the World Trade Center precipitated Operation Enduring Freedom in Afghanistan, and prior to the NATO intervention in Kosovo and the Monica Lewinsky scandal, Barry Levinson's film *Wag the Dog* (1997) told the story of a president compromised by sexual misconduct who deflects the scandal by engineering a foreign crisis in a faraway land. Based upon the plan of an intelligence operative (Conrad Brean, played by Robert de Niro), a Hollywood producer (Stanley Motts, played by Dustin Hoffman) is engaged to construct the appearance of a war. Disturbed by the notion that this ruse is untrue and will inevitably be exposed, both the nervous producer and anxious White House staffers are placated by Brean's belief that the truth makes no difference once the aura of a scandal takes hold.

Central to establishing the truth for both of the competing stories (the president's alleged affair and the emerging war) is the public use of photographs. News reports detailing the allegations of sexual misconduct are anchored by an image of the president with the girl who later made allegations against him. Likewise, in his effort to convince Motts that a Hollywood producer is ideally placed to simulate a war, Brean asserts that war is a performance remembered for its slogans rather than its specificities. After running through a series of iconic black and white images that are almost subliminally cut into the film – 'naked girl covered in napalm'; 'V for victory'; 'five marines raising the flag on Mount Surabachi' – Brean asserts 'you remember the picture 50 years from now; you will have forgotten the war'. Similarly for the Gulf War: 'smart bomb falling down a chimney; 2500 missions a day; 100 days; one video; one bomb . . . the American people bought that war . . . war is show business . . . that's why we're here', Brean says.

Brean directs Mott to think of the war as a pageant, something with a theme, song and visuals. Of course, given that the proposed war has no actuality, the images have to be created from scratch. First off, an enemy has to be put in place, and Brean opts for Albania on the grounds that no one has heard of it and no one knows anything about Albanians. This permits Brean to conclude they must therefore be shifty, standoff-ish and untrustworthy. On this foundation, Motts starts to weave a narrative of fundamentalist danger and the threat of nuclear proliferation, with Albanian terrorists attempting to smuggle a 'suitcase bomb' over the Canadian border into the US.

Embodying conflict often requires that someone be cast in the role of victim. To this end, Motts' constructs an image of a 'young girl in rubble . . . driven from her home by Albanian terrorists' as the pivot for popular support to justify the military mobilisation. Captivated by the idea of having grainy, hand-held news footage with her clutching a kitten while running from the ruins, a series of models' photographs are scanned to select the suitable candidate. Rejecting one for being 'too Texan', Motts and his staff settle on a beautiful young blonde and dress her to fit the stereotype of East European peasant, head scarf and all. After dismissing the make-up lady – because the victim has to look like 'she's been raped by terrorists' – the actress makes a couple of runs towards the camera against the standard blue TV background that allows images to be manipulated around her. The production staff, sitting on high in the control room perusing picture library files for suitable elements of the shot, digitally add the kitten along with a backdrop of a devastated village on fire, a bridge over a stream, and a soundtrack of screams and sirens. Mocked up in a few hours, the simulated news footage is leaked *via* satellite and instantaneously broadcast by a 24-hour news channel. After it is shown and described, the newscaster concludes, 'America has seldom witnessed a more poignant picture of the human race'. In place of the president's alleged affair, the news media had been fed a new story to consume endlessly.

News media and contemporary war

The propaganda practices that make up the plot of *Wag the Dog* may be crude and fictional, but they do highlight elements found in the news media's coverage of contemporary war. The insatiable appetite of a twenty-four hour news cycle, the proliferation of cable and satellite channels, the emotional value of feminised victims, the historical resonance of iconic images, and the official appreciation of all these factors, can all be located in recent coverage.

One of the lessons the Pentagon took from Vietnam was that the power of television meant control of the military's message was central to the success of their operations. As such, the combination of independent reporting and regular military briefings (the infamous 'five o'clock follies') US officials used to conduct daily in Saigon were to be restricted. Learning also from the British experience in the Falklands, the US developed constraints for media coverage of its operations in Grenada and Panama, before deploying them most successfully during the Gulf War of 1990–91. By arranging selected media representatives into pools – which would then be handled by military liaison staff and given only restricted access to the battlefield – and organising military briefings around video images the Pentagon itself produced, the Pentagon effectively controlled the story of its campaign.[3]

The success of military media management in the Gulf War led to the 1992 promulgation of the 'Principles of Coverage'. These principles state that the US military should, as quickly as is practicable, but cognisant of any possible impact on military operations, provide reporters with independent access to combat operations. In practice, those principles were not applied in Operation Enduring Freedom in Afghanistan.[4] According to *New York Times* columnist Maureen Dowd:

Military reporters say they are more handcuffed now than during Desert Storm. They have had only the most restricted and supervised access to Special Operations units. Even reporters who went to Afghanistan with Marines found themselves quarantined in warehouses and handed press releases from Central Command in Tampa about casualties less than 100 yards away. Some who got close to the action had film confiscated and guns pointed at them by Special Operations soldiers or their mujahedeen bullies.[5]

[3] See John J. Fialka, *Hotel Warriors: Covering the Gulf War* (Washington, DC: Woodrow Wilson Center, 1992).

[4] 'In the War on Terrorism, a Battle to Shape Public Opinion', *New York Times*, 11 November 2001, <http://nytimes.com/2001/11/11/politics/11PROP.html>

[5] Maureen Dowd, 'Coyote Rummy', *New York Times*, 24 February 2002, <http://www.nytimes.com/2002/02/24/opinion/24DOWD.html>. See examples of this given in Frank Rich, 'Freedom from the Press', *New York Times*, 2 March 2002, <http://www.nytimes.com/2002/03/02/opinion/02RICH.html>

In the place of independent journalism, the Pentagon produced its own material. To cope with the void of imagery in the opening weeks of the US military operation, the Defence Department provided its own pictures, among which the firing of a cruise missile from a navy ship, the American flag caught in the rocket's bright plume, was much used around the world. Phone interviews with groups of pilots fresh from bombing runs over Afghanistan were arranged and their patriotic sentiments broadcast far and wide.[6] Some operations were themselves designed for the images they could produce. When US Army Rangers parachuted into a Taliban airbase near Kandahar in late October 2001, the story of the first action by US ground forces was made possible by the green, grainy night video of troops in action released by the Pentagon. But the Rangers were not the first on the ground, as an Army Pathfinder team had already secured the base to ensure it was safe, leading a number of senior military officials to deride the much covered parachute jump as a 'television show' designed largely to influence public opinion.[7]

The military's desire to increasingly manage information was also made clear by the strange case of the proposed Office for Strategic Influence (OSI) in the Pentagon. Throughout the fighting in Afghanistan, the US and Britain established a series of 'Coalition Information Centres' in Washington, London and Islamabad in order to produce coordinated messages and rebuttals concerning alliance strategy, and have them available for the ceaseless global news cycle. Having been caught off guard by Osama Bin Laden's release of video messages to the media through Al-Jazeera, the Bush administration opted to expand the *ad hoc* wartime arrangements into a new office of global diplomacy run by a former advertising executive.[8] But it is the plans for the OSI that has been most revealing. Concerned with 'information operations' to influence foreign audiences, it was envisaged after September 11th that the OSI would coordinate everything from factual news releases to foreign advertising campaigns (billboards in Pakistan with images of the World Trade Centre under attack was one suggestion) to covert disinformation programmes designed to plant pro-American stories in the international media, sometimes using private firms to achieve the strategy.[9] The dilemma for the Pentagon, once OSI's existence had been revealed, was how to maintain the credibility of its public statements – how to make clear the Department of Defence was not engaging in spreading lies, while declaring that its strategy was to engage in 'tactical deception' of people beyond the US.[10] In an ironic outcome, Secretary of Defence Donald Rumsfeld claimed that 'the misinformation and adverse publicity'

[6] 'A Public Flooded with Images from Friend and Foe Alike', *New York Times*, 10 October 2001, <http://www.nytimes.com/2001/10/10/arts/television/10NOTE.html>

[7] For the images, see 'Revealed: How Bungled US Raid Came Close to Disaster', *The Guardian*, 6 November 2001, p. 1. For the background account of the raid and its filming, see Seymour M. Hersh, 'Escape and Evasion', *The New Yorker*, 12 November 2001, <http://www.newyorker.com/PRINTABLE/?FACT/011112fa_FACT>

[8] 'Bush Will Keep Wartime Office Promoting America', *New York Times*, 20 February 2002, <http://nytimes.com/2002/02/20/international/20INFO.html >

[9] 'Pentagon Readies Efforts to Sway Sentiment Abroad', *New York Times*, 19 February 2002, <http://www.nytimes.com/2002/02/19/international/19PENT.html>

[10] 'New Agency Will Not Lie, Top Pentagon Officials Say', *New York Times*, 21 February 2002, <http://www.nytimes.com/2002/02/21/international/21 INFO.html?>

OSI attracted meant that it had to be closed.[11] Which does not mean that its activities no longer occur, just that they take place within existing Pentagon offices or through private subcontractors to the US government.

One of those private domains and corporate spheres through which American strategic information operations has been and will be pursued is Hollywood. While reporters from ABC's news division (along with those from CNN and others) were not able to gain access to the military in the Afghan battlefield, the same restrictions did not apply to representatives from ABCs entertainment division. In the aftermath of September 11th, the satirical magazine *The Onion* ran an article entitled 'American Life Turns into Bad Jerry Bruckheimer Movie.'[12] It is a notion that was strangely prescient. Bruckheimer, the producer of successful blockbusters such as *Top Gun*, *Pearl Harbour*, and *Black Hawk Down*, joined forces with the television producer behind the reality programme 'Cops' to develop a 'patriotic' series about US soldiers fighting the war against terrorism. All Bruckheimer's films have portrayed the US military favourably, which is not surprising given they were made with the Pentagon's assistance and blessing (in the case of *Black Hawk Down*, they provided the Apache helicopters and one hundred soldiers on location in Morocco). Similar cooperation made the six hour-long episodes of the 'Profiles from the Frontline' project possible, with the Pentagon guaranteeing access to those US troops in Afghanistan and around the world previously shielded from news journalists.[13] Screened on network television in the month prior to the invasion of Iraq, 'Profiles' provided a visual link for the war on terror from Afghanistan to Iraq, and gave both the media and the viewers a clear idea as to how the strategy of 'embedding' journalists with military units would produce a paean to valour and virtue.[14]

The Bruckheimer production of the war on terrorism will not be the only Hollywood film effort in this new patriotic struggle. There is, of course, a long history of Hollywood's association with US military causes, so cooperation post-September 11th is hardly novel. Nonetheless, the willingness of all branches of the television and film industry to meet President Bush's top political advisor Karl Rove in November 2001 reflected, as the head of Paramount Pictures said, 'this incredible need, this incredible urge to do something.'[15] Notwithstanding the administration and industry's assertions that there is no question of the government control of content, it is clear from such views that official control, let alone censorship, would be redundant. Moreover, increasingly positive portrayals of US national security issues predate September 11th. After years of declining even media comment, let alone media assistance, and reaping a negative image in film and television as a

---

[11] 'Pentagon May Eliminate New Office of Influence', *The New York Times*, 25 February 2002, <http://www.nytimes.com/2002/02/25/politics/25CND-MILI.html>; 'Rumsfeld Formally Disbands Office of Strategic Influence,' *New York Times*, 26 February 2002, <http://www.nytimes.com/2002/02/26/national/26CND-PENTAG.html>

[12] 'American Life Turns Into Bad Jerry Bruckheimer Movie', *The Onion*, 26 September 2001, <http://www.theonion.com/onion3734/american_life_turns_into.html>

[13] '"Reality TV" About GIs on War Duty', *New York Times*, 21 February 2002, available from the New York Times on-line archive.

[14] For details of the show, see its official web site at <http://abc.go.com/primetime/profiles>

[15] 'Hollywood Signs on to Assist War Effort', *Los Angeles Times*, 12 November 2001, <http://www.latimes.com/news/local/la-111201holly.story>

result, the CIA appointed a former Latin American specialist as a full-time enter-tainment liaison officer. With the promise of official cooperation, scriptwriters and producers have submitted their work for approval, and incorporated suggestions from CIA staff. The result has been some three television series and five feature films in which the agency is flatteringly featured as hard-working and heroic, though some (such as the Robert Redford movie *Spy Game* and the television series *24*) were completed and shown even though agency approval was withheld.[16]

It is important to understand – so that we can appreciate the full extent of the challenge that faces those who want to develop a politically critical stance in relation to developments and issues such as those outlined here – that the interweaving and interdependence of the military, media and information industries is neither an unforeseen accident or a failure of nerve on the part of the participants (especially the media). This blurring of what previously appeared to be distinct domains is the core of the new military strategy that results from the ' Revolution in Military Affairs' (RMA) that has preoccupied the Pentagon for some time.[17] The RMA is concerned with how networked information technology is integrated into and changes the battlefield for the US military. One of the principal changes that result from this is a different understanding of the nature and extent of 'the battlefield'. No longer confined to a spatial or temporal exception, it stems from what James Der Derian has called the 'military-industrial-media-entertainment network (MIME-NET)'.[18] While the interaction of civilian and military technologies is not a recent development, what is new about MIME-NET, Der Derian argues, 'is the power of MIME-NET to seamlessly merge the production, representation, and execution of war. The result is not merely the copy of a copy, or the creation of something new: It represents a convergence of the means by which we distinguish the original and the new, the real from the reproduced.'[19] This seamless merging of production, representation and execution comes about because 'the new wars are fought in the same manner as they are represented, by military simulations and public dissimul-ations, by real-time surveillance and TV live-feeds. Virtuality collapses distance, between here and there, near and far, fact and fiction.'[20] As a result, the battlefield is now global and inclusive, overriding previous boundaries between the military and civilian, combatant and non-combatant, participant and observer. In such a world, the Pentagon's suffocating restrictions on the press, the demise of news programmes in the face of entertainment alternatives, intimate relations between Hollywood and the national security establishment, and the conduct of military operations for their information outcomes and representational value in the struggle for strategic influence, are the norm rather than the exception.

From the invasion of Iraq in 2003, the story of Private Jessica Lynch's 'rescue' demonstrates the ever-increasing cultural governance of the news media by the

---

[16] 'Hollywood Helps CIA Come in From the Cold', *The Guardian*, 6 September 2001, <http://www.guardian.co.uk/Archive/Article/0,4273,4251281,00.html>, 'The Caring, Sharing CIA', *The Guardian*, 5 October 2001, <http://www.guardian.co.uk/Archive/Article/0,4273,4270257,00.html>

[17] For details, see the on-line resource *The RMA Debate* at <http://www.comw.org/rma/index.html>

[18] James Der Derian, *Virtuous War: Mapping the Military-Industrial-Media-Entertainment Network* (Boulder, CO: Westview Press, 2001).

[19] Ibid, xx.

[20] Ibid, xviii.

military. Lynch's release was made public through the Coalition Media Centre (CMC) at the US Central Command headquarters in Qatar. This $1.5m briefing operation, with a futuristic, Hollywood-inspired set replete with plasma TV screens, is housed in a remote warehouse hundreds of miles from the battlefield, but offering the military overview desired by its US, UK, and Australian media minders. The CMC was integral to the strategy of embedding reporters with military units, for those on the front line provided images and stories from an unavoidably narrow perspective, while the journalists at the CMC were given what was said to be the broad overview but in effect only amplified the narrow perspective desired by the Pentagon and its partners. As one media critic observed, the 500 or more 'embeds' (with 100 cameras) were 'close up at the front' while the 600 CMC journalists were 'tied up in the rear'. This meant the military could be confidant journalists would produce 'maximum imagery with minimum insight'.[21]

The Lynch story demonstrated how well this operation could function. CMC journalists were roused from their sleep in the early hours of 2 April, thinking that a major story (such as the death of Saddam Hussein) was breaking. Instead they were presented with an edited five-minute military video – shot through a night lens, producing green, grainy images of silhouetted figures – detailing the Special Forces rescue of Private Lynch. The video encapsulated a narrative familiar to viewers of *Black Hawk Down* and *Behind Enemy Lines* – that the US military 'never leaves a fallen comrade'. A single still image was taken from this operation and circulated widely, showing Lynch lying on a stretcher aboard a US special forces helicopter, smiling grimly from under a US flag draped across her chest.

That Jessica Lynch is a fair-skinned, 19 year old blonde female from West Virginia helped spur the stories of heroism surrounding her captivity and rescue. Said to be suffering gun shot and stab wounds, and having been reportedly mistreated during her detention in an Iraqi hospital, a much used *Washington Post* story from 3 April cited unnamed sources as describing how Lynch had fought bravely during the battle of 23 March that led to her capture, firing a weapon repeatedly despite being hit and seeing many of her comrades killed.[22] Unsurprisingly, the cinematic quality of this description has led to quickly produced TV documentaries (the *Arts and Entertainment* network screened 'Saving Jessica Lynch' within two weeks of her rescue) and a massive effort to secure an exclusive interview upon her recovery, with CBS (which is part of the media conglomerate Viacom) offering a package of media inducements that included proposals for shows and publications from CBS News, CBS Entertainment, MTV (who dangled the prospect of Lynch co-hosting an hour long programme, with a concert held in her home town of Palestine, West Virginia), Paramount Pictures, and Simon and Schuster books.[23]

[21] John Kampfner, 'War Spin', *Correspondent*, BBC2, 18 May 2003. For critical accounts of the CMC operation, see Michael Wolff, 'You know less than when you arrived', *The Guardian (Media supplement)*, 31 March 2003, <http://media.guardian.co.uk/mediaguardian/story/0,7558,925900,00.html>; Wolff, 'I was only asking', *The Guardian (Media supplement)*, 14 April 2003, <http://media.guardian.co.uk/mediaguardian/story/0,7558,936087,00.html>

[22] 'Reporting Private Lynch', *Washington Post*, 20 April 2003, B6.

[23] 'In Hoopla Over a POW, A Mirror of US Society', *New York Times*, 18 April 2003; and 'To Interview Former POW, CBS Offers Stardom', *New York Times* 16 June 2003, available from the New York Times on-line archive.

Apparently Lynch cannot recall any aspect of her time in an Iraqi hospital or subsequent release. But later media investigations have discovered that most of the dramatic elements of the early accounts of Lynch's condition and return are open to serious question. A BBC documentary, which interviewed staff involved in Lynch's care after the war had been declared over, revealed that she had no war wounds but was diagnosed as a serious road traffic accident victim, had received the best available treatment from Iraqi medical staff, and that their attempt to return her to US forces in an ambulance had been repelled at a US military checkpoint.[24]

While the basic coordinates of Lynch's story were not invented (she was injured, captured then recovered), the account was staged, in so far as the particular narrative that was attached to and derived from the military film of her release was constructed by the Pentagon's media operation to convey a heroic and redemptive meaning (implicitly recalling the captivity narratives common in the early days of American settlement, with Iraq functioning as 'Indian country'). The power of the image – both the night-vision video, and the still of Lynch on the stretcher, redolent of the fair-haired victim in *Wag the Dog* – was key to the way this account represented part of the invasion of Iraq. But are there images resistant to such official discourses of cultural governance?

It is important to remember that, whatever the power of MIME-NET and information warfare strategies, alternative images to those released and broadcast are captured all the time. That is because a not insignificant number of cameramen and photographers operate independently and unilaterally in war zones. But even embedded cameramen have recorded shocking images of wars effects that counter the clean narratives of surgical strikes. The problem is that the media industry itself operates in terms of codes and norms that mesh with the military's restrictions and prevent the public release of such images by invoking conceptions of 'taste' and 'decency'. In this context, it is worth exploring one branch of the media that has not bowed to these conventions and continues to represent much of the unvarnished horror of war – the traditions of documentary photography and photojournalism. This necessitates reflecting on concerns about the truth of the photograph, before examining Don McCullin's photojournalism as an instance of potential pictorial resistance to the cultural governance of war's representation.

Photographs and the question of truth

It might seem anachronistic in the age of digital video and real-time news coverage to be concerned with the photojournalism of war and the politics of documentary photography. After all, it has been argued that Biafra (in 1968) was the last war in which newspapers scooped television, and black and white photographs played a

---

[24] Kampfner, 'War Spin', *Correspondent*, BBC2, 18 May 2003; Kampfner, 'The Truth about Jessica', *The Guardian* (G2 supplement), 15 May 2003, pp. 2–3. Many of these features were confirmed by the *Washington Post's* re-examination of the story two months after its initial account (which is no longer available in its online archives). See 'A Broken Body, a Broken Story', *Washington Post*, 17 June 2003, A1.

major role.[25] However, it is interesting to note – as the opening to *Wag the Dog* makes clear – when it comes to historical memory the photograph retains a considerable power. Indeed, as Susan Sontag has argued, it might be *precisely because of* the ubiquity of television's visual flow that the arrest of time in the photograph offers space for contemplation and critique.[26]

The digital age has, however, had an important impact on contemporary debates about photography. With the increased capacity for pictorial manipulation arising from the use of digital cameras and computer imaging, public laments about the associated loss of authority and truth are common. For example, the new technology has led Fred Ritchin to wonder how the photograph's documentary authority can be maintained when the computer provides no archival notion of an original photographic negative against which changes and tamperings could be checked. As a result, Ritchin speculates that ever-increasing digitisation might paradoxically mean 'a revival of the largely dormant photo essay taken by living, breathing, thinking photographers; the photograph, unchained from its simplistic role of authentication, will then be recognized for its linguistic subtlety and broader reach'.[27]

While computerisation might produce that paradoxical outcome, the resultant photographic product will not function as a stable referent of objective truth in contrast to the computer's indeterminate subjectivism. In large part, that is because the age of computer-based photography has heightened but not introduced the element of bias to an otherwise certain domain. Indeed, the digital revolution's most important effect has been to end the 'interlude of false innocence' in which the referential veracity of the photographic image was too often unquestioned.[28] But even those who did not assume that photography corresponded directly to the external world, have sometimes been moved by the computer to a different position. As John Roberts observes, 'one of the ironies of the debate on simulation and the chemical photograph is that all those who previously took documentary photography to task for believing in the 'truth-value' of the naturalistic image, now talk nostalgically about the disappearance of documentary's reportorial and archival role'.[29]

The irony of this situation is even more marked if we reflect on the way the truth-value of the photographic image has always been challenged through allegations of manipulation leading to fraud. Indeed, many of the most famous war photographs have been the subject of controversy, with at least elements of the alleged naturalism dispelled. For example, during the American civil war, photographers (such as Alexander Gardner and Matthew Brady) moved bodies around to make images;[30] Robert Capa's falling Spanish republican soldier is alleged to have been staged (or at

[25] Jonathan Benthall, *Disasters, Relief and the Media* (London: I.B. Tauris, 1993), p. 102.
[26] Susan Sontag, *On Photography* (New York: Anchor Books, 1990), pp. 17–18.
[27] Fred Ritchin, 'Photojournalism in the Age of Computers', in *The Critical Image: Essays on Contemporary Photography*, ed. Carol Squiers (Seattle, WA: Bay Press, 1990), pp. 35, 36.
[28] William J. Mitchell, *The Reconfigured Eye: Visual Truth in the Post-Photographic Era* (Cambridge MA: MIT Press 1992), p. 225.
[29] John Roberts, *The Art of Interruption: Realism, Photography and the Everyday* (Manchester: Manchester University Press, 1998), p. 221.
[30] Mitchell, *The Reconfigured Eye*, pp. 44–5; John Taylor, *Body Horror: Photojournalism, Catastrophe and War* (Manchester: Manchester University Press, 1998), p. 64.

least consistent with other interpretations, such as someone slipping during training);[31] the image of five marines raising the flag at Mt Surabachi, Iwo Jima on 23 February 1945 was re-enacted with a different flag some hours after the flag raising ceremony;[32] and General William Westmoreland, former US commander in Vietnam, claimed in a 1986 speech that Huynh Cong Ut's 1972 photo of the Vietnamese girl fleeing a napalm attack showed nothing more than a 'hibachi accident at a family bar-b-que'.[33] Recently, the still of the Bosnian prisoner Fikret Alic, emaciated and standing behind a barbed wire fence at the Bosnian Serb-run Trnjopolje camp – frame-grabbed from an ITN television news report in August 1992 by newspapers and magazines around the world – has (wrongly) been declared a misleading fabrication by those with an interest in denying the charge of genocide against Serbian commanders.[34]

In a similar vein is the controversy surrounding Arthur Rothstein's photographs of the South Dakota drought during the Depression. Rothstein placed a locally obtained cow skull against various backdrops to obtain an image of the economic and environmental plight of farmers in the area. As part of the famous Farm Security Administration's (FSA) photographic unit, which did so much to establish the reputation of documentary photography as a progressive social practice, Rothstein was part of the effort to visualise the Depression in such a way that enabled New Deal policies. As such, regional newspapers opposed to the economic strategies of the New Deal seized on Rothstein's work as a way of supposedly demonstrating that such policies were based on 'trickery'.[35]

Given the political stakes in the debate around Rothstein's image, the controversy almost brought a premature end to the FSA photographic unit by putting in doubt the aura of naturalist veracity its work had acquired.[36] Even some of Rothstein's colleagues were appalled by his action. Walker Evans, one of the FSA's most famous photographers and one of the most noteworthy photographers of the twentieth century, declared 'that that's where the word "documentary" holds: you don't touch a *thing*. You "manipulate", if you like, when you frame a picture – one foot one way or one foot another. But you're not sticking anything in.'[37]

Evans' stipulation that one can 'manipulate' in terms of picture selection and composition, but one cannot 'stick anything in', requires a fine but tenuous sense of legitimate practice. It flows, of course, from a conventional sense of the meaning of

---

[31] Mitchell, *The Reconfigured Eye*, pp. 40–2; Taylor, *Body Horror*, pp. 58–9.

[32] Mitchell, *The Reconfigured Eye*, p. 43.

[33] David D. Perlmutter, *Photojournalism and Foreign Policy: Icons of Outrage in International Crises* (Wesport, CT: Praeger, 1998), p. 23; Mitchell, *The Reconfigured Eye*, p. 43.

[34] For a full analysis of this controversy, see David Campbell, 'Atrocity, Memory, Photography: Imaging the Concentration Camps of Bosnia – The Case of ITN versus *Living Marxism*, Part I', *Journal of Human Rights*, 1:1 (2002), pp. 1–33; and 'Atrocity, Memory, Photography: Imaging the Concentration Camps of Bosnia – The Case of ITN versus *Living Marxism*, Part II', *Journal of Human Rights* 1:2 (2002), pp. 143–72. Both articles, and the relevant images and video, are available at <www.virtual-security-net>

[35] Martha Rosler, 'In, Around, and Afterthoughts (On Documentary Photography)', in *The Contest of Meaning: Critical Histories of Photography*, ed. by Richard Bolton (Cambridge MA: MIT Press, 1992), p. 337n.

[36] William Stott, *Documentary Expression and Thirties America* (Chicago, IL: University of Chicago Press, 1986), p. 61.

[37] Ibid, p. 269.

photography, a traditional understanding of the genre of documentary, and associated theories of reality and truth that undergird each. However, each of the above examples of controversial war pictures demonstrates the way in which these well understood realist accounts of photography are largely insufficient in making sense of the politics of photography. That is because in each of the cases there is no fraud equivalent to the obviously staged nineteenth-century images of fairies at the bottom of the garden, equivalent attempts to portray the Loch Ness monster or UFOs, or the manipulative construction of the Albanian victim in *Wag the Dog*. In each of the above cases, none of the critics doubt the basic elements of the images were there; what they doubt are the meanings most derive from the use of such images. Which raises the interesting prospect that a realist image may be a poorer conveyer of truth than either a heavily interpreted or even partially constructed image (such as Rothstein's cow skull). If we accept that, then what is the line – if any such line exists – between Rothstein's cow skull and *Wag the Dog's* Albanian beauty?

One of the major problems with war photography that focuses on victims as an antidote to heroic images is that it can produce a generalised and standardised visual account that anonymises victims and depoliticises conflict.[38] This results in what Allen Feldman calls 'cultural anaesthesia', and effects what Martha Rosler has termed *the revictimisation of victims*.[39] Moreover, given the importance of photography in the emergence of social science discourses such as anthropology and criminology in the late nineteenth century, the reduction of the mobile and multiple contingencies of personhood to the figure of a static, one-dimensional victim have a long history. As John Tagg observes, in turn-of-the-century social science 'the working classes, colonised peoples, the criminal, poor, ill-housed, sick or insane were constituted as the passive – or, in this structure, "feminised" – objects of knowledge. Subjected to a scrutinising gaze, forced to emit signs, yet cut off from command of meaning, such groups were represented as, and wishfully rendered, incapable of speaking, acting or organising for themselves.'[40]

The issue to consider, then, is whether being 'culturally anaesthetic' is an inevitable and unavoidable element of the photographic representation of victims of war, and to ask what are modes of photographic representation that can dissimulate if not dispense with such depoliticising effects? To locate this questioning, I will look at the work of noted British photojournalist Don McCullin.

Don McCullin and the ghosts of victims

Known in particular for his photographs of the conflict in Cyprus, the war-driven famine of Biafra, the fighting in Vietnam and the refugees created by the secession

---

[38] Allen Feldman, 'On Cultural Anaesthesia: From Desert Storm to Rodney King', *American Ethnologist*, 21:2 (May 1994), p. 407; and Liisa Malkki, 'Speechless Emissaries: Refugees, Humanitarianism, and Dehistoricization', *Cultural Anthropology*, 11:3 (1996), p. 386.

[39] Cited in Andrea Liss, *Trespassing Through the Shadows: Memory, Photography and the Holocaust* (Minneapolis, MN: University of Minnesota Press, 1998, p. xiv.

[40] John Tagg, *The Burden of Representation: Essays on Photographies and Histories* (Minneapolis, MN: University of Minnesota Press, 1993), p. 11.

of East Pakistan, Don McCullin readily acknowledges that his photography is preoccupied with often personalised images of atrocity. 'I thought of my pictures as atrocity pictures. They were not of war but of the dreadful plight of victims of war.'[41] Invariably, though not exclusively, composed of one or two individuals in a situation of distress, McCullin's dark, tonal images brood with a violence that exceeds the events being depicted.

The force of these images – what McCullin describes as their 'fist-like black and white' quality – is not something developed because of the fetishistic pleasure of death and disaster.[42] As Mark Haworth-Booth has observed, McCullin's 'photography of suffering has been a kind of *service*' to its audience.[43] The nature of that service? To be a *witness* – 'someone who epitomises the role of witness to the despair of our time',[44] '*our* eye-witness', a 'passionately eloquent witness' whose work is itself a 'witness to history'.[45]

Essential to the role of witness for McCullin is emotion. 'Photography for me is not looking, it's feeling. If you can't feel what you're looking at, then you're never going to get others to feel anything when they look at your pictures.'[46] What McCullin feels more often than not is a combination of disgust at the violent circumstances embracing the innocent, and an empathy with those who become the victims of war. Indeed, for McCullin that empathy is so strong he shares intimately the danger of those being fired upon. 'There were times', McCullin says, 'looking at those people when I felt I was looking at a mirror. There was an empathy because of my background. It never went away from me.'[47]

Empathetic witnessing, McCullin originally thought, would not be a political exercise. 'When I began as a photographer, I believed that my work would suffer if I allowed it to become political. In the event, it turned out to be nothing but political for I consistently took the side of the underdog and the under-privileged.'[48] This political exercise in photography was, however, for a clear purpose. By portraying 'the appalling things we are all capable of doing to our fellow human beings', McCullin's photojournalism sought 'to stir the conscience of others who can help'; to show those comfortably at home in Britain . . . how these people were suffering.'[49] But while political, McCullin's pictures, especially those of Biafra, 'were not partisan. I would like to think these images brought help to the beleaguered hospitals with their dying children. I knew my pictures had a message, but what it was precisely I couldn't have said – except perhaps, that I wanted to break the hearts and spirits of secure people.'[50]

---

[41] Don McCullin, *Unreasonable Behaviour: An Autobiography* (London, Vintage, 1992), p. 165.
[42] Quoted in Pam Roberts, 'War and Peace', in *Don McCullin: A Retrospective* (London: British Council, 1993), p. 7.
[43] Mark Haworth-Booth, 'Introduction', in Don McCullin, *Sleeping with Ghosts* (London: Jonathan Cape, 1994), p. 11.
[44] Mark Holborn, 'Don McCullin', at <http://www.hamiltonsgallery.com/>, 20 August 2003.
[45] Haworth-Booth, 'Introduction', p. 9. McCullin notes he has always tried to be an 'independent witness – though not an unemotional one'. McCullin, *Unreasonable Behaviour*, p. 101.
[46] Quoted in Peter Hamilton, 'Laying Some Ghosts to Rest', *Photographic Journal*, 137:7 (1997), p. 299.
[47] Chris Townsend, 'Ghostly Vision', *British Journal of Photography*, 7142 (1997), p. 16.
[48] McCullin, *Unreasonable Behaviour*, p. 270.
[49] Ibid., pp. 124, 82.
[50] Ibid., p. 125.

As the previous quote suggests, the clarity of purpose, in the face of abundant atrocity, articulated by McCullin, was not matched by the certainty that any of the images he produced contained within them a clear message, let alone a message that would automatically induce the sort of practical response required for the situations depicted. Perhaps for this reason, Don McCullin has been haunted by his work, often commenting on the presence of ghosts in his world. Reflecting on how he operated during the East Pakistan refugee crisis, McCullin has remarked, 'I felt as if I were using the camera as something to hide behind. I stood there feeling less than human, with no flesh on me, like a ghost that was present but invisible.'[51] The motif extends to the production of the print itself: 'If I'm printing a picture of a man whose wife lies dead before him, or the albino boy in Biafra, the moment I see them appearing through the fog of the developer it's as if they are still alive, and the full force of the tragedy comes flooding back'.[52] Not surprisingly, given that a photojournalist such as McCullin finds himself surrounded by an archive of still images of dead people who can be brought back to a limited form of pictorial life, the retrospective exhibition at the V & A Museum in London displaying McCullin's lifetime of work was entitled *Sleeping With Ghosts*.

Of course, one of the spectres hanging over the status of the documentary photograph as authentic witness is the code of practice articulated by Walker Evans and discussed earlier. Evans insisted that the truth of a realistic image can only be secured by the photographer refraining from meddling in any way with the subject (beyond the need to compose the shot), and declared that the whole point about documentary is 'that you don't touch a thing' and you certainly 'cannot stick anything in'. It is a view that McCullin – who has argued, 'what comes into the frame is truth' – endorses.[53]

However, in his role as eyewitness, trying to convey an image to a distant public that might disturb their collective conscience, McCullin has occasionally violated Evans' dictum in a manner akin to Arthur Rothstein's New Deal photograph. One case in point is his famous image of a dead North Vietnamese soldier lying, eyes fixed open and arm outstretched, next to his scattered personal effects – his wallet with the photo of a young child, along with a letter and other family photos strewn from an open tin. The placement of these personal effects alongside the body was something that McCullin created. As he has explained: 'I saw a whole bunch of [American] soldiers vandalising his body for souvenirs. I thought there's got to be something I can say about this. So I put these things together, I put them there to make the picture. It was the first time I thought I could justify it. And I don't have any shame about doing it. It wasn't the dead soldier that is the statement, it was the family photographs, the wallet. I was making a still-life.'[54]

McCullin experienced a similar moment in Biafra. One of his photographs from that conflict shows a solitary girl perched on a wooden bench. Smiling wanly, the image is notable in part for the girl's hands crossed in her lap, a pose that would not,

---

[51] Ibid., p. 165.
[52] Hamilton, 'Laying some Ghosts to Rest', p. 299.
[53] Ibid.
[54] Quoted Ibid., p. 300. The photograph – along with the preceding image showing two guilty-looking GI's looting the body (alongside which there are no personal effects) – can be found in McCullin, *Sleeping with Ghosts*, pp. 74–5.

save for the obvious distress her body has endured, be out of place in a formal portrait. McCullin has discussed how this picture was produced:

Before leaving I found a young girl of about sixteen sitting naked in a hut, looking ill and very frail, but beautiful. Her name, I was told, was Patience. I wanted to photograph her and asked the orderly if she would persuade the girl to cover the private parts of her body with her hands so that I could show her nakedness with as much dignity as possible. But the sight of her stripped me naked of any of the qualities I might have had as a human being. The whiplash of compassion and conscience never ceased to assail me in Biafra.[55]

In this case, as many others, the portrayal of the victim's *dignity* was McCullin's purpose. Commenting on his experience of covering a famine in the Bihar region of India, McCullin observed 'no heroics are possible when you are photographing people who are starving. All I could do was try to give the people caught up in this terrible disaster as much dignity as possible.'[56] In common with a photojournalist like Sebastiao Salgado, McCullin has made dignity the leitmotif of his work. Equally in common with Salgado, the portrayal of dignity has meant that McCullin's work has entered the debate about the place and role of aesthetic values in atrocity pictures.[57]

The identification of beauty in the midst of disaster is controversial and contestable. While the alleged timelessness and universality of images like the McCullin photograph of Patience are often taken to be the product of the aestheticisation of the image, and this is taken to be one way to make an image stand out despite its generalisable quality, critics such as Robin Andersen maintain that aestheticisation only further depoliticises the issue at hand, especially when tragedy is the product of agony beautified. As Andersen remarks, 'the beautification of squalid reality offers the viewer a certain amount of emotional distance. This distancing lessens the impact, and in the process the media have created a public which has learned not to care much.'[58]

Such effects would be contrary to most photojournalists' hopes. They would certainly be contrary to what McCullin has aimed for with his documentary work. Nonetheless, the standard critique of McCullin's work is that his overriding emphasis on subjects either alone, or framed with another in a similar state of suffering, is highly problematic. As Andersen writes:

In McCullin's work, and in much of the work of photographers who have come after him, neither starvation's victims nor victims of war are shown in a social context. They don't explain or inform. They become suffering individuals of the human condition. The social and political – human made – causes are not in appearance, and therefore not in the image. And many times, indeed most, the news context does not supply adequate information and explanations.[59]

---

[55] McCullin, *Unreasonable Behaviour*, p. 124. The photography can be found in McCullin, *Sleeping with Ghosts*, p. 86.

[56] McCullin, *Unreasonable Behaviour*, p. 82.

[57] See David Campbell, 'Salgado and the Sahel: Documentary Photography and the Imaging of Famine', in *Rituals of Mediation: International Politics and Social Meaning*, eds. Francois Debrix and Cynthia Weber (Minneapolis, MN: University of Minnesota Press, 2003).

[58] Robin K. Andersen, 'The Ideological Significance of News Photography: The Case of El Salvador', *Ideologies and Literature*, 3:2 (Fall 1988), p. 251.

[59] Ibid, pp. 237–8.

In Andersen's view, 'without a social or political context, and without information or explanations which would explain or account for suffering, photographs which document pain, misery and death *cannot* elicit public concern and empathy'.[60]

For one concerned to emphasise the importance of context, Andersen makes a definitive and emphatic judgement about what the photograph alone can and cannot do. It is, moreover, a judgement that differs in some respects from John Berger's meditation on the potential impact of what he calls atrocity photos. Moved to write after viewing a McCullin photo from Vietnam, Berger opined that such images had one predominant purpose:

They bring us up short. The most literal adjective that could be applied to them is *arresting*. We are seized by them . . . As we look at them, the moment of the other's suffering engulfs us. We are filled with either despair or indignation. Despair takes on some of the other's suffering to no purpose. Indignation demands action. We try to emerge from the moment of the photograph back into our lives. As we do so, the contrast is such that the resumption of our lives appears to be a hopelessly inadequate response to what we have just seen.[61]

The terms of Berger's reading are, of course, loaded, the only options for response being 'despair' *versus* 'indignation', with despair having no purpose. Berger is interested in whether a photograph can politicise understanding, and appears to endorse Roland Barthes' notion that 'photography is subversive not when it frightens, repels, or even stigmatises, but when it is *pensive*, when it thinks'.[62] In this context, Berger claims 'it is not possible for anyone to look pensively at such a moment [of agony, as in McCullin's photos] and emerge stronger'.[63]

Although he wants to rule out this possible effect, Berger nonetheless thinks that the war photo is contradictory. While it is assumed to awaken concern, once the reader who is arrested by the image emerges from it to carry on with her life, the disjuncture of the experience will leave her, says Berger, feeling morally inadequate. That inadequacy may now shock her as much as the war itself, and either she shrugs that paradox off or ' [s]he thinks of performing a kind of penance – of which the purest example would be to make a contribution to OXFAM or to UNICEF'. Whatever the response, concludes Berger, 'the issue of the war which had caused that moment is effectively depoliticised. The picture becomes evidence of the general human condition. It accuses nobody and everybody.'[64] Andersen thinks atrocity photos cannot elicit concern and sympathy, while Berger thinks they do provoke a response, but one that is misplaced and unhelpful.

Concluding reflections

Those differences notwithstanding, both Andersen's and Berger's accounts burden *the image itself* with the responsibility for politicisation, rather than viewing it in the

---

[60] Ibid, p. 238. Emphasis added.
[61] John Berger, 'Photographs of Agony', in Berger, *About Looking* (London: Writers and Readers Publishing Cooperative, 1980), p. 38.
[62] Roland Barthes, *Camera Lucida: Reflections on Photography*, trans. by Richard Howard (New York: Hill and Wang, 1981), p. 38.
[63] Berger, 'Photographs of Agony', p. 39.
[64] Ibid., 39–40.

intertextual context of the news, information, captions, layout, outlets and the like. This emphasis on the power of the image itself would be consistent with the thematic view that we are witnessing in social theory a 'pictorial turn' that is taking over from the 'linguistic turn' of twentieth century philosophy. However, this identification of the importance of the pictorial does not mean that we have to invent a new and singular mode of analysis for the visual.[65] As W. J. T. Mitchell argues, 'whatever the pictorial turn is, then, it should be clear that it is not a return to naïve mimesis, copy or correspondence theories of representation, or a renewed metaphysics of pictorial "presence"; it is rather a postlinguistic, postsemiotic rediscovery of the picture as a complex interplay between visuality, apparatus, institutions, discourse, bodies, and figurality'.[66] As such, Mitchell's argument chimes with Susan Sontag's view that while the photograph is significant because of its capacity to engender a space for thought, it cannot by itself be an instrument for change. Sontag maintains the image can help build or reinforce a moral position, but it cannot create such a position in the absence of 'an appropriate context of feeling and attitude'.[67] In other words, the photograph requires the politics produced by the interplay of image and context about which Mitchell writes. Moreover, the photograph requires the overt and committed politics of a photojournalist like Don McCullin.

As a practice of resistance, documentary photography has its work cut out. The speed at which (dis)information circulates in the media-managed battle space means the time for contemplation and critique offered by the still image is more compressed than ever. Nonetheless, while the images alone are unlikely to lead to change, especially in the short time available, they become part of what Sontag calls the vast repository of pictures that make it difficult to sustain the 'moral defectiveness' of ignorance or innocence in the face of suffering. Images may only be an invitation to pay attention. But the questions photographs of war and atrocity pose should be required of our leaders and us: 'Who caused what the picture shows? Who is responsible? Is it excusable? Was it inevitable? Is there some state of affairs which we have accepted up to now that ought to be challenged?'[68]

The conclusion Sontag reaches is a battle cry in which the picture functions as a ghost: 'Let the atrocious images haunt us. Even if they are only tokens, and cannot possibly encompass most of the reality to which they refer, they still perform a vital function. The images say: This is what human beings are capable of doing – may volunteer to do, enthusiastically, self-righteously. Don't forget.'[69] *The Guardian* used this Sontag quote in a short editorial to support its publication, twelve years after the event, of many previously unseen photographs from the Persian Gulf War.[70] Under the title 'Blood in the Sand' and edited by Don McCullin, these unsparing

[65] See Martin Jay, 'Vision in Context: Reflections and Refractions', in *Vision in Context: Historical and Contemporary Perspectives on Sight*, eds. Teresa Brennan and Martin Jay (London: Routledge, 1996), p. 3; and W. J. T. Mitchell, *Picture Theory: Essays on Verbal and Visual Representation* (Chicago, IL: University of Chicago Press, 1994), ch. 1.

[66] Mitchell, *Picture Theory*, pp. 4–5, 16.

[67] Sontag, *On Photography*, p. 17.

[68] Ibid., p. 117.

[69] Susan Sontag, *Regarding the Pain of Others* (New York: Farrar, Straus and Giroux, 2003), p. 115.

[70] 'The Pity of War: It is Right to Confront Images of Death', *The Guardian*, 14 February 2003, p. 23.

images 'reveal[ed] the true horror of the Gulf war', and their publication was timed to coincide with the global anti-war marches on 15 February 2003.[71]

One of the images in this selection was Keith Jarecke's famous image from the Gulf War of 1991 (published originally on the front page of *The Observer* under the title 'The Real Face of War') showing a charred Iraqi corpse still upright in his vehicle. As evidence of the infamous 'turkey shoot' on the Basra road – when allied jets devastated a vast convoy of Iraqi vehicles after they had fled Kuwait – this photograph immediately contested the well-established view of the conflict as casualty-free. Against the larger narrative of the conduct of the Gulf War, this image functioned as a point of disruption, a reminder of what that narrative hid. As a result, the publication of the photo was immediately controversial, with the political issues of reportage being contested by complaints of taste. Indeed, in most newspapers, issues of taste easily trumped the significance of the photograph as editors refused to contemplate its publication.[72]

Nonetheless, Kenneth Jarecke's photograph demonstrates the potential (through its publication both in 1991 and 2003) for such images to serve as a form of 'post-reportage', whereby one can speak in 'considered retrospect' of events narrated in contradictory ways.[73] In this context, what photographs can do is 'provide moments of silence, caught in the uneasy space between what was experienced *there* and what is being experienced *here*'.[74] Evocative of Barthes' contention that the photograph produces a different rendering of space-time, and is subversive when it is pensive, understanding photographs as opening critical spaces for thought (and political re-enactments) through their narrative *positioning* is suggestive of one way to promote photography's capacity to politicise war – especially when the power of MIME-NET propels us frighteningly close to the official promulgation of *Wag the Dog's* prop-aganda practices. It is a position that neither dismisses the art gallery as a critical site for public consumption (especially given the way a gallery and its commentary fosters contemplation rather than gratification), nor insists that a strict adherence to realist documentary protocols is essential for the truth-value of an image.

With the changing international political economy of the media – in which serious documentary reportage has given way to the fluff of consumerist lifestyle coverage – these alternative uses and locations of images are far from being irrelevant to the development of resistant political positions. Moreover, it demonstrates that pictorial resistance to the official practices of cultural governance can take place in a multitude of previously unacknowledged political spaces. What is required, however, is for that resistance to be timelier, more in tune with the speed of contemporary war.

---

[71] *The Guardian* (G2), 14 February 2003, pp. 1–17. For a similar series (two of which appeared in *The Guardian*) with a similar aim, see Peter Turnley, 'The Unseen Gulf War', *The Digital Journalist*, December 2002, at <http://www.digitaljournalist.org/issue0212/pt_intro.html>, 29 January 2003. For a discussion of the decision to print, see Ian Mayes, 'The Face of Reality', *The Guardian*, 17 February 2003, p. 21.

[72] Taylor, *Body Horror*, pp. 181–3.

[73] Ian Walker, 'Desert Stories or Faith in Facts', in Martin Lister (ed.), *The Photographic Image in Digital Culture* (London: Routledge, 1995), pp. 239–40.

[74] Ibid., p. 244. Walker considers the Jarecke photo at pp. 247–8.

Legitimacy in a global order

IAN CLARK*

'Principles of legitimacy are born, grow up, age, and die; sometimes they come into collision and clash. Their life cycles and their clashes are the invisible foundations of history'

G. Ferrero, *The Principles of Power*[1]

This is a study of legitimacy *in* a global order, not legitimacy *of* the global order. It explores the challenging issue of what legitimacy might mean within such a context, and on what basis that order could develop its own principles of legitimacy. Its purpose is to garner further insights into the nature of contemporary global governance, and resistance to it, inasmuch as the latter is widely deemed to be symptomatic of the legitimacy crisis at its heart. A multitude of writers, working from quite different perspectives, is in agreement that it is this lack of legitimacy that threatens the very fabric of the order.[2] Indeed, it is common to regard the emergence of concerns about the declining legitimacy of any system as itself indicative of some kind of failure within it: the concept tends to be associated with the 'politics of crisis'.[3] Accordingly, we are most likely to ask questions about the legitimacy of a system only when things appear to be going wrong. If this is so, legitimacy provides a vital key to understanding the tensions within the contemporary global order.

* This work has been completed during the author's tenure of a Major Research Fellowship from the Leverhulme Trust, and I wish to thank the Trust for its generous support. The article forms part of a larger project to be published as *Legitimacy in International Society* (Oxford University Press, forthcoming 2005). I am deeply grateful to my colleagues (Tim Dunne, Andrew Linklater and Nicholas Wheeler), and also to the Editors, for helpful comments on earlier drafts.

[1] G. Ferrero, *The Principles of Power: The Great Political Crises of History* (New York: Putnam's, 1942).
[2] Typical statements of the argument can be found in M. Bukovansky, *Legitimacy and Power Politics: The American and French Revolutions in International Political Culture* (Princeton, NJ: Princeton University Press, 2002), p. 233; J. A. Camilleri, K. Malhotra and M. Tehranian, *Re-imagining the Future: Towards Democratic Governance: A Report of the Global Governance Reform Project* (Bundoora, Melbourne: Department of Politics, La Trobe University, 2000), p. xvii; K. Nicolaidis, 'Conclusion: The Federal Vision Beyond the Federal State', in K. Nicolaidis and R. Howse (eds.), *Federal Vision: Legitimacy and Levels of Governance in the United States and the European Union* (Oxford: Oxford University Press, 2001), p. 477; V. Cable, *Globalization and Global Governance* (London: RIIA, Chatham House Paper, 1999); D. Held and A. McGrew, *Globalization/Anti-Globalization* (Cambridge: Polity, 2002); D. Held and A. McGrew (eds.), *Governing Globalization* (Cambridge: Polity, 2002); J. A. Nye and J. D. Donahue (eds.), *Governance in a Globalizing World* (Washington, DC: Brookings, 2000); R. Vayrynen (ed.), *Globalization and Global Governance* (Lanham, MD: Rowman and Littlefield, 1999). For one useful attempt to explore the concept of legitimacy in relation to global governance, see S. Bernstein, 'Legitimacy in Global Governance: Three Conceptions', Paper presented at American Political Science Association Conference, San Francisco, 2001.
[3] P. Kitromilides, 'Enlightenment and Legitimacy' in A. Moulakis (ed.), *Legitimacy/Legitimé* (Berlin: Walter de Gruyter, 1986), p. 61.

Any framing of the topic in terms of the 'politics of governance' and the 'politics of resistance' demands precisely such an exploration. This article will examine the generic issues that arise in the analysis of political legitimacy. It will then investigate how these have manifested themselves, and been responded to, in the specific context of IR. Finally, it will survey the problems that seem to be particular to its application within the framework of a global order, and to the development of mechanisms of global governance within it. As will become readily apparent, different conceptions of legitimacy are to be found within each of these settings. Given this, what will be demonstrated is that we can at least make a beginning in mapping out the concept of legitimacy in a global order, but that the politics of governance and resistance is not the most helpful frame of reference for this task.

The brief reasons for this rebuttal are as follows. In some respects, the concept of governance is less problematic than that of resistance, but the two nonetheless enjoy an unstable relationship. Global governance, in the conventional formulation, is the complex set of interlocking institutions and norms, both formal and informal, governmental and non-governmental, that serve to make the rules for the global order.[4] What is telling about such standard accounts is that they emphasise that governance is about authority and rule making. As Held and McGrew have expressed it, 'at the analytical core of the global governance approach is a concern with understanding and explaining the political significance of global, regional and transnational authority structures'.[5] For Rosenau, it is characterised 'by an extensive disaggregation of authority'.[6] The significance of this emphasis on authority will be returned to shortly.

The concept of resistance covers an even wider spectrum of possibilities, and its relationship to governance varies accordingly. To the one end, it may be thought of as functionally equivalent to a 'loyal' opposition in its acceptance of the basic system, even when it might advocate alternative policies and strategies within it. At the other end, resistance amounts to rejectionism. Typically, radical anti-capitalist groups regard present forms of global governance as the new imperialism. Resistance then demands a liberation struggle to bring about 'an alternative system of global governance, privileging people over profits, and the local over the global'.[7]

What follows from this variability is that any attempt to present governance and resistance as a sharp dichotomy suffers from two key problems. First, it operates on the mistaken assumption that governance and resistance are wholly separable categories, when in fact they are overlapping and crosscutting. Secondly, they dwell exclusively upon the system of rule in the global order, and thereby neglect the equally important underlying issue of the nature of the political community that is essential to any meaningful engagement with legitimacy. The force of this latter point will be developed in the final section of the article.

---

[4] J. Rosenau, 'Governance in a New Global Order', in D. Held and A. McGrew (eds.), *The Global Transformations Reader*, 2nd edn. (Cambridge: Polity Press, 2003), p. 225; F. Halliday, 'Global Governance: Prospects and Problems', ibid., p. 489.
[5] 'Introduction' in Held and McGrew, *Governing Globalization*, p. 9.
[6] 'Governance', p. 228.
[7] Held and McGrew, *Globalization/Anti-Globalization*, p. 64.

Accordingly, the starting point for this analysis is to dissent from an emerging, but increasingly facile, orthodoxy that holds this legitimacy deficit to be neatly captured in terms of the simple opposition between governance and resistance, as expressed for instance in Richard Falk's contrapuntal depiction of 'globalization-from-above' as distinct from 'globalization-from-below'.[8] Such a scheme reifies both in unhelpful ways, and does not begin to engage with the manifold dimensions of legitimacy that are at stake in those two domains. This would-be orthodoxy suggests an image in which illegitimate governance, implemented by states/IGOs/markets, is resisted by the combined forces of people/INGOs/civil society, and, as such, misses the rich and complex texture of both the governance, and the resistance, that is presently on display. Neither governance, nor resistance, is quite as monolithic as this classification would imply.

Typically, not all resistance demands the overthrow of state-centred governance. Indeed, much of the literature on the politics of resistance recurrently calls for the need to bring the state back in, not analytically, but politically, as a guarantor of existing social compacts against the depredations of the global economy. Even Richard Falk has diagnosed the principal danger to lie in the 'inability of the state to protect its own citizenry...in relation to the workings of the world economy'.[9] On the same premise, Barry Gills insists on the need for adequate social protection, and places the state amongst the countervailing forces that can act towards that end.[10] Similarly, Caroline Thomas, driven by concern about the nexus between social policy, development and human security, makes her own plea for an 'expansion of *meaningful state involvement* in global governance'.[11] Such positions stand in sharp contrast to the widely held view that it is in global civil society, acting *against* the state, that the rescue of global governance is to be found. Notably, champions of a human security perspective tend often to return to the theme that 'civil society has a critical role to play'.[12]

The sceptics, on the other hand, question the democratic credentials of civil society, and of the many INGOs established by it. In their critical appraisal, these bodies 'do not currently possess the requisite degree of legitimacy and accountability to be considered as democratic representatives in a globalized political community'.[13] Others have dismissed the notion that international civil society can be viewed as a 'global *demos*', since it is little more than 'a select and self-selecting mélange of individuals and organizations'.[14] On the contrary, on this assessment, if we want

---

[8] R. Falk, *Predatory Globalization: A Critique* (Cambridge: Polity Press, 1999), ch. 8.

[9] Falk, *Predatory Globalization*, pp. 144–5.

[10] B. K. Gills, 'Introduction: Globalization and the Politics of Resistance' in Gills (ed.), *Globalization and the Politics of Resistance* (Basingstoke: Palgrave, 2000), p. 8.

[11] C. Thomas, 'Global Governance and Human Security', in R. Wilkinson and S. Hughes (eds.), *Global Governance and Human Security* (London: Routledge, 2002), p. 125.

[12] F. O. Hampson et al., *Madness in the Multitude: Human Security and World Disorder* (Don Mills, Ontario: Oxford University Press, 2002), p. 7.

[13] A. Colas, *International Civil Society: Social Movements in World Politics* (Cambridge: Polity, 2002), p. 163. See also R. Devetak and R. Higgott, 'Justice Unbound? Globalization, States and the Transformation of the Social Bond', *International Affairs*, 75 (1999), p. 494.

[14] R. Howse, 'The Legitimacy of the World Trade Organization', in J. M. Coicaud and V. Heiskanen (eds.), *The Legitimacy of International Organizations* (Tokyo: United Nations University Press, 2001), p. 362.

democratic global governance, we have no choice but to act through the state as it remains 'the sturdiest base on which to build a genuinely democratic polity'.[15] In these complex, and often fractious arguments, it is difficult to remember who is performing the governance, where the sources of resistance are to be found, and whose corner it is that we are supposed to be cheering.

Any neat separation is further obscured by the realisation that civil society is by no means wholly excluded from the system of global governance, but is instead selectively coopted into it. It is this very 'selectivity' that gives rise to its own set of problems. This creates a tension, for example, within those international organis-ations that increasingly consult 'stakeholders', thereby undercutting their links to states and governments 'on whose political will and formal consent they are based'.[16] Such tendencies are currently resisted by a number of states, especially from the South. What these states object to is yet another manifestation of Western soft power, exercised through the means of private agencies, or INGOs, within which Western civil society is considered disproportionately represented. These agencies may be seen to foster secular and rights-based agendas at variance with communal values that, so some would claim, only the local state can protect.[17] Indeed, in some portrayals, global civil society should be regarded not as part of the resistance movement (as much Western liberal folklore would have it), but instead as the shock troops of Empire, and hence as very much an integral part of the fabric of gover-nance itself.[18] As succinctly put elsewhere, 'soldiers and humanitarians are trouble-shooters for an international society structured to sustain inequality and denial of human needs'.[19]

There is equally – and however paradoxical it might seem – a politics of resistance that comes from states generically, and manifests itself, for example, in present attempts to reassert the state's security-based legitimacy in the face of transnational terrorism's attempts to undermine it. It is certainly the case that attacks like those of September 11th have had the consequence, whether or not the specific intent, of eroding the state's 'ability to protect its citizens from direct attack',[20] and thus of subverting the legitimacy it has traditionally derived from this function. However, it is also the case that 'the war against terrorism will place in the hands of state authorities all sorts of powers of surveillance and regulation',[21] many of which are likely to be welcomed by nervous grass-roots publics, especially in the West. In this context, whose is the 'legitimate' voice of resistance? And while the war against terrorism might most obviously be thought of as an expression of global governance,

---

[15] Colas, *International Civil Society*, p. 158.
[16] V. Heiskanen, 'Introduction', in Coicaud and Heiskanen (eds), *Legitimacy of International Organizations*, pp. 10–11.
[17] See, for example, R. O'Brien, A. M. Goetz, J. A. Scholte and M. Williams, *Contesting Global Governance: Multilateral Economic Institutions and Global Social Movements* (Cambridge: Cambridge University Press, 2000), p. 219.
[18] M. Hardt and A. Negri, *Empire* (Cambridge, MA.: Harvard University Press, 2001), pp. 34–7.
[19] M. Pugh, 'Maintaining Peace and Security' in Held and McGrew (eds.), *Governing Globalization*, p. 228.
[20] A. K. Cronin, 'Rethinking Sovereignty: American Strategy in the Age of Terror', *Survival*, 44 (2002), p. 134.
[21] C. Brown, *Sovereignty, Rights and Justice: International Political Theory Today* (Cambridge: Polity, 2002), p. xiii.

its putative 're-territorialisation' of security can just as readily be portrayed as an act of resistance to this particular face of globalisation. The state too, in this regard, is part of the anti-globalisation movement when it suits it to be so. Likewise, those who would resist state-centred governance have been faced also by a similar dilemma in recent years with the emergence of 'new wars' that have placed civilians very much in the firing line. 'The less armed conflicts are structured and state-governed', Eric Hobsbawm has lamented, 'the more dangerous they become for the civilian populations'.[22] Is it better for human security that such wars remain 'deregulated', or, if not, what kind of global governance is needed to control them? Is the cause of civil society advanced, or retarded, by a diminution of the state's role in this area of global governance? For these many reasons, there is no simple tug of war between governance and resistance, but instead a multifaceted interaction involving a complex array of actors. It is this that makes the insertion of legitimacy into the discussion so difficult, and gives the lie to any crude notion that global governance suffers from a single legitimacy deficit, caused by the solitary fault line that runs between the reified representatives of governance, on the one hand, and those of resistance, on the other. Instead, these deficits are as plural as the multiple dimensions of governance and resistance themselves. To develop this further, we need to begin with some basic understandings of the general concept of legitimacy, and of its importance to political life.

Legitimacy

Political scientists have found themselves unable to live either comfortably with, or wholly without, this concept.[23] Since Max Weber, it has been commonplace to make the distinction between normative theories of legitimacy that set out general criteria in terms of which the right to rule can be appraised, and empirical theories which take as their focus the belief systems of those subject to government.[24] Weber described a form of social action that 'may be oriented by the actors to a *belief* in the existence of a "legitimate order"'. [25] Elsewhere, he based the prestige of modern states on 'the belief, held by their members, in a specific consecration: the "legitimacy" of that social action which is ordered and regulated by them'.[26] In this version, rule is legitimate when its subjects believe it to be so. This Weberian approach leaves to political philosophy the task of developing exogenous schemes for adjudging the legitimacy of any political system, and concentrates instead on the

[22] E. Hobsbawm, *The New Century* (London: Little, Brown, 2000), p. 15.
[23] Useful overviews are available in D. Beetham, *The Legitimation of Power* (Basingstoke: Macmillan, 1991) and R. Barker, *Political Legitimacy and the State* (Oxford: Oxford University Press, 1990).
[24] For an interesting attempt to find a middle way between these, by restoring values to Weber's positivist approach, see J.-M. Coicaud, *Legitimacy and Politics: A Contribution to the Study of Political Right and Political Responsibility* (Cambridge: Cambridge University Press, 2002).
[25] M. Weber, *On Charisma and Institution Building*, ed. S. N. Eisenstadt (Chicago, IL: University of Chicago Press, 1968), p. 11.
[26] M. Weber, *Economy and Society: An Outline of Interpretive Sociology*, vol. 1 (Berkeley, CA: University of California Press, 1968), pp. 903–4.

quality of the endogenous political relationship itself. The test for political legitimacy is then 'not the truth of the philosopher, but the belief of the people'.[27] When applied in IR, virtually all commentators begin by recognising some such distinction, and most end up by adopting a loosely-based Weberian approach.[28]

From such a starting point, it is generally concluded that the only practical way to study legitimacy is through the belief systems of the relevant actors. Legitimacy is thereby understood to refer 'not to some abstract conception of right but, rather, to the norms of a specific cultural system at a given time'.[29] Who then are the relevant actors? They are those participants in the system of rule, and it follows from this, as expressed by one international lawyer, that 'community' is the '*sine qua non*' of the entire enterprise of defining legitimacy'.[30] Legitimacy, in this sense, and employing Franck's own analogy, is tantamount to acceptance of Greenwich Mean Longitude – a social fact that is meaningful only to members of the community who accept it and, in turn, a fact that testifies to the existence of that particular community.[31] It is quite beside the point for any non-member of the community to dissent from any such convention.

In short, for there to be legitimacy there needs to be a community/society, and the fact that legitimacy makes sense within it is clear evidence that such a community/society actually exists. However, this does not mean that Franck's community *precedes* the inception of its principles of legitimacy. Arguably, just as there can be no concept of legitimacy outside of community, it can equally be held that a community does not exist without its own sense of legitimacy: both give rise to each other in mutual formation. This becomes pertinent, as will be seen below, in connection with international society. For example, two students of international society have explicitly claimed that principles of legitimacy are part of the 'constitutional structure', or fundamental 'institutions', of international society.[32] In that instance, Franck's stipulation is clearly met, since legitimacy is nested within a particular society. Can the same be said of the global order?

First, however, we need to consider why any of this might matter. Why should the existence or otherwise of legitimacy be thought important? Initially, this will be considered within the context of IR, and its particular frames of reference.

---

[27] T. Schabert, 'Power, Legitimacy and Truth: Reflections on the Impossibility to Legitimise Legitimations of Political Order', in Moulakis (ed.), *Legitimacy*, p. 102.

[28] See, typically, A. I. Applebaum, 'Culture, Identity, and Legitimacy', in Nye and Donahue (eds.), *Governance*, pp. 324–5; T. M. Franck, *The Power of Legitimacy Among Nations* (Oxford: Oxford University Press, 1990), p. 19; A. Watson, *The Evolution of International Society* (London: Routledge, 1992), p. 17; I. Hurd, 'Legitimacy and Authority in International Politics', *International Organization*, 53 (1999), p. 381; Bukovansky, *Legitimacy*, p. 24; J. Habermas, *Legitimation Crisis* (London: Heinemann, 1976), pp. 95–6; C. Reus-Smit, *Moral Purpose of the State* (Princeton, NJ: Princeton University Press, 1999), p. 136; Barker, *Political Legitimacy*, p. 28; R. Grafstein, 'The Failure of Weber's Conception of Legitimacy', *Journal of Politics*, 43 (1981), p. 456. One of the few exceptions is J. Williams, *Legitimacy in International Relations and the Rise and Fall of Yugoslavia* (Basingstoke: Macmillan,1998).

[29] Bukovansky, *Legitimacy*, p. 24.

[30] Franck, *The Power of Legitimacy*, p. 204.

[31] Ibid., pp. 204–5.

[32] A. Watson, *Evolution*, pp. 202–8; J. Donnelly, 'Ancient Greece and IR Theory', Paper presented at BISA Conference, London, December 2002, p. 15.

International legitimacy and the stability of international orders

A decade ago, Peter Wilson and the late John Vincent made a plea for 'the development of the notion of international legitimacy, a neglected idea in international relations thought'.[33] They would no doubt have been pleased at the high volume of legitimacy talk that is current these days. It is, of course, common to debate whether or not a particular policy or action is legitimate. For instance, as Chris Brown reminds us of the Gulf crisis in 1990–91, 'the United States and its coalition partners went to considerable pains to achieve council resolutions that legitimated their actions'.[34] Whether or not that war can be deemed legitimate is complex enough, but is a narrower issue than the legitimacy of the entire order of which it was a part. Equally, the public debate today about policy towards Iraq is suffused with questions about the legitimacy of undertaking war against that country. In turn, that basic question breaks down into a series of subsidiary engagements about legitimacy being embodied in a UN consensus, as expressed in duly authorising resolutions, or about the need to take action even if the UN is incapacitated, by appeal to more fundamental values embodied in the international order. It leads also to questioning of the legitimacy of Saddam Hussein's regime (and of the degree of licence to act against it that a verdict of illegitimacy might allow to the international community).

It remains, however, far from clear that all this talk is, as yet, underpinned by the kind of concept that could be usefully placed at the heart of theoretical discussions of international relations. We can begin with the conclusion, reached by English School theorists and others, that this legitimacy talk makes most sense within the specific framework of an international society. That is the pertinent community, and it is the belief system of its members that is crucial to the analysis of legitimacy. In a world of states, legitimacy is what states make of it. For this reason, Bobbitt is assuredly correct when he insists that 'only an international society could confer legitimacy' on the activities of the states system.[35] This is especially so when, as will be seen below, fundamental to the very concept of legitimacy is the stipulation of the right to membership within that society.[36]

There are essentially two kinds of claims that can be made for the importance of engagement with legitimacy by IR scholars. The first is a largely historical and theoretical one. It argues that the great historical turning points in the history of international society can be recounted as shifts in the prevailing conceptions of international legitimacy. In this way, we can undertake an archaeological excavation of international society by digging down through its successive layers of legitimacy principles. The second might appear to be a more immediately practical concern,

[33] R. J. Vincent and P. Wilson, 'Beyond Non-Intervention', in I. Forbes and M. Hoffman (eds.), *Political Theory, International Relations and the Ethics of Intervention* (Houndmills: Macmillan, 1993), p. 129. My thanks to Andrew Linklater for drawing my attention to this observation.

[34] Chris Brown, 'Moral Agency and International Society', *Ethics and International Affairs*, 15 (2001), p. 91.

[35] P. Bobbitt, *The Shield of Achilles: War, Peace and the Course of History* (London: Allen Lane, 2002), p. 121.

[36] D. Armstrong, *Revolution and World Order: The Revolutionary State in International Society* (Oxford: Oxford University Press, 1993), p. 36.

and this is the posited causal relationship between the degree of international legitimacy and the very stability of the international order itself. These two projects, of course, may be related in interesting ways: upheavals in legitimacy may be symptomatic of deep-seated systemic change, and correlated with high levels of instability.

So important is the concept now accepted to be that, in one recent analysis, the very idea of 'systemic change' – itself the battleground of competing IR perspectives – has been *defined* 'as a transformation of the parameters of political legitimacy'.[37] Legitimacy thereby becomes the decisive yardstick for measuring change within international society. Moreover, in this regard, it is worth stressing also that legitimacy has the advantage of being an ecumenical concept. It has been deployed by realists and liberals alike, but is also an important term in the constructivist lexicon. In recent decades, the dominant discussions of stability have been cast in terms of system polarity, and whether or not multipolar, bipolar, or unipolar distributions have innate qualities generating stability.[38] This was not a debate on which constructivism could find any purchase. Legitimacy, however, offers a radically different framework within which the question can be addressed, and is congenial to a wider set of theoretical perspectives. This focus on legitimacy follows from the persuasion of many political scientists that 'enhanced order, stability, effectiveness – these are the typical advantages that accrue to a legitimate system of power'.[39] Weber himself had made the same claim in distinguishing between those systems based on expediency or custom, on the one hand, and which are less stable, and, on the other, those which are more so because they enjoy 'the prestige of being considered binding, or, as it may be expressed, of "legitimacy" '.[40] In the context of different international societies, Adam Watson, for example, concluded that legitimacy was one of the key factors 'determining the stability of a system at a given time'.[41] Other historians, such as Andreas Osiander and Paul Schroeder, as well as political scientists, have reached similar conclusions.[42]

Not least of the virtues of investigating stability *via* legitimacy is, therefore, that all the major schools of theory can engage in these terms: legitimacy is not a concept that belongs to any school in particular. It is central to the entire corpus of writing of a realist such as Henry Kissinger, as expressed in his *locus classicus*.[43] It

---

[37] Bukovansky, *Legitimacy*, p. 50.

[38] Karl W. Deutsch and J. David Singer, 'Multipolar Power Systems and International Stability', *World Politics*, 16 (1964), pp. 390–406; Kenneth N. Waltz, 'The Stability of a Bipolar World', *Daedalus*, 93 (1964), pp. 881–909; William C. Wohlforth, 'The Stability of a Unipolar World', *International Security*, 24 (1999), pp. 5–41.

[39] Beetham, *Legitimation of Power*, p. 33.

[40] Weber, *Economy and Society*, vol. 3, p. 31.

[41] Watson, *Evolution*, p. 315.

[42] '...the degree of stability of the international system will depend on ... the degree of consensus present in the system'. A. Osiander, *The States System of Europe, 1640–1990: Peacemaking and the Condition of International Stability* (Oxford: Oxford University Press, 1994), p. 5; P. Schroeder writes of the new principles of legitimacy in the period 1815–48 as issuing in 'a more stable, peaceful era', *The Transformation of European Politics 1763–1848* (Oxford: Oxford University Press, 1994), p. 802; 'When legitimacy standards converge...the level of threat among states is reduced', H. R. Nau, 'Correspondence: Institutionalized Disagreements', *International Security*, 27 (2002), p. 180.

[43] Henry A. Kissinger, *A World Restored: The Politics of Conservatism in a Revolutionary Era* (London: Victor Gollancz, 1977 [1957]).

runs through a wide spectrum of liberal writings, such as its current exponents like G. John Ikenberry,[44] but embracing also a diverse body of 'English School' rationalists, as exemplified by the earlier work of Martin Wight.[45] It also extends to constructivist analyses of the shifting norms that have become embedded in historical international orders, and of the implications of these norms for the degree of stability that was to prove attainable within them.[46]

How does the matter of its legitimacy have a bearing upon the stability of an international order? In principle, it is perfectly possible for an international order to be considered both illegitimate, and yet highly stable (if measured crudely by avoidance of central or great-power war), as many would claim to have been the case during the Cold War. Nonetheless, historians, and IR scholars, have traditionally drawn associations between peace settlements and the stability of the international orders that have followed upon them, on grounds that the more legitimate the settlement, the better the prospects for ensuing stability.[47] In this respect, Vienna wins most plaudits, whereas Versailles is the most excoriated, because it was either too harsh, or not harsh enough. Either way, it failed to give rise to a legitimate order.

The classical expression of this argument is to be found in Kissinger's discussion of the post-1815 period: 'An order whose structure is accepted by all major powers is "legitimate"'.[48] The emphasis here is upon the existence of consensus, inasmuch as the order is acceptable to the great powers (but to them alone). In this version, legitimacy is attached to the procedural conventions devised by the great powers, and is present whenever these are acceptable to all concerned. It is the absence of such agreement that creates tension and instability in the system *because* the order, as a result, is illegitimate. This is explicitly set out in his suggestion that, after 1815, 'the period of stability which ensued was the best proof that a "legitimate" order had been constructed, an order accepted by all the major powers'.[49]

More recently, Robert Jackson has written from within essentially the same tradition. 'The debate on humanitarian intervention', he attests, 'is not a debate between those who are concerned about human rights and those who are indifferent or callous about human suffering … It is a debate about the basic values of international society … In my view, the stability of international society, especially

---

[44] Most recently in G. John Ikenberry, *After Victory: Institutions, Strategic Restraint, and the Rebuilding of Order after Major Wars* (Princeton, NJ: Princeton University Press, 2001).
[45] There are two published pieces on this by Wight, under the same title but in substantially different versions. See Martin Wight, 'International Legitimacy', *International Relations*, 4 (1972), pp. 1–28; and in Hedley Bull (ed.), *Systems of States* (Leicester: Leicester University Press, 1977), pp. 153–173.
[46] The best examples of this are to be found in Reus-Smit, *The Moral Purpose*; Rodney B. Hall, *National Collective Identity: Social Constructs and International Systems* (New York: Columbia University Press, 1999); D. Philpott, *Revolutions in Sovereignty: How Ideas Shaped Modern International Relations* (Princeton, NJ: Princeton University Press, 2001); and Bukovansky, *Legitimacy*.
[47] Representative examples can be found in Osiander, *The States System*, p. 5; Kissinger, *A World Restored*, p. 1; Schroeder, *The Transformation*, p. 802; Kal J. Holsti, *Peace and War: Armed Conflicts and International Order* (Cambridge: Cambridge University Press, 1991), p. 341; Sharam Chubin, 'The South and the New World Order', in Brad Roberts (ed.), *Order and Disorder after the Cold War: A Washington Quarterly Reader* (Cambridge: MIT Press, 1995), p. 434.
[48] Kissinger, *A World Restored*, p. 145.
[49] Ibid., p. 5.

the unity of the great powers, is more important, indeed far more important, than minority rights and humanitarian protection'.[50] He thereby makes the connection explicitly between stability and 'unity', and gives priority to that latter concern over other justice claims. In short, legitimacy is not to be understood as a statement about the 'fairness' or 'justice' of a particular order (which might be regarded as a solidarist benchmark), but only about the degree of consensus with which it is regarded by the principal states (Jackson's preferred pluralist paradigm). It is a matter of the pertinent 'beliefs' of the major powers concerned, and that is all there is to it.

G. John Ikenberry also shares some initial assumptions with this perspective, but develops from them a substantially different argument, resulting in a major rework-ing and application of the concept of legitimacy. For Ikenberry,[51] an order that is legitimate solely in the eyes of the great powers could not be stable. In its stead, he presents the idea of a highly institutionalised 'constitutional' order that is a compro-mise, and quasi contract, between the strong and the weak. Rather than impose its will, and pay the high costs of future coercion, the strong can pursue a strategy of restraint, whereby it makes concessions to the interests of the weak. The resulting order binds both victors and losers into a stable and consensual order. As has been pointed out by one reviewer, the essential characteristic of constitutional orders, so conceived, is that they 'are regarded as legitimate orders by *all* of its members'.[52] In that sense, the constituency has broadened out markedly from its initially narrow great-power confines, as found in Kissinger's version of the argument.

But for all their differences, this family of writers shares, at a fundamental level, an understanding of legitimacy as essentially about agreement and consensus in the international system, and additionally asserts this to be an important ingredient of stability. We can also take Osiander,[53] and his historical study of 'consensus principles' in peace settlements, as representative of the same broad approach. In a moment, we shall return to an assessment of this claim that legitimacy can *cause* stability, a notion shared by all these writers.

There is however an alternative, and distinct, tradition in thinking about inter-national legitimacy. Martin Wight demonstrates this second strand: 'By inter-national legitimacy I mean the collective judgment of international society about rightful membership of the family of nations'.[54] In this case, legitimacy takes on a different aspect. It is much more concerned with principles governing admission to, and recognition by, international society. This does not mean that there is no element of consensus in such a formulation. It remains residually concerned with the 'collective judgment' of international society (and thus with consensus by the back door). However, this consensus applies restrictively to the basis of international society, and the articulation of criteria for rightful membership of it. Ostensibly,

---

[50] Robert H. Jackson, *The Global Covenant: Human Conduct in a World of States* (Oxford: Oxford University Press, 2000), p. 291.
[51] Ikenberry, *After Victory*.
[52] Randall L. Schweller, 'The Problem of International Order Revisited: A Review Essay', *International Security*, 26 (2001), p. 166.
[53] Osiander, *The States System of Europe*.
[54] Wight, 'International Legitimacy' (1977), p. 153.

then, there is a distinction to be made between legitimacy understood as a principle about how international society is *formed* (the Wightian tradition), and legitimacy understood as a principle about how that society *behaves* (the consensus tradition). This distinction may be considered similar to that found in Franck's reworking of Hart's notion of primary and secondary rules. For Franck, the substantial difference between these resides in the fact that 'a community accepts its ultimate secondary rules of recognition not consensually, but as an inherent concomitant of member-ship status'.[55] From this perspective, it might be thought that the secondary rules, such as those of recognition, are more basic or constitutive.

Even if distinguishable, historically the two have often operated in tandem. Wight was to allude to the 'dislike for the variety and complexity of international society, and a belief that improved rules of legitimacy would lead to a greater uniformity'.[56] Its chosen instrument for doing so has been through the 'rightful membership' route. At the most basic level, this has been limited to requirements to meet the formalities of statehood, but, as Armstrong points out, it has also developed into preferences for certain *types* of state.[57] The application of the 'standard of civilization', as a test for fit membership, was a clear instance of this in the nineteenth century, as of course have been more recent tests for good government, and adherence to rights norms, as the 'conditionality' for enjoyment of certain of international society's privileges. When engaged in this practice, international society is regarded as a powerful source of state 'socialization',[58] or has taken on what has been called elsewhere a 'constabulary role'.[59] The important thing to note, however, is that this preference for greater 'uniformity' has not been considered an end in itself, but should be viewed rather as a means to greater international consensus. The under-lying belief has been the conventional liberal internationalist one that, the more alike in nature and value system, the more likely are states to discover a harmony of interests, and, in consequence, to live in greater tranquility and economic prosperity. States that are individually legitimate in the eyes of international society will collectively sustain legitimate patterns of behaviour.

Legitimacy, in this second sense of recognition, has thus been implemented in ways to further legitimacy in the first sense of international consensus. That there is an intimate connection between the two is nicely revealed in Wendt's discussion of the 'Lockean culture'. He reiterates the point above about the 'constabulary role' of international society in his claim that 'it has always been necessary also to conform to type identity criteria which define only certain *forms* of state as legitimate'. However, he goes beyond this to make the additional observation that the Lockean membership criteria are more stringent than the Hobbesian, and that the 'Lockean

---

[55] T. M. Franck, 'Legitimacy in the International System', *American Journal of International Law*, 82 (1988), p. 759. See also the related discussion in N. Onuf, *The Republican Legacy in International Thought* (Cambridge: Cambridge University Press, 1998), pp. 181–3.

[56] Wight, 'International Legitimacy' (1972), p. 27.

[57] Armstrong, *Revolution*, p. 36. See also I. Clark, ' "Another Double Movement": the Great Transformation after the Cold War?' *Review of International Studies,* 27 (2001), pp. 237–55.

[58] D. Armstrong, 'Globalization and the Social State', *Review of International Studies*, 24 (1998), pp. 461–78.

[59] Paul Keal, 'An "International Society"?' in G. Fry and C. O'Hagan (eds.), *Contending Images of World Politics* (Basingstoke: Macmillan, 2000), p. 69.

culture pays for its relative tranquillity with a less open membership policy'.[60] The comment is astute, and reveals how the two forms of international legitimacy have acted in concert with each other. It should, however, also be stressed that the relationship is two-way, and not unidirectional. While international society expresses preferences for the particular type of state, the emergence of a preponderance of states with new characteristics will, equally, leave its imprint on the face of international society. States facing a domestic legitimacy crisis may be forced to reinvent themselves, and, in doing so, contribute, over the longer term, to the reinvention of international society. In Bobbitt's recent words, 'a change in the constitutional order of states will eventually recreate the nature of the society of states and *its* constitutional order'.[61]

Let us finally return to an assessment of the case that legitimacy is the source of international stability, and consider the analysis provided by Kissinger in this context. His contention was that an order enjoying legitimacy is distinct from one reliant upon power alone. Although he is clear that it is the very legitimacy of an order that is the key to its stability, and hence to its durability (as after 1815), his own understanding of the relationship remains a complex one. This emerges in his various formulations of the order after the Vienna settlement:

> Thus the new international order came to be created with a sufficient awareness of the connection between power and morality; between security and legitimacy. No attempt was made to found it entirely on submission to a legitimizing principle ... Rather, there was created a balance of forces which, because it conferred a relative security, came to be generally accepted.[62]

Elsewhere, and more succinctly, he talks of the post-Vienna order being predicated on 'not only a physical equilibrium but a moral one'.[63] What all this seems to suggest is that a physical balance of power is necessary, but not sufficient, for a secure and stable order. What it needs, in addition, is a 'moral balance' which, given what is said elsewhere, presumably can express itself only through agreement and consensus.

What is so manifestly inadequate about this Kissingerian variant of the argument is that, in his account, we are given an explanation of stability that is based both on the balance of power and also on consensus, but in which it is hard to discern that legitimacy has a role as a separate causal factor. The order is stable because the great powers have the capacity to keep it so, and its definition of legitimacy is, in any case, explicitly derivative from power differentials (only the great need be satisfied). What work is not being done by the exercise of power, is otherwise being done by consensus amongst the great powers. The circularity in Kissinger's argument is to make stability a consequence of great-power agreement, while in effect explaining that

---

[60] A. Wendt, *Social Theory of International Politics* (Cambridge: Cambridge University Press, 1999), pp. 291–3. Note, in this context, Onuf's related comment: 'Scholars have wondered whether recognition is a declaratory or a constitutive act – declaratory insofar as recognition acknowledges that the material conditions of statehood have been met, constitutive insofar as statehood depends on acknowledgement and not just material conditions', N. Onuf, *The Republican Legacy*, 1998), p. 187.

[61] Bobbitt, *The Shield of Achilles*, p. 777. This is also the central theme of my *Globalization and International Relations Theory* (Oxford University Press: Oxford, 1999).

[62] Kissinger, *A World Restored*, p. 318.

[63] Henry A. Kissinger, *Diplomacy* (New York: Simon and Schuster, 1994), p. 79.

agreement in terms of the stable conditions that have made it possible. He does this by defining a stable international order as being in the interests of great powers, but this holds true only as long as it holds true. In a stable international order, the great powers may well reach such agreement, but his analysis does not explain the conditions which make it possible, nor what role legitimacy can play in sustaining it. Legitimacy, in this version, is not a reason for compliance, beyond the continuing agreement amongst the great powers that no one of them will challenge the *status quo* in unacceptable ways.[64] Once any individual power decides that it has interests in doing precisely that, the order loses its stability, but not because of any decline in its legitimacy, simply because that power's definition of its interests has changed. Legitimacy, so understood, is no more than a restatement of an extant consensus (as long as it lasts), but gives us no additional insight into why the consensus exists in the first place, nor any account of how it can inhibit its own demise. From that point of view, it is merely descriptive of stability, and not an explanation of it. Indeed, it makes just as much sense to argue that it is the stability of the order that gives rise to the possibility of shared principles of legitimacy, as it does to posit the causality working in the opposite direction.

In short, this mode of reasoning that legitimacy is a cause of stability is at best half of an argument. This does not mean that the concept of legitimacy is unhelpful – far from it – but that the full force of this argument remains to be worked out in greater detail. If this is so in relation to the international order, where does this leave our understanding of legitimacy in relation to the global order? Does it at all matter? And if it does, is it simply about forging consensus? If so, amongst whom is it required? If it is also about membership and recognition, what does that actually mean within the context of a global order?

Legitimacy in a global order

In this final section, an attempt will be made to develop a framework for under-standing legitimacy in a global order that steps outside the governance/resistance duality, while building upon the categories already explored in the IR context. To begin the discussion with a generic concept of resistance is to start from the wrong place, since this does not make clear whether the resistance is on the part of those whose entitlement to speak is recognised (but who dissent from specific policies nonetheless), or on the part of those who feel excluded (and whose demand is to be treated as part of the constituency). The first relates to issues of consent and/or

---

[64] There are, of course, constructivist arguments that attempt to deal with this issue, but this is not the position that Kissinger himself stakes out, and hence these will not be pursued at this point. The general constructivist response to the above is that the wish to sustain the consensus, by acting 'legitimately' within it, shapes new identities, and hence interests, and that this is conducive to stability. The interesting question is then why, historically, such phases have periodically broken down. The answer must presumably be couched in the language of the costs and benefits of defection *versus* continued cooperation, and the moot point is whether such a calculation of *interests* is compatible with what legitimacy means, or not, even if the practice of cooperation has helped to redefine those interests. See, on this, the discussion in Hurd, 'Legitimacy and Authority'.

consensus, and the latter is a matter of membership. The implications for legitimacy are not the same in each case.

How then might this part of the argument be developed? Franck's claim that legitimacy is to be found only in the context of community is the obvious starting point, and stumbling block, for any consideration of the relevance of legitimacy to the global order. What is the pertinent community within which the sense of legitimacy is nested? One manifestation of the problem arises, for example, in discussion of the legitimacy of international organisations, where the particular perspective adopted yields differing conclusions about the proper constituency (governments, citizens, stakeholding groups, humankind), whose 'beliefs' about legitimacy should count.[65] Jackson attempts to solve the problem by his claim that 'today everybody is an insider of international society'.[66] This might be more plausible if, following Bull's interpretation of Grotius, we were to concede that 'international society ... is not just the society of states, it is the great society of all mankind'.[67] This, however, is not Jackson's position, and his admission elsewhere that today's international society differs in density from one global sector to another – with some regions taking on solidarist characteristics - calls the utility of any such move into question. As these regions hover uncertainly along different parts of the spectrum between *societas* and *universitas*, to employ Jackson's own terminology,[68] there is surely the prospect that principles of legitimacy will not be universally shared, or shared with the same intensity, even within his framework of an all-embracing international society.

If not to international society, can we appeal to some other 'community' that is coextensive with the global order, and within which we might talk meaningfully of 'the norms of a specific cultural system'? From the available literature, a number of distinct possibilities emerge. Some of these derive from efforts to overcome the so-called communitarian/cosmopolitan divide, and express themselves in the form of enquiries into meaningful normative communities 'beyond borders'. Illustrative of these are the arguments predicated on interdependence, transformations in the nature of community in the context of globalisation, and such variants that focus on the notion of all-embracing communities of fate.[69] There is also a separate strand of literature that comes at the global governance issue from within the distinctive perspective – not of global normative communities, extant or imagined – but instead of really existing networks of global power which unify the globe within systems of

[65] G. C. A. Junne, 'International Organizations in a Period of Globalization: New (Problems of) Legitimacy', in Coicaud and Heiskenen (eds.), *Legitimacy of International Organizations*, pp. 191–2.

[66] Jackson , *Global Covenant*, p. 13.

[67] H. Bull, 'The Importance of Grotius in the Study of International Relations', in H. Bull, B. Kingsbury and A. Roberts (eds.), *Hugo Grotius and International Relations* (Oxford: Oxford University Press, 1990), p. 83.

[68] Jackson, *Global Covenant*, pp.127-8.

[69] For example, C. Beitz, *Political Theory and International Relations* (Princeton, NJ: Princeton University Press, 1979); C. Brown, *Sovereignty, Rights*; T. Erskine, ' "Citizen of Nowhere" or "The Point where Circles Intersect"? Impartialist and Embedded Cosmopolitanisms', *Review of International Studies*, 28 (2002), pp. 457–78; A. Linklater, *The Transformation of Political Community* (Cambridge: Polity, 1998); D. Archibugi, D. Held and M. Kohler (eds.), *Re-imagining Political Community* (Cambridge: Polity, 1998); M. Frost, *Towards a Normative Theory of International Relations* (Cambridge: Cambridge University Press, 1986); M. Cochran, *Normative Theory in International Relations: A Pragmatic Approach* (Cambridge: Cambridge University Press, 1999).

rule. The stereotypical manifestations of this position are those works that make appeal to Empire, or to versions of the global or international state.[70] Might any one of these provide us with a credible social framework within which the emergence and evolution of legitimacy principles could be traced? Does thinking about global governance as morally interdependent communities of fate, on the one hand, or as Empire, on the other, offer a convincing sociological framework for a theory of legitimacy within the global order?

One possible analytical strategy for dealing with these weighty issues can be developed from Weber's treatment of the topic. It has been noted that there is in Weber's account of legitimacy, over and above what he says about authority specifically, also 'an apparently unrelated discussion of legitimacy concerned with "orders" '.[71] In elaboration, one writer makes the further distinction between norms and authority. In the former, actors orient their behaviour towards the same norms; in the latter, 'the *commands* of certain actors are treated as binding by the others'.[72] The query suggested by this is whether it is 'possible to separate discussion of the legitimacy of orders from the legitimacy of authority'.[73] Certainly, while Weber wrote extensively about legitimate forms and sources of authority (and it is for this that he is routinely invoked), he did also write some short passages about legitimate orders. He avers that 'legitimacy may be ascribed to an order' in several ways (tradition, affectual attitude, rational belief in value, legality).[74] This distinction will be adopted, without in any way entering into a detailed discussion of the precise sense in which Weber employed this terminology, and simply as an organising device for the remainder of this analysis. The tentative scheme that can be drawn from this suggestion is that legitimacy has purchase in two arenas: one is that of authority and focuses upon commands; the other is the broader normative order within which that nexus of command may exist. For the purposes of further analysis, these will be discussed, respectively, as the legitimacy of authority, and as the legitimacy of order. The argument will be that, globally speaking, we can distinguish between two emerging discourses of legitimacy, each appropriate to differing facets of the global order. The first is the authority structures of that order and the legitimacy of its systems of rule. The second is the normative principles that define membership and inclusion within that order, and entitlement to consultation and participation, but are not yet (fully) articulated in a system of commands. Since, as stated, the concept of global governance is firmly tied to structures and processes of authority, the framework of governance and resistance delivers some mileage in dealing with the first. It remains, however, largely unhelpful in understanding the second.

There are various lines of argument that can be drawn upon in support of this distinction. According to the widely cited version found in Thomas Franck, part of

---

[70] Hardt and Negri, *Empire*; M. Shaw, *Theory of the Global State: Globality as an Unfinished Revolution* (Cambridge: Cambridge University Press, 2000); T. Barkawi and M. Laffey, 'Retrieving the Imperial: Empire and International Relations', *Millennium*, 31 (2002), pp. 109–27; 'Exchange: What Empire? Whose Empire', *Millennium*, 31 (2002), pp. 318–45.

[71] M. E. Spencer, 'Weber on Legitimate Norms and Authority', *British Journal of Sociology*, 21 (1970), pp. 123–4.

[72] Spencer, 'Weber', p. 124.

[73] Ibid., pp. 123–4.

[74] Weber, *Economy and Society*, p. 12.

the definition of legitimacy is that 'it is a property of a rule or rule-making institution'.[75] In any such account, discussion of legitimacy can take place only within a context of rules and rule making. Its focus is naturally upon the authority with which the rules are made and applied. Typically, standard discussions of legitimacy draw attention to its three key dimensions: conformity to established rules, justifiability of the rules themselves, and consent to the power relation expressed in this system of rule.[76] All of these criteria relate directly to rule, command and authority. It is from this angle that Adam Watson felt able to describe legitimacy as 'the acceptance of authority, the right of a rule or a ruler to be obeyed'.[77]

When this is placed in juxtaposition to some classic accounts of international order, interesting results begin to emerge. Most famously, Hedley Bull insisted that order was a 'pattern of human activity that sustains elementary, primary or universal goals of social life'.[78] Significantly, he was at pains to detach order from rules as such. While rules were frequently the basis of orderly human conduct, he believed that 'order in social life can exist in principle without rules', and it was therefore best to regard rules as a 'means of creating order', not as 'part of the definition of order itself'.[79] If we allow this much, and combine it with the reasoning of Franck, then it follows that legitimacy pertains to the realm of rules and rule making, but not necessarily to the social order as a whole. This circle of reasoning is completed when Bull offers his account of international society within which states bind themselves 'by a common set of rules', as the defining quality of that society.[80] Within the confines of international society, we are again entitled to engage in legitimacy talk because we are back in the realm of rules. Does this mean that Bull would have regarded legitimacy as irrelevant to the wider concept of global order? This seems unlikely. Such a conclusion would sit uncomfortably with other elements of his thought. For example, he accepted the reality of a global political system (based on the global system of states, but also moving beyond it), and perhaps more pertinently he accepted also the notion of 'world order' as something 'wider than order among states; something more fundamental and primordial than it; and also, I should argue, something morally prior to it'.[81] Given such a moral hierarchy, it seems implausible that Bull would have felt wholly at ease with the notion that legitimacy could be expressed within an international society, but not as part of the global order as a whole. If such a conclusion is to be avoided, there must be scope for a separate discourse of legitimacy pertaining, not to global rules and authority as such, but instead to the distinct terrain of community and membership within the global order.

Global authority

The first idea treats the global order as a system of rule, and hence gives rise to an agenda about the legitimacy of authority. This is most clearly to be found in the

[75] Franck, *The Power of Legitimacy*, p. 16.
[76] Beetham, *Legitimation of Power*, p. 16.
[77] Watson, *Evolution*, p. 17.
[78] H. Bull, *The Anarchical Society: A Study of Order in World Politics* (London: Macmillan, 1977), p. 5.
[79] Bull, *Anarchical Society*, p. 7.
[80] Ibid., p. 13.
[81] Ibid., p. 21.

various ideas about Empire or the global/international/world state,[82] albeit that all of those cluster very much to the 'hierarchy', as opposed to 'anarchy', end of the global governance spectrum. Central to these sundry claims is that, whether or not a global community exists in any kind of normative sense, we are all increasingly subject to common and integrated forms of political and economic rule. Hardt and Negri define the global order as an Empire, by which they mean that 'sovereignty has taken a new form, composed of a series of national and supranational organisations united under a single logic of rule'.[83] Note here, in particular, that the concentration is upon a 'logic of rule'. This global order, we are told, is 'still virtual' but, nonetheless, applies 'actually to us'.[84] Moreover, this unified logic of network power is spawning its own forms of legitimacy that are endogenous to it. It makes no appeal to traditional principles of international legitimacy, such as those expressed through international organisations. Instead, the 'legitimation of the imperial machine is born at least in part of the communications industries' and is a 'subject that produces its own image of authority'. It is self-referential and self-validating.[85] It evokes its own distinctive forms of resistance to this type of governance. The somewhat idiosyncratic appeal that these authors make to the 'multitude' is for it to take advantage of the 'new possibilities to the forces of liberation'. The imperial order cannot be overturned, they insist, by local forms of resistance to it. Instead, it can only be reshaped, at a global level, by 'constructing a counter-Empire, an alternative political organization of global forces and exchanges'.[86] What is interesting about this formulation, and what reinforces the above contention about the bewildering variety of the politics of resistance on offer, is that the task is construed, not really as one of resisting Empire at all, but instead of supplanting it with an alternative, but equally global, system. This would entail reconfiguring it, to be sure, but very much in its own original image. There can be no more compelling illustration of the general thesis that anti-globalisation is a strategy of globalisation by other means.

Theories of Empire and the global state assuredly lie towards the extreme end of those perspectives on global governance that insist upon the reality of an extant network of rule, claimed to be shaping our lives. But similar ideas are to be found throughout the global governance literature more generally. What we face, it has been suggested, is not the reality of a 'single institution', but nonetheless 'the networks and linkages that bring together different organizations, interest groups and forms of authority in relation to specific regulatory tasks'.[87]

Thus viewed, legitimacy – considered as a problem about the authority to rule – is deemed reducible to that of democratisation. What current arrangements lack is robust channels of consent and accountability, resulting in a 'global democratic deficit that must be reduced if world-wide arrangements are to be legitimate'.[88]

---

[82] On the former, see Hardt and Negri, *Empire*. On the latter, see variously Shaw, *Global State*; Barkawi and Laffey, 'Retrieving the Imperial'.

[83] Hardt and Negri, *Empire*, p. xii.

[84] Ibid., 19.

[85] Ibid., p. 33.

[86] Ibid., p. xv.

[87] M. Duffield, *Global Governance and the New Wars: The Merging of Development and Security* (London: Zed Books, 2001), p. 44.

[88] A. Linklater, 'The Evolving Spheres of International Justice', *International Affairs*, 75: 3 (July 1999), p. 477.

Conceived as an issue in the authority of rule, legitimacy boils down to the need to institute effective democratic procedures.[89] The problem lies in knowing what this might look like. If, as seems plausible, it is the case that 'legitimate political activity is inseparable from responsibility',[90] then to whom should the myriad of policy-makers that contribute to global regulation in one way or another be held account-able? This is the core issue facing democratisation,[91] and what it is above all concerned with is the definition of the affected constituency.

Global order

This second debate – about the legitimacy of order – is more inchoate in form, but revolves around notions of community, citizenship and participation. At stake here is not the authority of rule, but the quest for a normative account of what it means to be part of this order, who is entitled to membership of it, and of the various rights and responsibilities entailed by such membership. By analogy with the earlier discussion of legitimacy within international society, this discussion of legitimacy within the global order is largely preoccupied with its constitutive basis, including rightful membership, and is not yet about the legitimacy of its procedures and systems of rule. The key theme that runs through this debate is 'who has a right to have rights?'[92] It is nonetheless the emergence of this dialogue that gives expression to the more obvious legitimacy deficits experienced in relation to the rule-making aspects of global governance. We cannot know what rule-making structures are suitable to be put in place until we have settled the primary issues of who is to count for membership, within what context, and for what purpose. Although the common diagnosis is of a legitimacy crisis in global governance, widely construed as a crisis of authority, it might more properly be said that the pressing legitimacy crisis, in terms of the global order, is actually about the nature of the community linked by the order, and about whose voice is entitled to be heard on what issues.

We return here to Franck's account of the secondary rules, and how they are not dependent upon explicit consent or consensus, and hence not directly about issues of democratisation. States, he avers, are obligated 'as part of their own validation; that is, as an inseparable aspect of "joining" a community of states'.[93] The same might be said of participation in the global order. Its more fundamental problem is less about the terms of authority, and more to do with the nature of this 'joining', and how to provide a coherent account of its terms of recognition. As a specific illustration, we can note the observation that the *ad hoc* consultation of various individuals and

---

[89] D. Held, *Democracy and the Global Order: From the Modern State to Cosmopolitan Governance* (Cambridge: Polity, 1995); B. J. Barber, 'Democracy and Terror in the Era of Jihad *vs.* McWorld', in K. Booth and T. Dunne (eds.), *Worlds in Collision: Terror and the Future of the Global Order* (Basingstoke: Palgrave, 2002), p. 255; C. N. Murphy, 'Global Governance: Poorly Done and Poorly Understood', *International Affairs*, 76 (2000), p. 790; Devetak and Higgott, 'Justice Unbound?' p. 490.

[90] Coicaud, *Legitimacy and Politics*, p. 33.

[91] See C. Hill, *The Changing Politics of Foreign Policy* (Basingstoke: Palgrave, 2003), pp. 298–300.

[92] Coicaud, *Legitimacy and Politics*, p. 234.

[93] Franck, 'Legitimacy in the International System', p. 758.

INGOs by international organisations rests 'on the quintessentially corporate concept of the stakeholder', and not on any concept of 'popular sovereignty, or a universal citizenship'.[94] What this highlights is that the problem has less to do with the structure of authority, than it is with finding the relevant model in terms of which those embraced by the order will be recognised, and their entitlements understood.

These thoughts can be reinforced by appeal to the equally 'incoherent' nature of the international order, appearances to the contrary notwithstanding. If order is a 'pattern' that sustains certain 'goals', it is, in principle, distinct from a system that 'authoritatively allocates' these values, and hence from rule and command. Order in this sense, and detached from rule as such, has been argued by others to be the very bedrock of international legitimacy. It constitutes the basic values in accordance with which legitimacy can be said to exist at all, and adherence to it adjudged. As argued by one exponent of this view, order 'provides an international value system against which it is possible to make judgments about the legitimacy of international institutions and international practices and procedures'.[95] However, even within a specifically 'international' setting, this value system is far from definitive, and embraces tensions and possible contradictions. The amalgam of sovereignty, non-intervention, self-determination and human rights – let alone the shifting bases of rightful membership, such as dynastic, popular and national – that looms large in the evolving international society raises questions about the coherence of the value system that underpins even that society. It comprehends a number of distinct 'legitimacies' since, in Coicaud's words, this 'kind of normative indeterminacy results when international principles constitute a normative order', but one that 'represents a relative plurality of values that is not entirely convergent'.[96] Yet others regard this tension as being even more deep-seated. It has recently been suggested that international society's concept of order is itself based on a fundamental ambivalence, since it espouses the values of both 'toleration' and of 'civilization'. By this is meant that it has been pluralistic towards its core members, and tolerant of difference between them, while at the same time seeking to impart civilisation to those outside.[97]

On these grounds, we should not dismiss talk of legitimacy in a global order because it appears nebulous. If these arguments are allowed, then even within the parameters of international order there is no clear and unambiguous set of basic values to be found, but only shifting compromises and tentative adjustments. To the extent that international legitimacy rests on the values embodied in any order, it rests on shifting sands. It is likely to be equally so with the search for the values embodied in any emerging global order. Thus viewed, the emergence of legitimacy within the global order is likely to be no more and no less the result of political processes – conflict and accommodation – than has been the quest for legitimacy

---

[94] Heiskanen, 'Introduction', in Coicaud and Heiskanen (eds.), *Legitimacy of International Organizations*, p. 12.

[95] Williams, *Legitimacy in International Relations*, p. 12.

[96] Coicaud, 'Conclusion' in Coicaud and Heiskanen (eds.), *Legitimacy of International Organizations*, p. 538.

[97] E. Keene, *Beyond the Anarchical Society: Grotius, Colonialism and Order in World Politics* (Cambridge: Cambridge University Press, 2002), esp. pp. 122, 148.

within international society. This conflict and accommodation is too multi-layered and diffuse sensibly to be portrayed in terms of governance and resistance.

Here the parallel with the earlier discussion of international order can again be drawn. If much mainstream IR theory is incomplete in its suggestion that legitimacy causes stability, it is for the reason that it misconstrues legitimacy as a 'thing', separate from the process by which agreements about basic values are attained. The notion of legitimacy is our shorthand description of that process, and not something separate whereby legitimacy produces those results. By analogy, we should not imagine that there is a magical path by which the global order can acquire legitimacy, and thereby solve all its contingent problems of instability. This is to get it the wrong way round. Only once the global order is sufficiently stabilised – meaning by this which actors will be recognised and for which purposes, and how authority to decide is to be parcelled out amongst its various institutions – will this begin to express itself in the appropriate principles of legitimacy. The correct analysis must be, not that the system of global governance is illegitimate (since that assumes that its principles of legitimacy *already* exist, but are in some sense being disregarded or violated), but instead that they have not yet been 'constructed', or articulated in a developed form. Only when they have been so will we know that the order has become 'stable'. It is the working out of the politics of legitimacy that lies at the heart of contemporary global governance, and the manifold evidences of resistance at the present time. Actors within the global order are searching for, and competing about, the principles of legitimacy that deserve respect. When the massive and dynamic upheavals that currently beset us have reached some new point of political equilibrium, this stability will become manifest in the deployment of more coherent accounts of the global order's own legitimacy principles.[98] We might, at that stage, also feel comfortable to speak of a global society instead.

Conclusion

The issue of legitimacy is a central one in the current development of systems of global governance. However, this article has dissented from the view that we can simply subtract the resistance from the governance to reach an accurate measure of the legitimacy deficit under which the global order currently labours. In its stead, it has set out two key provenances of legitimacy – that pertaining to authority (and largely focused on the right to rule), and that pertaining to order (and largely focused on issues of community). It concludes that the debate about legitimacy in the global order has been overly concentrated upon the former, at the expense of the relative neglect of the latter.

At the level of international society, it has been demonstrated that the existing arguments for a causal relationship between legitimacy and international stability remain unpersuasive: it is just as convincing that a consensus about legitimacy

---

[98] It is important to stress the role of power in such recognition outcomes, as acknowledged in earlier legitimacy struggles of this kind. See H. Spruyt, *The Sovereign State and its Competitors: An Analysis of Systems Change* (Princeton, NJ: Princeton University Press, 1994); and Bukovansky, *Legitimacy*.

emerges because of new conditions of political stability and equilibrium than that the causality works in the opposite direction. Alternatively expressed, the language of legitimacy is a way of describing what we mean by international stability, rather than a separate source of it. For that reason, any simple prescription that we need to make the global order legitimate, thereby to stabilise it, is doomed to be inadequate as policy, and incoherent as theory.

More specifically, when we explore the constituents of international legitimacy in historical international societies, we discover a recurrent fusion between its two separate, but profoundly intertwined, notions of consensus and fit membership. It is the political bargains on these two core issues that form the basis of any equilibrium in a political system, and allow us to describe its indigenous legitimacy principles.

By the same token, the quest for legitimacy principles within the wider global order encounters two major obstacles of its own. The first is the search for reasonable working principles around which the key players – both state and non-state actors – can coalesce. These concern the right to rule, and the procedural principles that will be accepted as signifying consent, if not consensus. More fundamentally, however, the order remains unsettled by its inability, as yet, to develop agreed conceptions of rightful membership: the entitlement to be heard. If the global order ever comes up with satisfactory solutions to these two sets of problems, it will have taken greater strides towards enduring stability. This will not have been caused by greater legitimacy, but will reflect the political bargains that have allowed these consensual legitimacy principles to be expressed in the first place. Hurrell is certainly correct to emphasise the inescapably political nature of legitimacy, as grounded in compromise, when he stresses its role as the 'pragmatic meeting point between political effectiveness and the need for moral consensus'.[99] Legitimacy cannot solve the problems of global governance, but will begin to emerge only when these problems are on the way to finding a solution. There is no simple, and bipolar, struggle between governance and resistance, but instead a multi-level politics directed at both. Legitimacy has no power to bring an end to this complex political process, but can emerge only, if at all, when that process has run its temporary course, and reached a new point of equilibrium which can find expression in such agreed principles. The pervasive sense of illegitimacy within the current global order is but a measure of the long distance this process still has to run.

---

[99] A. Hurrell, ' "There Are No Rules" (George W. Bush): International Order after September 11', *International Relations*, 16 (2002), p. 202.

The power of representation: democratic politics and global governance

ALEJANDRO COLÁS*

The notion of democracy has been invoked in the past decade by both opponents and proponents of global governance. Many in the so-called 'anti-globalisation' movement have underlined the inherently unaccountable, opaque and unrepresentative nature of global governance, whilst those more sympathetic to the pluralising dynamics of the phenomenon have emphasised the potentially democratic aspects of this new form of rule, especially with reference to the incorporation of a putative 'global civil society' into the structures of global governance and the accompanying diversification of sources of international political authority. Yet both critics and advocates also tend to agree that there are two basic challenges to (on some accounts, causes of) global governance: the global capitalist market and the concomitant system of sovereign states. The disjunctures generated by the operation of these two structures of power, so both liberal defenders of global governance and their radical, anti-capitalist contenders argue, have created the conditions for decentralised, multilateral mechanisms of socioeconomic and political management of world affairs, that is, 'global governance'. It therefore seems that the question on both sides of this divide, is not so much whether to do away with transnational, multilateral forms of political authority altogether (although that is certainly one aim in some quarters of the anti-globalisation movement) but rather, how to render these democratic, that is, how to democratise global governance.

I understand democracy as entailing both formal guarantees of individual and collective autonomy and equality (broadly, civil liberties), and substantive control over our own social reproduction (crudely put, socioeconomic rights). On this reading, the substantive democratisation of global governance necessitates the simultaneous politicisation of the private economic sphere of civil society, and the delineation of concrete 'communities of fate' (or put more conventionally, delimitating the space of political communities). Democracy, then, requires the collective, public regulation of those activities responsible for our social reproduction, which in most parts of the world are currently effected through the capitalist market. Yet if such political regulation is to be democratic – if it is to be subject to free and public scrutiny, deliberation and authorisation – it must also identify the membership of its constituency, that is, who 'the public', 'the community', or the *demos* is. The overarching aim of this essay therefore is to make a case for a conception of global democratic resistance and transformation which places the modern territorial state at the centre of

* Earlier versions of this article were presented at the University of Alberta, Canada and the University of Aalborg, Denmark, in 2003. I wish to thank all those who offered comments and critiques on those occasions, especially Stella Gaon, Alfredo Saad-Filho, Susanne Soederberg, Marcus Taylor and the late Paul Q. Hirst, who has left a lasting imprint even on those of us who had barely got to know him.

its political project. I wish to insist – through recourse to the related concepts of *representation* and *mediation* – that movements seeking to democratise global governance should reject the radical opposition between resistance and authority; movement and stability; or transgression and closure, and instead begin with a conception of democratic protest where forms of political authority are recognised as being inherent to the modes of resistance. Such a conception of democratic politics, it will be further suggested, emphasises the power of the territorial state in subordinating the undemocratic operations of the global capitalist system to collective needs, whilst at the same time recognising the dangers of fetishising existing national states as the sole source of democratic power. It is precisely this attempt at reconciling the persistent contradiction between the power of representation and territory on the one hand, and the dynamic force of transnational resistance and movement on the other, which, I shall argue, can be the unique source of strength and legitimacy in struggles for a democratic, and therefore anti-capitalist global governance.

On democratic politics, capitalism and representation

The central impulse behind the project for global governance as it is currently conceived is arguably to manage through public, political means what are generally private interactions between agents of civil society. As was just mentioned, such a project initially emerged during the 1990s in response to a perceived set of tensions or 'disjunctures' between the spatial determinants of political authority (including, naturally, 'democracy') and the largely temporal dynamics of transboundary or 'global' phenomena, particularly those effected through the global capitalist market. Thus, the challenge of global governance is primarily to control and set limits on what appear to be unruly, unbounded and transgressive global flows – instantaneous financial transactions, international trafficking, global warming and of course, most recently, 'global terror'. Although these myriad expressions of a 'runaway world' are not all reducible to the workings of the capitalist market, there can be little doubt that it is the capitalist drive to constantly and everywhere appropriate time – not just labour-time, but care-time and recreational time too – which has relentlessly challenged and unsettled modern notions of bounded space over the past couple of centuries or so. At first sight, therefore, there is considerable plausibility to the 'hyperglobalist' argument to the effect that the dynamics of socioeconomic globalisation are subverting the stasis of political community; that the power of markets is trumping the authority of states. As we shall see further below, this is a view held across the ideological spectrum, especially amongst many of the theorists and activists of the global anti-capitalist movement.

Though retaining the notion that the tendency of capital accumulation is infinite, whilst that of political authority is bounded, the rest of this article will assume that this tension has historically been resolved (though not erased) in capitalist societies through the medium of the sovereign state and its attendant institutions of law and order.[1] For, since capitalism is above all a system of *social relations* (and not a reified

---

[1] Here, the argument resembles that presented by Rob Walker in his various works on the spatiotemporal sources of modern sovereignty. Such modern 'resolutions' of the tensions between space and time, however, are ascribed in this essay to concrete sociopolitical struggles over the nature of authority, including, but not limited to, discursive conceptions of sovereignty.

power somehow existing outside intersubjective human relations), it too unfolds in concrete social spaces through the interaction of spatially-situated collectivities and social institutions. To use David Harvey's more elegant formulation, despite its structural dependence on the appropriation of time, capitalism also requires 'spatial fixes'.[2] An obvious example being the institution of private property under capitalism, which is at once premised on the temporal exploitation of nature and labour-power, and the spatial ownership of a delimited area and its physical contents, guaranteed through the political authority of the law and its enforcers. Over the past two centuries, the sovereign, territorial state has emerged as the dominant – though not exclusive – expression of such a 'spatial fix': it is the modern state in its multiple manifestations (both 'domestic' and 'international') that has historically guaranteed the reproduction of capitalist social relations. The first basic assumption of this article, then, is that the global reproduction of capital is heavily mediated by political institutions, foremost among them the sovereign state. Contrary to many liberal and radical libertarian (that is, anti-statist) renditions of global governance which see this phenomenon as an expression of the increasingly smooth, flat and decentred surface created by the world capitalist market, I start from an understanding of global capitalism as a hierarchical, striated space where the political institutions associated with state sovereignty mediate the interactions of a seemingly globalised civil society.

A second core proposition of this essay is that since capitalist social relations – like most power relations – are politically contested, democratic struggles over the nature and content of specific political communities have played – and continue to play – a central role in the rise and consolidation of the sovereign state as the prevailing form of political organisation in the modern epoch. As Geoff Eley has demonstrated in his brilliant new book, *Forging Democracy*, it is the historical unfolding of class struggles for democracy which led to the consolidation of modern state sovereignty in nineteenth and twentieth-century Europe.[3] Similarly, the struggles for representative democracy in Latin America, East Asia or Southern Africa have also focused upon and refashioned the various organs of the state. On this reading, the modern sociopolitical struggles over democracy have essentially been about 'representation' and 'inclusion' within a bounded political community; that is, they have been sociopolitical struggles over, literally, 'making present' the interests, opinions and perspectives of sectors of society previously excluded from the exercise of social power. The concept of social and political 'representation' is of course a fraught and contested one, so it will not be broached here at any great length. For our purposes it may suffice to simply highlight two points which will hopefully contextualise its usage in the rest of the article.

Firstly, the notion of representation is not inherently democratic. Its contemporary origins lie in medieval and early-modern notions of corporatism, where the different members of the 'body politic' are brought together in a Parliament, Diet, *audiencia* or similar assembly, with the dual aim of receiving instructions from the

---

[2] 'The free market, if it is to work, requires a bundle of institutional arrangements and rules that can be guaranteed only by something akin to state power'. D. Harvey, *Spaces of Hope* (Edinburgh: Edinburgh University Press, 2000), p. 178.

[3] G. Eley, *Forging Democracy: The History of the Left in Europe, 1850-2000* (Oxford: Oxford University Press, 2002).

monarch or 'head' of the realm, and of conveying the petitions from the relevant communities. Speaking of the evolution of parliamentary representation in England from the fourteenth to the seventeenth century, Hannah Fenichel Pitkin suggests that 'At first the crucial thing was that they [knights and burgesses] come with the authority to bind their communities to the taxes to be imposed. Somewhat later they began to be used by the communities as a way of presenting grievances to the king, and there were attempts to insist on the redress of grievances before consenting to taxes. With this development began a gradual recognition that the member could further the interest of his community, in addition to committing it to taxation.'[4] Such an understanding of representation was thus chiefly functional to the tributary modes of surplus appropriation and the rigidly hierarchical forms of political rule which accompanied them: '[t]he representative roles within the medieval political assembly were conceived of as the stones within a mosaic which reproduced organically the interests and social conditions of the various classes which made up the world of the people. The right to representation did not therefore belong to single individuals but only to towns, classes, corporations, collegiate bodies and so forth.'[5] The democratic requirement of autonomy and equality was therefore absent from these representative institutions, as European medieval societies were structurally reproduced through formally hierarchical social relations and heteronomous political institutions. (This observation will have some bearing on a later discussion of contemporary neocorporatist proposals for a 'stakeholder' or 'functional' democratic governance).

Secondly, even after representation became associated with the equal franchise of (male) adults, there remained some dispute over the nature and extent of the representative's freedom, with some conceptions advocating a *mandatory* relation between a delegate and the represented body, whilst others defended the autonomy of the representative as someone who is *entrusted* or *authorised* to act on behalf of his or her constituency as they see fit. Historically, as Bernard Manin reminds us, the first option has rarely materialised: 'None of the representative governments established since the end of the eighteenth century has authorized imperative mandates or granted a legally binding status to the instructions given by the electorate'.[6] The second variant of representation has now become dominant in most liberal democracies (albeit obviously conditional on periodic elections and other mechanisms of accountability). It has most recently been complemented – and in some cases challenged – by the assumption of an identity between constituents and representatives, so that some proportional correspondence between the gender, colour, religion or national composition of the representative assembly and its constituency or membership is deemed to be a requirement of democracy.

In what follows, I shall understand 'representation' in its modern incarnation: as a way of entrusting or authorising the exercise of power by a self-defined political community of formally equal members – be it a neighbourhood association, a

---

[4] H.F. Pitkin, *The Concept of Representation* (Berkeley and Los Angeles, CA: University of California Press, 1967), p. 244.

[5] D. Zolo, *Democracy and Complexity: A Realist Approach* (Cambridge: Polity Press, 1992), p. 78.

[6] B. Manin, *The Principles of Representative Government* (Cambridge: Cambridge University Press, 1997), p. 163.

transnational social movement or a federal state. Short of invoking an implausible and largely mythical 'direct democracy' in the governance of world affairs, what this amounts to in the context of the present discussion is an insistence on the mediating role of existing representative institutions – most notably, but not exclusively the territorial state – in the democratisation of global governance. Successful struggles for the democratisation of global governance, it will be suggested, must be attentive to both the mediating power of political institutions in the reproduction of global capitalism, and to the centrality of representation in the legitimation of such a democratic politics.

It is worth emphasising that this is *not* an argument to the effect that all meaningful resistance *must* everywhere and always be mediated through the representative institutions of the state. Clearly, sociopolitical resistance finds multiple expressions – from hidden, 'everyday' forms of resistance such as gossip, irreverence or sabotage, to frontal, revolutionary destruction of existing institutions of authority, be they the Church, the state or private property. Rather, the claim is that *democratic* resistance and transformation has both historically and conceptually been associated with the powerful socioeconomic and political resources mustered by institutions of political representation and by the modern state.

Posing the challenge of democratic politics to global governance in this way once again raises difficult questions on how to avoid static and reified conceptions of political action and community, built on purely formal institutions and settled notions of identity which so often lead to persecution, oppression and outright genocide. This is especially so for an argument like the one developed in this essay, which places much of the burden of democratic politics on the activity of self-organised sociopolitical *movements*, and the accompanying popular *participation* in the exercise of democratic political authority. Yet, following Iris Marion Young,[7] it is possible to make a case for a substantive, participatory form of democratic politics which engages with, and in the process often transforms, representative institutions. One instance referred to below will be that of experiments in 'participatory budgeting' in several Brazilian cities, where the symbiosis between state and civil society in the extension of a participatory, democratic politics is especially relevant.

Finally, and in line with arguments presented by David Harvey in the context of his discussion of utopian political communities, it is worth noting that a contestation or resistance premised on an ever open-ended process and uninterrupted movement is destined toward debilitation and exhaustion: 'The history of all realized utopias points to the issue of closure as both fundamental and unavoidable, even if disillusionment through foreclosure is the inevitable consequence. If, therefore, alternatives are to be realized the problem of closure (and the authority it presupposes) cannot endlessly be evaded.'[8] A viable democratic politics, then, must start from the requirement of closure and boundaries – the recognition that democratic inclusion also implies exclusion – and from this knowledge, develop inclusive, accountable, representative and dynamic forms of political resistance and authority. The timing and place of closure is, of course, itself a matter of contestation and should not therefore be naturalised or limited to the existing forms

---

[7] I. M. Young, *Democracy and Inclusion* (Cambridge: Cambridge University Press, 2002).
[8] Harvey, *Spaces of Hope*, p. 160.

of *national* states. Yet, in a world dominated by capitalist social relations, political contestation – democratic or otherwise – is always subject to the hierarchical constraints of both the market and the bourgeois state: we can deliberate on the time and place of political closure, but not under the conditions of our own choosing.[9]

Since most of these assertions are neither novel nor uncontroversial, the larger part of what follows is dedicated to their elaboration and substantiation with reference to two interrelated problems: that of power and representation on the one hand, and that of democracy and territory on the other.

The power of representation

One of the striking aspects of the anti-capitalist activism within the global movement for justice and solidarity (many of those associated with this 'movement of movements' are of course not anti-capitalist) is the retrieval of libertarian or anarchist language and tactics of protest. Direct action; decentred, anti-hierarchical (dis)organisation through loose networks of activists; a rejection of strategic discourses which set medium or long-term political objectives or seek to channel protest into coherent bodies through representative organisations; and a deep scepticism toward any progressive potential of the state, are all salient features of recent global anti-capitalist protest. Indeed, prominent Marxist theorists like Antonio Negri or John Holloway have, together with their intellectual and political associates, expressed this libertarian impulse in their innovative treatment of concepts such as 'multitude', 'immanence' and 'transcendence', '*potestas*' and '*potentia*', or 'constitution' and 'existence', all with concrete reference to the international struggles against capitalist globalisation, especially that of the Mexican Zapatistas and their global supporters.[10]

The thrust of these rich and complex analyses is, as we shall see below, a celebration of the immediate, ubiquitous and antagonistic political subjectivity of the 'multitude' and a correspondingly deep suspicion of mediated, representative institutions built around the 'People' – most notable amongst these, the modern state.[11] On this reading, democratic resistance to capitalist globalisation and global governance must shed the discourses and practices associated with representative politics – be they local or international – and instead focus its energies on '[s]truggle as a process of ever renewed experiment, as creative, as negating the cold hand of Tradition, as

---

[9] With apologies to Marx.

[10] A. Negri, *The Savage Anomaly: The Power of Spinoza's Metaphysics and Politics* (Minneapolis, MN and Oxford: University of Minnesota Press, 1991), M. Hardt and A. Negri, *Empire* (Cambridge, MA: Harvard University Press, 2000), and J. Holloway, *Change the World Without Taking Power: The Meaning of Revolution Today* (London and Sterling, VA: Pluto Press, 2002). See also John Holloway, 'Global Capital and the National State' in W. Bonefeld and J. Holloway (eds.), *Global Capital, National State and the Politics of Money* (Basingtoke: Macmillan/St Martin's Press, 1995), pp. 116–40.

[11] For a good overview of Antonio Negri's conception of power and politics see Jason Read, 'The Antagonistic Ground of Constitutive Power: An Essay on the Thought of Antonio Negri', *Rethinking Marxism*, 11:2 (Summer 1999), pp. 1–17.

constantly moving a step beyond the absorbing identification that capitalism imposes'.[12] In the alternative formulation of one of Negri's associates, Paolo Virno: 'Democracy today has to be framed in terms of construction and experimentation of forms of non-representation and extraparliamentary democracy'.

Such conceptions of democratic (for Negri and Holloway, communist) resistance are predicated upon a very specific understanding of power and politics in capitalist societies, which will be briefly elucidated below. Such an overview of Negri's 'autonomist' and Holloway's 'open' Marxism will hopefully serve as a prelude to outlining why their rejection of political mediation and representation as democratic mechanisms debilitates the very struggles for democracy and against capitalism they seek to further. To anticipate, my own argument is twofold: firstly, because global capitalism relies on mediating political structures for its own reproduction, struggles for the democratisation of global governance would do well to focus on 'the political' in its various manifestations as a key site of anti-capitalist contestation and transformation; secondly, if such struggles are to be democratic in their practice as well as in their programme, some conception of representation – a clear answer to the question of who or what is 'the demos'? – is imperative. As we shall see shortly, Negri and Holloway – together with large segments of the anti-globalisation movement – understand this emphasis on representation as yet another undesirable instance of 'power-over' or *Potestas*, whilst I wish to insist that it is an inescapable component of any democratic project involving the 'power-to' or *potentia* of a putative global multitude.

The power of negation: Negri and Holloway on capitalism and politics

The interpretation of capitalism developed by both Negri and Holloway begins with the recognition of capital's radical dependence on labour: the reliance of capital on the exploitation of commodified labour for its very existence. From this fairly uncontroversial first premise, the 'autonomist' and 'open' Marxist approaches both go on to suggest that labour, or the capacity to consciously transform our environment, is much more powerful in capitalist societies than is generally accepted. For Holloway, the secret of capital's durability lies in its capacity to reify or fetishise the separation between what he calls 'the doing' and 'the done'; the 'separation of the constitution of the object from its existence'.[13] This 'breaking of the social flow of the doing' through the crystallisation of labour-power into private property, in turn generates a distinction between *potentia* (power-to) and *potestas* (power-over): 'Whereas power-to is a uniting, a bringing together of my doing with the doing of others, the exercise of power-over is a separation. The exercise of power-over separates conception from realisation, done from doing, one person's doing from another's, subject from object'.[14] Once this separation is contested, however; once labour ('the doers') negates its own objectification into 'the done', capital's con-

[12] Holloway, *Change the World*, p. 213.
[13] Ibid., p. 31.
[14] Ibid., p. 29.

tinued existence becomes precarious: 'No matter how much the done dominates the doing, it depends absolutely on that doing for its existence... That which exists depends for its existence on that which exists only in the form of its denial. That is the weakness of any system of rule and the key to understanding its dynamic. That is the basis of hope.'[15]

In a similar vein, the writings of Antonio Negri and his collaborators also aim to recover the radical subjectivity of labour under capitalism, and the consequent power of negation. Negri's conception of power is somewhat more baroque since it emerges through the idiosyncratic reinterpretation of Benedict Spinoza's early-modern philosophy. With the backdrop of the general crisis in seventeenth century Europe, Negri contrasts Spinoza's conception of power as constituent and generative *potentia* to that of his more influential contemporary, Thomas Hobbes, whose *Leviathan* is the archetype of power as constituted and suppressive *Potestas*:

> There are, at this point, two possible solutions [to the seventeenth-century crisis]: either restore the linearity and the essentiality of the constitutive process by means of the mediation and the overdetermination offered by a function of command – and this is the master line of the bourgeois utopia of the market – or, rather, – and this is the Spinozian line – identify in the passage from a philosophy of surfaces to a theory of the constitution of praxis the route that passes beyond the crisis, the route of the continuity of the revolutionary process. In Hobbes the crisis implies the ontological horizon and subsumes it; in Spinoza the crisis is subsumed in the ontological horizon. Here the models of appropriative society are differentiated in ontological terms: in Hobbes freedom yields to Power (*potestas*); in Spinoza Power yields to freedom.[16]

Leaving aside considerations of textual interpretation, the important point here is to identify the conceptions of power which Negri develops in relation to modern, capitalist society. As his translator and most recent associate suggests: 'In general, Power denotes the centralized, mediating, transcendental force of command, whereas power is the local, immediate, actual force of constitution . . . In the context of the Marxist tradition the antagonism between Power and power can be applied in relatively unproblematic terms, and we often find the central axis of Negri's work oriented to the opposition of the Power of capitalist relations of production and the power of proletarian productive forces.'[17] Indeed, in the latest rotation of this intellectual axis – the enormously influential *Empire* – Hardt and Negri deploy this understanding of power to insist that not only have capitalist relations really subsumed the world, creating in its wake a smooth space where 'Capital and labor are opposed in a directly antagonistic form', but also that the sovereign, territorial state is being replaced as a form of authority by the global and hybrid 'constitution of Empire' as a decentred and deterritorialised 'non-place' or *ou-topia*.[18] On this account, the constituted, transcendental power of the sovereign state as it emerged in seventeenth-century Europe has in recent decades been replaced by the immanent authority of a global 'society of control'.

It will hopefully be apparent from this brief overview that, despite significant differences in the detail of their theories, both 'autonomist' and 'open' Marxist

---

[15] Ibid., p. 36.
[16] Negri, *The Savage Anomaly* p. 20
[17] Ibid, Translator's Preface, p. xiii.
[18] Hardt and Negri, *Empire*, p. 237.

renditions of the contemporary world share an emphasis on the increasingly unmediated nature of global social relations, and indeed celebrate this as a potentially liberating development in the struggle for democracy. For Holloway, democracy must express itself as a movement of 'anti-power' which through everyday modes of resistance that reconstitute and 'rebraid' the 'flow of social doing', everywhere and always negates existence and definition. Representative organisations which aim to seize control over what is the constituted Power of the State will necessarily mirror the static, objective expressions of *Potestas*. Instead, Holloway invokes the Zapatista insurgency in Mexico as an instance of a movement of anti-power which defies identity and closure, and which consequently salvages 'revolution from the collapse of the state illusion and from the collapse of the power illusion.'[19]

Hardt and Negri for their part reappropriate the early-modern notion of 'multitude' and after giving it the obligatory Spinozian inflection, identify it with that indeterminate, expansive and constituent plethora of movements which corresponds to the new imperial form of rule. Since, under the rule of Empire, 'The social conflicts that constitute the political confront one another directly, without mediations of any sort' it is the global 'multitude', and not the national 'People' which is now the constituent subject of democracy: 'The multitude is a multiplicity, a plane of singularities, an open set of relations, which is not homogenous or identical with itself and bears an indistinct, inclusive relation to those outside of it. Whereas the multitude is an inconclusive constituent relation, the people is a constituted synthesis that is prepared for sovereignty.'[20]

Global capitalism, local mediations

Dressed up in this fashion, and in the heady context of mass protest, such formulations of libertarian vitalism are extremely seductive. Struggles for democracy and against capitalism must always contain an element of fantasy, desire and impulsive abandon. Equally however, as Marx once suggested, communists must always 'dream with sober senses'. After the exhilarating celebration of protest we generally wake up once more to face the dull compulsion of the market, and in the stark light of day, the attraction of the global multitude and a globalised politics of negation is diminished by two basic realities: the continuing tenacity of mediating structures of global capitalism and the accompanying power of political institutions of representation.

In referring to the mediating structures of capitalism, I mean to suggest that this mode of production has historically reproduced itself across the globe in variegated forms. Contrary to the more evolutionist passages in the *Communist Manifesto*, and indeed the hyperglobalist appropriations of this text by the likes of Hardt and Negri, capitalism has not compelled '[a]ll nations, on pain of extinction, to adopt the bourgeois mode of production' but instead, has encountered forms of socio-political and economic resistance and collaboration in the course of its expansion which have led to an uneven extension of capitalist social relations, and indeed to an

---

[19] Holloway, *Change the World*, p. 21.
[20] Hardt and Negri, *Empire*, p. 103.

uneasy coexistence with non-capitalist social relations in many parts of the world. Eric Wolf's magisterial *Europe and the People Without History* provides a lucid summary of how the combined and uneven reproduction of capitalism since the nineteenth century engendered a 'differentiated' mode of production on a global scale:

> The outcome of this process was a complex hierarchical system controlled by the capitalist mode of production, but including a vast array of subsidiary regions that exhibited different combinations of the capitalist mode with other modes. The carrier industries of the capitalist mode dominated the system, but these rested upon variable and shifting supports that were often embedded in different modes of production.[21]

This characterisation of global capitalism as a 'differentiated' mode of production radically contradicts the thesis of *Empire* as an expression of the real subsumption of labour under global capital and instead underlines how labour in many parts of the world is only formally subsumed to capital, and in significant instances is exploited through non-capitalist social relations, that is, it underlines how pre-capitalist structures of kinship, sex, caste, ethnicity, colour or religion still play a significant role in the global reproduction of capitalism.

As the first truly global mode of production, capitalism certainly imposes its overarching logic of accumulation upon all peoples in the world; but it does so in the context of particular social formations that often include pre-capitalist modes of exploitation and domination. Recent studies by Laura Raynolds and Jenny B. White, for example, demonstrate the intricate combination of exploitative relations which obtain at the point of production in Caribbean agri-businesses and Istanbuli garment production, and how these are linked through successive mediations (extended family, middlemen, organs of the state) to the global capitalist market.[22] Similarly, an emphasis on global capitalism as an articulated mode of production allows us to address the divergent forms of political domination in say, the Middle East, with reference to the historical combination of capitalism with pre-capitalist modes of social reproduction which in turn generate class interests peculiar to that specific social formation. To take but one example: the initial instalment and subsequent persistence of dynastic monarchies in the Arabian peninsula (and the corresponding lack of civil liberties of the indigenous population, let alone the sizeable population of 'guest workers') could be explained through an analysis of how British imperialism grafted (and the USA later sustained) the general dynamics of capitalist exchange and production upon pre-existing social relations, and how this specific combination has produced rentier social formations with very particular class antagonisms and indeed, inter-class alliances.[23]

---

[21] Ibid, pp. 296–7.

[22] Laura Raynolds 'Restructuring National Agriculture, Agro-Food Trade, and Agrarian Livelihoods in the Caribbean', in D. Goodman and M.J. Watts (eds.), *Globalising Food: Agrarian Questions and Global Restructuring* (London and New York: Routledge, 1997), pp. 119–132, at 129; Jenny B. White *Money Makes Us Relatives: Women's Labor in Urban Turkey* (Austin, TX: University of Texas Press, 1994), p. 108.

[23] For an up-to-date analysis of how these particularities play themselves out in one of the more dynamic societies in the peninsula, see M.-A. Tétreault, *Stories of Democracy: Politics and Society in Contemporary Kuwait* (New York, NY: Columbia University Press, 2000). For a consideration of the 'invention' and subsequent persistence of dynastic monarchies in that region, see J. Kostiner (ed.), *Middle East Monarchies: the Challenge of Modernity* (Boulder, CO and London: Lynne Rienner, 2000).

The upshot of these illustrations is simply to suggest that far from facing each other in a direct, unmediated form, capital and labour clash on the global plane through the mediation of various sociopolitical institutions. These institutions are of course, neither neutral nor unhierarchical – but they do represent necessary sites of contestation between capital and labour, and indeed between these and pre-capitalist forms of domination. To that extent, and insofar as democracy involves the gradual subordination of capital to the collective needs of labour, the latter must simultaneously engage with and transform these mediating structures. The democratic state, and the citizenship it confers on its population, is in this respect a crucial resource of power for subordinated collectivities, and it is the representative institutions of the working class in particular that have secured this power. The experiments in 'participatory budgeting' (PB) in urban Brazil are especially illuminating in this regard. Here we have an instance of how collective struggles for representative democracy, led by working class organisations, have both widened and deepened forms of local democracy in one of the world's largest economies.

Participatory representation: an illustration

The history, development and consequences of PB are complex and contradictory, and so they will not be broached here in any great detail. For our purposes, four aspects of the process are worth highlighting. First, local experiments in PB have to be seen in the broader context of nationwide and indeed, international constraints – most notably, those enforced by the US Administration. The scores of municipalities which have adopted PB in Brazil are of course heavily dependent on transfers from the State and Federal governments, and like most major cities in the world, also rely on private sector and multilateral agency credit.[24] This reliance on external transfers and credit (be it domestic or international) therefore makes experiments in local democracy highly sensitive to the political and socioeconomic vicissitudes of other, more powerful institutions: the backing and resources of larger political entities such as the Brazilian Federal Government appear to be central to the viability of experiments in local PB. It follows that the more democratic and resourceful the Federal Government, the more likely it is that the transfers necessary to fund PB locally will make themselves available. Local democracy, to adapt a phrase, 'is not an oasis in the neoliberal desert'[25] and its fate is clearly tied to the democratisation or policy orientation of larger political entities – be they national, regional or global.

Secondly, for all the infrastructural power of state institutions in delivering and spending PBs in Brazilian cities, it is the mobilisation and participation of individual citizens, 'grassroots' associations and political, cultural and religious organisations which is the lifeblood of PB. Although overall participation in the various stages

---

[24] Porto Alegre, the flagship city for PB, derived 52 per cent of its annual revenue from local sources (taxation and tariffs) and 48 per cent from State or Federal transfers. See Boaventura de Sousa Santos, 'Participatory Budgeting in Porto Alegre: Toward a Redistributive Democracy', *Politics and Society*, 26:4 (December 1998), pp. 461–510, fn. 13.

[25] Sérgio Baierle, 'The Porto Alegre Thermidor?': Brazil's "Participatory Budget" at the Crossroads', *Social Register, 2002* (London: Merlin Press, 2002).

associated with PB appears to be relatively low (in Porto Alegre it has remained at under 10 per cent of the total population[26]), in absolute terms the level and intensity of civic participation in government is by all accounts unprecedented in Latin America. More importantly, the democratic aspiration of inclusion, autonomy and equality has been fostered through the PB processes. To take the flagship case of Porto Alegre once again, the breakdown of participants by gender, income, ethnic origin and age for the participatory meetings of the year 2000 indicates a remarkably representative forum with the ratio between women and men participants close to 60/40 (with the notable exception of city councillors, where only 27.3 per cent were women); 54 per cent of plenary participants officially considered as 'poor'; and close to a quarter of those plenary participants, assembly delegates and councillors identifying themselves as black and indigenous citizens.[27] The local government-led PB experiment has certainly provided an 'opportunity structure' for civic participation, but there can be little doubt that it is the various autonomous neighbourhood associations and religious, cultural or political organisations which have mobilised such participation.

The PB initiatives have extended the scope of local democracy in Brazil by including previously marginalised social sectors, increasing transparency and accountability, and securing civil society participation in the budgetary process. But they have also developed a third aspect of democracy by significantly increasing public revenue and allocating it according to criteria which privilege collective need over private interests. This substantive dimension of democratisation is especially important in Latin America (and indeed in the Third World more broadly) where sharp income inequalities coexist with extensive tax evasion by the rich and extremely low tax burdens.[28] Although strictly speaking, the PB institutions have no tax-raising powers (these are formally the prerogative of the city legislature), and their remit only covers funds earmarked for public works and procurement, the PB assemblies have in the past been essential in legitimising executive-led tax rises amounting to a 48 per cent increase in the city's revenue over the space of a decade.[29] Moreover, PB has seen the redistribution of investment funds to the poorest and most marginalised sectors of the population, substantially improving the provision of basic needs such as sanitation, housing, street paving, and elementary and secondary education.[30]

---

[26] For Porto Alegre, this would amount to over 100,000 participants. See de Sousa Santos, p. 486.

[27] See Baierle, p. 307 and for previous years, de Sousa Santos, pp. 485–91.

[28] As Atilio Borón reminds us, ' Despite the allegations of the neoliberal zealots, the tax burden (measured as percent of the GDP and excluding social security contributions) of the more developed countries of Latin America is around 17% while in the OECD countries the proportion is twice as much, averaging 37.7%', in 'State Decay and Democratic Decadence in Latin America', *Socialist Register 1999* (London: Merlin Press, 1999), pp. 209–26, p. 218.

[29] The 1990 tax reform in Port Alegre introduced a property tax which accounted for 18% of the municipality's revenue in the late 1990s, up from a mere 5.8% in 1990. According to de Sousa Santos, 'The tax reform, which was crucial to relaunch the popular administration [in 1990], had to be approved by the Câmara de Vereadores [city legislature]. Because the Popular Front did not have a majority in the Câmara, the PT [Worker's Party] and the executive promoted a massive mobilization of the popular classes to pressurise the legislators to approve the tax reform law.' 'Participatory Budgeting', p. 477.

[30] Ibid., p. 285.

Finally, and perhaps most relevant for the argument of this essay, it is important to note that the PB process necessarily involves a territorial allocation of power. Aside from the obvious point that the limits of PB coincide with those of the municipality (de Sousa Santos mentions the case of a neighbouring town wishing to join the municipality of Porto Alegre so as to benefit from PB), the delegation, deliberation and implementation of the PB is organised along regional, as well as 'thematic' lines. Thus, the division of Porto Alegre into sixteen regions fixes the spatial representation of the city, thereby effectively delimiting 'communities' or 'the demos' by area.

The PB policies in Porto Alegre and elsewhere are not easily transferable to the domain of global governance, as we shall see in a moment; nor is the desirability and viability of these policies a foregone conclusion. But the example of PB does offer an important illustration of how state and civil society, or *Potestas* and *potentia* need not be at odds with each other. It is clear from the experiments in Porto Alegre that the broadening and deepening of democracy cannot take place without either the institutional mechanisms of representational politics (regional and thematic delegation, voting procedures, engagement with legislative and executive authority and so forth), or the substantive resources procured by the state which accompany it in the form of revenue, transfers and credit-raising powers. As Rebecca Abers has suggested, 'The Porto Alegre policy has combined substantial amount of government investment in social programs with a successful state-sponsored effort at capacitating civic groups to control that investment and, in doing so, to dramatically improve their quality of life.'[31] A conception of political power like that of Negri and Holloway which sees any mediating, representative power as an absolute expression of *Potestas* or 'power-over' overlooks how the latter can, under appropriate circumstances, *facilitate* the vital democratic expressions of 'power-to' or *potestas*. More seriously, simply counterpoising the constituent *potentia* of labour to the constituted *Potestas* of capital and the state misses the crucial relational dimension of power under capitalist society, and in particular, the subordinate position of labour in that relation. Such subordination, as the struggles for democracy in Brazil and elsewhere have demonstrated, is most likely to be reversed through political means: that is, by mobilising civil society through democratic associations, engaging with and transforming the representative power of existing institutions and, crucially, harnessing the resources of the state at its various levels in securing such a reversal.

Democracy and territory

This understanding of democratic resistance as an internationalised struggle for state power was of course that adopted by and embodied in the internationalist organisations of the nineteenth and twentieth century. Working-class internationalism

---

[31] Rebecca Abers, 'From Clientelism to Cooperation: Local Government, Participatory Policy and Civic Organizing in Porto Alegre, Brazil', *Politics and Society*, 26:4 (December 1998), pp. 511–37, at p. 511.

in particular, offers in this regard the most developed and influential historical form of international, democratic anti-capitalism. Yet, in investing so much of their political capital in the institutions of the territorial state, such expressions of globalised democratic politics have also often succumbed to the trappings of essentialised identities, parochial politics and excessively formalised conceptions of democracy. One clear consequence of this today is the polarisation within the global anti-capitalist movement between deterritorialised, decentred conceptions of protest as unfolding within a 'global space', and those that still retain what one critic has called a 'nostalgic idealism of territorial democracy'.[32] Indeed, Michael Hardt, one of the prominent advocates of the latter position, drew the following conclusions from his participation at the second World Social Forum in Porto Alegre: 'There are . . . two primary positions in the response to today's dominant forces of globalization: either one can work to reinforce the sovereignty of nation-states as a defensive barrier against the control of foreign and global capital, or one can strive towards a non-national alternative to the present form of globalization that is equally global.'[33]

Clearly, the position outlined thus far in this essay is closest to the first of the responses Hardt identifies within the global anti-capitalist movement. Arguments have already been made in the first section of the article as to why engaging with and harnessing state sovereignty, political representation and other mediating mechanisms in anti-capitalist campaigns is crucial to a successful democratic politics. The purpose of this section is to focus more narrowly on the relationship between the organisation of political space and projects aimed at democratising global governance. Specifically, I wish to make two arguments. Firstly, that liberal programmes for cosmopolitan governance have much to offer a radical democratic politics insofar as they stimulate our reimagination of political communities. But in order to deliver substantive democratisation, such projects must also be accompanied by a correspondingly radical transformation in our modes of social reproduction. I shall suggest that even the most sophisticated liberal arguments stop short of making an internal or structural link between these two spheres of democratic transformation. Thus, the challenge for cosmopolitan democrats – whatever our ideological persuasion – lies not only in reimagining the national state as the predominant form of political community, but also, more dauntingly, in transcending capitalism as the dominant mode of social reproduction.

Secondly, and in contrast to the broadly-conceived libertarian reconceptualisations of global political space, I shall contend that social movements and political organisations seeking the substantive democratisation of global governance will, as in the past, have to organise and mobilise simultaneously at national and transnational levels. This is so, it will be suggested, for the strategic reasons outlined in the first part of the article, but also because such movements cannot themselves be deemed democratic unless they determine the limits of their own constituency. Such limits, it will be further suggested, are necessarily territorial.

---

[32] William E. Connolly, 'Democracy and Territoriality', *Millennium*, 20:3 (1991), pp. 463–84.
[33] Michael Hardt, 'Today's Bandung?', *New Left Review*, 14 (New Series), March/April 2002, pp. 112–18, at p. 114.

Beyond territorialism: the challenges of cosmopolitan democracy

The last decade has witnessed an impressive international effort by liberal thinkers to move beyond the 'territorial trap' of conventional IR analysis and to propose models of global governance which recast the boundaries of democratic politics. The issue at stake – to adopt the evocative title of one influential collection of proposals – is that of 'Democracy's Edges': 'An enduring embarrassment of democratic theory is that it seems impotent when faced with questions about its own scope. By its terms democracy seems to take the existence of units within which it operates for granted. It depends on a decision rule, usually some variant of majority rule, but the rule's operation assumes that the question "majority of whom"? has already been settled.'[34]

One rather conservative way of addressing this question is by accepting existing nation-states as the only relevant democratic units and *extending* the membership or national representation *within* the existing institutions of global governance. Several campaigns for the democratisation of global governance have over the years called for the greater accountability, transparency and equity of multilateral institutions. From this perspective, global governance must be rendered democratic by way of a more equitable representation of member-states in multilateral decision-making bodies like the UN Security Council, the Board of Governors of the World Bank or the General Council of the WTO.[35] Member-states here clearly replace the role of the electorate in a domestic setting as the chief source of representative legitimacy. However, in recognising that most UN member-states are, at best, imperfectly representative of their populations, such proposals for democratisation often also include calls for 'popular representation' in the form of a 'Second UN Chamber' or the presence of member-government's opposition organisations in the relevant multilateral bodies. Notwithstanding the variety and occasional sophistication of many such proposals, they essentially operate through the suspect 'domestic analogy' whereby democratic principles and practices that obtain within liberal states can be transposed to the international sphere fairly unproblematically. Moreover, they tend to omit any reference to a substantive deepening or widening of global democracy – their operative unit is that of the nation-state. In both these senses, such proposals contribute precious little to the mobilisations for the radical democratisation of global governance.

An alternative approach to the issue of democracy and global governance – associated with the work of James N. Rosenau – vigorously rejects domestic analogies, suggesting that '[i]n the absence of fixed boundaries in Globalized Space, processes of representation and responsibility normally associated with democratic institutions are of limited relevance'.[36] Instead, Rosenau identifies a number of 'functional

---

[34] Ian Shapiro and Casiano Hacker-Cordón, 'Outer Edges and Inner Edges', in I. Shapiro and C. Hacker-Cordón (eds.), *Democracy's Edges* (Cambridge: Cambridge University Press, 1999), pp. 1–17, at p. 1.

[35] See for instance, Boutros Boutros Ghali, *Agenda for Democratization* (New York: UN Publications, 1996); H. Kovach, Caroline Neligan and Simon Burrall, *Power Without Accountability: The Global Accountability Report* (London: One World Trust, 2003).

[36] James N. Rosenau, 'Governance and Democracy in a Globalizing World', in D. Archibugi, D. Held and M. Köhler, *Re-Imagining Political Community: Studies in Cosmopolitan Democracy* (Cambridge: Polity Press, 1998), p. 40.

equivalents of the basic precepts of territorial democracy' – 'disaggregation', INGOs, social movements, cities and micro-regions, electronic technologies – which might act as checks and balances, and 'inhibit unrestrained exercise of power'.[37] It is unclear whether Rosenau is here rejecting the possibility of democratic representation *tout court*, or whether he is endorsing an updated version of the medieval corporatism identified earlier which, shorn of its tributary and hierarchical properties, gives INGOs, social movements, cities, micro-regions and so on a right to represent their functional community in the fragmented Globalized Space – a kind of globalised version of the Q.O.T. principle.[38] Either way, it is clear that for Rosenau, the dispersal of political authority away from the territorial state and its diffusion across a broad range of agents in 'Globalized Space' is potentially democratic by virtue simply of the constraints such disaggregation poses on the concentration of power.

Once again, such proposals eschew the question of how democracy may be deepened on a global scale, and by assuming uncritically 'the absence of fixed boundaries' actually confuse the *diffusion* or *pluralisation* of democracy with *widening* its scope. Like other 'stakeholder' conceptions of global governance, Rosenau's proposals simply shift the crucial question of the limits or scope of democracy, to a functional instead of a territorial domain. For the 'functional communities' which are to replace territorial representation will themselves have to be delimited, and so the issue of who or what the (functional) *demos* is emerges once again. All this arguably reduces the attraction of Rosenau's model for struggles seeking to radically democratise global governance as it reproduces the problem of inclusion and exclusion, whilst simultaneously undermining the modern democratic principle that all citizens have a say in the running of their public, collective affairs.

A third, and more powerful, liberal engagement with the problems of democracy and territoriality, is that generally associated with models of 'cosmopolitan demo-cracy' or 'cosmopolitan governance'.[39] These ideas have informed various experiments in transnational governance – from Kofi Annan's 'Global Compact' to regional arrangements such as the now virtually defunct Euro-Mediterranean Partnership. Independently of their actual success, such projects for cosmopolitan democracy merit our critical scrutiny simply for their audacious attempt at concretising alternative ways of thinking about democracy in a so-called age of globalisation.

The starting-point for these concrete utopias, as we saw earlier, is the disjuncture or misalignment between the political organisation of the world into discrete territorial states and the transnational flows of the global economy. Now that the globalised world has outgrown the territorial state, so the argument runs, it is time

---

[37] Ibid., p. 47.

[38] *'Quod omnes tangit, ab omnibus tractari et approbat debet'* ('What touches all should be considered and approved by all'). Manin suggests that the invocation of this Roman principle in medieval Europe '[d]id not imply that the consent of the governed was deemed the sole principal source of legitimacy . . . Rather it meant that a wish from "above" had to meet with approval from "below" in order to become a fully legitimate directive that carried obligation. Nor did the principle entail any notion of choice among candidates by the people or proposals by the assembly. It was rather that the people were being asked to give their seal of approval to what the authorities . . . had proposed.' Manin, *Principles*, p. 88.

[39] Representative texts include: D. Archibugi and D. Held (eds.), *Cosmopolitan Democracy: An Agenda for a New World Order* (Cambridge: Polity Press, 1995); Archibugi et al. (eds.), *Re-Imagining*; and D. Held, *Democracy and the Global Order: From the Modern State to Cosmopolitan Governance* (Cambridge: Polity, 1995).

to design a new set of democratic institutions that fit the increased size of global interdependence. However, two contestable premises – one historical, the other conceptual – in my view undermine the power of these critiques of a territorial conception of democracy.

The first of such assumptions relates to a surprisingly ahistorical and undialectical narrative of modern history, and in particular, of modern sovereignty. For, in order to intellectually legitimise the shift from modern territorialised conceptions of democratic sovereignty to a late- or postmodern notion of deterritorialised democracy or a post-Westphalian political order, cosmopolitan democrats tend to rely on an implausibly static and absolute understanding of modern state sovereignty. On this account, the modern conception of state sovereignty which crystallised in Europe with the end of the Thirty Year's War in 1648, was consolidated and universalised in the course of the following three centuries and has only been challenged by the forces of globalisation since the end of World War II. It is an account of the expansion of international society which, following the more conservative histories, uses order rather than crisis as the signpost of historical change.

Yet if we invert some crucial aspects of such a narrative so as to emphasise, for instance, the ordering power of imperial rule, or the impact of 1776–1848 or 1905–19 as moments of world-historical change, the history of modern sovereignty appears as a far more contested, unstable and indeed unfinished process than is often acknowledged. On this reading, the global reproduction of the modern state form becomes a highly uneven, unsettled and crisis-ridden process where non-capitalist structures of transnational imperial authority display considerable staying power in Europe, the Middle East and east Asia; where the allegedly fixed boundaries of the modern state actually ebb and flow with the related phenomena of wars and social revolutions; and where the seemingly homogenous identity of the nation-state is recurrently contested and negotiated through both socioeconomic flows associated to the globalisation of capitalism and the political struggles for recognition and inclusion. Here, the understanding of democratic sovereignty eschews a cumulative, Whiggish conception of change and instead suggests that the consolidation of the sovereign state as the dominant form of geopolitical organisation is the variegated, protracted and often contingent outcome of internationalised socio-political struggles which are still underway today. Cast in this light, the realisation of cosmopolitan democracy becomes part of a broader historical process initiated with the Atlantic revolutions of the late eighteenth century, and which is therefore associated less with rethinking the sovereign state as the dominant political community, and much more with the struggles for the fulfilment of the modern state's democratic potential.

A second and related objection to the liberal conception of cosmopolitan governance is its tendency to naturalise the separation between politics and economics – between states and markets – which characterises capitalist social relations. This assumption overlooks the internal, or structural relation between modern state sovereignty and capitalist exploitation and instead presses on with a conception of global governance where the political forms of authority can be decoupled from the modes of social reproduction. To be sure, sophisticated models of cosmopolitan democracy like that found in David Held's *Democracy and Global Order*, acknowledge that such a political project must be accompanied by a radical reform of the global capitalist economy. Yet in characteristically liberal fashion, Held (like most of his colleagues) reduces capitalist social relations to one of seven sites of power – that of 'production' or 'economics' – thereby foregoing the opportunity to associate the various disjunctures explored to the dynamics of a broader totality of *social* (not just 'productive' or 'economic') relations which characterise capitalism. In other words, Held fails to establish the crucial link between the structural requirement for capitalism to constantly generate surplus value and the diverse sociohistorical disjunctures which he rightly claims define the contemporary democratic predicament. This in turn leads – crucially – to a misplaced emphasis on the territorial, 'Westphalian model' of sovereignty as the major source of such a predicament, instead of on the broader system of surplus appropriation responsible for the disjunctures of globalisation. Held, in short, falls into the trap of fetishising the political expressions of global capitalism by assuming that the political forms of rule it throws up can be transformed in isolation from the social relations that underpin this system.

Far from representing a minor (and predictable) theoretical quibble between liberal and Marxist notions of 'production' or 'social relations', these considerations are germane to the present discussion in that they underline how even projects for a cosmopolitan democracy will be unable to overcome the 'disjunctures' generated by global capitalism unless they address the structural basis of that mode of production. To use Held's own terminology, insofar as global capitalism necessarily feeds off 'nautonomic' social relations,[40] the challenge for any project of cosmopolitan *democracy* lies not only in the rearticulation of political community, but in the overhaul of the social relations that generate such 'nautonomy' – that is, exploitation and alienation – in the first place. In other words, so long as it is *capitalist* social relations that are being regulated, no amount of global governance will do away with the 'nautonomic' relations that characterise the contemporary international system.[41]

Of the various liberal approaches to democracy and territoriality outlined above, it is Held's model of cosmopolitan governance which seems most promising for the realisation of democracy on a global scale. For, while it eschews the crude 'domestic analogy' of those that seek to democratise global governance by simply changing the composition of state representation in multilateral agencies, it also acknowledges – *contra* Rosenau – that democracy requires some delimitation of the represented *demos* if it is to avoid either the naïve democratic pluralism of the 'Globalized Space' or the functional-corporatist democratisation of global governance through the medium of specialised interest groups or operational facilitators. More importantly, it recognises that any democratic deliberation and authorisation also requires democratic *implementation*; that is, the administrative authority to make binding decisions, to enact the authority of 'the people' – especially when such decisions aim to regulate the relentless movement of capital:

A cosmopolitan democracy would not call for a diminution per se of state power and capacity across the globe. Rather, it would seek to entrench and develop democratic institutions at regional and global levels as a necessary complement to those at the level of

---

[40] '[t]he asymmetrical production and distribution of life-chances which limit and erode the possibilities of political participation', *Democracy and Global Order*, p. 171.

[41] For a similar critique of Held's programme for global socioeconomic reform, see Tony Smith, 'Globalisation and Capitalist Property Relations: A Critical Assessment of Held's Cosmopolitan Theory', *Historical Materialism*, 11:2 (2003), pp. 3–35.

the nation-state. This conception of democracy is based on the recognition of the continuing significance of nation-states, while arguing for a layer of governance to constitute a limitation on national sovereignty.[42]

If democratic politics is conceived as a struggle over inclusion and exclusion, the necessity for closure and boundaries cannot be wished away. Such closure need not be timeless or indeed exclusively bound by the sovereign state: it is not *what* type of spatial delimitation corresponds to democracy that is at stake here, but rather *that* democracy requires spatial delimitation. Liberal theories of cosmopolitan democracy offer plausible models for the reorganisation of political communities in ways that can facilitate the democratic control over our collective fates. They highlight the transnational and interdependent dimensions to our daily lives and identify possible mechanisms for the political regulation of such phenomena beyond the confines of a particular region. Yet, in the end, they too evade the crucial paradox whereby it is only a territorially bounded entity, containing a defined constituency, which can democratically hold to account those very social forces that constantly undermine the authority of the democratic political community. So long as global capitalism continues as the dominant mode of social reproduction, any political community, whatever its size or scope, that aims to democratically regulate the boundless dynamics of value-accumulation must come to terms with the necessity of closure.

Mobilising democratically for a democratic global governance

The question of closure, of setting the limits to inclusion, is one in which democratic social movements are heavily implicated. For, as was illustrated with reference to the Brazilian experiments in participatory budgeting, democratic associations of civil society need in the course of their struggles to engage with the political authority of the state. Similarly, any political authority which aims to widen and deepen democracy requires the participation of various agents of civil society. Both state and civil society, therefore constantly encounter the problem of delimiting 'democracy's edges': of establishing the limits of their own political legitimacy.

Such a problem is especially acute in a global context, where the 'pluriverse' of political authority famously delivers an 'anarchical' international system where there is no superior authority to that of the state. As was just indicated, a simple reproduction of local or national experiments in participatory democracy is therefore unsatisfactory in that there is no simple equivalent at the international level of the domestic breakdown in jurisdiction, between say Federal, regional and local government. What *does* currently exist is a variety of multilateral institutions and international organisations, which through the mediation of states constitutes that *nébuleuse* of political authority known as global governance. Social movements seeking to democratise such global governance will therefore have to challenge the interests, policies and decision-making structures which, *via* the authority entrusted to them by states, manage this form of political rule. And it follows that in order to

---

[42] David Held, 'Democracy and Globalization', in Archibugi, *Re-Imagining*, p. 88.

do so legitimately and effectively, these very movements must themselves develop forms of democratic mobilisation which can serve as the basis for future models of democratic global governance.

There are essentially two opposing (though by no means entirely incompatible) forms of global democratic resistance to follow here. In the report cited earlier, Michael Hardt echoes many observers of (and participants in) global anti-capitalist resistance in proposing the first model: a globalised 'network resistance' which '[c]an allow a full expression of differences within the common context of open exchange. They displace contradictions and operate instead a kind of alchemy, or rather a sea change, the flow of movements transforming the traditional fixed positions; networks imposing their force through a kind of irresistible undertow.'[43] One concrete expression of this libertarian celebration of 'flows', 'openess' and 'difference' in socio-political resistance has been that of the Mexican EZLN and its supporting networks. Another (cited by Hardt in his piece) is that of the Argentinian *asambleario* movement emerging out of the recent legitimacy crisis in that country.

Notwithstanding their important differences, what these forms of resistance offer to the global anti-capitalist movement is a model of anti-sovereign, deterritorialised and flatly unhierarchical anti-politics which, according to many activists, presents the only means of democratically contesting the ubiquitous and unmediated power of global capital, or *Empire*. This model of network resistance therefore conceives of political space as a 'rhizomatic' structure – one that has no centre or hierarchy – and which is epitomised by the solidarity of the 'cyberactivist'. Here, democratic contestation is not about seizing power but about creating it afresh as 'power-to'; not about national or international organisations and representation, but rather about constantly upsetting our received conceptions of space and making the local and the global simultaneous; and it is not about defending national sovereignty, but about rejecting any fixed and firm identity. Solidarity expresses itself as an autonomous and open-ended process of 'networking' where 'no two nodes face each other in contradiction; rather, they are always triangulated by a third, and then a fourth, and then by an infinite number of others in the web'.[44]

A fair range of objections could be raised against this self-presentation of 'network resistance' – including the deeply hierarchical character of many so-called indigenous movements which form part of the EZLN; the famous 'tyranny of structurelessness' and the fact that many of these network movements in fact emerge in contexts where there is no state power to contest or engage with in the first place. But the central shortcoming of such forms of resistance lies in their (literal) incapacity to *implement* democratic measures, or put differently, their self-imposed lack of *political authority*. As will have hopefully become evident from the first part of the article, this is especially damaging to any project aimed at democratising global governance, as any such programme will require a sizeable mobilisation of political authority in favour of collective needs and against the powerful interests of capital and its ruling classes. Put very bluntly: resistance without authority is a recipe for perennial domination; authoritative resistance empowers the dominated. The democratic challenge is to transform authority through resistance in ways that do away with domination.

[43] Hardt, 'Today's Bandung?', p. 117.
[44] Ibid., p. 117.

This is clearly a tall order, and one for which there is no ready-made blueprint or predetermined road-map. But if the arguments and illustrations presented above are in any way compelling, there is much to be learned for the democratisation of global governance from contemporary struggles – like those of the Brazilian Worker's Party and its supporters – for forms of exercising political authority which are both representative and participatory. In the context of the present discussion, this second model implies a continued emphasis on forms of global resistance which – like their more classically 'internationalist' forebears – understand democracy as the process of deepening and broadening the collective regulation of social life and therefore seek to further this goal through international campaigns for democratic sovereignty *within* as well as *between* states. The various worldwide and regional social forums which have taken place since the late 1990s offer in this regard an example of how the more traditional working-class movements – be they the PT in Porto Alegre, the various communist organisations at Florence or those likely to be steering meetings in St Denis and Bombay – can offer the logistical and organisational resources for an inclusive, participatory yet representative and territorialised form of global democratic politics.

Some concluding reflections

The liberal euphoria which accompanied the collapse of the Soviet bloc in the period immediately after 1989 has been dampened in recent years by the multiple financial crises in several nodal points of the global capitalist system, the sluggish performance of the core capitalist economies and the emergence of a new generation of activists intent on puncturing the global triumphalism of capital. The terrorist attacks on Washington and New York and the ensuing 'war on terror' have further compounded a sense of international crisis – at least for the minority of us for whom socioeconomic and political breakdown is not a fact of everyday life.

It is in this context that the so-called Global Movement for Justice and Solidarity which has crystallised around successive counter-summits and social forums, offers the first glimpse since the end of historical communism of a globalised resistance to capitalism. There is no question that if such an anti-capitalist movement is to make political inroads in future, it must above all be a *democratic* movement. It must build the support of the mass of the world's population which carries the burden of global capital's manifold crises, and it must channel such support through open, representative and accountable mobilisations. Yet it must also offer viable and durable alternatives to the existing socioeconomic and political mechanisms which manage such crises. Such alternative forms of political authority, it has been suggested, are unlikely to develop without first democratising existing political institutions across the world – primarily, but not exclusively, nation-states.

I have tried in this article to indicate how the two moments in the process of democratic struggle – the moment of protest and the moment of authority – are intertwined: how the temporal politics of resistance, inclusion, *potentia* and movement is necessarily linked to the spatial Politics of the state, closure, *Potestas* and stability. On this view, any future realisation of global democracy will be immanent in the sociopolitical movements which struggle for such democracy. Yet equally, the radical transformation of capitalist globalisation will have to be predicated on actually-existing social and political relations, and their accompanying mediating structures and hierarchies. It is these mediating structures, I have further argued, which constitute the primary site of contestation between the two major antagonists in capitalist societies (capital and labour), and between those who represent capital in non-capitalist relations (landlords, patriarchs, middlemen) and their subordinates (bonded labourers, household workers, sharecroppers). Because of their mediating power, these structures are potentially the weakest link in the expanded reproduction of capital, and so the power of representation manifests itself in the capacity of such subordinated classes to engage with and transform these mediating structures. In the context of global governance, it has been suggested, it is the modern sovereign state and its representative institutions – be they local, regional or global – which should be the strategic site of anti-capitalist mobilisation. And it is in the process of building up such movements that the full potential of future, democratic global governance will hopefully emerge.

Global civil society: a liberal-republican argument

MICHAEL KENNY*

Introduction

This article highlights two of the most influential normative perspectives upon the ethical character of global civil society in Anglo-American political thought. These are considered under the headings of liberal cosmopolitanism and subalternist radicalism. Within international political theory, the main alternative to cosmopolitan arguments is usually regarded as provided by moral theories that invoke the continuing significance of national boundaries in relation to political community.[1] The rivalry between cosmopolitan convictions and nationalist ethics is deeply entrenched within Anglo-American thinking. As a result, international political theory seems to throw up a fundamentally antinomian choice: *either* we possess overriding duties and obligations to others, irrespective of our nationhood; *or* the borders of a settled nation-state substantially define our sense of political identity and justify a marked ethical partiality towards our fellow nationals. Such is the hold of this antinomy upon the Western political imagination, it seems, that alternative conceptions of the relationship between territory, community and ethicality have been neglected or dismissed as unduly heterodox. Given the continuing purchase of this dualistic approach on international political ethics, the recovery and normative evaluation of various alternatives is a task of some intellectual importance.

This article aims to contribute to this wider project, first, through a critical examination of liberal idealisations of global civil society – an increasingly familiar term of use in journalism, public debate and academic analysis.[2] It then considers an

* I am particularly grateful to the Review's two anonymous referees for their perceptive comments on an earlier draft of this article, and to Bice Maiguashca, for the editorial skill and valuable suggestions that she has offered. I also received helpful advice from: Ian Bache, Andrew Gamble, Randall Germain, Jean Grugel, Graham Harrison, Kimberley Hutchings, Duncan Kelly, Petr Kopecky, Tony Payne, Rajiv Prabhakar, and Jan Aart Scholte. Earlier versions of this argument were delivered to audiences at Birmingham and Kingston Universities, and Goldsmith's College, in the UK. Kevin Gillan provided invaluable bibliographical assistance.
[1] For a thoughtful discussion of the influence of this and other related dualisms in international political theory, see Kimberley Hutchings, *International Political Theory: Rethinking Ethics in a Global Era* (London: Sage, 1999).
[2] Divergent accounts of the origins and implications of the term 'global civil society' can be found in Helmut Anheier, Marlies Glasius, and Mary Kaldor, 'Introducing Global Civil Society', in Anheier, Glasius and Kaldor (eds.), *Global Civil Society* (Oxford: Oxford University Press, 2001), pp. 3–22; Alejandro Colás, *International Civil Society: Social Movement in World Politics* (Oxford: Polity, 2002); and John Dunn, 'Indiscreet as War on Terror', *The Times Higher Educational Supplement*, 22: 3 (2002), p. 27.

alternative interpretation of this ideal – that developed by various subalternist radicals. Despite their opposition to liberal conceptions of international politics and society, their approach is unable to surmount the weaknesses of liberal models: it fails to offer a plausible response to the dilemmas of moral pluralism in an international setting and marginalises forms of social enterprise and cultural expression that do not fit with its normative presuppositions. By contrast, the author considers the various merits of an unduly neglected alternative in international political theory – the broad tradition of liberal-republicanism. This is the source of critical insights and questions that might well support coherent normative understandings of the ethical character of transnational society beyond the confines of either liberal cosmopolitanism or subaltern radicalism.[3]

The argument that follows is, then, shaped by two overriding aims. Its primary, minimalist, ambition is to establish that some of the most familiar understandings of global civil society should be critically re-examined, rather than unreflectively deployed, by students and scholars of international politics and society. A second, more ambitious, purpose is to establish that republican liberalism is worthy of serious consideration as a source of moral understanding and persuasive normative arguments about the dilemmas and changes associated with transnational civil society. These dilemmas include such issues as whether the development of global public spaces entails and legitimates the ethos of world citizenship. Among the various changes associated with the idea of global civil society are the growth of transnational social and political networks, and the involvement of civil society actors in some of the key networks of the new globalised governance.

The arguments considered here are closely related to the two perspectives highlighted in this Special Issue. Liberal proponents of global civil society are often advocates of global governance, and the subalternist arguments that I consider rest upon a celebration of various kinds of resistance to globalisation. Neither of these broad approaches, I argue, is sufficiently attuned to the power dynamics that give associational life its shape and character, and to the social relations through, and against, which group identity and collective action take shape. As a result, both offer one-dimensional accounts of the moral implications of transnational activity. I therefore explore the merits of a neglected political-ethical alternative to them, highlighting a liberal-republican tradition that makes central such questions as: what makes a political order legitimate; how group identities and interests bear upon citizenship; and the relationships between spatial scales and political authority.

Characterising global civil society: liberal perspectives

Prevailing understandings of global civil society emerge from two counter-opposed perspectives in Anglophone political theory. The first of these coheres around the ongoing efforts of various liberal theorists to delineate and idealise the emergence of

---

[3] For a discussion of the contribution of liberal republicanism to the theorisation of civil society, see Alan Thomas, 'Liberal Republicanism and the Role of Civil Society', *Democratization*, 4: 3 (1997), pp. 26–44.

a genuinely global social terrain and accompanying sense of civic community.[4] While there are more dimensions to these liberal ideas than can be adequately represented here, it is possible to discern the outlines of an ideal-typical Anglophone liberal account. This has succeeded in exercising an influence upon the moral and political thinking of key political actors and public intellectuals, as well as academic theorists.[5]

For liberal thinkers, the notion of a global civil society is widely used to describe the proliferation of forms of associational activity and social agency that reach beyond the borders of individual nation-states. The term is conventionally taken to refer to the increasing salience of non-governmental organisations (NGOs) in international political life since the early 1990s. These have, in some cases, become important players in emergent networks of global governance. The transnational focus and activities of other kinds of civil society organisation (CSO), campaigning group and network are also seen by liberals as signs that the associational dynamics of civil society have spread beyond the bounds of the nation-state.[6] A third sense in which this term figures in liberal commentary is as a descriptor of various trans-national public spaces and forums within which, it is suggested, a genuinely global civic culture is developing.

Some important normative claims are advanced by Anglo-American liberals through the ideal of a transnational civil society. For some international theorists, this concept has helped relegitimate the aspirations of moral cosmopolitanism.[7] Moral cosmopolitans have appropriated Kantian theory to suggest that the division of the world into political communities located in distinct national territories represents an artificial carapace blunting the realisation of universalisable moral principles.[8] For many liberals, the notion that individuals possess a bundle of inviolable natural rights irrespective of their national background has remained an important counter-weight to the discourses of realism and liberal nationalism that were prominent in international political life throughout much of the twentieth century. For some contemporary political philosophers, the universalisable character of the principles of right implies that the whole of humanity constitutes the most meaningful moral community.[9] Recent sociopolitical developments are viewed as precursors to an overdue alignment of political realities with moral principle.

This has not, of course, been the prevalent position adopted by Anglophone liberals since the eighteenth century. Most have sought to establish a moral com-

---

[4] For a critical discussion of liberal approaches to global civil society, see Laura Macdonald, 'Globalising Civil Society: Interpreting International NGOs in Central America', *Millennium*, 23: 2 (1994), pp. 267–85.

[5] For instance: Madelaine Albright, *Focus on the Issues: Strengthening Civil Society and the Rule of Law. Excerpts of testimony, speeches and remarks by US Secretary of State Madeleine K. Albright* (Washington, DC, 2000); and Michael De Oliveira, 'The Case for Global Civil Society', *National Civic Review*, 84 (1995), pp. 130–2.

[6] Jan Aart Scholte, 'Global Civil Society', in Ngaire Woods (ed.), *The Political Economy of Globalization* (Basingstoke: Macmillan, 2000), pp. 173–200.

[7] See Nigel Dower, 'The Idea of Global Citizenship – A Sympathetic Assessment', *Global Society*, 14: 4 (2000), pp. 553–67.

[8] See, for instance, Jeremy Waldron, 'Minority Cultures and the Cosmopolitan Alternative', *University of Michigan Journal of Law Reform*, 25 (1992), pp. 751–93.

[9] See the important contributions of, for instance, Charles Beitz, *Political Theory and International Relations* (Princeton, NJ: Princeton University Press, 1999); and Thomas Pogge, *World Poverty and Human Rights: Cosmopolitan Responsibilities and Reforms* (Cambridge: Polity, 2002).

promise between the priority of our obligations to fellow nationals and the duties that our moral beliefs imply that we owe to 'others' beyond the borders of our nation. The philosophical basis of this balancing has varied enormously as disagreement about the basis and scope of political obligation has been a central topic of debate among Anglo-American theorists during this period.[10] Of late, there has been a renewal of liberal theorising about the possibilities and importance of community and ethical life at scales other than the national, and it is against this backdrop that the once marginal cosmopolitan strain of liberalism has been powerfully revived.

Some of the leading moral accounts of the post-Westphalian political order associated with the economic and cultural processes of globalisation echo this cosmopolitan vision. These theorists typically suggest that new forms of social and economic interdependence, developments in communication technologies, and the appearance of relatively autonomous transnational public spaces, have cleared the way for the realisation of an ethos of global citizenship.[11] As nation-states supposedly wane in power and moral authority, the ideal of the world citizen has moved closer to realisation.[12] For such theorists, the state can be expected to 'wither away' as new kinds of transnational political arrangements emerge.

The renewal of moral cosmopolitanism has been enabled by, and has helped legitimate, the idea that a global society, and transnational public spheres, are taking shape irrespective of national borders. While liberal theorists characterise these developments in different ways, a common feature of such theorising is the claim that an inexorable, zero-sum transfer of legitimacy is taking place from the nation-state to the new representatives of global society. This legitimacy claim figures prominently in cosmopolitan thinking.[13] For liberals anxious that the turbo-capitalist global economy is outstripping the regulative capacities of individual states and damaging the long-term interests of peoples and social groups, the development of transnational society is highly significant. Through an analogy with the liberal capitalist state, some liberals suggest that the dynamic and unstable global economy needs to be re-embedded in the social networks and cultures of global society.[14] Various elite actors and decision-makers see in the formation of transnational ties, affiliations and civic spaces, the possibility of plugging the legitimacy deficit facing elite international institutions and decision-making bodies, such as the G7 or WTO. This idea has been politically taken up in moves to incorporate NGOs and other civil society voices in the decision-making processes of these organisations.[15] Liberal actors and commentators are accordingly keen to emphasise the increasing visibility

---

[10] Important contributions to these debates include: David Miller, *On Nationhood* (Oxford: Clarendon Press, 1995), and Andrew Mason, *Community, Solidarity and Belonging: Levels of Community and their Normative Significance* (Cambridge: Cambridge University Press, 2000).

[11] Dower, 'The Idea of Global Citizenship – A Sympathetic Assessment'; and 'Situating Global Citizenship', in Randall Germain and Michael Kenny (eds.), *Global Civil Society: Ethics, Citizenship and Governance* (forthcoming, 2004).

[12] Ronald Lipschutz, 'Reconstructing World Politics: The Emergence of Global Civil Society', *Millennium*, 21: 3 (1992), pp. 389–420, at 392.

[13] For a critical analysis of this legitimacy claim, see Gideon Baker 'Problems in the Theorisation of Global Civil Society', *Political Studies*, 50 (2002), pp. 928–43.

[14] De Oliveira, 'The Case for Global Civil Society'.

[15] See, for instance, John Lloyd, 'The New Deal', *Prospect* (December 2000), pp. 24–8; and Mary Kaldor, ' "Civilising" Globalisation? The Implications of the "Battle in Seattle" ', *Millennium*, 29: 1 (2000), pp. 105–114.

of, and moral authority exercised by, different kinds of non-state actor in, for instance, forums and programmes sponsored by the United Nations. A variety of established NGOs and civil society organisations (CSOs) have been included in significant international negotiations, global crises, and elite decision-making networks. And some have effectively become incorporated into the governance of particular regions and localities, when local state machinery and political elites have either collapsed or become deeply distrusted by such institutions as the IMF.[16] For some commentators, there is a natural synergy between the growing legitimacy of groups in international politics and the emergence of new systems and layers of governance in which state actors are participants with various non-state groups in complex, loosely interlocking networks.[17]

The idea that civil society is integral to the emergent architecture of global governance is a central part of the liberal internationalism favoured by some Western political actors. For liberal political theorists, this idea is yoked together with the claim that transnational civil society represents an important step towards the realisation of established moral truths.[18] Global civil society is, in fact, invoked in two distinct, but related, senses by liberals keen to demonstrate that the principle of right can be justified on a transcultural basis.[19] First, some of its most salient and powerful groups are regarded as important 'carriers' of ideas about universal human rights and freedoms.[20] Their relative autonomy from particular states means that they can introduce such ideas in zones where powerful Western states are regarded with suspicion. Thomas Risse provides a compelling account of the role of leading NGOs within the virtuous circles that he locates at the heart of struggles for democratisation in Latin America during the 1980s.[21] Many CSOs have, indeed, become highly adept at orchestrating international opinion and pressurising Western, as well as non-Western states, on human rights and environmental issues. For some Anglo-American liberals, lodged within the heart of this kind of transnational interchange is an inexorable expansion of moral community beyond the nation-state, a process that is, for some, synonymous with the increasing acquiescence by states to the conventions, laws and global institutions that promote liberal ideas of human rights.

A second liberal argument about global civil society and the nature of moral community is also salient. This turns upon the conviction that, as Alexis de Tocqueville argued about the United States in the eighteenth century, secondary

---

[16] Scholte 'Global Civil Society'.

[17] See, for instance, the Report of the Commission on Global Governance, *Our Global Neighbourhood* (Oxford: Oxford University Press, 1995); and T. G. Wiess and L. Gordenker (eds.), *NGOs, the UN and Global Governance* (Boulder, CO: Lynne Rienner, 1996).

[18] Dower, 'The Idea of Global Citizenship'.

[19] For a critical discussion of different liberal philosophical attempts to establish such a norm, see David Miller and Cecile Fabre, 'Justice and Culture: Rawls, Sen, Nussbaum and O'Neill', *Political Studies Review*, 1 (2003), pp. 4–17.

[20] See Diane Otto, 'Nongovernmental Organizations in the United Nations System; the Emerging Role of International Civil Society', *Human Rights Quarterly*, 18 (1996), pp. 197–241.

[21] Risse, 'The Power of Norms versus the Norms of Power: Transnational Civil Society and Human Rights', in A. Florini (ed.), *The Third Force: The Rise of Transnational Civil Society* (Tokyo/Washington DC: Japan Center for International Exchange and Carnegie Endowment for International Peace, 2000), pp. 177–209.

associations are the bulwarks of a democratic order because of their potential as 'schools of civic virtue'.[22] This approach, which has been powerfully revived within recent American liberal theory, has been deployed to suggest that transnational civil society is enabling the achievement of a sense of citizenship that spans national boundaries. It draws attention, above all, to the civic dispositions and attributes appropriate to the practice and status of citizenship, and to the particular kinds of moral learning and affective solidarity promoted in associational life. The 'morality of association', for liberal political theorists, provides a crucible within which the dispositions and character required of liberal citizens takes shape.[23]

These different understandings have, over the last decade, been developed by liberal theorists and, in a more rudimentary but powerful vernacular, by strategic thinkers and planners in the World Bank, IMF and WTO.[24] The notion that deeply entrenched moral, cultural, and ethnic differences might be offset by the establishment of ties of trust and the discovery of common values, which global society promises, is likely to become a popular motif among liberal intellectuals following the new wave of geopolitical conflicts that erupted in world politics on, and after, 11 September 2001.

Evaluating liberal arguments

Perhaps the most familiar critical reaction to these ideas comes from those who see in them an attempt to project the ideals associated with Western, and specifically American, democracy as the universal future of mankind.[25] Some critics have linked the projection of the merits of a global civil society with the Anglo-American assertion of the superiority of Western conceptions of human rights, seeing these as ideological devices designed to justify a new period of American geopolitical domination. But critics are wrong to see liberalism as inherently insensitive to differences of moral perspective, cultural tradition and social identity. The challenges posed by cultural diversity and moral disagreement have been placed centre-stage in Anglophone liberal philosophy in the last twenty years.[26] Moreover, the individualistic bias that its critics lament has been countered by pluralist and communitarian attempts to reintroduce into liberal thinking a greater commitment to the plurality of ends

---

[22] For a perceptive discussion of the continuing influence of de Tocqueville's understanding of the democratic potential of secondary associations, see Mark Warren, *Democracy and Association* (Princeton, NJ: Princeton University Press, 2001).

[23] These arguments are critically reviewed in Michael Kenny, *The Politics of Identity* (Cambridge: Polity Press, forthcoming 2004).

[24] Steven Hopgood, 'Reading the Small Print in Global Civil Society: the Inexorable Hegemony of the Liberal Self', *Millennium*, 29: 1 (2000), pp. 1–25; and Tom Young, ' "A Project to be Realised": Global Liberalism and Contemporary Africa', *Millennium*, 24: 3 (1995), pp. 527–46.

[25] Young, 'A Project to be Realised'.

[26] See, for instance, John Rawls, *Political Liberalism* (New York: Columbia University Press, 1993); Will Kymlicka, *Liberalism, Community and Culture* (Oxford: Oxford University Press, 1989); Iris Marion Young, *Justice and the Politics of Difference* (Princeton, NJ: Princeton University Press, 1990); and Charles Taylor, 'The Politics of Recognition', in A.Gutmann (ed.), *Multiculturalism: Examining the Politics of Recognition* (Princeton, NJ: Princeton University Press), pp. 25–73.

that persons and groups hold dear, as well as a sense of the constitutive value of social solidarity.[27]

Similarly, the idea that global civil society only makes sense against the backdrop of a form of Enlightenment liberalism that posits all non-liberal cultures and practices as irrational and backward, ignores the importance of ongoing disagreements about the epistemological and ethical foundations of liberalism.[28] It also overlooks the major rift that has opened in Anglophone political theory between those seeking to emphasise liberalism's 'Reformation' character as opposed to its Enlightenment heritage. The former invokes liberalism as a doctrine that offered principled and peaceful terms of coexistence in contexts where groups were prepared to engage in murderous conflict over rival theological beliefs.[29] Various liberal philosophers claim to have separated liberalism from 'Enlightenment' commitments to what John Rawls termed the comprehensive doctrines of autonomy and individuality.[30] Whether liberal political theory, and any particular liberal culture, can evade the heritage of the Enlightenment entirely, remains a controversial philosophical question. But the justification of liberalism offered by 'political liberals' – in terms of the establishment of principles of social cooperation that draw upon a range of 'reasonable', comprehensive, moral perspectives in diverse societies – has become a leading position in Anglophone liberal political thought. In the wake of these debates, there have emerged various accounts of both domestic and international civil society that give a greater accent to the plurality of 'reasonable', non-liberal values and purposes that associational membership promotes.[31] Indeed, the claim that global civil society can *only* be advanced in respect of a particular brand of Enlightenment liberalism has drawn attention away from other normative difficulties lodged within the arguments of liberal cosmopolitans. In particular, two contentious normative claims arise from liberal proclamations of global civil society.

Global democracy?

It has become increasingly familiar for liberals to suggest that with the generation of transnational networks of social and political activism, the politicisation of questions

---

[27] Among the various recent pluralist interpretations of liberalism, see George Crowder, *Liberalism and Value Pluralism* (London: Routledge, 2002); John Kekes, *The Morality of Pluralism* (Princeton, NJ: Princeton University Press, 2001); and Charles Larmore, *Patterns of Moral Complexity* (Cambridge: Cambridge University Press, 1987). For a discussion of the turn towards the themes of civic unity and social solidarity in recent liberal political theory, see Will Kymlicka and Wayne Norman, 'Citizenship in Culturally Diverse Societies: Issues, Contexts, Concepts', in Will Kymlicka and Wayne Norman (eds.), *Citizenship in Diverse Societies* (Oxford: Oxford University Press, 2000), pp. 1–41.

[28] This critical reaction has been enunciated, in terms of global civil society, by Young, 'A Project to be Realised'; and M.K.Pasha and D.L.Blaney 'Elusive Paradism: the Promise and Peril of Global Civil Society', *Alternatives*, 23 (1998), pp. 417–60.

[29] See, for instance, William Galston, *Liberal Purposes: Goods, Virtues, and Diversity in the Liberal State* (Cambridge: Cambridge University Press, 1991); and Rawls, *Political Liberalism*, p. xxv.

[30] Rawls, *Political Liberalism*, pp. 48–86.

[31] See, for instance, Percy Lehning, 'Towards a Multicultural Civil Society: The Role of Social Capital and Democratic Citizenship', *Government and Opposition*, 33: 1 (1998), pp. 221–42; and Nancy Rosenblum, 'Civil Societies: Liberalism and the Moral Uses of Pluralism', *Social Research*, 61: 3 (1994), pp. 539–62.

with a strongly international dimension, and the emergence of networks of global governance, the dynamics of liberal democracy have shifted from the nation-state to transnational levels of political life. One version of this argument posits a transnational civil order as a necessary step towards the creation of a democratic global polity. On this view, transnational civil society acts as a *necessary* spur to global democratisation.[32]

Is it axiomatic, however, that the growing standing and moral authority of NGOs in international politics and society represents a step down the path to a democratic global polity? Various observers note the lack of transparency and accountability that belie the idea of these organisations as agents of democracy.[33] Moreover, the groups that have become salient in global society are themselves reflections of structurally entrenched imbalances in power, resource and access between North and South. Were human rights groups, for instance, rather than states, to be deployed as agencies that monitored and enforced particular states' treatment of their peoples' rights, the question of how to ensure their accountability, transparency and openness to different cultural perspectives would in some respects be much harder to address than is the case with state actors bound by internationally ratified agreements that reflect the formal equality of nations.[34] The particular geographic concentration and inequitable standing of various international campaigns and organisations reinforces, as much as it offsets, the lack of representation of the world's most marginalised and oppressed communities.[35]

Liberal models of global civil society tend to take the marked inequalities of resource and influence among civil society actors as a social given. Echoing earlier radical arguments, Neera Chandhoke observes the tendency of liberal theorists to promote the ideal of civil society in the image of particular kinds of non-political groups.[36] Much the same is true of the ideal of global civil society. According to the neoliberal consensus that has become prevalent within various global institutions, respectable NGOs that help legitimate the ideal of 'good governance' and the virtues of unregulated markets, need to be distinguished from other kinds of civil society organisation and campaigning group. The latter, Chandhoke suggests, are viewed from the heights of the new global order as 'problems that have to be resolved through managerial techniques'.[37]

Liberal approaches to civil society that privilege the moral value of associational freedom, prior to the duties and obligations that equal citizens owe to each other, tend to overlook the inequalities that shape group activities. Thus, the hierarchies that commentators observe among, and within, international civil society organisations are frequently absent from liberal accounts. So too is the fraught question of

---

[32] The prevalence of this linkage is critically discussed in Petr Kopecky, 'Civil Society, Uncivil Society and Contentious Politics', in Kopecky and Cas Mudde (eds.), *Contentious Politics in Eastern Europe* (London: Routledge, 2002).

[33] Scholte, 'Global Civil Society'.

[34] These issues are discussed in Baker, 'Problems in the Theorisation of Global Civil Society', pp. 934–6.

[35] The geographical concentration of NGOs and international CSOs is well documented in the first two volumes of the *Global Civil Society Yearbook*: Anheier, Glasius and Kaldor (eds.), *Global Civil Society 2001*; and Glasius, Kaldor, and Anheier (eds.), *Global Civil Society 2002* (Oxford: Oxford University Press, 2002).

[36] Chandhoke, 'The Limits of Global Civil Society'.

[37] Ibid., p. 54.

how civil society organisations relate to the constituencies in whose name they speak. As Chandhoke remarks, 'Associational activity at the global level tends therefore to acquire a life of its own, a life that is quite distinct from the everyday lives of the people who do not speak but who are spoken for'.[38] As organisations feel the pressure to adopt increasingly specialised forms of expertise and professionalised modes of operation, they are ever more likely to distance themselves from the daily lives and experiences of their social constituents. From this critical perspective, the neo-Tocquevillian idea of a transnational political society arising from the trust, goodwill and peaceful interactions spread by groups, represents a mystification of unyielding social realities. For this Tocquevillian picture to be plausible at transnational scales of operation, a much greater variety of associational groupings, and some kind of equality of standing between them, would be necessary.

Global citizenship?

A different interpretation of the ethical character of global society is favoured by some liberal cosmopolitans. This arises from the idea that the associational activities that increasingly stretch beyond national borders are contributing to the social realisation of the truth that the virtues of democratic citizenship derive from universal moral principles. This argument is advanced in two distinct forms.

1. *Groups as world citizens*. One version of the cosmopolitan argument for world citizenship advances the idea that it might be possible to treat NGOs as informal representatives of the global demos in a putative world legislature.[39] This idea remains troubling in several respects. Does it make sense, David Miller asks, to treat as citizens collectivities that are established to pursue particular group purposes, compete over resources, or pursue sectional interests?[40] Groups, he suggests, are unlikely to possess the will or capacity to deliberate, like individual citizens, in ways designed to evoke common moral values and shared interests. Civil society organisations are appealing, in part because they act in ways unlike individual citizens who need to learn the arts of compromise and restraint in their deliberative engagements.[41]

Other objections to the conversion of NGOs into political representatives also raise doubts about the democratic potentiality of this idea. What kinds of procedures can ensure that groups actively represent the communities from which they emerge, or the constituencies and interests on whose behalf they speak? Commentators have commonly observed the absence of internal mechanisms of accountability and the hier-

---

[38] Ibid., p. 46.
[39] For a useful critical discussion of this idea, see Kimberley Hutchings, 'The Idea of International Citizenship', in Hutchings and Roland Dannreuther (eds.), *Cosmopolitan Citizenship* (Basingstoke: Macmillan, 1998), pp. 113–34.
[40] David Miller, 'Bounded Citizenship', in Hutchings and Dannreuther (eds.), *Cosmopolitan Citizenship*, pp. 60–79.
[41] On the various, non-democratic purposes and methods of groups in democratic society, see Nancy Rosenblum, *Membership and Morals: the Personal Uses of Pluralism in America* (Princeton, NJ: Princeton University Press, 1995).

archical character of many international campaigns and NGOs.[42] And, in normative terms, there is an inherent difficulty with a representative model if these representatives have only sporadic access to, and influence upon, policymaking at a global level.

2. *The telos of global citizenship.* The idea of groups as citizens is only one manifestation of the cosmopolitan liberal claim that global citizenship is advancing with the rise of transnational civil society. Some liberal thinkers stress the variety of opportunities and activities that are enabling many citizens to experience a wider sense of moral community.[43] Three particular social trends assume significance in such arguments – computer mediated technological developments that permit individuals to share information and deliberate with others, unhindered by constraints of time and space; the rise of a global media system that encourages new kinds of inter-dependency and mutual understanding; and the increasing propensity for groups and individuals to take part in forms of collective action that span national borders.

These are all undoubtedly significant kinds of activity that are growing in frequency and, possibly, political effect. But their meanings are more ethically ambiguous than teleological cosmopolitanism assumes. In particular, some of the most visible instances of transnational collective action and protest in recent years have used new technologies to advance a profound distrust of cosmopolitan values. Rapidly co-ordinated protest campaigns against, for instance, the Iraq War of 2003, typically invoke ideas of national sovereignty and self-determination as much as an ethos of global fraternity or citizenship.

The teleological outlook of moral cosmopolitanism leaves its adherents prone to overstate the significance and inexorability of the shift from community at the national to the global level.[44] The tendency to read social, political and cultural developments through the prior conviction that a universal morality is already latent in the world can generate implausibly benign and overconfident accounts of global society. The shift towards a moral and political awareness of the global plane of human existence in fact generates moral dilemmas and paradoxical reactions that teleological cosmopolitanism ignores. Among these are the revival of forms of political identity founded upon regional, national and/or ethnic forms of belonging. Global citizenship is one 'rational' response to globalisation, but the search for meaning and identity through the politics of ethnic purity or national exclusivity makes as much political and economic sense to many. It may well be the case that the interests of individual citizens are increasingly affected by processes and decisions taken beyond the state, and that the exercise of political autonomy requires some say in these decisions.[45] Yet many citizens and theorists remain convinced that in an economic order characterised by such uncertainty and rapidity of change, the best way in which to pursue individual and group interests is to exert an impact at those political levels at which one has a reasonable hope of making a difference, and to ensure that perceived threats and alien 'others' are kept out of one's locality or

---

[42] Scholte, 'Global Civil Society'; Chandhoke, 'The Limits of Global Civil Society'.
[43] Dower, 'The Idea of Global Citizenship – A Sympathetic Assessment'; and 'Situating Global Citizenship'.
[44] See Hutchings, *International Political Theory*.
[45] This position is developed in David Held, *Democracy in the Global Order* (Cambridge: Polity, 1995).

nation. While global civil society can plausibly be adduced to support one of the premises of arguments for global citizenship – that it is a mistake to regard our ethical obligations as exhausted by membership of bounded political communities, the further claim that it embodies the advance of world citizenship is less convincing.

Subalternist approaches

In his essay on the rival conceptions of civil society in modern European thought, Charles Taylor observes the popularisation of the notion that this is the domain in which unimpeded communication and authentic communal relations flourish.[46] To this observation we may add the more recent tendency to invoke transnational civil society as a quasi-unitary actor that advances the sovereign will of the global demos against the machinations and manipulation of corrupt political elites and self-serving bureaucracies. Taylor suggests that the origins of such ideas can be traced back as far as the seventeenth century, to John Locke's account of civil society as a 'sphere of independent self-regulation by spontaneously associating groups'.[47] This dream is at the heart of recent accounts that regard civil association as a haven of progressive social mobilisation; and hence as an alternative source of political dynamism and moral vision to the compromised world of conventional politics.[48] Such ideas have been powerfully revived through the radical conception of a global civil society that is taking shape freed from the malign influence of political and corporate elites. In this rendition, the civil society ideal offers both a source of radical political inspiration and profound scepticism about politics itself.

Two particular claims are advanced through the subalternist reading of global society. The first suggests that social mobilisation and political rebellion constitute its authentic core, as opposed to liberal cosmopolitan interpretations that stress the importance of rights, law and global governance.[49] This radical interpretation has gained considerable ground due to the hopes raised by various mass protests held at meetings of the G7, the WTO and the IMF in recent years.[50] As the American author Elaine Bernard argued following the protests against the WTO at Seattle, the international advocacy networks through which these were organised were of long-term significance because they offered a 'forum for debating, negotiating and deliberating global solidarity'. These, she and others suggest, represent the glimmerings of an emerging international civil society that 'provides space for the development of public values, and is the process by which a public self, or citizenry, is created'.[51]

---

[46] Charles Taylor, 'Invoking Civil Society', in Taylor, *Philosophical Arguments* (Cambridge, MA/London: Harvard University Press, 1995), pp. 204–23.

[47] Taylor, 'Invoking Civil Society', p. 209.

[48] Ibid., pp. 217–19.

[49] See Baker, 'Problems in the Theorisation of Global Civil Society'.

[50] Judith Garber, 'The Public Sphere and the Antiglobalization Protests', *The Good Society*, 10: 2 (2001), pp. 16–20.

[51] Cited in Mark Rupert, *Ideologies of Globalization: Contending Visions of a New World Order* (London: Routledge, 2000), p. 152.

The leading 'organic intellectual' of this subalternist conception of global civil society is Richard Falk. In his writings, a reactive, different kind of globalisation is now taking shape 'from below'.[52] This is emerging through the struggles and ideas generated by indigenous movements of resistance as well as cosmopolitan campaigns for human rights, that are all aimed at displacing the established, neoliberal project of globalisation 'from above'.

Interpretations from this paradigm emphasise the carving out of new channels and spaces by movements and protest coalitions, and the exchange of ideas and information among these.[53] Some authors see the prototype for these activities in earlier social movements that reached beyond the borders of the states that contained them. The contacts forged between networks of peace activists during the 1980s led to the construction of a European movement for Nuclear Disarmament which opened up a transnational space founded upon a distinctive political identity – as European peaceniks opposed to both sides in the Cold War.[54] More recently, the internationally conscious and technologically up-to-date Zapatistas figure prominently as exemplars of subaltern forces engaged in indigenous struggle as well as innovative, transnational forms of communicative expression.[55]

A second, distinctive normative feature of subalternist arguments is their commitment to the intrinsic virtues of the unconventional and dynamic character of social mobilisation. This idea has been advanced through a counter-opposition between the spontaneous and organic character of social mobilisation 'from below', and the legalistic and statist assumptions that are taken to be central to the liberal vision of international society. In several recent accounts, much has been made of the purportedly subversive character of forces that do not respect the binary conceptual distinctions – 'inside/outside', or the national/international – that have been central to liberal conceptions of international politics.[56] Gideon Baker provides a challenging version of these arguments when he contrasts 'the standpoint of global civil society' to the inadequacies of arguments for cosmopolitan democracy.[57] He echoes R.B.J. Walker in suggesting that, despite appearances, cosmopolitan liberalism merely extends the model of liberal democracy to the global level, rather than breaking from its legalism and statism.[58] Falk has influenced many with his argument that at the heart of the various protests, struggles and alternative programmes animating opposition to the neoliberal project of globalisation, a 'law of humanity' is immanent.

---

[52] Falk, *On Humane Governance; Toward a New Global Politics* (Cambridge: Polity, 1995); 'Global Civil Society: Perspectives, Initiatives, Movements', *Oxford Development Studies*, 26: 1 (1998), pp. 99–110; and Joseph Camilleri and Falk, *The End of Sovereignty* (London: Edward Elgar, 1992).

[53] Macdonald, 'Globalising Civil Society: Interpreting International NGOs in Central America', *Millennium*, 23: 2 (1994), pp. 267–85.

[54] Mary Kaldor, 'Transnational Civil Society', in T.Dunne and N.J.Wheeler (eds.), *Human Rights in Global Politics* (Cambridge: Cambridge University Press, 1999), pp. 195–213.

[55] See, for instance, Baker, 'Problems in the Theorisation of Global Civil Society', pp. 941–2.

[56] This deconstructionist approach is developed in R.B.J. Walker, *Inside/Outside: International Relations as Political Theory* (Cambridge: Cambridge University Press, 1993). An important source for these ideas is post-colonial theory, for instance: Gayatri Spivak, *A Critique of Postcolonial Reason: Towards a History of the Vanishing Present* (Cambridge, MA/London: Harvard University Press, 1999).

[57] Baker, 'Problems in the Theorisation of Global Civil Society'.

[58] Walker, 'Social Movements/World Politics', *Millennium,* 23: 3 (1994), pp. 669–700.

Global society and the politics of resistance

Thinkers who subscribe to this kind of position see the social dynamics and political rebellions of the transnational society that is being forged 'from below' as signs of a new ethos of resistance in global politics. Resistance movements forge agendas that are informed by, and in turn influence, the ambitions of other indigenous struggles. From these subaltern interchanges, there arises a confidence in the possibility of a counter-attack upon neoliberal globalisation. A profound political challenge and alternative morality is discerned by some radicals within those groups and campaigns opposed to multinational capitalism in general, and free trade in particular.[59] This constellation of protests has raised the hope that one outcome of 'globalisation from below' will be the promotion of a coherent social dynamic capable of taming neoliberal globalisation.

Such readings are typically presented as the antithesis to mainstream liberal approaches to international society.[60] In at least one respect, however, they provide their echo. This arises from the underlying assumption that it is in civil society that authentic self-assertion occurs and identity is established. This chimes with the liberal idea that civil society should be insulated from the worlds of bureaucratic control, constitutional guarantee and political deliberation. Subalternists differ from liberals both in their appropriation of the emancipatory readings of civil society that were popularised by leftist intellectuals in the 1980s, and in their particular idealisation of social movements.[61] These emphases underlie the belief that the genesis of a global civil society must signal a progressive shift in the balance of social forces within the current world order.

The particular faith placed in social movement is an important, and contentious, aspect of this argument. In particular, the propensity to read very different kinds of social mobilisation as the authors of a coherent set of moral beliefs is problematic. This is partly because these forces are usually associated with the dissemination of a multiplicity of ideas, rather than a singular oppositional ethos.[62] As Nicholas Onuf suggests, even when particular movements develop sufficient dynamism and strength to escape the limitations of their particular state, and to promote particular values more widely, they are unlikely to distil an ordered ideological alternative.[63] The social movements of modernity, and in particular those that rise, fragment and recombine with quite dizzying alacrity – in what Manuel Castells terms the age of

---

[59] See, for instance, the essays collected in the special issue of *New Political Economy*, edited by Barry Gills: 'Globalisation and the Politics of Resistance', 2: 1 (1997).

[60] Macdonald, 'Globalising Civil Society'; and Baker, 'Problems in the Theorisation of Global Civil Society'.

[61] These political readings of civil society are thoughtfully discussed by one of the leading scholarly proponents of this theme: John Keane, *Civil Society: Old Images, New Visions* (Cambridge: Polity, 1998).

[62] This theme is elaborated by one of the leading historians of social movements: Charles Tilly, 'Models and Realities of Popular Collective Action', *Social Research,* 52: 4 (1985), pp. 717–47; and 'Social Movements as Historically Specific Clusters of Political Performances', *Berkeley Journal of Sociology*, 39: (1994), pp. 1–30.

[63] Nicholas Onuf, *The Republican Legacy in International Thought* (Cambridge: Cambridge University Press, 1998). For a similar argument in relation to anti-globalisation politics, see Fred Halliday, 'Getting Real about Seattle', *Millennium*, 29: 1 (2000), pp. 123–29.

informational capitalism[64] – are inherently mercurial: 'They mutate, combine and dissolve. If they survive their protean tendencies, then they suffer another fate ...'.[65] The ethical dimensions of these social and political forces are typically mediated through the influence of intellectuals and parties, and are rarely as unambiguous, or as novel, as subalternist commentary implies.

Opposition to neoliberal ideas about globalisation emerges from a host of moral and political vantage points, a fact that has belied efforts to construct a singular social movement opposed to it. When Falk argues that a new ethical paradigm is immanent within the forces seeking a humane alternative to neoliberal globalisation, he overlooks the problem that many of the values he deems central to this project are anathema to other groups and traditions also opposed to Western globalisation.[66] This resistance narrative, as much as its liberal counterpart, neglects the challenges posed by moral pluralisation and cultural diversity in the context of global society. These issues are illustrated by the increasingly intense conflicts generated by the attempts of Western-based groups to present human rights and environmentalist concerns as 'trumps' that override the concerns and beliefs emanating from non-liberal cultures, and the resistance such claims generate.

Subalternist approaches to civil society can be contrasted with a broad European intellectual tradition that posits this domain as one in which ineradicable differences – of belief, identity and interest – are located. An important watershed, in this regard, was established in the history of Western thought during the late eighteenth century in the work of leading political economists – Adam Ferguson and Adam Smith above all. These thinkers advanced upon the Lockean distinction between natural and civil society, drawing a distinction between the spheres of legitimate governmental and legal authority, on the one hand, and the semi-public arenas in which associational freedom is exercised, on the other.[67] Various social sites were seen as the domain where virtues were instilled – the 'habits of the heart' charted by de Tocqueville in his magisterial study of American society – and also where commercial activity flourished.[68] The idea that economic activity and civil association were intertwined was taken up by some of the leading nineteenth- and twentieth-century theorists of civil society – Hegel and Marx included.[69] Though they differed in many respects, some of the major thinkers who deployed this term favoured an understanding of civil society as an arena in which there co-exist antagonistic interests and moral perspectives.

Re-engaging with this heritage suggests that the apparently transparent references to the ethical significance of transnational civil society offered by cosmopolitan

---

[64] Castells, *The Information Age*, vol. I: *The Rise of the Network Society*; and vol. II: *The Power of Identity* (Malden, MA/Oxford: Blackwell, 1997).

[65] Onuf, *The Republican Legacy in International Thought*, p. 278.

[66] Falk, *On Humane Governance*, p. 113.

[67] Andrew Lively and Jack Reeve, 'The Emergence of the Idea of Civil Society: the Artificial Political Order and Natural Social Orders', *Democratization*, 4: 1 (1997), pp. 68–80; and Keane (ed.), *Civil Society and the State: New European Perspectives* (London: Verso, 1988).

[68] Alexis de Tocqueville, *Democracy in America* (New York: Harper & Row, 1969); Adam Seligman, *The Idea of Civil Society* (Princeton, NJ: Princeton University Press, 1995).

[69] See, for instance, Robert Fine, 'Civil Society Theory, Enlightenment and Critique', *Democratization*, 4: 1 (1997), pp. 7–28; and Adam Seligman, *The Idea of Civil Society* (Princeton, NJ: Princeton University Press, 1995).

liberals and subalternists should be regarded with some scepticism. The tendency of both to approach transnational society with a simple moral hierarchy of groups in mind – with NGOs at the apex for liberals, and protest networks for radicals – implies a rather narrow, distorting reading of this domain. Other observers note the sheer variety of agencies, and the different cultural, economic and political purposes, that shape social and civic enterprises of a transnational kind.[70] Only by filtering out a vast number of groupings can the cosmopolitan and resistance readings of civil society be sustained.[71] Their exclusion from the interpretations offered by these perspectives not only diminishes understanding of the complex character of transnational publics and groups, but also limits the purchase of their ethical accounts of global society. Economic actors have played a role as carriers of liberal values, and as the providers of infrastructural developments on which NGOs and pressure groups have relied. Powerful socioeconomic interests have campaigned for free-trade agreements, and have joined both sides of the argument about the merits of state controls over the movement of capital.[72] As well as the personnel of aid agencies or NGOs, corporate giants constitute the face of global civil society that many people living in some of the poorest countries are likely to encounter. Accounts of civil society that filter out the commercial and economic aspects of civil association, and stress only a limited range of civic or radical activities, occlude recognition of the power dynamics and social relations that shape associational life. Without attention to these, we easily lose sight of the discrepancies of power, influence and voice that civil society necessarily involves.[73]

Towards a liberal-republican approach

An important question arises from this argument: can the ethical and political implications of global civil society be meaningfully addressed outside these paradigms? Or, are ethical nationalists right to suggest that global civil society is a hubristic fantasy dreamed up by metropolitan intellectuals? This is a large question, with important moral and intellectual ramifications. In the remainder of this article, I offer one particular pathway into the tangle of issues it signals, and ask whether a broadly liberal-republican sensibility offers a more promising basis from which to reflect upon the social developments and moral relationships pertinent to transnational civil society. Republicanism appears at first sight an inappropriate source in relation to the idea of an ethical life beyond national borders. Yet this is an internally diverse intellectual lineage, I will suggest, that offers some fascinating and useful intellectual resources to those considering the character of transnational public spaces, the importance of international civil association and the problematic of legitimacy in relation to emergent political authority.

---

[70] Keane, 'Global Civil Society?', in Anheier, Glasius and Kaldor (eds.), *Global Civil Society 2001*, pp. 23–50.

[71] A similar perspective is offered in Robert Fine and Shirin Rai, 'Understanding Civil Society: A Preface', *Democratization*, 4: 1 (1997), pp. 1–6.

[72] The ideological aspects of these struggles are captured in Rupert, *Ideologies of Globalization*.

[73] Macdonald, 'Globalising Civil Society'.

The republican legacy

For some political theorists, the idea that the insights of this tradition are applicable at a scale of social interaction greater than the nation-state is troubling.[74] A political community, republicans tend to argue, needs clearly demarcated boundaries separating outsiders from insiders in order that the mutuality required for democratic citizenship is achievable, and so that a viable sense of political identity can be established.[75] Many republican theorists have been cautious about the possibility of establishing a political community in territories that are too large or culturally diverse. This concern underpins a valid objection to one supposed projection of republican ideas beyond the national domain – the utopian fantasy of a singular global republic governed by a world government, in which states and nations have withered away.[76] While there are, as Onuf suggests, more overlaps between republican and cosmopolitan ideas than conventional demarcations in political thought suggest, this is a project that remains substantially out of kilter with the basic tenets of different strands of modern republicanism.[77]

The implausibility of this particular model, and its dubious republican heritage, should not be taken to imply that republican thinking is inherently inapplicable or inappropriate as a framework for conceiving ethical and political relationships beyond the world of states. Two grounds for justifying the deployment of republican themes in relation to transnational developments are especially promising. The first stems from the genealogy of this tradition. Modern republicanism represents an abridgement of several different intellectual lineages that have their roots in periods prior to the establishment of the nation-state.[78] Republicans have disagreed about the particular scale that provides the optimal framework for political community, with a variety of candidates being promoted – among them the city-states of Ancient Greece, the republics of Renaissance Italy and the cantons of eighteenth-century Geneva. Rather than conceiving republicanism as committed to any particular scale(s) over others, however, its interpretative legacy is better postulated in terms of a generic tendency to pose questions about what constitute the limits and conditions – such as scale, territorial size and boundaries – for a political community to prosper as a 'free state'.[79] As leading historians of the republican tradition, such as Quentin Skinner and John Pocock have shown, the answers supplied by republicans from different national contexts and in historical periods, often involved discussion of the character of the public spaces, political institutions

---

[74] See, for instance, Miller, *On Nationhood*; and Maurizio Viroli, *Republicanism* (London: Holt, 2002).

[75] Adrian Oldfield, *Citizenship and Community: Civic Republicanism and the Modern World* (London: Routledge, 1990).

[76] Such a vision enjoys a lengthy pedigree in modern Western thought. See the discussion of these ideas in Derek Heater, *World Citizenship* (London: Continuum, 2002).

[77] Onuf, *The Republican Legacy in International Thought*.

[78] See the seminal historical studies by: J.G.A.Pocock, *The Machiavellian Moment: Florentine Political Thought and the Atlantic Republican Tradition* (Princeton, NJ/London: Princeton University Press, 1975); Quentin Skinner, *Liberty before Liberalism* (Cambridge University Press: Cambridge, 1998); and Viroli, *Republicanism*.

[79] On the conception of the 'free state' in neo-Roman republicanism, see Quentin Skinner, *Machiavelli* (Oxford: Oxford University Press, 1981); and *Liberty before Liberalism*.

and constitutional mechanisms that propagate a sense of public duty among citizens, and promote the exercise of individual liberty.[80] In contemporary terms, such a focus suggests an alternative perspective upon the 'problematic' of global citizenship. Rather than seeking to locate the figure of the world citizen in the realms of moral philosophy, or in heroic moments of resistance to globalisation, adherents of this approach enjoin us to consider the civic possibilities bound up in the expansion of institutional structures, legal frameworks, and a shared political culture, beyond the boundaries of the nation-state. In contemporary terms, this implies the kind of normative project proposed by some 'political' cosmopolitans, and by those, like Jürgen Habermas, who advocate the merits of a postnational citizenship in relation to regionally constituted spaces like the European Union.[81] Liberal-republicanism leads us to ask whether these developments are sufficiently embedded, legitimate and stable to sustain the relationships and roles that we might plausibly conceive as conducive to the ideals and practice of global citizenship.

These themes in republican discourse are especially pertinent for contemporary theorising since this lineage was once an important influence upon the ways in which Western liberalism conceived the character of international life. Nicholas Onuf identifies republican liberalism as a leading liberal variant.[82] It contributed important and influential insights into the character and purposes of politics prior to the world of states. Above all, it offered to modern liberalism the idea that human association is what makes society possible. As Onuf illustrates, the assignation of the republican lineage to the domestic, *as opposed to* the international, arena reflects a particular, recent phase in its historical evolution.[83] He observes too the combination in some brands of republican thinking of intellectual elements that contemporary liberal philosophy tends to separate and keep apart – a sense of the value of locally grounded centres of civic activism and a heightened sense of cosmopolitan aspiration: 'the twinned concern for the local and the universal is a republican legacy'.[84] This aspect of the republican heritage is well represented in the work of scholarly analyses that illustrate how globally constituted norms have worked their ways into, and alter the character of, the fabric of locally constituted struggles for power and resource. This process is ably documented in Risse's discussion of the appeal of Latin American NGOs to internationally recognised norms and principles.[85] Considered as a multiple lineage that has developed through a series of interwoven, but separable, phases, republicanism appears replete with different insights into the dilemmas and possibilities of political community beyond the world of states. These can be translated, in contemporary terms, into a set of distinctive normative questions for those considering the uneven formation of transnational networks and relations signalled by the concept of global civil society.

---

[80] Skinner, *Liberty before Liberalism*; and Pocock, *The Machiavellian Moment*.

[81] Held, *Democracy in the Global Order*; Habermas, *Post-National Constellations* (Cambridge: Polity, 2001; and *The Inclusion of the Other: Studies in Political Theory* (Cambridge, MA: MIT Press, 1998). See also Klaus Eder and Berhard Giesen (eds.), *European Citizenship: between National Legacies and Postnational Projects* (Oxford: Oxford University Press, 2001).

[82] Onuf, *The Republican Legacy in International Thought*, p. 2.

[83] Ibid., p. 6.

[84] Ibid., p. 18.

[85] Risse, 'The Power of Norms'.

Republicanism is also, as Taylor suggests, one source of a rather different tradition of theorising about civil society.[86] This too has exercised an important pull upon liberalism. In his overview of the main rival visions of civil society in modern European thought, he contrasts those thinkers who have, since at least John Locke, regarded an independent civil society as prior to, and independent of, the constraints upon individual liberty represented by the state and the law, on the one hand, and a continuing counter-tradition to which republican thinkers contributed, on the other. The latter argues that the emergence of a democratic society is guaranteed by the prior achievement of a particular kind of political and constitutional order. As opposed to the classical liberal ideal that counter-opposes the exercise of individual liberty to the duties of the citizen, liberal republicanism suggests a more intertwined relationship between political institutions, citizenship and freedom. Hegel's conception of the partiality and moral insufficiency of civil society in relation to citizenship was blended with a complex account of the ethical significance of the moral lessons learned through the roles, offices and statuses of associational life.[87] Such an approach suggests the merits of an analytical focus upon the significance and character of the various forms of interconnectedness and cooperative enterprise that shape transnational social life. Approaching global politics through this republican lens would, for instance, lend emphasis to the importance of fostering forms of social interaction that are likely to promote some of the values – trust, reciprocity, self-respect and civility, most notably – congruent with a *democratically orientated* global society. Such a domain implies the acceptance of a set of shared basic political and moral values that undergird the ethos of peaceful coexistence with those whose culture, ethnicity and religious outlook are radically different. Republican forms of liberalism, in other words, promote an awareness of the dynamics of interdependence *and* separation that shape the state-society relationship.[88] For Hegel, the rights and duties we possess as citizens build upon those implied by our status as members of civil society.[89] States have thus been vital agencies serving the common interests of citizens, providing a legitimate agency capable of mediating social conflicts and offering remedies for socioeconomic inequalities.

In terms of the democratic potential of a putative transnational society, re-acquaintance with this lineage reminds us of the limitations of 'classical' liberal positions, such as the idea that society and state are morally antithetical. In the context of global society, we should wonder whether it is appropriate to consider the growth of the social capital and political influence of civil society actors as necessarily resulting in a loss of authority and power for states, as liberals often assume. The growing involvement of Western NGOs in, for instance, developing and monitoring aid programmes, may well enhance the influence and power of leading

---

[86] Taylor, 'Invoking Civil Society'.

[87] For a stimulating discussion of Hegelian thought in relation to these issues, see Nicholas Onuf, 'Agency, Institutions and Structuration in Late Modern Society', in Germain and Kenny (eds.), *Global Civil Society*. See also Jean Cohen and Andrew Arato, *Civil Society and Political Theory* (Cambridge, MA/London: MIT Press, 1992), pp. 83–116.

[88] See the account of the republican liberal tradition offered by Richard Dagger, *Civic Virtues* (Oxford/New York: Oxford University Press, 1997).

[89] For a perceptive discussion of these ideas in relation to the question of international citizenship, see Hutchings, 'The Idea of International Citizenship'.

donor states, because the latter are able to stand at one remove from groups that are often implementing their agenda. Equally, as John Keane observes, many groups and campaigning bodies have come into being because of decisions made, and resources supplied, by states:

If the institutions of global civil society are not merely the products of civic initiative and market forces, then is there a third force at work in nurturing and shaping it? It can be argued that global civil society is also the by-product of state or inter-state action, or inaction.[90]

As well as highlighting the question of what makes political authority legitimate, a liberal-republican sensibility leads us to ask whether any particular claim about transnational citizenship – for instance within the European Union – is underpinned by a sufficient density of forms of interdependence and shared understandings arising from the social experiences and interchanges of citizens. These are indispensable if citizenship is to signal more than an abstract legal status. This is especially so if a civic ethos is to be sufficiently robust to engender a sense of obligation and duty towards other citizens, especially when these are unlikely to share one's religious sensibility, ethnic background or cultural tradition. Republicanism prompts liberals to give greater priority to consideration of the social and civic sources of the mutuality that needs to be sustained if rights-entitlements are to be meaningful and legitimate. This tradition also demands of cosmopolitans that they attend to the question of what exactly constitutes the equivalent to the civic unity that neo-Roman theorists regarded as the prerequisite for the observance and exercise of individual liberty.[91]

In a global context in which vast disparities of income, resource and opportunity are structurally embedded in economic and social processes, this might well be taken to imply the public consideration of processes and relationships that sustain the entrenched domination of some groups over others, and the moral priority of questions of global injustice. Were this liberal-republican emphasis to become politically influential, we might expect to see global institutions, such as the United Nations, prioritise policies designed to redress the different kinds of inequity that inhibit peoples in various parts of the world from enjoying the basic capabilities implied by a universal citizenship. This could, in practice, mean the public promotion of something akin to the quality of life measure associated with the work of Amartya Sen and Martha Nussbaum.[92] While this focus upon entrenched relations of inequality is clearly not unique to this paradigm, the connection it suggests between a sense of the basic goods pertinent to any meaningful sense of individual well-being and social agency across the globe, and the moral obligations of states and citizens in wealthy countries, represents an important part of liberal-republicanism's contribution to international political theorising.

---

[90] Keane, 'Global Civil Society?', p. 35.

[91] Skinner, *Liberty before Liberalism*; and 'The Republican Ideal of Political Liberty', in Gisella Bock, Quentin Skinner, and MaurizoViroli (eds.), *Machiavelli and Republicanism* (Cambridge: Cambridge University Press).

[92] Nussbaum and Sen (eds.), *The Quality of Life: WIDER Studies in Development Economics* (Oxford: Clarendon Press, 1993); Sen, *Development as Freedom* (Oxford: Oxford University Press, 2001); and Nussbaum, *Women and Human Development: the Capabilities Approach* (Cambridge: Cambridge University Press, 2000).

Liberal republicanism also suggests a different moral slant to the subalternist conviction that a global society is organically emerging through the interstices and dynamics of established political conflict. On what basis, we might ask, are the different voices and traditions opposed to Western globalism to be engaged and distinguished by proponents of an alternative international society? Aside from the particular dilemmas this question suggests about how Western radicals should relate to terroristic groups, as well as non-liberal forms of religious practice and cultural tradition, it signals the larger moral problem of how to balance the pluralism dear to opponents of globalisation with some of the core values in, say, Falk's 'law of peoples'. These include such principles as equality between the genders – about which swathes of global opinion are in profound disagreement.[93] Republicans have admittedly proffered very different answers about where to set the limits to pluralism in different political societies, and they have invoked different principles governing the trade-off between civic unity and cultural diversity.[94]

But liberal republicanism also offers a particular conceptual contribution to contemporary international thought in this area – its distinctive conception of the virtue of civility. In the most general terms, the value of 'toleration' is typically presented by Anglophone liberals as an outcome and signature of a healthy, pluralist associational culture, and a moral disposition towards which individuals in a liberal democracy will naturally gravitate. In recent republican thinking, by contrast, the related, but different, value of civility is advanced as an indispensable moral ingredient for the exercise of democratic citizenship in culturally diverse and morally plural societies, and one of the core civic capacities that the state needs to promote.[95] Civility figures prominently in the work of some democratic theorists who seek to delineate the social and philosophical conditions appropriate to republican-style deliberative engagement. It is invoked by these thinkers to suggest something other than the idea of social politeness, which it signals in everyday English parlance.[96] In relation to the problem of transnational community, the value of civility represents a fertile addition to current debate. Whereas toleration obliges liberal citizens to show nothing more than indifference to the values and projects of their fellows, civility implies a readiness to accord those whose culture, appearance and values seem at first sight alien, and even threatening, the status of equals in a common enterprise. Civility, it has been suggested, represents the signature and outcome of civil societies in which the liberal principle of equality of respect is central not just in the public culture and institutions of the state, but is reflected in many of the informal interactions of its citizens.[97] An important consequence of a democratic culture in which civility is publicly valued is a readiness to inhabit the public domain alongside

---

[93] The problem of moral disagreement in relation to this principle is central to the Rawlsian-influenced argument developed by Nussbaum in *Women and Human Development*. For a critique of the very notion of global civil society on the grounds of cultural diversity, see Peter Marden, 'Geographies of Dissent: Globalization, Identity and the Nation', *Political Geography*, 16: 1 (1997), pp. 37–64.

[94] Dagger, *Civic Virtues*.

[95] See, for instance, Philip Pettit, *Republicanism: A Theory of Freedom and Government* (Oxford: Clarendon Press, 1997), pp. 245–61; and Edward Banfield, *Civility and Citizenship in Liberal Democratic Societies* (New York: Paragon House, 1992).

[96] Mark Kingwell, *A Civil Tongue: Justice, Dialogue and the Politics of Pluralism* (University Park, PA.: Pennsylvania State University Press, 1995).

[97] R. Bauböck, 'Social and Cultural Integration in Civil Society', in C. McKinnon and I. Hampsher-Monk (eds.), *The Demands of Citizenship* (London/New York: Continuum, 2000), pp. 91–119.

those whose beliefs and values are different, and to treat others with the presumption that they are one's moral equals.

Feminist arguments for the equal treatment of women in the workplace typically invoke the principle of non-discrimination against various kinds of unjust practice. But they also imply the norm of 'civility' – that women should be treated with a certain kind of respect and presumption of equal worth, in terms of the background culture and everyday interactions that shape working life.[98] Civility, in this perspective, is both the analogue of non-discrimination as well as a normative condition for compliance to this principle.[99] As Will Kymlicka observes, this value enjoins democratic communities to consider the social bases of political life, and specifically whether patterns of civil association promote the values of civility and mutual respect: 'whether people have genuinely equal opportunities depends not only on government actions, but also on the actions of institutions within civil society – corporations, schools, stores, landlords, and so forth'.[100] Such an argument suggests a particularly important role, in transnational settings, for social forces and groups that highlight the consequences and character of profound kinds of incivility to various minority groups. Those forces, campaigns and organisations that highlight, and protest against, the uncivil behaviour and cultures that inhibit the civic capacities and self-respect of citizens, have a particularly important role to play in global political life, according to the liberal-republican tradition. On this view, civility is closely interwoven with the patterning of social interaction and communicative interchange between geographically and culturally differentiated persons and groups, and is a value that can be promoted within international and global societies. It plays an important bridging-role as a value that links the 'ethicality' of various kinds of social exchange and intersubjective relation, with the legitimisation of other, closely related, universally applicable principles – the dignity of the individual, and equality of respect, for example.

A liberal-republican agenda

As well as providing pertinent critical reflections upon, and supplements to, the two main political perspectives upon global society, a liberal-republican dispensation might well suggest several distinctive lines of enquiry for those considering the ethical implications of transnational civil society. These are outlined, in indicative form, below.

Public spaces

One of the most important legacies of modern republican theory has been to promote the idea that unimpeded deliberation is both an indispensable part of the

---

[98] Nussbaunm, *Women and Human Development*.
[99] Banfield, *Civility and Citizenship*, p. xii.
[100] Will Kymlicka, 'Ethnic Associations and Democratic Citizenship', in A. Gutmann (ed.), *Freedom of Association* (Princeton, NJ: Princeton University Press, 1998), pp. 177–213.

process whereby shared interests and values can be discovered in a diverse political community, and the means by which citizens learn the merits of engaging in public forms of reasoning. While the ideal of a singular public conversation is clearly inappropriate at the international and global political levels, a liberal-republican sensibility leads us to consider carefully the various kinds of public space and deliberative interchange that have become established on a transnational basis. Analysts might fruitfully ask whether transcultural dialogues – be these the events and forums sponsored by the United Nations, or more informal exchanges organised by global media outlets – 'naturally' conform to consensually agreed procedures, or yield more substantive common values such as equality of respect. Some important critical questions accompany this focus. How broadly based, in both moral and cultural terms, are these conversations? And, what kinds of transnational forum ought to be sponsored by those keen to promote a liberal-republican sensibility? Should they argue, for instance, for the creation of regional legislative assemblies and constitutional arrangements? What, too, has been the impact of various global and international forums in establishing the legitimacy and moral worth of dialogic exchanges across some of the major religious and cultural cleavages in international society?[101] Does the rise of the global media represent the established supremacy of commercial rationality over communicative possibility in international life, or provide opportunities for the broadening and deepening of public dialogues?[102]

Though often accused of promoting the homogenising ideal of the singular public conversation, republican theorists have tended to proclaim the importance of many different kinds of public space and sphere – from formally constituted legislative assemblies, to informally constituted 'counter-spheres' where alternative voices gain the strength and confidence to join the wider public conversation.[103] An important recent philosophical development arises from the blending of the republican stress upon the merits of deliberative engagement with a more pronounced emphasis upon group differentiation and subaltern social struggle. In particular, Nancy Fraser's suggestion of the significance of 'counter-spheres' developed by subaltern groups in civil society carries an important resonance for current debates about the character of various kinds of transnational public space.[104] It suggests the long-term democratic merits of promoting various alternative forums and sources of opinion – Southern based NGOs and campaigning groups, for example, as counterweights to the influence of voices favoured by Western media conglomerates.[105]

---

[101] For some interesting analysis of various international initiatives of this sort, see Marc Lynch, 'The Dialogue of Civilisations and International Public Spheres', *Millennium*, 29 (2000), pp. 307–330. Also, see E. J. Clarm, E. J. Friedman and K. Hochstetler, 'The Sovereign Limits of Global Civil Society: A Comparison of NGO Participation in UN World Conferences on the Environment, Human Rights, and Women', *World Politics*, 51: 1 (1998), pp. 1–21.

[102] These themes are especially associated with the republican-influenced writings of Jürgen Habermas on the public sphere. See, especially, Habermas, *The Structural Transformation of the Public Sphere: An Inquiry into a Category of Bourgeois Society* (Cambridge: Polity, 1989); *The Inclusion of the Other*; and the essays collected in Calhoun (ed.) *Habermas and the Public Sphere* (Cambridge, MA/London: MIT Press, 1992).

[103] See Taylor, 'Liberal Politics and the Public Sphere', in Taylor, *Philosophical Arguments* (Cambridge, MA/London: Harvard University Press, 1995), pp. 257–87.

[104] Fraser, 'Rethinking the Public Sphere: A Contribution to the Critique of Actually Existing Democracy', in Calhoun (ed.), *Habermas and the Public Sphere*, pp. 109–142.

[105] A similar argument is advanced, from a pluralist perspective, by Iris Young, *Inclusion and Democracy* (Cambridge: Cambridge University Press, 2000), pp. 236–76.

Politicising global society

Republicanism is typically associated with the idea that politics plays a constitutive role in respect of human flourishing. As Skinner, however, has argued, this Aristotelian-inspired conception of the integral relationship between politics and virtue, in fact represents only one variant of modern republican thinking.[106] Yet, this neo-Aristotelian republican strain sustains a valuable critique of Anglophone liberal understandings of civil society. Classical liberalism, in particular, invokes a distinction between civil society as the realm of individual liberty and choice, and politics as the domain of the legitimate coercion upon the individual will. Reviving the Aristotelian linkage between the principles and processes of self-government and the moral ideal of self-realisation suggests, in contrast, that we ask whether international initiatives and the decisions of global institutions are likely to promote the autonomy and political capacity of oppressed and subordinated peoples affected by them. As opposed to the subalternist suspicion towards all projects of governance and legal regulation that arise 'from above', this perspective prioritises the question of the moral ends towards which executive decisions, governing networks, and legal developments point, and the values towards which these might be directed. As such, it offers an important regulative ideal against which the worth of, for example, development initiatives and aid programmes in particular regions can be assessed: to what degree are these premised upon, or liable to contribute to, the self-government and empowerment of groups and peoples that they affect?

Legitimacy

The third area of normative thinking and critical questioning that republican thinking suggests concerns political legitimacy. This represents a blind-spot in both the liberal and subalternist visions of global society. While moral cosmopolitanism encourages liberal theorists to read off the inexorable realisation of established moral truths from what are, in fact, ambiguous and uneven sociopolitical developments, subalternist radicals assume that the subordination of oppressed or marginalised groups secures the legitimacy of their demands. This assumption neglects the fundamental incompatibility of some of the claims advanced by these groupings, and the differentiated character of the conceptions of 'the good' from which these arise.

Modern republicanism, in its various guises, draws attention to the importance of the constitutional and political order that makes the enjoyment of individual liberty possible.[107] This 'neo-Roman' (as Skinner puts it) emphasis is revived by recent republican theorists who continue to stress the necessity of a 'free state' as a

---

[106] Skinner, *Liberty before Liberalism*.

[107] See the reconstruction of the lineages of European and American republican constitutionalism in Dario Castiglione, 'The Political Theory of the Constitution', *Political Studies*, 44: 3 (1995), pp. 417–35; and Richard Bellamy, 'The Political Form of the Constitution: the Separation of Powers, Rights, and Representative Democracy', *Political Studies*, 44: 3 (1995), pp. 436–56.

condition for individual liberty.[108] In relation to debates about the implications of transnational civil association, this implies a critical questioning of the basis of the legitimacy of the mélange of global institutions, international legal regulations, regional bodies and state actors that currently constitute some of the main executive authorities in a globalising world. As various forms of commercial, civil and social exchange have assumed a degree of autonomy from extant national boundaries, the moral challenge of designing and enforcing laws that will simultaneously promote individual liberty, represent a range of social interests, and offset the domination of some parties over others, becomes especially important.[109]

The contribution of republican thinking to modern Western understandings of the relationship between sovereignty, legitimacy and political community, deserves re-evaluation by analysts concerned with the question of what makes a particular governance arrangement legitimate to those under its jurisdiction. In the current 'neo-medieval' global order, where international, transnational and state jurisdictions intersect and overlap, often uncomfortably, republican thinking may be an important alternative resource to cosmopolitan theorising. It encourages a critical evaluation of whether emergent systems of global governance have secured the consent of, and some kind of input from, citizens they claim to represent.

It may well be worthwhile, therefore, to distinguish more carefully between the aspirations of moral cosmopolitans from various projects that reflect the ambitions of 'political' cosmopolitanism.[110] Some of the latter are broadly consonant with a liberal-republican approach. In particular, if the relationship of civil society to democratisation is best conceived as contingent in kind, as I have suggested above, then the question of which political and legal arrangements might best inflect the ethical potentiality immanent within the networks, activities, and protests associated with an array of transnational groups, is of considerable significance. This suggests the centrality of institutional and constitutional considerations in relation to the establishment and preservation of public spaces. It also signals the importance of the development of international law and accompanying institutions that will reflect and legitimate such values as the dignity of the person.[111] Some of the programmatic suggestions associated with the cosmopolitan democracy programme developed by David Held and Daniele Archibugi,[112] for example, might be fruitfully examined as continuations of liberal-republican ambitions. For Andrew Linklater too, the Kantian model of international law is insufficient since, 'The deontological duties defined by the modern cosmopolitan moral law cannot be willed in isolation. They are known only through active democratic procedures and they take on a social,

[108] Skinner, *Liberty before Liberalism*; and 'The Republican Ideal of Political Liberty', in Gisella Bock, Quentin Skinner, and MaurizoViroli (eds.), *Machiavelli and Republicanism* (Cambridge: Cambridge University Press).

[109] For an assertion of the centrality of the principle of non-domination in republican political thinking, see Pettit, *Republicanism*.

[110] This distinction is, for instance, absent from Baker, 'Problems in the Theorisation of Global Civil Society', but is discussed in Hutchings, *International Political Theory*.

[111] The normative relevance of this principle to global civil society is elaborated in Mervyn Frost, *Ethics in International Relations* (Cambridge: Cambridge University Press, 1996); and 'Global Civil Society: Civilians and Citizens'.

[112] Held and Archibugi (eds.), *Cosmopolitan Democracy: An Agenda for a New World Order* (Cambridge: Polity, 1995).

economic and cultural dimension'.[113] In this powerful argument, cosmopolitanism is found wanting in terms of an active conception of political agency – a central motif in republican thought.

This focus upon institutional and constitutional design in order to realise demo-cratic potential at a variety of spatial scales arises from different strands of republican political thought. In this respect, a liberal-republican anchorage appears to offer a more promising vantage point upon global society than the romantic ideal animating subalternism. Advocates of the latter revive an antinomy between organic community and law that ultimately hampers the realisation of some of their core normative values. Global civil society offers a cacophony of protesting and dissenting voices and vital sources for alternative thinking. These can suggest, but not themselves legitimately constitute, the kinds of regulatory authority needed to call the forces of the global economy to order. Transnational society will not spontaneously produce a new democratic order without the agency of national and supranational governmental structures and political authorities.

Conclusions

The outlines of the liberal-republican argument sketched here have an important bearing upon the broader ambition of this article – to consider whether we can engage the idea of a global civil society from a politico-ethical vantage point other than the positions associated with liberal cosmopolitanism and subaltern radicalism. These represent two of the most influential frames through which this notion has been projected within Anglophone political theory. Despite their differences, they invite their adherents to imagine, and indeed celebrate, the idea that a globally constituted society has outstripped the moral and political capacities of states. But in a world in which multiple levels of authority and public space are emerging, and in which nation-states are likely to remain highly significant moral and political communities, the teleological and romantic elements of these frameworks remain problematic. By contrast, republican-liberalism offers a promising '*via media*' between the liberal idea that law is the highest embodiment of the ethicality of a society, on the one hand, and the subalternist suspicion of rights on the other.

Some of the leading figures in the liberal-republican lineage have pointed to the likelihood that in modern conditions citizens pursue 'the good' in a variety of arenas and at different social scales. The citizens of Hegel's *Philosophy of Right*, for example, learn to manage the competing demands and obligations suggested by a pattern of relative identities – represented through the spheres of family, civil society and state.[114] The dilemmas and opportunities posed for individuals by the 'weak' solidarities implied by transnational civility may well represent a further con-tinuation of, not a break from, the dispersal of the sites at which ethical life is experienced in an increasingly interdependent, yet profoundly differentiated, world.

---

[113] Linklater, *The Transformation of Political Community: Ethical Foundations of the post-Westphalian Era* (Oxford: Polity, 1998), p. 207.

[114] Hegel, *Hegel's Philosophy of Right;* translated with notes by T.M. Knox (London: Oxford University Press, 1967).

Challenging globalisation: toward a feminist understanding of resistance

MARIANNE H. MARCHAND[1]

Introduction

'Given the success of Naomi Klein with her book *No Logo*[2] and Noreena Hertz's *The Silent Takeover*[3], can we infer from this that feminists are finding themselves in the limelight of the anti-globalisation movement?' With this question a reporter of the Dutch magazine *Op Gelijke Voet*[4] approached me about two years ago.

It is an extremely interesting question and one which cannot that easily be answered. For one, do Hertz and Klein identify with feminism and label themselves feminists? Secondly, even if they do, it is not clear whether both authors are being perceived as feminists and as promoting feminist causes. Both issues are not easily resolved and pinpoint the complex relationship(s) among feminism, gender and the politics of resistance (against globalisation).

The reporter's question brought to mind two related concerns which have interested me for some time: (1) what does a gender analysis of the politics of resistance entail? And (2) what involves a gendered politics of resistance? A quick perusal of the literature on the politics of resistance[5] reveals that there are quite a few publications on, for instance, global feminism or the transnationalisation of women's movements, but that these tend to be case-study driven. As such they do not provide a gender analysis but rather a social movement analysis. Moreover few, if any, studies directly address the possibly gendered nature of a politics of resistance.

The possibly gendered nature of the politics of resistance against globalisation has not attracted a great deal of attention in academic and policy debates either. Can we conclude from this that the gender dimensions of the politics of resistance have followed the well-known path of being silenced? The answer to this question is

[1] I wish to thank in particular Barbara Hobson and those present at the Gender and Globalization Seminar, University of Stockholm, for their wonderful feedback and input. I am also indebted to Abel Gómez Gutiérrez for his assistance in preparing this manuscript.
[2] Naomi Klein, *No Logo* (London: Flamingo, 2001).
[3] Noreena Hertz, *The Silent Takeover* (London: Arrow Books, 2001).
[4] This magazine is published by the Directorate of Co-ordination of Emancipation Policy, Ministry of Social Affairs and Work and provides information about governmental emancipation policy.
[5] Amrita Basu (ed.), *The Challenge of Local Feminisms: Women's Movements in Global Perspective* (Boulder, CO: Westview Press, 1995); Inderpal Grewal and Caren Kaplan, *Scattered Hegemonies* (Minneapolis, MI: University of Minnesota Press, 1994); *New Political Economy*, Special Issue 'Globalisation and the Politics of Resistance', ed. Barry K. Gills, 2:1 (March 1997); Margaret E. Keck and Kathryn Sikkink, *Activists Beyond Borders* (Ithaca, NY and London: Cornell University Press, 1998); Mark Rupert, *Ideologies of Globalization: Contending Visions of a New World Order* (London: Routledge, 2002).

not as straightforward as one might think. Media representations of the anti- or critical globalisation movement (CGM) have not been entirely disembodied (which is usually an indication that gender dimensions are being silenced). For example, the cover of a recent *El País Semanal*[6] shows the face of a young woman with a red and yellow peace sign painted on it. Moreover, the lead article accompanying the cover provides an overview of various critical globalisation and anti-war groups and activists, which includes quite a few women. Added to these are the prominent places occupied by Susan George, Noreena Hertz and Naomi Klein among the gurus of the CGM. Does this mean that the CGM has successfully engaged in gender mainstreaming? Again the answer is not straightforward, as the presence of women does not necessarily imply a gender-sensitive politics of resistance.

In short, it is important to deepen our understanding of the connections among feminism, gender and the politics of resistance against globalisation. The objective of this article is to do just that and to develop a gendered analysis of the politics of resistance as well as explore its gendered nature. In the next section I will address some recent debates and conceptualisations of the politics of resistance. The following section will elaborate the main tenets of a gender analysis. This will be used as the starting point for discussing gendered practices, strategies and sites of resistance. This last section of the article will use various examples for illustration.

Conceptualising the politics of resistance

The discipline of International Relations has traditionally been state-centred and, therefore, not very much focused on non-state actors, in particular non-governmental organisations (NGOs) and social movements. The increasing importance of transnational corporations (TNCs) in the global political economy placed non-state actors on the agenda, at least in the sub-field of international political economy. Although this attention to TNCs meant a shift away from the state-centred focus, it still reflected an overall bias toward the powerbrokers in and of international relations.

It was not until the mid- to late 1980s that civil society and NGOs started to receive some attention from international relations scholars. A combination of factors contributed to this. For one, environmental concerns spurred the emergence of an environmental movement with such outspoken organisations as Greenpeace and think-tanks like the World Watch Institute. In addition, human rights groups like Amnesty International and the 'Crazy Mothers of the Plaza de Mayo' in Argentina were important not only in raising awareness about dictatorial regimes but also contributed to them being ousted. Neoliberal discourse also served to empower civil society because of its attack on the role of the state in the marketplace and its emphasis on liberal individualism as well as citizenship. Paradoxically, however, many of the most outspoken groups in civil society have tended to oppose neoliberal economic policies.

The widespread opposition of a 'people's movement' to the communist regimes in Central and Eastern Europe, as well as the force of 'people's power' against the

---

[6] This is the Sunday magazine of the newspaper *El País*, 16 March 2003.

Marcos dictatorship in the Philippines, made it yet more difficult for IR scholars to ignore civil society and social movements. Moreover, the social and cultural implications of profound economic and political restructuring or globalisation, have foregrounded discussions about an emerging global civil society. Optimists have tended to see the emergence of a global civil society as a positive development, which to a large extent has been stimulated and aided by the new information and communication technologies (ICT). The United Nations report *Our Global Neighborhood*[7] reflects this positive stance. Pessimists, or rather opponents, have in contrast emphasised the negative effects of globalisation on local culture and traditions, arguing that it leads to either homogenisation or fragmentation.[8]

In short, (global) civil society, social movements and the politics of resistance have now become accepted subjects of study within the IR community. Despite the recent interest in these subjects very few attempts have been made to use new conceptual tools and engage in new ways of 'seeing' and framing. This lack of conceptualising and framing has been noted by Rob Walker.[9] However, as I have argued elsewhere, his attempt to reframe and conceptualise is problematic from a feminist point of view.[10]

In general there have been several issues raised in the emerging literature on social movements.[11] One area of concern is related to the question of power. Here the concern is how powerful are social movements in their opposition to global restructuring and whether they are not too fragmented or even single-issue oriented to be effective political actors. Related to this, and as already discussed above, a second concern for IR scholars has been their state-centrism. This has prevented many within the discipline from understanding and valuing the different politics and articulations of power by grassroots movements. Another main concern has been to discuss and define the nature of social movements. This can be, for instance, by distinguishing new from old social movements or exploring the emancipatory potential of social movements. Also the internal organisational structure of social movements in terms of their democratic calibre has been scrutinised. Finally, various scholars have been interested in the question of transnationalisation of social movements.[12]

Gendering the politics of resistance

What entails a gender perspective on the politics of resistance? In the previous section we have seen how the politics of resistance against globalisation is being framed. However, such framing does not take gender into account. As argued

---

[7] The Commission on Global Governance, *Our Global Neighborhood: The Report of the Commission on Global Governance* (New York, NY: Oxford University Press, 1995).

[8] Mike Featherstone, Scott Lash and Roland Robertson (eds.), *Global Modernities* (London: Sage Publications, 1995).

[9] Rob B. J. Walker, *One World, Many Worlds: Struggles for a Just World Peace* (Boulder, CO: Lynne Rienner Publishers, 1984).

[10] Marianne H. Marchand 'Some Theoretical Musings about Gender and Resistance', in Robin L. Teske and Mary Ann Tétrault (eds.), *Conscious Acts and the Politics of Social Change* (Columbia, SC: University of South Carolina Press, 2000), p. 60.

[11] This discussion is a summary from Marchand, 'Some Theoretical Musings', pp. 57–60.

[12] Keck and Sikkink, *Activists Beyond Borders*.

elsewhere,[13] gender operates at three interconnected levels: the ideological, the physical (body) and the social. A gender analysis of the politics of resistance against globalisation should incorporate these three levels or dimensions. If we revisit the processes of globalisation we can easily detect these three dimensions. For instance, ideologically globalisation is being valorised and represented through such terms as 'the final frontier'.[14] As Charlotte Hooper shows, these are not gender-neutral terms; rather they are associated with a new form of masculinity, which she calls 'entrepreneurial frontier masculinity'.[15] Borrowing from Robert Connell she asserts that this is a new hegemonic masculinity associated with globalisation.[16] At the same time new spaces associated with globalisation, such as the global financial and high tech sectors, tend to be primarily embodied by men. In other words, these spaces or flows, in Manuel Castells' words, are predominantly masculine spaces.[17]

Yet, there are also different embodiments associated with less visible and prestigious spaces and activities such as domestic labour and working in free-trade zones or maquiladoras.[18] As Kimberley Chang and Lily Ling[19] argue, this is global restructuring too, producing a 'regime of labor intimacy'. These are the racialised and feminised spaces of globalisation, associated with 'Third World' women and men, women of colour and minorities in general.

Processes of globalisation have also affected the social, in other words gender relations including the gender contract. For instance there has been a rearticulation of the public-private divide, not just in terms of a shift from the public sector to the market, but also to the household or domestic sphere.[20] This is most clearly manifested in the increased burden on women in terms of caring for family members or additional community-related activities due to structural adjustment programmes.[21] But even in high-income countries such as the Netherlands, women are either directly or indirectly called upon to care for family members, be a reading parent at school or engage in other 'voluntary' unpaid work.

Looking through a gender lens[22] at globalisation brings to the fore how profound a transformation it entails in terms of the day-to-day lived realities of people. This is why it is more appropriate to speak of global restructuring than of globalisation.[23]

---

[13] Marianne H. Marchand and Anne S. Runyan (eds.), Introduction. 'Feminist Sightings of Global Restructuring: Conceptualizations and Reconceptualizatons', in *Gender and Global Restructuring: Sightings, Sites and Resistances* (London: Routledge, 2000), p. 8.

[14] Charlotte Hooper, 'Masculinities in Transition: The Case of Globalization', in Marchand and Runyan (eds.), *Gender and Global Restructuring*, p. 68.

[15] Hooper, 'Masculinities', p. 67.

[16] Ibid., pp. 70–71.

[17] Manuel Castells, *The Information Age: Economy, Society and Culture*, vol. 1: *The Network Society*, (Oxford: Blackwell, 1996).

[18] Maquiladoras is the term used in Mexico and Central America for factories located in free trade zones. In the case of Mexico they are now located in virtually all parts of the country, not just in the border zone with the United States.

[19] Kimberly A. Chang and Lily H. M. Ling, 'Globalization and its Intimate Other: Filipina Domestic Workers in Hong Kong', in Marchand and Runyan (eds), *Gender and Global Restructuring*, p. 33.

[20] Marchand and Runyan, 'Introduction. Feminist Sightings', pp. 17–18.

[21] Caroline Moser, *Gender Planning and Development* (London: Routledge, 1993).

[22] V. Spike Peterson and Anne S. Runyan, *Global Gender Issues*, 2nd edn. (Boulder, CO: Westview Press, 1999).

[23] Marianne H. Marchand, 'Reconceptualising "Gender and Development" in an Era of "Globalisation"', *Millennium*, 25: 3 (1996), pp. 577–603.

The latter term is too broad and vague and tends to obfuscate the profound transformations that are occurring in people's lives. Global restructuring, instead, indicates a process of partially breaking down an old and constructing a new order. As such it involves the renegotiation and rearticulation of boundaries.[24] These boundaries include the public/private/domestic, national/international/global, state/society/market, and so on.

Global restructuring and its concomitant boundary renegotiation and rearticulation provide the context for the politics of resistance. It is exactly around the rearticulations and renegotiations of these boundaries as well as at their interstices that resistances occur. The question we need to ask, then, is how are these resistances around such boundary renegotiations and rearticulations gendered?

First, it is important to recognise the contextual and embedded nature of the resistances. In other words, resistances are as much structured by global restructuring as resistances are structuring global restructuring.[25] From a feminist point of view context is important because it provides a framework within which we can place and understand certain kinds of resistances, taking into account different histories and existing structures of inequality along the lines of class, race ethnicity and so on as they intersect with gender.[26] This may involve a politics of location which

As a practice of affiliation, [. . .] identifies the grounds for historically specific differences and similarities between women in diverse and asymmetrical relations, creating alternative histories, identities and possibilities for alliances.[27]

Related to the politics of location is the notion of positionality. Positionality usually refers to the relationship between researcher, in particular ethnographer, and the person or individuals who are the subject of the research. Positionality involves a reflexive stance on behalf of the researcher and is seen as a way to identify situated knowledges.[28] As such positionality connects subjectivity with different and possibly changing positions within structures of inequality, geopolitics and histories.

Gendering resistance involves a recognition of the politics of location as well as positionality in the way resistances are being articulated. Taking these dimensions into account may serve to identify specific masculine and feminine practices of resistance. Obviously, the notions of 'feminine' and 'masculine' are culturally as well as historically coded constructs and may not necessarily reflect the actual behaviour and activities of individual men and women.[29] However, if we loosely follow Judith Butler's ideas about gender as performance, it can be argued that the categories of masculine and feminine are constructed through 'a stylized repetition of acts'.[30]

---

[24] Janine Brodie, 'Shifting the Boundaries: Gender and the Politics of Restructuring', in Isabella Bakker (ed.), *The Strategic Silence: Gender and Economic Policy* (London: Zed Books, 1994).

[25] Marchand and Runyan, 'Introduction. Feminist Sightings', p. 19.

[26] Gillian Rose, 'Situating Knowledges: Positionality, Reflexivities and Other Tactics', *Progress in Human Geography*, 21: 3 (1997), pp. 305–20.

[27] Caren Kaplan, 'The Politics of Location as Transnational Feminist Practice', in Inderpal Grewal and Caren Kaplan (eds.), *Scattered Hegemonies* (London: University of Minnesota Press, 1994), p. 139.

[28] Rose, 'Situating Knowledges', *passim*.

[29] Robert W. Connell, *Masculinities* (Cambridge: Polity Press, 1995).

[30] Judith Butler, *Gender Trouble: Feminism and the Subversion of Identity* (New York, NY: Routledge, 1990), p. 140.

According to Butler, the repetitive performances ultimately result in their (gendered) embodiment.[31] At the same we should not discard the possibility of a politics of resistance which tends to be relatively 'gender-neutral', that is, one that does not relate to any specific masculine or feminine embodied or coded politics of location or positionality.

A second important dimension of a gendered politics of resistance involves a concern with relating content to form. Content refers to the actual articulation of issues, their prioritisation and the political agenda they reflect. However, a feminist politics is also concerned with the question of how these issues are being formulated, how they get on to the agenda and how priorities are being established. In other words, internal democratic decision-making structures and organisation are important aspects of feminist politics. The question is whether this can be contrasted to a masculinist politics of resistance which, then, supposedly, tends to focus on content and ignore its relation to form.[32]

In addition to the organisational and decision-making dimensions of form, we can also think about form in terms of how the actual protest is being articulated. In this respect it is important to analyse how particular protests are connected to content and whether they invoke a specific gender identity or are gender-coded. This aspect of form (and its relationship to content) may be reflected in resistance practices.

The final dimension of a gender analysis of resistance involves a focus on identity politics. What kinds of identities are being articulated through resistances and to what extent do they involve gender identities? For instance, are women organising as women when they participate in protests against globalisation or do other identities prevail? And what about the men? What kinds of identities do they invoke when organising?

In sum, a gender analysis of the politics of resistance involves relational thinking. Relational thinking tries to connect the (material) context, perceptions or particular views with subjectivities and identities.[33] In the next section we will turn to the issue of what entails a gendered politics of resistance against globalisation.

Gendered practices, strategies and sites of resistance

As is argued in the previous section, global restructuring has entailed profound political, economic, social and cultural transformations, which affect our daily lives. Obviously, not everyone is affected in the same way, and not all changes that have occurred in the context of global restructuring are necessarily for the worse. Yet since the 1990s we have witnessed a significant and increasing level of opposition to globalisation. However, if we take a closer look it appears that before the emergence

---

[31] Butler, *Gender Trouble.*

[32] Anne C. Snyder, *Setting the Agenda for Global Peace: Conflict and Consensus Building* (Aldershot, UK: Ashgate Publishing, 2003).

[33] V. Spike Peterson, 'Whose Crisis? Early and Post-modern Masculinism', in S. Gill and J.H. Mittelman (eds.), *Innovation and Transformation in International Studies* (Cambridge: Cambridge University Press, 1997).

of the highly visible CGM there has been substantial opposition to different dimensions of global restructuring. For instance, during the 1980s there have already been the so-called IMF riots against structural adjustment programmes as well as the organising of neighbourhood soup kitchens in Lima, Peru. At first sight the latter activity may not appear to be an instance of resistance. Yet, a closer look reveals that it can be (and often has been) interpreted as an act of defiance, on the one hand to the failure of local government to provide for basic needs and, on the other, to *Sendero Luminoso* which tended to target leaders of grassroots groups for refusing to side with the revolution.[34] In other words, opposition to globalisation did not start in Seattle during the third ministerial meeting of the World Trade Organisation (WTO), nor is the CGM the only form of resistance against globalisation. Adopting a gender lens allows us to perceive the multiple practices, strategies and sites of resistance.

Practices of resistance

From a gender perspective it is interesting to explore whether there are gendered practices of resistance. In other words, is it possible to distinguish between masculine and feminine practices? And if so, how are they articulated? As mentioned before, masculinity and femininity are culturally and socially coded constructs and may not reflect the actual behaviour of individual people. However, it is possible to identify such practices when they are either explicitly constructed as masculine or feminine or perceived as such.

Recent organising in the Americas, in particular around the Free Trade Area of the Americas (FTAA) and the World Social Forum in Porto Alegre, serves as example to illustrate possibly gendered practices of resistance. One of the first interesting distinctions to be observed is that certain feminist and women's groups or networks organize *as women* within the CGM, but that men are not organising as men. The latter organise on the basis of such identities as workers, environmentalists, indigenous, *campesinos*, anarchists (the 'autonomous'), and so on.

Obviously, there are also women who do not organise as women but who identify themselves with some of the groups just mentioned. In this context it would be interesting to investigate whether there is a strategy of gender mainstreaming implemented to make sure that gender issues are being addressed in the overall strategies. With respect to resistance practices it is more difficult to think in terms of gender mainstreaming although not impossible. Ideally such gender mainstreamed practices would be contextualised, for instance by invoking a global-local nexus, involve the articulation of inclusive identities which allow for difference and the engagement in so-called transversal politics, which is articulated at the intersection of peoples' different realities, backgrounds, experiences and priorities.[35]

[34] Human Rights Watch, 'Threats and Murder of Women Leaders', *Human Rights Watch Global Report on Women's Human Rights (New York, 1998)*. <http://www.hrw.org/about/projects/womrep/General-57.htm#TopOfPage>, downloaded on 25 August 2003.
[35] Marjorie Pryse, 'Trans/Feminist Methodology: Bridges to Interdisciplinary Thinking', *National Women's Studies Association Journal*, 12: 2 (2001), pp. 105–18.

There are quite a few examples of women organising as women in the overall protest movement against the FTAA. These activities range from developing position papers, claiming an autonomous women's space within the movement, to a declaration on behalf of the Network of Women Parliamentarians of the Americas. One of the most outspoken feminist actions took place in Quebec City during the 2001 Summit of the Americas on the FTAA. A few months prior to the meeting a call went out to women's groups throughout the hemisphere to participate in creating or weaving a web of solidarity. As was stated in the call to action:

We are taking action because we will no longer tolerate the web of corporate control that binds us down and constricts our lives. We will not allow this system to continue. We have taken this measure: its time is done. Instead, we will become spiders, spinning a new web of connection, of solidarity out of our rage, out of our love.

We will, as women, weave together our hopes and dreams, our aspirations, our indictments, our testimony, our witnessing, our demands, our visions. We will write on ribbons, on strips of cloth, on rags. We will draw, paint, knot cords, braid yarn, whisper into pieces of string. And from these materials we will weave our web.[36]

At the meeting in Quebec City (April 2001) about 300–500 women gathered to actually weave such a web of solidarity. To this end they used all the materials that had been sent or brought. With this web the group women marched from the women's space to the security perimeter of the old part of town. Barbara Walker Graham describes the symbolism(s) used during the rally as follows:

She towered 10 feet over us, her hair flaming orange, her hands grasping . . . when she moved, her green skirts billowed, flaring out in the cool Quebec breeze. She is Nemesis—the angry and proud spirit of all the women of the Western Hemisphere. Women laboring under hazardous and illegal working conditions, women who struggle daily to feed their children and keep their loved ones alive often under brutish political regimes and a declining standard of living.[37]

This Nemesis puppet was at the head of the rally, which also carried the Web of Solidarity. Once the group reached the security parameter at René Levesque Boulevard, a few representatives talked with the police present and were allowed to attach the 'Women's Mural Against the FTAA' to the fence.[38] Near the fence, a small group of woman also created a weaving by performing a weaving dance using poles.[39] During the rally women used other symbols as well, including faking pregnancy to reflect the sacredness of life and having a women's clothes-line for hanging alternatives to the FTAA.[40]

What does this example of feminist organising within the CGM reveal in terms of resistance practices? There seems to be implicit references to different strands of

---

[36] *Women s Call to Action*, April 2001, <http://www.nadir.org/nadir/initiativ/agp/free/ftaa/womens. html>, downloaded on 27 August 2003, p. 1.

[37] Barbara Walker Graham, 'Whose Nemesis? Feminist Action against the FTAA', *Awakened Woman e-magazine*, <http://www.awakenedwoman.com/walker_report.htm>, 16 May 2001 (downloaded on 6 March 2003.

[38] Walker Graham, 'Whose Nemesis?', p. 2.

[39] The Association for Women's Rights in Development (AWID), interview with Anna Kruzynski, *The AWID resource net* <http://www.awid.org/fridayfile/msg00023.html>, 4 May 2001, p. 2, downloaded on 6 March 2003.

[40] Walker Graham, 'Whose Nemesis?', p. 2.

feminism, including cultural, radical and ecofeminism. The appeals to the sacredness of life, using 'fake' pregnancies to evoke this, can be interpreted as expressions of radical and ecofeminism. Similarly, the Web of Solidarity symbolised the inter-connectedness of life, while the Nemesis puppet appears to fit with radical feminist concerns about exploitation. The symbolism of weaving a quilt-like mural or web, using a clothes-line for hanging alternatives, reflects in part cultural feminist concerns. And having a feminist space within the overall movement seems to have been informed by cultural and radical feminist ideas. Finally, the protest rally ended with a 'ritual calling for healing energy and empowerment for all the protesters'[41] which seems to have been inspired by a combination of ecofeminism and new age.

Interestingly, the women's rally was apparently not perceived as threatening or dangerous by the security forces. According to eyewitness accounts[42] women were allowed to scale the fence and get on the inside of the security perimeter. This reaction to the women's rally reminds of the initial attitude by the Argentinean military dictatorship toward the 'Mothers of the Plaza de Mayo' who were marching on behalf of their disappeared daughters and sons. As they were women (with diapers as headscarves to symbolise motherhood), the women appeared to be 'a-political' and, thus, invisible and non-threatening to the military.[43] It was not until later, when it was too late to repress the movement, that the 'Crazy Mothers' were seen as a threat. A similar attitude appears to have been adopted by the security forces in Quebec City. Although there was a forceful reaction toward the protest of the overall CGM, the women's rally did not evoke the same reaction by the security forces. Apparently, the symbolic protest involving the Nemesis puppet and the Web of Solidarity, were perceived as non-threatening.

In sum, the example discussed here suggests that we can identify certain gendered practices of resistance. The first dimension involves an explicit articulation of identity. However, this articulation of (gender) identity is one-sided as certain (groups of) women organise *as women*, but as far as I have been able to detect, men do not explicitly organise *as men* (at least not in the context of the CGM). The women's protest also involved an explicit contextualisation, especially through the call for action in which women were asked to create something that represented the way in which globalisation impacts their lives, families and communities. Finally, the symbolic protests tended to be perceived as being non-threatening by the security forces, which allowed the women to enter the security perimeter.

Strategies of resistance

Much attention has been focused on the large-scale protests against globalisation, as embodied by international organisations such as the WTO, the International Financial Institutions as well as meetings by the G8 and the World Economic Forum. The question we need to ask is to what extent this focus may reflect a certain

[41] Ibid., p. 3.
[42] Ibid., p. 3.
[43] Marysa Navarro, 'The Personal is Political: Las Madres de la Plaza de Mayo', in Susan Eckstein (ed.), *Power and Popular Protest* (Berkeley, CA: University of California Press, 1989).

bias and overlook or make invisible (other) resistance strategies used by women. The large-scale protests have attracted so much attention not only because they make, to speak in newspaper terms, 'good copy' but also because of their novelty. For one, the CGM has been able to organise effectively due to the use of the Internet and e-mail. Also, the ability to get a transnational movement organised is something new. From a social science perspective the CGM may provide the beginnings of a global civil society, in which the use of new ICT and the emergence of transnationalism are important developments.[44] Moreover, the resonance of the CGM with many groups and individuals in various parts of the world reflects a certain frustration with the lack of possibilities or channels to influence decision-making in the area of global economic policy. In sum, it is quite understandable why so much attention is being paid to the CGM.

However, what about resistance strategies that are less spectacular? From a gender perspective it is important to reveal possible gender biases in which we conceptualise social phenomena. In the case of resistance strategies it is important to take into account what range of possible resistance strategies exist, in what ways they are tied to the issue of positionality and to what extent they involve a challenge, problematisation and renegotiation of boundaries.

As argued elsewhere[45] women engage in a range of resistance strategies. Such strategies can be individualised and involve everyday resistances[46] or coping strategies to face a worsening economic environment. Coping strategies often involve some kind of pooling of resources at the household level. This can be in the form of remittances from (female) family members abroad[47] or the pooling of income, by living in a multi-generational household.

Some of the most interesting or innovative strategies of resistance have been the creation of neighbourhood soup kitchens and the giving of testimonials, which was in the 1980s and early 1990s quite a popular strategy of voicing opposition in Latin America. The testimonies were often given in opposition to repressive military regimes, which made any other form of resistance very difficult and dangerous. However, under certain circumstances even the giving of a testimony was a dangerous enterprise as the continued threats to Rigoberta Menchu's life show.[48] To this date, Nobel prize winner and peace activist Menchu can not live in her home country Guatemala for fear of her life.

The soup kitchens which were set up during the 1980s in Lima, Peru, have been an often cited example of how women became politically mobilised. Set up to meet the basic needs of many families living in low income *barrios* the soup kitchens helped to galvanise participating women to formulate demands directed at municipal authorities to improve the living conditions in the neighbourhood.

---

[44] Keck and Sikkink, *Activists Beyond Borders*.
[45] Marchand and Runyan, 'Introduction. Feminist Sightings', pp. 18–20.
[46] James C. Scott, *Weapons of the Weak: Everyday Forms of Peasant Resistance* (New Haven, CT: Yale University Press, 1985).
[47] Mayke Kromhout, 'Women and Livelihood Strategies: A Case of Coping with Economic Crisis Through Household Management in Paramarimbo, Suriname', in Marchand and Runyan, *Gender and Global Restructuring*
[48] Elisabeth Burgos-Debray, *Rigoberta Menchu* (New York: Verso, 1984).

Interestingly, both resistance strategies – one individualised but speaking on behalf of a community and one collective strategy at the community level – involve a rearticulation of boundaries and an explicit reference to the gender identity of the women involved and their positionality. In both instances, women are organising as women using their role as mothers and family caretakers as the foundation for their involvement. In so doing they are rearticulating the boundaries between public and private. Community organising is being redefined as an extension of the household or private sphere and, therefore, interpreted as non-political. Likewise, the testimonies reflect a politicisation on the basis of values usually associated with women. Not being able to fulfill their roles as caretakers, nurturers, (re-)producers of life and the community has been a major reason for women's politicisation. In addition to their day-to-day activities at the community level, women who have given their testimonies also chose a strategy or voice, which would make them heard at the global level.[49]

In addition to the resistances at the local and household levels, women have engaged as well in gendered strategies of resistance within the CGM. The most salient strategy is the so-called transversal politics, which rejects a homogenising global feminist or global sisterhood perspective. An example of such attempt is the 'Women of the Americas Gathering Toward Porto Alegre, 2003'. The meeting was held in Cuenca, Ecuador from 24–26 October, 2002. The groups present at the meeting were from different parts of Latin America and used the meeting to brainstorm about how to introduce a feminist and gender perspective to the World Social Forum.[50] At the meeting the following strategy was formulated in response to African-Ecuadorian complaints that they are made invisible:

The women of the gathering concluded that the struggle must be transversal, in other words, constructed on the intersections of women's different realities, priorities and experiences. It is impossible to put an end to oppression without also examining the differences in privileges amongst women; therefore, these differences must be recognized and debated. A true plurality must be put into practice, constructing spaces of inclusion that also respect our autonomy and uniqueness. Crossing the question of race with class, gender and sexuality women can propose a model of diversity and solidarity to confront the homogenizing effects of neoliberal and authoritarian thought.[51]

In sum, the examples provided give an idea of the range of resistance strategies in which women are involved and also of the importance of positionality, identity and the renegotiation as well as challenging and problematising of boundaries. This does not mean that men are not involved at the local level or may be engaging in boundary renegotiation. It appears, however, that women are predominantly involved at the community level.[52] In many instances, women explicitly connect

---

[49] For a detailed analysis of testimonies, see Marianne H. Marchand, 'Latin American Voices of Resistance: Women's Movements and Development Debates', in Stephen J. Rosow, Naeem Inayatullah, and Mark Rupert (eds.), *The Global Economy as Political Space* (Boulder, CO: Lynne Riener, 1994) and Marchand, 'Some Theoretical Musings'.

[50] Centro de Medios Independientes, 28 October 2002, 'The Women of the Americas Gathering', <http://ecuador.indymedia.org/es/2002/10/464.shtml>, downloaded 6 March 2003.

[51] Centro de Medios Independientes, 'The Women of the Americas', p. 3.

[52] See also Moser, *Gender Planning*.

reproductive issues, which tend to be very pressing at the local level, to the overall transformations of the global political economy. Moreover, women tend to also be much more explicitly concerned about how their positionality affects the resistance strategies they choose. The focus on transversal politics is an illustration of this.

Sites of resistance

Although discussed here separately, it is clear that resistance practices, strategies and sites are intricately connected. While strategies and practices are aimed at renegotiating boundaries between (social) spheres affected by global restructuring, the sites are located at the interstices of such boundaries as the public-private, domestic-international and global-local. For instance, women involved in community organising to demand the delivery of public services or the provision of basic needs are situating their struggle simultaneously at the interstices of the public-private, economic-societal and global-local. In terms of the public-private boundary, community organisations are challenging the privatisation of public services, which often lead to higher prices being charged for such basic provisions as health services, clean drinking water, transportation and garbage collection. In fact, a double privatisation has been taking place. Budget cuts in government spending and concomitant privatising of public services have lead to a situation where many women are taking up the slack by, for instance, caring for sick family members. In other words, provisions which fell until recently within the public domain have been privatised, not only in the sense that private companies are now providing these services, but also because many of these tasks are now being performed for free by women.[53]

At the same time, opposition to such policies by the state involves a challenging of the boundary between the economy and society. The demand for basic affordable provisions is questioning their marketisation. Instead of such marketisation, many community/local women's organisations are arguing that these basic needs should be provided by the state because they involve the minimum requirements for human and social development. In other words, such provisions should not be subjected to an economic rationale, but should rather be seen as basic economic and social economic rights.

Such framing also relates to the global-local boundary. As many states have engaged in budget cuts and privatisation policies in response to pressures from International Financial Institutions to introduce structural adjustment programmes, the community-based resistances also address the global. The following passages from the report on 'The Women of the Americas Gathering' reflect this:

Women must overcome their differences and find a way to unite in the struggle against global capitalism and its destructive effects on populations, cultures, and the economies of the south.

The indigenous women were also present, speaking about the reality in their communities where globalisation is trying to erase their cultures, traditional knowledge, and subsistence-based economies. They insisted on the importance of valuing and developing their ethnic

[53] Marchand and Runyan, 'Introduction. Feminist Sightings'.

identity as a form of resistance against the attacks of capitalism; for example, they spoke of rescuing their traditional medicine, fighting for food sovereignty, refusing genetically-modified seeds, and combating all types of discrimination.[54]

What these passages illustrate is not only how the indigenous women's groups at the meeting see the articulation of their ethnic identity as a strategy of resistance, but also how they connect their local struggle to the global. In defending traditional medicine, calling for food security and opposing genetically modified seeds they are redrawing the boundaries between their local communities and the global economy. They oppose in particular the direction taken by the WTO and the FTAA on such issues as Trade Related Intellectual Property Rights, trade liberalisation concerning agricultural products as well as food safety and the preservation of biodiversity.

As the discussion above indicates, the public-private boundary is an important, if not the most important, site for women's resistances. The major contribution to public debate made by feminist thought and women's organising is a reconceptualisation of the public-private to include not only the public=state and private=market spheres, but also the domestic=household sphere. As Margaret Keck and Kathryn Sikkink[55] suggest, there is no better illustration of this than the organising around the issue of violence against women. Before the rearticulation of the private-public divide could be addressed there was first the need to define the term 'violence against women'. This was done by finding an overall category which could absorb separate, local campaigns against such diverse issues as dowry deaths, rape and battery, female genital mutilation and sexual slavery.[56] The construction of the overall category of violence against women helped to make people see similarities and even sameness among diverse issues. It was only then that people could be mobilised on a large scale and start campaigning internationally.[57]

But, as Keck and Sikkink argue, the contribution of women's organising around the issue of violence against women went further:

A new focus on violence in the private sphere was the major conceptual innovation that the issue of violence against women contributed to the international human rights discourse. Traditional human rights work had focused on trying to get governments to stop doing something (for instance, torturing or imprisoning people). Certainly some violence against women is carried out by the state, as when rape is used as an instrument of ethnic cleansing in Bosnia, or prison guards are particularly abusive in their treatment of women prisoners; but most violence against women is carried out by private individuals within the household or community. In cases like female genital mutilation or dowry death, the key perpetrators may even be other women, including mothers or mothers-in-law. The new international attention to violence against women implied rethinking the boundaries between public and private (as had the antislavery and anti-footbinding movements).[58]

As the above passage suggests, the campaign to stop violence against women implies a rearticulation of the public-private. However, it also involves to some extent a reordering of hierarchies among boundaries and domains. For instance the human

---

[54] Centro de Medios Independientes, 'The Women of the Americas', p. 2.
[55] Keck and Sikkink, *Activists Beyond Borders*.
[56] Ibid., p. 171.
[57] Ibid., p. 172.
[58] Ibid., pp. 172–3.

rights discourse had to be reconceptualised to also include women's rights. This did not just involve the addition of the category 'women'. It involved a serious rethinking of when and where human rights violations take place. Moreover, it implied a recognition that state authorities are not the only perpetrators of human rights abuses.

Violence against women is not directly linked to (economic) globalisation, although the campaign definitely has a global reach.[59] Indirectly however, there is some evidence that, for instance, economic crises may lead to increases in domestic violence. Recently, a particular form of violence against women, which appears to be linked to global restructuring, has received international attention. It concerns the serial murders of young women, most of whom have come to Ciudad Juárez, Mexico to work in the *maquiladoras*.

These murders have been going on for some ten years and the estimates are that 300–400 women have been murdered and 400–1,000 missing.[60] The murders are particularly gruesome because they involve torture of the victims and gang rape. When the bodies are found they 'are usually mutilated, laid out in cross formation, and branded with signature carvings on various parts of their bodies'.[61] One of the major problems is that in all those years none of the murders has been solved, primarily because of police incompetence and disinterest. Some of the police spokespeople have even gone as far as blaming the victims by suggesting that they were 'loose women' or involved in drug trafficking.[62]

Despite the organising by local groups, such as *Nuestras Hijas de las Casas* (May Our Daughters Return Home) and women's crisis centre *Casa Amiga*, it was very difficult to make these murders and disappearances into a political priority. Even the local media have not been very cooperative in putting the issue on the political agenda.

This situation has recently changed, however. For one, the documentary *Señorita Extraviada* (Missing Young Woman) by Lourdes Portillo, which relates these murders, has been aired nationally and internationally.[63] Moreover, the issue of these gender-specific murders has been recast into a human rights frame through the interventions of Amnesty International and the Inter-American Commission on Human Rights. In October 2002 the Inter-American Commission on Human Rights held a hearing on the murders and Amnesty International recently started an international campaign.

The changes in the campaign against the gender-specific murders in Ciudad Juárez involve an interesting shift in sites of resistance. Local organisations have focused primarily on the public-private boundary. They have done so, on the one hand, by showing that these young women have homes and families and are, therefore, not 'rootless' and loose women, a twist that the local police force has been trying to impose. On the other hand, these organisations have demanded that the private multinational companies provide more security to their female employees

---

[59] Ibid.
[60] Donnah Baynton, 'Murder in Juárez and Beyond', <http://americas.org/News/Features/ 200304_MayJune/CiudadJuarez.htm>, downloaded on 6 March 2003.
[61] Baynton, 'Murder in Juárez', p. 1.
[62] Ibid.
[63] Ibid.

when they travel to and from work. So far the companies have resisted by invoking Chapter 11 of the North American Free Trade Agreement, which provides protection to investors. This chapter can be read as prohibiting the Mexican government from implementing policies which oblige North American companies to provide protection or transportation for their workers.[64]

With the intervention by human rights organisations, the site of resistance has shifted from the public-private to the global-local boundary. Invoking a human rights dimension implies certain obligations on behalf of the Mexican state. The state not only has to take more serious action in persecuting and bringing to trial the perpetrators of these murders, but is also bound to provide more security for the *maquiladora* women. This can be done by ensuring that the streets are safe(r) and by requiring the *maquiladoras* owners to provide more security.

In terms of gendered sites of resistances we can conclude that the public-private boundary has been the primary site for women's groups and feminism. Interestingly, the public-private boundary has been reconceptualised through such resistances to include the domestic sphere or household. This is not to say that feminist and women's opposition has not been located at other sites. Often, however, it involves an expansion to other boundaries rather than leaving the public-private. It appears, however, from some of the examples concerning violence against women, that for a real breakthrough in terms of political attention and action there needs to be a reframing of the issue. In the example provided by Keck and Sikkink and in the case of the murders in Ciudad Juárez this involved a recasting into a human rights frame.

This section on gendered resistances did not address the possibility of masculine sites of resistances against globalisation. In part this is because men have not really organised *as men* to counter the negative effects of global restructuring. However, one can speculate that certain sites are more attractive to men and others to women. For instance, women seem to be very active at the local or community level. Because of their different positionality(ies) men may be more inclined to situate their resistances at the domestic-international boundary. One example of this could be the opposition of organised labour to free trade agreements. Being at least until recently (and to some degree still) male-dominated, labour unions appear to reflect a different politics of location and engagement. They have predominantly been drawn into a nationalist and protectionist discourse, defending national industry against the invasion of foreign investment. At the same time they have fought against the erosion of labour standards due to national TNCs moving abroad. These struggles have been concentrated at the domestic-international boundary as they are aimed at persuading the (national) state to intervene in the face of international competition.

Conclusion

This article started with the question whether feminists find themselves in the limelight of the CGM. From that question emerged two concerns, which I have tried to address: What does a gender analysis of a politics of resistance against globalisation entail? And, can we identify a gendered politics of resistance against globalisation?

---

[64] Ibid.

The analysis suggests that it is possible not only to develop a gender perspective on globalisation or global restructuring, but that there seem to be some gender differences as far as the politics of resistance are concerned. A gender analysis involves an understanding that gender operates at various levels, the ideological, physical and the social. From this follows that resistances should be contextualised and that we need to explore the linkages among them. As the different examples of resistance suggest, there are multiple practices, strategies and sites of resistance. It is, therefore important that we look beyond the CGM, especially since this is not a homogenous movement at all.

Moreover, feminist literature has informed us that gender is a significant boundary ma(r)ker and identity producer. As such it is a focal point not only for and of global restructuring, but also in articulating resistances against such processes. One of the interesting findings in this respect is that women are organising *as women*, but men are not organising *as men* in their struggle against global restructuring. In other words, gendered resistances against global restructuring involve a renegotiation and rearticulation of identities and boundaries.

The gendered politics is also reflected in the choice of practices, like weaving a web of solidarity, and strategies such as giving testimony. Most of the examples discussed in this article show that a gendered politics of resistance is primarily concerned with the renegotiation and reconceptualisation of the public-private boundary. This renegotiation can be related to other boundary renegotiations. There is even some evidence, which suggests that a multi-sited resistance may be more effective than one that only involves a single site.

Human rights and the global politics of resistance: feminist perspectives

FIONA ROBINSON

> While there is much talk these days around the United Nations about global governance, there is not yet talk about global governance that includes our half of the population.
>
> (Charlotte Bunch, 1995:25).[1]

Introduction

Talk of human rights is, currently, nearly as ubiquitous as talk of globalisation. While globalisation has been described as 'the most over used and under specified term in the international policy sciences since the end of the Cold War', the same could reasonably be said of 'human rights'.[2] Human rights are a product of the immediate aftermath of World War II, and thus they developed, in their contemporary form, in the context of the Cold War. The philosophical and political roots of human rights, of course, date back at least to the seventeenth and eighteenth centuries, and some would say even further, to the Stoics of Ancient Greece. Globalisation, too, has unfolded mainly in the late twentieth-century and has reached a position of prominence in the post-Cold War context; at this juncture, and according to popular perception, the spread of market capitalism, Western culture and modern technology fit comfortably with the death of socialism and the 'end of history'. But globalisation too has roots that date back much earlier – as early as, it has been argued, the fourteenth century.[3]

During the past two decades, one important feature of globalisation has been the unprecedented growth in international non-governmental organisations and global social movements; together, these groups are often described as comprising the new 'global' civil society. Many of these groups seek to challenge the neoliberal logic of economic globalisation and also to contest the policies and practices of the institutions of contemporary global governance. Human rights discourse has played a central role in articulating this challenge from transnational non-state actors.

---

[1] Charlotte Bunch, 'Through women's eyes: global forces facing women in the 21st century', speech delivered at the Plenary Proceedings of the NGO Forum on Women, Beijing, 1995, in Eva Friedlander (ed.), *Look at the World Through Women's Eyes: Plenary Speeches from the NGO Forum on Women, Beijing, '95* (New York: Women, Ink., 1996), p. 25.
[2] Richard Devetak and Richard Higgott, 'Justice Unbound: Globalization, States and the Transformation of the Social Bond', *International Affairs*, 75:3 (1999).
[3] Jan Aart Scholte, 'Globalisation: Prospects for a Paradigm Shift', in Martin Shaw, *Globalisation: Knowledge, Ethics and Agency* (London: Routledge, 1999), p. 14.

Indeed, almost without exception, the organisations of global civil society – regardless of their self-designation as anti-globalisation, peace or environmental groups – voice their resistance using the moral, legal and political language of human rights. Moreover, in addition to these broad-based groups, there also exists a highly developed 'global' human rights movement, consisting of a large number of transnational, non-state, human rights actors.

It is in the light of this context that this article seeks to conduct a gender-based analysis of the use of human rights discourse and strategies by global civil society, and of the nature and effects of human rights activism as a form of resistance against globalisation. The article will comprise three parts. The first part looks briefly at the nature of globalisation and makes a case for the need for a gender-based analysis of the processes of globalisation, including its various facets, and its diverse effects. The second part explores the 'global civil society' literature, examining and critiquing the ways in which the realm of non-state actors is currently understood in much recent literature in International Relations (IR). Much contemporary 'critical' literature within IR focuses on the positive and progressive role to be played by non-state actors and by 'global civil society' more generally. This is especially evident in constructivist scholarship which makes a case for the ability of these groups to influence states and state policy through norm promotion and 'entrepreneurship'.

In particular, constructivist research has shown how transnational non-state actors in the field of human rights have been successful in bringing 'new ideas, norms, and discourses' into policy debates and in promoting norm implementation among 'target actors'.[4] But upon closer examination, it becomes clear that these norms, ideas and discourses are not entirely 'new'; on the contrary, they are often articulations of conventional liberal accounts of human rights which merge, at a general level, with the expectations and policy goals of powerful states. Thus, in spite of their widespread use and proliferating scope, orthodox understandings of human rights cannot provide the necessary discursive or strategic tools to mount serious resistance to globalisation for those who are most vulnerable to it.

This section will also include an analysis of the dominant discourse of human rights, which is widely accepted by many IR scholars, especially many constructivists, as the central and most important normative or 'moral' discourse in world politics. I will argue, however, that many of the most influential organisations of global civil society – mainly northern NGOs and social movements – have relied on an ostensibly universal discourse of human rights to promote a set of values that are heavily gendered and which reflect a Western bias. As such, it could be argued that 'human rights' – as a normative and strategic concept – has limited applicability for those individuals and groups – especially women from the South – who are made most vulnerable by the processes of globalisation.

The third and final part of the article will explore feminist reconceptualisations of rights, as well as the ways in which women's groups have employed their own brand of rights discourse. Indeed, it is evident that women *are* employing rights discourse; concurrently with the rise of global civil society, more situated, local, 'grassroots'

---

[4] Margaret E. Keck and Kathryn Sikkink (eds.), *Activists Beyond Borders: Advocacy Networks in International Politics* (Ithaca, NY: Cornell University Press, 1998), p. 3.

movements are emerging, led by women – especially non-Western women – around the world. But because these groups do not always fit into the prescribed definition of 'global civil society' – often because their work originates in or is focused on developing countries, and thus may be more locally-based – their resistance to globalisation is less visible. Thus, while women are using the language of rights to articulate their goals, they are expanding and reshaping it in order that it may address their concerns and needs. While this can be seen as a positive step, it is also the case that the claims of these women are often disregarded or ignored by the institutions of global governance, which seek a liberal, masculinist view of human rights to converge with their aims: liberal democracy and 'good governance' in the context of market-based economic development.

While there can be no single discursive or moral or political strategy against globalisation, I will, however, suggest that feminist reworkings of human rights may offer a fundamentally new understanding of what it means to challenge globalisation, based on two key factors: first, the recognition of relationships as a fundamental ontological feature of human social life, and second, a scepticism of 'universal humanity' and moral universalism, tied to a commitment to the recognition of difference and specificity. Reconceptualised to take account of these two alternative understandings, human rights may have a strategic and rhetorical role to play in challenging globalisation, but they will no longer be able to articulate 'human' goods – such as democracy and environmental security – as 'genuinely universal, consensual aspects of a global "common good"'.[5] I do not suggest this approach as an ethical or legal strategy strictly 'for' women; rather, it should be understood as a normative and strategic approach with widespread relevance for groups and individuals, and as one which questions the necessity of globalisation without replacing it with yet another set of moral and political absolutes.

Globalisation, human rights and resistance

It is now widely accepted that globalisation is a set of processes not restricted to any single sphere, but rather spanning across economics, culture and politics. While corporate symbols and brands – McDonald's, NIKE, Coca-Cola – have become icons of globalisation, they capture only a small part of a set of complex global transformations. Scholte's notion of 'deterritorialization', for example, suggests a profound shift from a world organised around clearly demarcated territories, to a 'borderless', 'distance-less' world, inexorably linked by instantaneous ('time-less') communications.[6] The effects of this transformation on 'culture', individual and group identity and personal and social relations are clearly profound, and their extent remains as yet unknown. In terms of politics, deterritorialisation is directly linked to the transformation of sovereignty and the nature of the sovereign state – once central to the material and discursive organisation of 'national' and 'inter-

---

[5] Mustapha Pasha and David Blaney, 'Elusive Paradise: The Promise and Peril of Global Civil Society', *Alternatives*, 23 (1998), pp. 436–7.
[6] Jan Aarte Scholte, *Globalization: A Critical Introduction* (Basingstoke: Macmillan, 2000), p. 46.

national' political life, the nature of sovereign authority is now, if not necessarily diminished, certainly substantially altered.

This has led many commentators to argue that governance is becoming, in some important sense, global. This is not to suggest, however, that the state is no longer an important site of governance, nor that governance has simply been transferred to some single, global entity. On the contrary, governance has become more 'multi-layered' – increasingly 'diffused across substate (municipal and provincial) and suprastate (regional and transworld) agencies as well as state organs'.[7] International organisations, including international financial institutions, as well as non-governmental organisations, social movements and transnational corporations have become important agencies of governance and regulation in a globalising world.

Many of these changes to governance are related – in terms of both cause and effect – to the economic aspects of globalisation. Economic globalisation – in the realms of production, trade and, finance – is, to a large extent, responsible for transformations in the nature of time and space, and in the nature and role of sovereignty and the sovereign state. Moreover, technology, especially information and communications technology, is regarded as the key 'enabling and contributing factor to globalisation processes'. As Marchand and Runyan point out:

> ... without the advent of computers and other new means of communication, financial markets would, for instance, never have been able to integrate into one global financial market. Likewise, firms' integrated production networks and strategies of just-in-time (JIT) delivery would have been impossible without computers.[8]

Thus, while the revolutions in technology have facilitated the globalisation processes, it is widely agreed that a particular set of actors, including transnational corporations, international financial institutions and states, constitute the 'main driving forces' behind globalisation.[9] It is the agency of these actors, combined with the structural forces of global capitalism, which are propelling the increasing integration of financial markets, production processes and trade.

Recognising the significance of economic globalisation must avoid, however, the slide into reductionism. As Marchand and Runyan argue, many conventional representations and interpretations of globalisation are too narrowly economistic, and thus pay little attention to attendant 'global/local restructurings of social, cultural, racial, ethnic, gender, national, and familial identities, roles and relations'.[10] In particular, they argue that gender analysis is especially well-equipped for developing a better understanding of the various dimensions of globalisation. They provide a useful classification of three sets of interrelated issues and concerns which can be illuminated through gender analysis. First, questions concerning the conceptualisation of globalisation and global restructuring, such as 'what are the gendered constructions of the new global political economy'; second, questions concerning the sites or spaces of global restructuring; and third, questions addressing the

---

[7] Ibid., p. 22.
[8] Marianne Marchand and Anne Sisson Runyan, 'Introduction. Feminist Sightings of Global Restructuring: Conceptualizations and Reconceptualizations', in Marchand and Runyan (eds.), *Gender and Global Restructuring: Sightings, Sites and Resistances* (London: Routledge, 2000), p. 5.
[9] Ibid., p. 4.
[10] Ibid., p. 1.

responses and forms of resistance which global restructuring has evoked, such as 'does gender analysis enable us to formulate, and even advocate, varying kinds of resistance strategies which make sense from a feminist perspective'?[11]

While this article cannot address all of these issues, it is primarily concerned with the final set of questions regarding the responses and forms of resistance which global restructuring has evoked. In particular, the following sections will examine the prevalence of human rights-centred responses to globalisation and global restructuring, focusing on the extent to which these forms of resistance may be gendered, and whether they have been, or indeed can be, inclusive of the needs and concerns of women.

Global civil society and human rights

The existence and nature of contemporary global civil society is currently the subject of much debate. Proponents of the term 'global civil society' argue that, while in the early modern period civil society was socially and territorially bounded, what is new about the contemporary use of civil society is both its transnational character and its emphasis on participation. On one characterisation, transnational or global civil society represents a 'demand for a radical extension of democracy across national and social boundaries'.[12] Martin Shaw has suggested that global civil society corresponds to an emerging 'global state' which reflects the 'pooling of the monopoly of violence among major states'.[13] On this view, then, global civil society in the contemporary world is not so much a collection of already existing and often strong national civil societies; rather, it is a single 'society' which corresponds to a 'global state'. This emerging global state represents the convergence – in terms of policy and action in the fields of both security and economy – of the so-called 'major' states; as such the global state must be understood as Western and powerful – both militarily and economically. On this view, the new social movements – for peace, human rights, democracy and the environment – represent a new potential for 'global consciousness'; they are about the growth of new forms of action which are seen as 'spearheading globalism'.[14]

Constructivism in IR has been at the forefront of the analysis of global or 'transnational' civil society, especially with respect to international human rights. Constructivists have sought to demonstrate how norms may shape state interests, and thus have an important impact on their conduct within the international system. In particular, they have focused on emergent norms relating to human rights, demonstrating how these norms can mitigate states' self-interested behaviour, and can thus act as a powerful constraint on the established norms of

---

[11] Ibid., p. 2.
[12] Mary Kaldor, 'Transnational Civil Society', in Tim Dunne and Nicholas J. Wheeler (eds.), *Human Rights in Global Politics* (Cambridge: Cambridge University Press, 1999), p. 195.
[13] Martin Shaw, 'Global Voices: Civil Society and the Media in Global Crises', in Tim Dunne and Nicholas J. Wheeler (eds.), *Human Rights in Global Politics* (Cambridge: Cambridge University Press, 1999), p. 217.
[14] Ibid., p. 221.

sovereignty.[15] In most of the literature, the norms of human rights – characteristically interventionist, cosmopolitan, and morally 'good', are contrasted to the
norms of sovereignty – state-centric, communitarian, and self-interested.[16] As
Rodger Payne and Nayef Samhat assert, '... human rights NGOs, broadly defined,
are acquiring a degree of authority in world politics that challenges the
unquestioned place of the state'.[17]

While this constructivist research is diverse in both substantive and conceptual
content, there is a central theoretical argument which is widely shared: that
'transnational human rights pressures and policies, including the activities of
advocacy networks, have made a very significant difference in bringing about
improvements in human rights practices in diverse countries around the world'.[18]
Most of these authors focus on what is referred to as a 'central core of rights' – the
right to be free from extrajudicial execution and disappearance, and the right to be
free from torture and arbitrary arrest and detention. Risse, Ropp and Sikkink,
whose work has such a focus, claim that they do not wish to suggest that other rights
in the Declaration are unimportant; rather, they argue that their focus reflects the
fact that these basic 'rights of the person' have been 'most accepted as universal
rights, and not simply rights associated with a particular ideology or system'.[19]

Another constructivist scholar, Ann Marie Clark, has explored the role of
Amnesty International in creating and implementing international human rights
norms. She argues that, since its beginning, Amnesty International has demonstrated
leadership in the emergence of specific international norms concerning torture,
disappearances and extrajudicial executions.[20] In practical terms, AI had two related
yet distinct goals: the long-term goal of the development of international human
rights norms, and the more immediate goal of relief for individual prisoners of state
repression.[21] It is this case study which is used to illustrate her wider theoretical
argument: that the autonomous nature of NGOs, which keeps them independent of
state interests, also places them in a position to act as legitimate advocates of
principled norms in the international system.[22]

While all of these works offer meticulous research and careful analysis of the
development of these norms, and of the theory of 'norm-construction' by non-state
actors, I would argue that there are inherent limitations in the constructivist approach
to global civil society and human rights. First, there appears to be remarkably little

---

[15] See Thomas Risse, Stephen C. Ropp and Kathryn Sikkink (eds.), *The Power of Human Rights:
International Norms and Domestic Change* (Cambridge: Cambridge University Press, 1999); Anne
Marie Clark, *Diplomacy of Conscience: Amnesty International and Changing Human Rights Norms*
(Princeton, NJ: Princeton University Press, 2001).

[16] For one significant exception to this, see Christian Reus-Smit, 'Human Rights and the Social
Construction of Sovereignty', *Review of International Studies*, 27: 4 (2001).

[17] Rodger A. Payne and Nayef H. Samhat, 'Democratizing Global Politics: Comparing Models and
Practice', Paper delivered at the Annual Conference of the International Studies Association, New
Orleans, LA, March 2002, pp. 27–8.

[18] Thomas Risse and Stephen C. Ropp, 'International Human Rights Norms and Domestic Change:
Conclusions', in Risse *et al.* (eds.), *Power of Human Rights*, p. 275.

[19] Thomas Risse and Kathryn Sikkink, 'The Socialization of Human Rights Norms into Domestic
Practices: Introduction', in Risse *et al,* (eds.), *Power of Human Rights*, p. 2.

[20] Clark, *Diplomacy of Conscience*, p. 125.

[21] Ibid., p. 126.

[22] Ibid.

critical analysis of the norms themselves in this work. The norms developed by Amnesty and other NGOs surrounding human rights are described by Clark as 'principled norms' – norms based on moral principles.[23] Indeed, the progressive and 'good' nature of these norms is taken for granted, based largely on their association with 'human rights', an historically rich and theoretically complex concept which remains opaque and under-theorised in much of the literature. Second, the decision to focus on 'core' civil and political rights reflects a bias which has been inherent in many of the large NGOs themselves, as well as in global civil society more generally. The assertion that these rights have been 'most accepted as universal' reflects gender and Western-centric biases, and overlooks the profound criticisms that have been waged against this individual-state model of human rights by women and non-Western peoples the world over. To suggest that these types of rights have not been associated with a particular 'ideology or system', moreover, fails to acknowledge the important historical, philosophical and ideological connections between the rise of individual political rights and liberalism, in both its classical and contemporary forms. Third, in spite of the central constructivist argument – that norms modify state behaviour and sovereign practices – a strict dichotomy is nevertheless drawn between states and NGOs/civil society. There is an assumption that, were they not influenced by the moral principles of NGOs, states would continue to act in their interests, defined in terms of power. NGOs like Amnesty, by contrast, are regarded as independent of state interests and thus act '(i)n defiance of power consider-ations'.[24] This overlooks the extent to which human rights themselves and the principles that give rise to them cannot be extracted from considerations of power.[25]

It is worth noting, moreover, that many of these assumptions about the inherently progressive role of civil society groups in international politics are mirrored in the work of other analysts of global civil society and international politics working from outside the constructivist theoretical orientation. For many advocates of GCS, for example, the term is not simply an analytical or descriptive one; indeed, GCS represents a 'political project'. The nature of the project is that it is eclipsing familiar yet outdated ideological cleavages between left and right, and replacing them with a national/international divide. As Mary Kaldor explains:

> … in the post-Cold War period, the fundamental political cleavage, which could define the way in which we view contemporary society .. (is the) division between *those who stand for internationalist, Europeanist, democratic values, including human rights, and those who remain wedded to national or exclusivist thinking*.[26]

Here, there is no attempt to disguise the nature of the 'project'. Indeed, it is those modern, Western (or Europeanist) values which are progressive, and which correspond to the movements towards 'globalism'. Human rights, moreover, are at the forefront of this project. On this formulation, the most crucial kinds of rights are clearly those rights of the person which protect and enhance the Western model of 'democratic citizenship' – freedom of speech, movement, political participation,

---

[23] Ibid., p. 4.
[24] Ibid., p. 126.
[25] See especially Neil Stammers, 'Human Rights and Power', *Political Studies*, 41 (1993), pp. 70–82.
[26] Kaldor, 'Transnational Civil Society', p. 195, emphasis added.

and so on. For many advocates of the transformative potential of GCS, the fact that global civil society originated among Western social elites appears to be only a minor problem. Martin Shaw, for example, suggests that this is a problem solely of 'representativeness'. Although he worries about how far global civil society actually involves people across the globe, he seems convinced that globalist ideas represent 'inclusive global interests in an ideological sense'.[27] Thus, those who do not stand for the internationalist, Europeanist, democratic values that Kaldor describes (such as human rights) are victims of either false consciousness or pathology; in spite of their lack of participation and voice, however, we can be assured that their true interests are being represented by global civil society nevertheless.

Moreover, although the use of the human rights discourse by global civil society is widespread, the perceived links between global civil society and human rights are more than discursive. Mary Kaldor has argued that to be part of civil society implies a shared commitment to common human values and, in this sense, the concept of global civil society might, in fact, be *equated* with the notion of a global human rights culture. Indeed, she sees the two notions as convergent:

Some would argue that civil society is broader since it encompasses issues such as peace, gender equality and the environment. But these can easily, and in some cases rather usefully, be reconceptualized as human rights issues. Hence, Russian human rights groups who campaign against the war in Chechnya argue that the war is a massive violation of human rights. Likewise, independent trade unions in Russia argue that they are human rights organisations concerned with workers' rights. The advantage of the human rights discourse is its globalist character and its emphasis on the individual – the 'last child' as Gandhi put it.[28]

I would argue, however, in direct contrast to this view, that the 'globalist' (and also 'universalist') character of human rights may be its disadvantage – especially, as I will explain below, in the case of individuals and groups for whom the dominant conceptions of human rights are irrelevant or even potentially harmful. Certainly, for many of the NGOs which most readily come to mind when thinking about global civil society, the terms 'universal', and 'Western' aptly describe their understanding of human rights. For example, although groups such as Amnesty International and Human Rights Watch have recently begun to pay lip-service to economic, social and cultural rights, these rights remain secondary to 'first generation' civil and political rights – rights which have always been prioritised by Western states, international organisations, and international NGOs.[29]

While the voices of these large, global human rights NGOs are certainly being heard by state actors and multilateral institutions, the norms that they are advocating are closely aligned with the norms of 'democracy' and 'good governance' being promoted by many Western states and multilateral institutions in an era of globalisation. For those whose needs and interests are not addressed by these broad goals – including most women and especially women of the South – these conventional articulations of human rights by large 'global' NGOs may prove to be a less than effective normative and discursive strategy for representation, organisation and resistance.

---

[27] Shaw, 'Global Voices', p. 221.
[28] Kaldor, 'Transnational Civil Society', pp. 210–11.
[29] See Fiona Robinson, 'NGOs and the Advancement of Economic and Social Rights: Philosophical and Practical Controversies', *International Relations*, 17:1 (2003).

It is in the light of realisations such as this that some recent research has shown caution, and even pessimism, regarding the extent to which global civil society can truly challenge globalisation and global governance. For example, it is crucial to recognise that NGOs are often dependent for financial support from governments and other international institutions; thus, the NGOs may serve more to support existing systems of governance than to replace them.[30] Spivak has suggested that 'international civil society' is, in fact, a creation of the agents of what she calls 'transnational financialization'; these agents name the collectivity of collaborative non-governmental organisations an 'international civil society', bypassing individual states, and then 'attempt to appropriate these NGOs by much publicized particip-ation at UN conferences'.[31]

Moreover, it has also been argued that civil society, with its voluntarist ethos and emphasis on extra-state groups and associations, is now being lauded as a substitute for state power, particularly in the areas of state activity being rolled back by neoliber-alism: welfare, education, and health.[32] 'Civil society', argues William Graf, 'liberates citizens from the fetters of state regulations and oppression, while good governance does away with whole areas of state activity and reduces its functions in the interests of greater efficiency'.[33] It has been demonstrated by many feminists that cutbacks in areas such as these are especially hard-hitting on women and children; this is because women and children are the major recipients (and women are the major providers) of services such as health care in both developed and developing countries.[34]

Seen in this way, it is a confusion to claim that global civil society is *necessarily* a site and source of resistance to globalisation. While 'progressive' forces look to civil society as a site for mounting challenges to globalisation, it is important to remember that a strengthened civil society is itself a goal of neoliberal forces. For neoliberals, a strengthened civil society translates into a reduced state. Indeed, it has been argued that NGOs, promoted by the World Bank and other agencies, are driving a wedge between the NGOs and governmental departments, and are thus restraining the role of the state and eroding its legitimacy. On this view, NGOs are complicit in global capitalism, and are instruments of the 'new thrust of the neoliberal dogma in which the state itself … is given a back seat'.[35] As Marchand and Runyan argue,

… the elements of civil society neoliberals wish to privilege over the state are precisely those which will broaden and deepen relations of domination in the absence of any recourse to democratic governance at the local, national and global levels.[36]

---

[30] Pasha and Blaney, 'Elusive Paradise', pp. 432–3.
[31] Gayatri Chakravorti Spivak, 'Cultural Talks in the Hot Peace: Revisiting the Global Village', in Pheng Cheah and Bruce Robbins (eds.), *Cosmopolitics: Thinking and Feeling Beyond the Nation* (Minneapolis, MI: University of Minnesota Press, 1998), p. 339.
[32] William Graf, 'Democratization "for" the Third World: Critique of a Hegemonic Project', *Canadian Journal of Development Studies*, Special Issue (1996), reprinted in Mark Charlton (ed.), *Crosscurrents: International Relations in the Post-Cold War Era*, 2nd edn. (Toronto: ITP Nelson, 1999), p. 549.
[33] Ibid.
[34] See D. Dahlerup, 'Learning to Live with the State – State, Market and Civil Society: Women's Need for State Intervention in East and West', *Women's Studies International Forum*, 17 (1994) and Mona Harrington, 'What Exactly's Wrong with the Liberal State as an Agent of Change', in V. Spike Peterson (eds.), *Gendered States: Feminist (Re)Visions of International Relations Theory* (Boulder, CO: Lynne Rienner, 1992).
[35] Rajni Kothari, 'Globalisation: A World Adrift', *Alternatives*, 22: 2 (1997), pp. 231–2.
[36] Marchand and Runyan, 'Feminist Sightings', p. 20.

This is not to say, however, that there are no 'oppositional structures' or counter-hegemonic forces in place within civil society; nor is to suggest that these groups are not often influential and effective, especially at the local level. Clearly, civil society is one of the most familiar grounds for feminist activists and women's NGOs; strengthening civil society, for example, is often regarded as an important objective in the struggle to improve women's human rights.[37] However, it is also the case that because of the nature of these groups, and also due to their often unorthodox understandings of women's rights, their claims often go unheard. To quote Spivak once again:

Alternative development collectivities, national-local health care, ecology and literacy collectivities have been in place for a long time, and play a critical role at the grassroots level. Why are they seldom heard? These oppositional structures are indigenous NGOs, or non-governmental organisations.[38]

The NGOs that surface at the 'NGO Forums' of the UN conferences have been so thoroughly vetted by the donor countries, and the content of their presentations so organized by categories furnished by the United Nations, that neither subject nor object bears much resemblance to the 'real thing', if you will pardon the expression.[39]

It could be argued, then, that the activities of 'global civil society' – meaning the civil society that is seen and heard – are thus neither autonomous from nor particularly challenging to the processes of globalisation. While there is certainly *potential* for resistance and transformation inherent within both the idea of human rights and the organisations and strategies of global civil society, their current incarnations have not, as yet, moved beyond the dominant, broadly liberal framework. As Scholte argues, the non-state actors that influence global economic governance are disproportionately Northern, Western, white, males who are also propertied, professional, computer-literate, English-speaking urban residents.[40] Not surprisingly, the values that tend to be put forward by these members are largely homogeneous. As Mustapha Pasha and David Blaney point out, 'envisioning a democratic global society requires resisting not only the existing oligarchical organisation of global life, but also the impulse to rectify that situation with a *prefigured set of global values* sponsored by the transnational extensions of actors from advanced industrial societies'. That values such as human rights and democracy (the values associated with GCS by virtually all of its proponents) are genuinely universal, consensual aspects of a global 'common good' is by no means beyond question.[41] This is especially the case when we consider the needs and interests of women, who are among the poorest of the poor in many developing countries.

Women reshaping human rights

The systematic exclusion of women from the political theory, and the ethics and law of human rights in particular, is now well-documented. Most commonly, it is argued

[37] Ibid.
[38] Spivak, 'Cultural Talks', p. 333.
[39] Ibid.
[40] See Jan Aart Scholte, 'Cautionary Reflections on Seattle', *Millennium: Journal of International Studies*, 29: 1 (2000), p. 119.
[41] Pasha and Blaney, 'Elusive Paradise', pp. 436–7.

that so-called 'human' rights are, in theory and in practice, 'men's' rights. As a consequence, exclusions, constraints and abuses more typical of women's lives are neither recognised nor protected by human rights instruments.[42] While there are many explanations offered for the gendering of 'universal' human rights, most can be traced back to the public/private dichotomy first advanced by the early liberals of the eighteenth century – theorists who were, not surprisingly, the authors of the historical antecedents to our contemporary Western understanding of human rights. Ursula O'Hare suggests that along these lines, two main arguments have emerged:

One argument suggests that the failure of the human rights system to reach women results from the deference it maintains towards the private sphere – human rights law privileges the public world while the private sphere is considered outside the scope of legal regulation. Others argue that the myth of nonintervention in the private sphere, which has grown up in human rights discourse, simply masks the gendered application of human rights law. ... In either case, both theories argue that women's issues have not been taken seriously by the human rights community.[43]

As many commentators have noted, the problematic nature of the public/private dichotomy is most starkly demonstrated by the issue of violence. From the systematic rape of women in the former Yugoslavia, to the less visible, but more pervasive 'intimate' violence committed against women in the home by their partners or other family members, violence against women has not been perceived as a human rights issue.[44]

Defenders of universal human rights would likely point to the enormous ground that has been gained in the struggle to ensure that women's human rights are recognised in both theory and practice. Indeed, when the UN's Commission on Human Rights failed to recognise women's aspirations adequately, women delegates and the NGOs that supported them managed to obtain a freestanding Commission on the Status of Women (CSW). By 1979, the CSW, with the support of women delegates and NGOs and a new wave of feminism underway, had drafted and successfully lobbied the adoption of the Convention on the Elimination of All Forms of Discrimination Against Women. By 1980, the Convention became an international women's human rights treaty.[45]

Perhaps even more important than the changes that have taken place within formal UN and state legal mechanisms is the work done by women towards reshaping the discourse and strategies of human rights within the realm of civil society. Indeed, as Marguerite Guzman Bouvard points out, women have long been active in the fight for human rights at all levels and on many fronts: in resistance during wartime, in struggles against colonialism and authoritarian governments, and,

---

[42] V. Spike Peterson and Laura Parisi, 'Are Women Human ? It's Not an Academic Question', in Tony Evans (ed.), *Human Rights Fifty Years On: A Reappraisal* (Manchester: Manchester University Press, 1998), p. 132.

[43] Ursula A. O'Hare, 'Realizing Human Rights for Women', *Human Rights Quarterly*, 21 (1999), p. 368.

[44] Ibid., pp. 369–71. While rape of women during war has recently been recognised by the International Criminal Court as a war crime, for centuries it was regarded as a regrettable yet inevitable 'by-product' of war, rather than a particularly gendered violation of women not as 'human beings', but as *women*.

[45] Arvonne Fraser, 'Becoming Human: The Origins and Development of Women's Human Rights', *Human Rights Quarterly*, 21 (1999), p. 857.

within democratic societies, in seeking their just claims and those of people excluded from the political community as defined by the largely male elite. [46] Importantly, many of the women engaged in these struggles made use of radical and alternative approaches to human rights based upon female views of the polity and of morality as well as a continuity between the public and private spheres.

These women regard human rights as enmeshed in all the factors that impinge upon our daily lives not only at the state level but also in the economic, social and religious arenas. Women activists are seeking to transform the assumptions, discourse and goals of the international human rights movement and, by implication, the power structures of states and international organisations. While recognizing the importance of liberal theory in rescuing the individual from governmental and nationalistic tyranny, they believe that there is another stage to traverse in order for democracy to achieve its full realization. Individual dignity must be part of relationships characterized by mutual respect, which foster both personal growth and the ongoing development of these ties.[47]

There are numerous examples of women's activist groups which have reshaped the human rights discourse so that it can more effectively address their needs and goals. Indeed, this is especially evident in the context of neoliberal development strategies. Many women's movements in developing countries have directed their protests around the daily impacts of restructuring as it affects their roles in production and reproduction. For example, in 1992, neighbourhood women's organisations in Ecuador were active in protesting against Citibank's freeze on US $800m from the Ecuadorian Central Bank's account.[48] While this protest could be viewed simply as a public response to the economic crisis that the country faced, it is important to recognise the different levels on which this protest, and its participants, can be understood. These women positioned themselves as rights-holders in opposition to the Ecuadorian state; that said, however, they deviated from the dominant understanding of rights as civil and political rights. As Amy Lind points out, the participants invoked a 'politicized notion of reproduction based on women's roles as consumers, as those most affected by the changes in consumer prices which accompany adjustment measures'.[49] Thus, although they acted as rights-holders, their understanding of rights challenged two dichotomies: first, between the 'public' and 'private' spheres, and second, between civil and political rights and economic, social and cultural rights.

Another better-known women's group whose actions have reshaped the nature of human rights are the Mothers of the Plaza de Mayo in Argentina. This group was first formed in 1977, when a group of women refused to accept the 'disappearance' of their children by the then ruling military regime. Each Thursday afternoon, the mothers appeared wearing white kerchiefs, embroidered with the names of their missing relatives and the dates of their disappearances. In a tight circle, the group would orbit a monument at the centre of the Plaza de Mayo in

---

[46] Marguerite Guzman Bouvard, *Women Reshaping Human Rights: How Extraordinary Activists are Changing the World* (Wilmington, DE: SR Books, 1996), p. xi.

[47] Ibid., p. xiii.

[48] Amy Lind, 'Negotiating Boundaries: Women's Organizations and the Politics of Restructuring in Ecuador', in Marchand and Runyan (eds.), *Gender and Global Restructuring*, p. 164.

[49] Ibid., p. 165,

absolute silence.[50] While the activities of the Mothers have broadened in scope since then, their goals, and their methods, remain the struggle for the rights of their missing children.

The Mothers represent an interesting use of rights. As Catherine Eschele has argued, they are an example of women articulating a public presence, and a demand for rights, through their maternal responsibilities, not despite them.[51] She points out that women acting politically in the form of social movements may draw on roles and skills learned within the family and domestic sphere, such as cooperative modes or organisation, maternal authority and the protection of children. While Eschele focuses here on how the movement form of political action can bridge the public and private spheres, the same arguments can be made regarding that which groups like the Mothers have acted upon in order to create a revised understanding of the nature of rights, and of rights-holders. Here, the agency of the rights holder is based on an experience specific to women – motherhood – rather than in some kind of universal humanity.[52]

It is important to remember, moreover, that since feminism is not an homogenous movement, women's groups have made, and will continue to make use of rights in many different ways. The sources of this diversity are evident in feminist theory, where critiques of rights are diverse and contentious. Some feminists focus on the conceptual limitations of rights in ethics, legal and political theory; for example, cultural feminists and those who embrace the ethics of care are concerned with the overly abstract nature of rights, as well as the selfish and atomistic vision of human nature and the contractual and usually conflictual view of social life that rights entail. In addition, feminist post-structuralists focus on the socio-linguistic hierarchies of rights discourse, and target the 'unitary self' for criticism. Others, by contrast, have focused on the strategic value of rights, and the contribution that rights can make towards feminist goals of emancipation and empowerment.[53]

For example, Celina Romany has argued that a feminist critique of human rights discourse has to grapple with the current dichotomisation of political/civil rights and economic/social rights. Doing so would 'underscore the social structural framework's role in the construction of gender subordination'.[54]

In order minimally to comply with women's civil and political rights, in order to ensure the minimum rights of citizenship, the dichotomy that exists in the current human rights discourse needs to be transcended. Thus, in ensuring women's civil and political rights, the state must be held to an affirmative duty to ensure the eradication of those social and economic conditions that maintain and perpetuate subordination.[55]

---

[50] Ravi Mattu, 'Las Madres de Plaza de Mayo: Civil Society in Argentina', *Latitudes*, 4 (1995).

[51] Catherine Eschele, Global Democracy, Social Movements and Feminism (Boulder, CO: Westview Press, 2001), p. 111.

[52] Ibid.

[53] Elizabeth Kiss, 'Alchemy or Fool's Gold? Assessing Feminist Doubts About Rights', in Mary Lyndon Shanley and Uma Narayan (eds.), *Reconstructing Political Theory: Feminist Perspectives* (Cambridge: Polity Press, 1997), p. 2.

[54] Celina Romany, 'State Responsibility Goes Private: A Feminist Critique of the Public/Private Distinction in International Human Rights Law', in Rebecca J. Cook (ed.), *Human Rights of Women: National and International Perspectives* (Philadelphia, PA: University of Pennsylvania Press, 1994), p. 107.

[55] Ibid., p. 108.

But many feminists have gone beyond this critique of certain aspects of the dominant human rights discourse, and have argued instead for an abandonment of rights as the primary normative framework for women's resistance. As Hilary Charlesworth points out, feminists have argued that a continuing focus on the acquisition of rights may not be beneficial: women's experiences and concerns are not easily translated into the narrow, individualistic language of rights. Rights discourse, she argues, overly simplifies complex power relations and their promise may be thwarted by structural inequalities of power; in addition, the balancing of 'competing' rights by decision-making bodies often reduces women's power; and particular rights, such as the right to freedom of religion or the protection of the family, can in fact justify the oppression of women.[56]

Such an analysis suggests rather bleak prospects for the potential of rights discourse to be instrumental to women's resistance and, ultimately, to the transformation of women's lives. That said, many women and women's groups are reluctant simply to abandon rights discourse and rights-based strategies. As Charlesworth explains:

Because women in most societies operate from such a disadvantaged position, rights discourse offers a recognized vocabulary to frame political and social wrongs. ... The empowering function of rights discourse for women, particularly in the international sphere where we are still almost completely invisible, is a crucial aspect of its value.[57]

This argument is reinforced by Laura Macdonald and Cathy Blacklock in their work on the nature of women's resistance in Mexico and Guatemala. The authors point out how, in their recent engagement with the issues of domestic and sexual violence in the private sphere and the socioeconomic violence of the feminisation of impoverishment perpetrated in the public sphere, women's organisations in these two countries have come face to face with the gendered silence of the discourse of human rights. Moreover, in the case of Mexico, the authors explore how indigenous organisations are encountering the limits to the 'use-value' of the discourse of human rights to recognise and support *specificity and difference*.[58]

Interestingly, while recognising these deficiencies, Blacklock and Macdonald remain persuaded by the discursive force of human rights. They correctly point out that, limited though it may be, international and domestic events have pushed popular sector activists to adopt a discourse of universal human rights as part of their citizenship demands. In other words, women and indigenous organisations are actually *using* this discourse; thus, it is suggested, our best course of action is to search for alternative conceptions of human rights, so that difference, subjectivity and specificity can be 'incorporated rather than silenced in struggles for political inclusion and effective participation'.[59] In Charlesworth's words, '(t)he need to develop a feminist rights discourse so that it acknowledges gendered disparities of power, rather than assuming all people are equal in relation to all rights, is crucial'.[60]

---

[56] Hilary Charlesworth, 'What are "Women's International Human Rights"?', in Cook (ed.), *Human Rights of Women*, p. 61.

[57] Ibid., p. 61.

[58] Cathy Blacklock and Laura Macdonald, 'Human Rights and Citizenship in Guatemala and Mexico: From 'Strategic' to 'New' Universalism? *Social Politics* (Summer 1998), p. 134, emphasis added.

[59] Charlesworth, 'Women's International Human Rights', p. 153.

[60] Ibid.

Clearly, the idea of simply jettisoning the discourse of human rights seems untenable to many feminists – from academics to activists. However, it would seem that, to be truly effective as a discursive and strategic basis for women's resistance in an era of globalisation, the concept requires substantial revision.

Towards a feminist conception of human rights and resistance

Undoubtedly, the work that has been done by academics and activists to expand and reconstruct international human rights to include the specific vulnerabilities and concerns of women has been, and continues to be, extremely valuable. However, it remains the case that, when the most influential and powerful organisations of global civil society make use of the unexamined discourse of rights, they draw on a totalising ethical discourse which, so constructed, fails to address the needs of most women. In the context of the challenge to globalisation from a feminist perspective, it may be that the orthodox discourse of rights must give way not to another universal language, but to a wide variety of norms and ethical practices that can speak to women, especially in the 'developing' world. I would suggest that work on feminist legal theory/jurisprudence and feminist ethics can provide a starting point for thinking about reconceptualising human rights as a basis for resistance to globalisation. This approach involves a shift in thinking with regard to two key theoretical features of rights-based ethics and rights discourse: first, the notion of equality, and second, the ontology of individualism.

Equality, difference and power

In her analysis of gender equity in Canadian courts, Kathleen Mahoney has argued that, in most countries of the world, if equality for women is legally acknowledged at all, it is understood in the Aristotelian sense: equality norms require that likes be treated alike and permit unalikes to be treated differently. This is a problem for women, she argues, 'because their social reality consists of systemic deprivation of power, resources and respect. Thus, it makes little sense to require them to be the "same" as socially advantaged men in order to be entitled to be treated equally.'[61] In addition, she points out that when equality is defined according to this 'sameness/ difference' model, the assumption is made that 'equality is the norm and that, from time to time, autonomous individuals are discriminated against. Systemic, persistent disadvantage is not contemplated.'

The Aristotelian model is incapable of proposing or restructuring or even identifying systematic discrimination in educational institutions, the workplace, the professions, the family, or the welfare system. It assumes these societal institutions should continue to exist as they are. To be equal, women just need the same chance as men to be able to participate in

---

[61] Kathleen E. Mahoney, 'Canadian Approaches to Equality Rights and Gender Equity in the Courts', in Cook (ed.), *Human Rights of Women*, p. 442.

them. This universalistic, gender-neutral approach does not recognize that institutional structures may impinge differently on men and women.[62]

In contrast to this model, Mahoney outlines the new notion of equality, first adopted in the Canadian Supreme Court in 1989, which determines discrimination in terms of disadvantage. If a person is a member of a persistently disadvantaged group, and can show that a distinction based on personal characteristics of the individual or group not imposed on others continues or worsens that disadvantage, the distinction is deemed discriminatory.[63] The importance of this for women cannot be overstated:

> Unlike the test of 'similarity and difference,' the test of 'disadvantage' requires judges to look at women or other claimants in their place in the real world and to confront the reality that the systemic abuse and deprivation of power women experience is because of their place in the sexual hierarchy.[64]

This is an approach which 'favors context rather than detached objectivity'; it demonstrates that 'equality must be taken beyond formalistic abstract principles'. Moreover, it permits 'flexibility, understanding and empathy' in the formulation of judicial responses to inequality.[65]

Like the work in feminist jurisprudence, research in the field of feminist ethics in the context of world politics has been equally critical of the idea of equality as sameness/universality in international human rights. For example, Kimberly Hutchings has argued that the idea of human rights is premised on the recognition that in crucial respects, human beings are the same. If instead we point to gender differences in the meanings of a human right, we are exposing the fact that global ethical life is structured by and through *gendered relations of power*. Thus, our understanding of rights is premised not on an ontology of universality and equality, but on difference and inequality. Once this is appreciated, Hutchings argues, the strategic value as well as the ethical significance of drawing on a rights discourse in order to protect women's interests changes.[66]

> At the deeper level of ethical significance the strategic necessity of grounding rights on difference can be understood ... as putting into question the grounding of fundamental human rights in humanity as such – rights become conceptualized always as a strategic weapon in the construction of a form of ethical life which is no more ethically necessary, though for many (including many feminists) it may be preferable, than any other. In such an ethics the notion of human rights cannot act as an ethical trump card. Instead, specific human rights must be interrogated and judged in terms of the ways in which they function in the broader values, structures and institutions of world politics.[67]

The key point here is worth restating. It must be recognised that, on this view, to call for 'women's human rights' is to challenge and undermine the foundation of human rights – the notion of 'humanity as such'. It is, therefore, to undermine their claim to

---

[62] Ibid., pp. 442–3.
[63] Ibid., p. 445.
[64] Ibid.
[65] Ibid., pp. 448–9.
[66] Kimberly Hutchings, 'Towards a Feminist International Ethics', *Review of International Studies*, 26, Special Issue (December 2000), p. 127, emphasis added.
[67] Ibid., p. 128.

'ethical necessity' – which is the basis of their claim to be universal, absolute, inalienable 'trump cards'. It could be argued that, once this is undermined, the moral and political force of rights is lost; indeed, some would undoubtedly argue that human rights are, by definition, universal, and that without this requirement, they cease to be human rights at all. Hutchings, however, argues that their force becomes radically rethought; rights become, as she states above, *strategic* weapons in the construction of a form of ethical life which is not absolutely and universally good, but which, hopefully, is useful for many, if not all women, living in particular moments in time and space.

It is not difficult to see how this revision of the traditional understanding of rights gives the concept the flexibility that is required to make it more relevant for the lives of many women, especially women in the developing world. Such a conceptualisation of rights makes room for the fact that it is precisely women's *difference* – their unique social roles as workers in the paid labour force, in the community, and in the home, and as nurturers and caregivers – which demands that their view of rights addresses the needs and requirements of these women and their families on a day-to-day basis. Thus, women's rights must take account of issues such as health, reproductive rights, and violence – all of which are experienced by women in ways that are very different from men. Indeed, for many women in a globalising world, including the women of Ecuador cited above, human rights are not about the exceptional circumstances of torture, arbitrary arrest, detention or killing, but rather about the daily struggle to provide for themselves and their family in an environment which is safe and secure. This is not to say, of course, that men do not engage in this struggle, or that 'men's rights' are only civil and political rights. Rather, it is simply to suggest that the feminist reshaping of rights discourse involves the recognition that individual abuses of rights are inseparable from the social and economic structures that perpetuate or create injustices.[68]

Relationships and responsibilities

The autonomous, rational subject is at the heart of modern moral theory, and thus, of human rights discourse. In challenging this understanding of subjectivity, and, indeed, the entire ontology that it implies, feminists are setting out the groundwork for a revised understanding of the nature of rights. As Susan Hekman argues, the dominant concept of the self in theories of moral development is that of the separate self. Moral psychologists such as Piaget and Kohlberg assume that development towards autonomy and separation is the paradigm of healthy subjectivity. Object-relations theory, by contrast, understands the self as constituted through relations with others. Indeed, even the differentiated, autonomous self is understood as a product of relational forces – a particular way of being connected to others.[69]

Although Hekman argues that the impact of this theory is limited to psychology, it is clear that, in recent years, this understanding of the self has had an important

---

[68] Guzman Bouvard, *Women Reshaping Human Rights*, p. x.
[69] Susan Hekman, *Moral Voices, Moral Selves: Carol Gilligan and Feminist Moral Theory* (Cambridge: Polity Press, 1995), pp. 72–3.

influence on feminist moral, political and legal theory. For example, Gayle Binion has pointed out that feminist legal theorists have wondered whether the dichotomous and adversarial character of rights is not alien to women's experience. This has lead to the application of a 'responsibility' approach to the human rights arena.[70] Following this approach, she argues, the central question concerning international human rights would then become 'what are the conditions of human freedom, dignity, health and safety that are fundamental to an experientially meaningful theory of 'rights'. Such a view, she argues, would focus on the needs of the disempowered by focusing on outcomes and actual experience. And while this model might have general benefits – in terms of thinking in terms of positive incentives to change and a worldwide responsibility for the human condition – it is also likely that women's particular needs for social reordering would fare better under a model of this type. [71]

Thus, by taking this fully relational ontology of social life as the starting point for thinking about ethics and politics, feminists are revising both the conceptual nature of rights, and the substance and effects of those rights. While traditional accounts of justice tend to neglect basic issues of child-rearing and care for dependents, feminist work on law, justice and politics takes more seriously the facts of human dependency, neediness and vulnerability, and hence the moral value and social importance of care.[72] Thus, while the Mothers of the Plazo de Mayo were, in one sense, fighting for rights as traditionally understood – for freedom of the (usually male) individual from arbitrary arrest, detention and killing – they were articulating these claims in a way which foregrounded not individual autonomy, but relationship. For the Mothers, caring for their children meant doing whatever was necessary to fight for their return, and hence to restore and maintain the relationship. This is not to say, however, that care and the qualities associated with it are necessarily 'superior' moral virtues. It is simply to recognise the widespread and ever-present nature of caring values and caring practices in the everyday lives of most people, and the importance of integrating these into our accounts of the nature of morality, law and justice, as well as into our political and legal strategies for human well-being.

Thus, the project of rethinking rights as a strategy for resistance must begin at the conceptual level, but must not remain there. Blindly criticising rights strategies or, worse still, abandoning rights as a political tool altogether, is bound to be counterproductive, in that it disregards the ongoing practical importance of rights for members of all subordinate groups, including women.[73] Existing outside the formal structures of domestic and international law, civil society groups face an even bigger challenge in the articulation and implementation of revised conceptualisations of rights. That said, women's social movements have the advantage of being able, ultimately, to influence and interface with the law – as in the revised definitions of equality described above – while not being constrained by it. At both the local and the global level, women's groups in civil society need to focus on both the rethinking of legal definitions and policy priorities, as well as the broader processes of social education and the shifting of cultural norms about the way we view, and value, the reality of human interdependence and the importance of care in our daily lives.

---

[70] Gayle Binion, 'Human Rights: A Feminist Perspective', *Human Rights Quarterly*, 17:3 (1995), p. 525.
[71] Ibid., p. 526.
[72] Kiss, 'Alchemy or Fool's Gold?', p. 11.
[73] Ibid., p. 3.

Conclusion

This article has sought to examine the discursive and ethical construction of rights within 'global civil society' as a basis for resistance to globalisation. In particular, I have argued, along with many feminist theorists, that 'human rights' is a gendered and Western-centric concept with pretensions to universality. As such, it fits comfortably, at the present stage, with the general ideology and goals not only of the advocates of neoliberal globalisation, but also of 'global civil society'. Advocates of global civil society as a 'political project' readily admit that it is driven by values which originated in the West (but which are now purportedly 'global') and is comprised largely of Western groups and individuals.[74] They admit that 'large parts of Africa or Latin America are virtually excluded from globalised activities', and that those who support civic internationalist values are ' the cosmopolitan young people' who work in international organisations or the media, or who join Greenpeace or Amnesty International, or who offer 'voluntary contributions' to 'cosmopolitan causes'. The 'courageous territorially tied people' who work in local institutions are said to be 'equally important', yet there is a strong suggestion that these people remain 'behind', still locked in the 'nationalist and exclusivist' ideologies of yesteryear, and as yet insufficiently tuned in to the dynamics of transnational values and activism.[75]

Human rights is the obvious discursive framework for this 'political project' of global civil society, which is modernist, Western-centric, and gendered in its approach. It is, paradoxically, also the logical discursive framework for neoliberals and indeed all advocates of greater economic liberalisation and globalisation, who seek 'open', stable political societies as a basis for open markets. Critics of this comparison would argue, of course, that neoliberals remain focused on a narrow definition of rights which limits them to civil and political rights; global civil society, and in particular the anti-globalisation movement, it could be argued, reject this narrow definition in favour of a broader definition of rights which encompasses economic, social and cultural rights as well as 'women's human rights'.

I have argued, however, that the dominant discourse of rights remains a feature of, rather than a challenge to, globalisation and global governance, and that, as such, it is complicit in the continued silencing of the needs and interests of women, especially in developing countries. In spite of conceptual and practical developments, rights still remains a concept which is tied to the individual and which articulates his freedoms from intervention, primarily from the state. As such it is a skeleton moral concept, not in the sense that what it articulates is basic or 'fundamental', but in the sense that it is about the procedure that must be followed for individuals to pursue and enjoy freely their own conception of the good. It lacks the ability to 'flesh out', or put features on that skeleton; as a result, it is ill-equipped to respond to the needs and interests of most women, who are made most vulnerable by the processes of globalisation.

The notion of human rights is based on a moral foundation of universality, which cannot accompany the feminist requirement of the recognition of difference, diver-

---

74 See especially Shaw, 'Global Voices', and Kaldor, 'Transnational Civil Society'.
75 Kaldor, 'Transnational Civil Society', pp. 208–9.

sity and specificity. Moreover, it is based on an individualist, atomistic ontology, which regards objects and individuals as fundamentally separate, existing only in legalistic or contractual relations with others. The voices of global civil society have embraced universality in the form of 'transnational' or 'cosmopolitan' values, and have upheld the individualistic picture of human existence, in line with neoliberal strategies of privatisation. I have argued, by contrast, that a feminist reconceptualisation of rights would fundamentally revise these two basic features of rights-based ethics and rights discourse. In order that rights can truly address the needs and interests of women, there must be a shift away from universalism towards a recognition of difference, specificity and context. This would also involve, importantly, addressing the inequalities in terms of power relations between men and women. In addition, a feminist reworking of the concept of rights would have as its starting point a social or relational moral ontology based on the belief that human beings exist and live their lives in the context of patterns of relationship, rather than as isolated, atomistic individuals. This ontological premise, moreover, leads to the recognition of the ubiquity of other moral values and practices in society beyond rights and duties, including care, attentiveness, responsibility, trust and empathy.

In no way is this argument meant to degrade or disparage the moral and political progress that has been achieved through the discursive and legal power of human rights; nor is it to overlook the tremendous role played by social movements and non-governmental organisations – both in the West and, more quietly, at the grassroots, community-based level in the South and East – in combating exclusion and hierarchy in the effort to achieve more just and equitable societies. Rather, my quarrel is with the unreflective acceptance of the 'global' in global civil society, and the assumption that the dominant discourse of international human rights can provide a discursive, ethical and political strategy for combating globalisation. In an era when there is a proliferation of new kinds of rights and new rights holders, and an increasingly widespread use of the discourse, we must explore the possibilities of alternative discursive and ethical categories to offer real challenges to globalisation.

Globalising common sense: a Marxian-Gramscian (re-)vision of the politics of governance/resistance

MARK RUPERT

The impoverishment of mainstream International Relations (IR) scholarship, especially as it is practised in the bastions of academic power and respectability in the United States, can be registered in terms of its wilful and continuing conceptual blindness to mutually constitutive relations of governance/resistance at work in the production of global politics. This has been underscored in recent years by the rise of powerful transnational social movements seeking to reform or transform global capitalism, a coalition of coalitions recently reincarnated in the form of a global peace movement opposing the blatantly neo-imperial turn in US foreign policy.[1] As the essays in this Special Issue attest, critical scholars of world politics have developed conceptual vocabularies with which to (re-)construct, from various analytical-political perspectives, aspects of these governance/resistance relations. My task in this article is to argue that – under historical circumstances of capitalist modernity – a dialectical understanding of class-based powers is necessary, if by no means sufficient, for understanding social powers more generally, and issues of global governance and resistance which implicate those powers. Although it is not without its tensions and limitations, I have found re-envisionings of Marxian political theory inspired by Western Marxism – and in particular by interpretations of Antonio Gramsci – to be enabling for such a project. Marxian theory provides critical leverage for understanding the structures and dynamics of capitalism, its integral if complex relationship to the modern form of state, the class-based powers it enables and the resistances these engender; and Gramsci's rich if eternally inchoate legacy suggests a conceptual vocabulary for a transformative politics in which a variety of anti-capitalist movements might coalesce in order to produce any number of future possible worlds whose very possibility is occluded by capitalism. In the present context of globalising capitalism and neo-imperialism, such resistance has taken the form of a transnational confluence of movements for global justice and peace.

---

[1] The literature on the global justice movement has grown too vast to attempt encapsulation here. Extensive references may be found in my own work on this transnational movement: M. Rupert, *Ideologies of Globalisation* (London: Routledge, 2000); 'Class Powers and the Politics of Global Governance', chapter prepared for *Power and Global Governance*, edited by Michael Barnett and Raymond Duvall (Cambridge: Cambridge University Press, forthcoming); 'Anti-Capitalist Convergence? Anarchism, Socialism, and the Global Justice Movement', in Manfred Steger (ed.), *Rethinking Globalism* (Lanham, MD: Romwan & Littlefield, forthcoming); 'The Global Justice Movement in a Neo-Imperial Moment', chapter prepared for *Critical Theories, World Politics, and the 'Anti-Globalisation Movement'*, edited by Catherine Eschle and Bice Maiguashca (London: Routledge, forthcoming).

Marx: social power and class relations

One of the enduring insights of Marxian theory is that the seemingly apolitical economic spaces generated by capitalism – within and across juridical states – are permeated by structured relations of social power deeply consequential for political life and, indeed, for the (re)production of social life as a whole. These powers may be ideologically depoliticised – and thus rendered democratically unaccountable – in liberal representations separating a naturalised and privatised economy from the formally political sphere. The operation this economy (and the implicit social powers residing within it) may then be represented as something approaching a universal social good, the engine of economic growth and a generalised prosperity.[2] However another of these enduring Marxian insights is that social power relations are also *processes* – dynamic, contradictory and contestable.

As usefully emphasised by Scott Solomon,[3] Marx's capitalism is not a seamless web of oppression, but rather represents a contradictory life of 'dual freedom'. On such a dialectical Marxian view, capitalism entails liberation from the relations of direct politico-economic dependence characteristic of feudalism and other pre-capitalist forms, and hence presents possibilities for social individuation and 'political emancipation' within the parameters of republican forms of state. But capitalism simultaneously limits the historically real emancipatory possibilities it brings into being by (re-)subjecting persons to social domination through the compulsions of market dependence and the disabling effects of fetishism and reification. Under historical conditions of capitalism, social relations are mediated by things – commodities. Although the social division of labour under capitalism has brought together and collectively empowered human producers as never before, it simultaneously divides and disables them by representing their social relations as naturalised relations of exchange between commodities. To the extent that social relations are subsumed into a world of putatively independent objects – 'things' – human producers are correspondingly disempowered. Inhabitants of the capitalist market, the subjects of capitalist modernity, are represented to themselves as abstract individuals who, as such, are largely unable to discern – much less communally to govern – the social division of labour in which they are embedded. In the words of Derek Sayer's apt summary: 'People appear to be independent of one another because their mutual dependence assumes the unrecognisable form of relations between commodities.'[4] Further, even as capitalism realises 'political emancipation' through the development of the liberal republic in which citizens are formally equal, it effectively privatises and depoliticises class-based social powers and thereby eviscerates political democracy.[5] These dialectics of freedom and unfreedom, the powers they

[2] Rupert, *Ideologies of Globalization*, ch. 3; also Manfred Steger, *Globalism: The New Market Ideology* (Lanham, MD: Rowman and Littlefield, 2002).

[3] Scott Solomon, 'Marx's 'Dual Freedom' Thesis and Globalization', paper presented at the workshop *The Politics of Protest in the Age of Globalization*, University of Sussex, UK, 26–27 September 2002.

[4] Derek Sayer, *Capitalism and Modernity* (London: Routledge, 1991), pp. 64; the *locus classicus* is of course Karl Marx, *Capital*, vol. I (New York: Vintage, 1977), ch. 1.

[5] Karl Marx, 'On The Jewish Question', in *Karl Marx: Early Writings* (New York: Vintage, 1975); also Sayer, *Capitalism and Modernity*, ch. 2; Paul Thomas, *Alien Politics: Marxist State Theory Retrieved* (London: Routledge, 1994); and Ellen Meiksins Wood, *Democracy versus Capitalism* (Cambridge: Cambridge University Press, 1995).

generate and resistances they engender, have produced families of capitalist historical structures which are fraught with tension and possibilities for change. Whether any such possibilities are realised, and in what particular ways, depend upon open-ended political struggles in which the power relations of capitalism will necessarily be implicated.

Ellen Wood has argued consistently and with great force that the critical leverage of a Marxian critique of capitalism is generated by its explicit focus on the social power relations which inhere in, and yet are obscured by, the structures and practices of capitalist production and exchange.

> The fundamental secret of capitalist production disclosed by Marx . . . concerns the social relation and the disposition of power that obtains between workers and the capitalist to whom they sell their labor power. This secret has a corollary: that the disposition of power between the individual capitalist and the worker has as its condition the political configuration of society as a whole – the balance of class forces and the powers of the state which permit the expropriation of the direct producer, the maintenance of absolute private property for the capitalist, and his control over production and appropriation. . . . for Marx, the ultimate secret of capitalist production is a political one.[6]

Capitalist social relations generate the possibility of asymmetrical social powers distributed according to class. Socially necessary means of production are constituted as private property, exclusively owned by one class of people. The other class, whose exclusion from ownership of social means of production is integral to the latter's constitution as private property, are then compelled to sell that which they do own – labour-power, that is, their capacity for productive activity – in order to gain access to those means of production and hence – through the wage – their own means of survival. As consumer of labour-power, the capitalist may control the actual activity of labour – the labour process – and appropriate its product, which is then subsumed into capital itself. In Jeffrey Isaac's apt summary, 'The capitalist class thus possesses two basic powers: the power of control over investment, or appropriation; and the power to direct and supervise the labour process . . .'[7]

As *employers*, capitalists and their managerial agents attempt to assert control over the transformation of labour-power – the abstract, commodified capacity for labour – into actual labour. They seek to maximise the output of workers in relation to wages paid for labour-power, and may lengthen the work day or transform the labour process itself in order to do so.[8] In the social position of *investors*, their decisions directly determine the social allocation of labour and resources – the pace

---

[6] Wood, *Democracy versus Capitalism*, pp. 20–21. It is possible, I would argue, to mount a political critique of capitalism without committing oneself to Wood's more fundamentalist claims about the universal and overriding significance of class relative to other social relations of domination; see the arguments developed below and in Rupert, 'Globalising Gramsci', paper prepared for the workshop *Images of Gramsci: Connections and Contentions in Political Theory and International Relations*, convened by Andreas Bieler and Adam Morton, University of Nottingham, UK, 24–25 October 2003; compare Wood, *Democracy versus Capitalism*, pp. 256–63, 266–70, 282–3.

[7] Jeffrey Isaac, *Power and Marxist Theory* (Ithaca, NY: Cornell University Press, 1987), p. 126; the *locus classicus* is Marx, *Capital*, vol. 1, pp. 291–2; see also Samuel Bowles and Herbert Gintis, *Democracy and Capitalism* (New York, Basic Books, 1986), pp. 64–91; and Wood, *Democracy versus Capitalism*, pp. 28–31, 40–44.

[8] Marx, *Capital*, vol. 1, pp. 948–1084; on the latter tendency as it was instantiated in struggles surrounding Fordist workplace regimes, see M. Rupert, *Producing Hegemony* (Cambridge: Cambridge University Press, 1995).

of aggregate economic activity and the shape of the social division of labour – and indirectly limit the scope of public policy through the constraint of 'business confidence' and the implicit threat of 'capital strike'. Insofar as these social powers are effectively privatised – associated with private ownership and exchange of property among juridically equal individuals in an apparently depoliticised economic sphere – they are ideologically mystified and democratically unaccountable.[9]

Anti-democratic and disabling as they might be, these class-based powers are neither uncontestable in principle nor uncontested in fact. Like all relations of social power, capitalist power relations are reciprocal, constituting a 'dialectic of power', subject to ongoing contestation, renegotiation and restructuring.[10] They represent, in short, historically particular forms of social power. As such, class powers must be actualised in various concrete sites of social production where class is articulated with other socially meaningful identities resident and effective in those historical circumstances. Capitalist power over waged labour has been historically articulated with gendered and raced forms of power: separation of workplace from residence and the construction of ideologies of feminised domesticity rationalising unpaid labour; ideologies of white supremacy rationalising racial segregation and inequality; gendered and raced divisions of labour; and so forth. These relations of race and gender have had important effects on class formation.[11] This implies that in concrete contexts class cannot be effectively determining without itself being determined. However this is not to say, in some pluralist sense, that class is only one of a number of possible social identities all of which are equally contingent. Insofar as productive interaction with the natural world remains a necessary condition of all human social life,[12] I would maintain that understandings of social power relations which abstract from the social organisation of production must be radically incomplete.

To the extent that capitalism and its putatively private relations of power organise crucial parts of social life on a transnational scale, the struggles surrounding these relations and their various articulations in sites around the world merit serious study as part of the question of global governance and resistance. Critical analyses of class-based powers and their historical interweaving with gender, race-based and other relations of privilege may shed new light not only on issues of transnational power and global governance but also on possibilities for democratising projects and the social production of alternative possible worlds.

Gramsci: common sense and transformative politics

If Marx left us with incisive theorisations of capitalism, its core relations and constitutive tensions, it was the Italian political theorist and communist leader

---

[9] On the constraint of 'business confidence' and the implicit threat of 'capital strike', see Fred Block, (1977), 'The Ruling Class does not Rule', *Socialist Revolution*, 33 (1977), p. 16; and Bowles and Gintis, *Democracy and Capitalism*, pp. 88–90; on the anti-democratic character of capitalist politics more generally, see Thomas, *Alien Politics*, and Wood, *Democracy versus Capitalism*.

[10] Isaac, *Power*.

[11] See, for example, Michelle Barrett, *Women's Oppression Today* (London, Verso: 1988); Johanna Brenner; 'The Best of Times, the Worst of Times: US Feminism Today', *New Left Review*, 200 (1993), pp. 101–59; and Michael Goldfield, *The Color of Politics* (New York, New Press, 1997).

[12] Marx, *Capital I*, p. 290.

Antonio Gramsci who contributed to the historical materialist tradition a conceptual vocabulary with which to enable processes of transformative politics. Marx suggested that socialist transformation might emerge out of the confluence of capitalism's endemic crisis tendencies, the polarisation of its class structure and the relative immiseration of the proletariat and, most importantly, the emergence of the latter as a collective agent through the realisation of its socially productive power, heretofore developed in distorted and self-limiting form under the conditions of concentrated capitalist production. Gramsci accepted in broad outline Marx's analysis of the structure and dynamics of capitalism, but was unwilling to embrace the more mechanical and economistic interpretations of Marx circulating in the international socialist movement.[13]

Contrary to vulgar Marxist dogma, progressive social change would not automatically follow in train behind economic developments, but must instead be produced by historically situated social agents whose actions are enabled and constrained by their social self-understandings.[14] Thus, for Gramsci, popular 'common sense' becomes a critical terrain of political struggle.[15] His theorisation of a social politics of ideological struggle – which he called 'war of position' to distinguish it from a Bolshevik strategy of frontal assault on the state – contributed to the historical materialist project of dereifying capitalist social relations (including narrowly state-based conceptions of politics) and constructing an alternative – more enabling, participatory, intrinsically democratic – social order out of the historical conditions of capitalism.[16]

Popular common sense could become a ground of struggle because it is an amalgam of historically effective ideologies, scientific doctrines and social mythologies. Gramsci understood popular common sense not to be monolithic or univocal, nor was hegemony an unproblematically dominant ideology which simply shut out all alternative visions or political projects. Rather, common sense was understood to be a syncretic historical residue, fragmentary and contradictory, open to multiple interpretations and potentially supportive of very different kinds of social visions and political projects. And hegemony was understood as the unstable product of a continuous process of struggle, 'war of position', 'reciprocal siege'.[17]

Gramsci's political project thus entailed addressing the popular common sense operative in particular times and places, making explicit the tensions and contradictions within it as well as the sociopolitical implications of these, in order to enable critical social analysis and transformative political practice. His aim was 'to construct an intellectual-moral bloc which can make politically possible the intellectual progress of the mass and not only of small intellectual groups', and thereby 'to create the conditions in which this division [leaders/led] is no longer necessary', and in which 'the subaltern element' is 'no longer a thing [objectified, reified] but an historical person . . . an agent, necessarily active and taking the

[13] Antonio Gramsci, *Selections from the Prison Notebooks* (New York: International Publishers, 1971), pp. 34, 201–2, 419–72.
[14] Gramsci, *Selections*, pp. 164–5, 172, 326, 344, 375–7, 407–8, 420, 438.
[15] Ibid., pp. 323–34, 419–25.
[16] Ibid., pp. 229–39, 242–3; on 'statolatry', see p. 268.
[17] Ibid., pp. 182, 210, 239, 323–34, 350, 419–25.

initiative.'[18] At the core of Gramsci's project was a critical pedagogy which took as its starting point the tensions and possibilities latent within popular common sense, and which sought to build out of the materials of popular common sense an emancipatory political culture and a social movement to enact it – not simply another hegemony rearranging occupants of superior/subordinate social positions, but a *transformative* counter-hegemony.[19]

Gramsci's historical materialism understands history as a complex and contradictory story of social self-production under specific social circumstances. The meaning of this social history, then, resists reduction to simple formulae: 'The experience on which the philosophy of praxis is based cannot be schematised; it is history in all its infinite variety and multiplicity'.[20] But while history is infinitely complex, from within the context of capitalist modernity it is possible to imagine grounds for emancipatory collective action and more meaningful social self-determination. Gramsci's historical materialism thus envisions a process of 'becoming which . . . does not start from unity, but contains in itself the reasons for a possible unity':

> . . . The unity of history (what the idealists call unity of the spirit) is not a presupposition, but a continuously developing process. Identity in concrete reality determines identity in thought, and not vice versa. . . . every truth, even if it is universal, and even if it can be expressed by an abstract formula of a mathematical kind (for the sake of the theoreticians), owes its effectiveness to its being expressed in the language appropriate to specific concrete situations. If it cannot be expressed in such specific terms, it is a Byzantine and scholastic abstraction, good only for phrase-mongers to toy with.[21]

I understand this to mean that the class-based relations of production under capitalism create the *possibility* of particular kinds of collective agency, but this potential can only be realised through the political practices and struggles of concretely situated social actors, practices which must negotiate the tensions and possibilities – the multiple social identities, powers, and forms of agency – resident within popular common sense.

Gramsci was, of course, a Marxist, and assigned to class identity a relatively privileged position in his vision of transformative politics.[22] But Gramsci's Marxism was an historicism which explicitly disavowed the notion that historical materialism represented trans-historical or universal truth. Rather, he insisted that historical materialism was a *situated knowledge*, constructed within and relevant to the historical relations of capitalism in particular times and places: upon the historical supercession of capitalism, then, historical materialism would be superceded by other forms of knowledge relevant to their own socio-historical context.[23] This understanding of historical materialism as situated knowledge implies, at the very least, the potential for productive political dialogue with other forms of situated knowledge constructed in contexts where capitalism has been articulated with various kinds of social identities and relations not reducible to class.

---

[18] Ibid., pp. 332–5, 144, 337; also 346, 349, 418.
[19] This argument is developed more fully in Rupert, 'Globalizing Gramsci'.
[20] Gramsci, *Selections*, p. 428.
[21] Ibid., p. 201; the preceding quote is from pp. 355–6.
[22] Ibid., pp. 139–40, 148, 151, 227, 259, 263.
[23] Ibid., pp. 152, 201, 248–9, 404–7, 436–7, 445–6.

Despite Gramsci's insistence that a counter-hegemonic bloc should be led by anti-capitalist forces, his vision of this historic bloc in terms of a dialogic process creates openings for engagement with other situated knowledges in ways which, his relational ontology implies, will reshape the identities of all participants in the conversation. Gramsci emphasises the transformative potential of such a relational vision by interpreting politics – entailing the historical problem of leaders/led – in terms of education – which to the extent that it is successful is transformative of the teacher/student relation along with the parties embedded within that relation.[24]

An historical act can only be performed by 'collective man', and this presupposes the attainment of a 'cultural-social' unity through which a multiplicity of dispersed wills, with heterogeneous aims, are welded together with a single aim, on the basis of an equal and common conception of the world. . . . This problem can and must be related to the modern way of considering educational doctrine and practice, according to which the relationship between teacher and pupil is *active and reciprocal* so that every teacher is always a pupil and every pupil a teacher. . . . Every relationship of 'hegemony' is necessarily an educational relationship and occurs not only within a nation, between the various forces of which the nation is composed, but in the international and world-wide field, between complexes of national and continental civilizations.[25]

The political-educational process he envisions is to be distinguished from indoctrination insofar as the former entails reciprocal development and seeks to enable the student to construct new truths independent of his/her teacher and, in the process, to teach the teacher, thereby transforming their relation. The relation teacher/student (and leader/led) is then reciprocal but (in the context of capitalist modernity) initially asymmetrical: Gramsci envisions developing the reciprocity of the relation until the asymmetry approaches the vanishing point. I am claiming, in other words, that Gramsci's political project aims at overcoming the historical division between leaders and led through 'active and reciprocal' processes of transformative dialogue and the concomitant reconstruction of social relations and identities. This is why, I believe, he emphasises (contrary to more economistic Marxisms and their mechanical interpretations of Marx's base/superstructure metaphor) that the core of his pivotal concept of 'historic bloc' entails 'a necessary reciprocity between structure and superstructure, a reciprocity which is nothing other than the real dialectical process'.[26]

How then to account for his insistence that this process should be led, initially at least, by class-based social forces[27] and that the counter-hegemonic historic bloc should be '100 percent homogeneous on the level of ideology' in order to effect a social transformation?[28] It is interesting to observe that the assertion of reciprocity between structure and superstructure quoted in the paragraph above occurs immediately following Gramsci's suggestion that an historic bloc must be '100 percent homogeneous on the level of ideology' and so on, and hence implies a

---

[24] For the leading role of anti-capitalist forces, see Gramsci, *Selections*, pp. 259, 263, also 139–40, 148, 151, 227; on transformative politics as education, see pp. 227, 242, 247.

[25] Gramsci, *Selections*, pp. 665–66; my emphasis.

[26] Ibid., p. 366.

[27] Ibid., pp. 139–40, 148, 151, 227.

[28] Ibid., pp. 366; also, less categorically, 158, 168, 328, 445; but compare the seemingly much more rigid formulation on 265.

critique of economism[29] which would undercut a simple class-reductionist interpretation of what he meant by 'homogeneous'. Rather than reading Gramsci as straight-
forwardly (and, in light of his larger project, perversely) reasserting the economistic
Marxist eschatology of the 'universal class' as historical messiah, I would make
sense of these claims in the context of the relational theory of transformative
process sketched out here. I understand Gramsci to be suggesting that, in a capitalist
social context, the necessary condition for any sort of transformative project
whatever is a re-opening of political horizons effectively foreclosed by capitalist
social relations. Whatever else they may be or become (that is, 'history in all its
infinite variety and multiplicity'), transformative politics from within a capitalist
context must necessarily entail shared anti-capitalist commitments in order to open
up future possible worlds which are obscured by the social identities of abstract
individualism and disabling ideologies of fetishism and reification produced by
capitalism.

But the counter-hegemonic historic bloc should not be 'homogeneous' in the
sense of annihilation of meaningful political difference, a unitary and uniform class-
based identity imposed by a party uniquely in possession of a full understanding of
history.[30] Indeed this would entail a self-defeating refusal to engage with and learn
from potential allies (a position of 'intransigence') which Gramsci derisively
identifies with 'economistic superstition'.

It is clear that this aversion on principle to compromise is closely linked to economism. For
the conception on which this aversion is based can only be the iron conviction that there exist
objective laws of historical development similar in kind to natural laws, together with a belief
in a predetermined teleology like that of a religion.[31]

If the historical supercession of capitalism is to be achieved, this will entail a
relational transformation not just of the social-structural environment but of the
participants in the struggle themselves. Gramsci's vehicle for the realisation of this
kind of transformation was the historic bloc, led/educated – initially at least – by a
class-identified political party:

Although every party is the expression of a social group, and of one social group only,
nevertheless in certain given conditions [a counter-hegemonic bloc] certain parties [the party
of the non-owners of capital] *represent a single social group precisely insofar as they exercise a
balancing and arbitrating function between the interests of their group and those of other
groups, and succeed in securing the development of the group which they represent with the
consent and assistance of the allied groups.*[32]

In other words, the party of those subordinated under capitalism's class-based
dominance relations can realise its potential as such only by transcending a narrow,
instrumental or sectarian approach to politics and by attaining hegemonic leadership of a bloc of social forces committed to attaining post-capitalist futures.[33]

---

[29] Gramsci's critique of economism is sharply made elsewhere in the Notebooks: see pp. 158–68,
419–72.
[30] Although see Gramsci, *Selections*, p. 265 for a passage which, if abstracted out of the larger relational
context I am suggesting here, might be read as an instance of economistic class-determinism.
[31] Gramsci, *Selections*, pp. 167–8; for 'economistic superstition', see p. 164; and on the undialectical
Marxist 'religion'of determinism and teleology, see Gramsci's critique of Bukharin, esp. pp. 434-48.
[32] Ibid., p. 148, my emphasis.
[33] Ibid., pp. 180–2.

Gramsci's historic bloc is not a one-way street, nor is it based on an instrumental understanding of compromise in which the constituent groups and their core interests remain essentially the same even as they accommodate one another. Rather the counter-hegemonic historic bloc involves the transformation of all parties actively involved in its construction, including the leading party:

The development of the party into a State [that is, a new form of collective social self-determination, 'an integral state, and not into a government technically understood'] reacts upon the party and requires of it a continuous reorganization and development, just as the development of the party and State into a conception of the world, i.e., into a total and molecular (individual) transformation of the ways of thinking and acting, reacts upon the State and party, compelling them to reorganize continually and confronting them with new and original problems to solve.[34]

The goal of this process is not the permanent institutionalisation of the rule of one particular, preconstituted social group or its party over all others, but the transformation of capitalist social relations and their characteristic structural separations of state/society, politics/economics, in order to enable the devolution of implicitly class-based political rule into a more generalised social self-determination – a future for which the democratisation of economic relations would be a necessary, if not sufficient, condition: 'the [new, integral] State's goal is its own end, its own disappearance, in other words the re-absorption of political society into civil society'.[35]

In light of all this, I suggest that Gramsci's counter-hegemonic bloc may be understood as 'homogeneous' to the degree that it shares a rejection of capitalism's abstract individuals in favour of more socially-grounded relational ontologies, process-oriented visions of social reality, and acknowledgements of the historical situatedness of political knowledge and practice. Once developed within popular common sense, these elements of a 'homogeneous – in other words, coherent and systematic – philosophy'[36] constitute the necessary common ground for forging an anti-capitalist bloc which would, if successful, construct new forms of political community and open doors to a rich variety of possible futures, all of which are occluded by capitalism's reification of social life. Once this post-capitalist political horizon was approached, the anti-capitalist bloc would lose its historical reason for existence and its social condition of intelligibility, it would transform itself in ways appropriate to the new social context and new identities it had brought into being, and would thus be superceded by new forms of social self-determination.[37]

This is, I confess, not an innocent reading of Gramsci (I doubt whether any such thing is possible). Rather, my reading is motivated by a desire to reappropriate his thinking in order to enable a politics of solidarity in the increasingly unified, but at the same time nonetheless plural world, of globalising capitalism. I do not mean to suggest by this that Gramsci's thinking entirely escapes the potential pitfalls of Marxian teleology; only that there are resources within his thought for auto-critique and continual reopening of political possibility. And, in the present context of globalising capitalism and neo-imperialism, such resources are no less important than they were when Gramsci wrote.

---

[34] Ibid., p. 267.
[35] Ibid., p. 253, also 260.
[36] Ibid., p. 769.
[37] Ibid., p. 152.

Globalising capitalism, governance, resistance

While I would agree with the claim that capitalist class powers have never been more effectively global, I am equally persuaded that these powers have never been contained within the confines of particular states. Recent Marxian scholarship has argued persuasively that capitalism may be fruitfully understood as a transnational social system which has encompassed the system of sovereign states as well as the seemingly discrete sphere of the capitalist economy: 'The separation of the political and the economic indicates precisely the central institutional linkage between the capitalist economy and the nation state: that is, the legal structure of property rights which removes market relationships from directly political control or contestation and allows the flow of investment capital across national boundaries'.[38] It is through these latter processes of transnational economic activity that the privatised powers of capital have been projected on an increasingly global scale. 'For under this new arrangement, while relations of citizenship and jurisdiction define state borders, any aspects of social life which are mediated by relations of exchange in principle no longer receive a political definition (though they are still overseen by the state in various ways) and hence may extend across these borders'.[39]

Scholars sharing a broadly historical materialist perspective have identified historical processes through which internationally active segments of the capitalist class have organised to frame common interests, project a universalising worldview which effectively depoliticises the economic sphere, and coordinate their own political action to realise their interests and visions.[40] Capitalism's globalising tendencies have been substantially realised in a particular historical context, and this has been the political project of a tendentially transnational – if also US-led – historic bloc comprised of particular fractions of the capitalist class, state managers and international bureaucrats, journalists, and mainstream labour leaders.

Constructing the institutional infrastructure of international trade and finance, this historic bloc fostered the growth of international trade and investment through the postwar decades, especially within and between the so-called 'triad' regions. Moreover, with the founding of the World Trade Organisation in 1995, the infrastructure of liberalisation has been substantially strengthened and extended. The WTO wields unprecedented powers of surveillance and enforcement, and has extended its ambit to include trade in services as well as trade-related investment and

[38] Justin Rosenberg, *Empire of Civil Society* (London: Routledge, 1994), p. 14; but for an important qualification to this line of argument compare Hannes Lacher, 'Making Sense of the International System: The Promises and Pitfalls of the Newest Marxist Theories of International Relations', in M. Rupert and H. Smith (eds.), *Historical Materialism and Globalization* (London: Routledge 2002).

[39] Rosenberg, *Empire*, p. 129.

[40] Kees van der Pijl, *Making of an Atlantic Ruling Class* (London, Verso 1984) and *Transnational Classes and International Relations* (London, Routledge 1998); Stephen Gill, *American Hegemony and the Trilateral Commission* (Cambridge: Cambridge University Press, 1990), and 'Globalization, Market Civilization, and Disciplinary Neoliberalism', *Millennium*, 24:3 (1995), pp. 399–423; William Robinson, 'Capitalist Globalization and the Transnationalization of the State', in Rupert and Smith (eds.), *Historical Materialism and Globalization*; Robinson and Jerry Harris, 'Towards a Global Ruling Class', *Science and Society*, 64:1 (2000), pp. 11–54; Rupert, *Ideologies*; Leslie Sklair, *The Transnational Capitalist Class* (Oxford: Blackwell, 2001). The significance of globalisation within an historical materialist frame is, however, very much a matter of debate: some important positions are staked out by contributors to Rupert and Smith (eds.), *Historical Materialism and Globalization*.

intellectual property issues.[41] This reflects a broadening of the agenda of liberalisation beyond tariff reduction to encompass 'harmonisation' of (formerly 'domestic') rules and regulations governing business insofar as these appear, from the liberal perspective, as potential non-tariff barriers to trade.

A second aspect of postwar processes of globalisation has been the emergence of multinational firms and the transnational organisation of production.[42] Developing countries have been increasingly, if unevenly, incorporated into these global production networks. This globalisation of production has substantially enhanced the powers of employers in relation to their workers. For workers in developed countries, globalisation means that employers are able more credibly to threaten plant relocation and job loss when faced with collective bargaining situations, and there is strong evidence to suggest that this is increasingly widespread.[43] For workers in developing countries, globalisation may imply opportunities for employment which might not otherwise be available, but along with that come the subordination and exploitation entailed in the capitalist labour process.[44]

In the realm of finance, excess liquidity from consistent US balance of payments deficits, the collapse of the Bretton Woods fixed rate regime and its associated capital controls, the recycling of petrodollars and the emergence of offshore xeno-currency markets, together resulted in breathtaking volumes of foreign exchange trading and speculative international investment which now dwarf the currency reserves of governments and can readily swamp, or leave high and dry, the financial markets of particular nations.[45] Responding to short-term differences in perceived conditions of profitability and variations in business confidence between one place and another, as well as speculative guesses about future market fluctuations, these enormous flows are highly volatile. These developments have been consequential, for the emerging historical structures of neoliberal capitalism embody an enhancement of the social powers of capital, especially finance capital, which can discourage or deter expansionary macro-policies aimed at increasing employment or wage levels. Accordingly, the globalisation of finance has been accompanied by a resurgence of *laissez-faire* fundamentalism since the late 1970s, as neoliberal austerity has largely eclipsed the growth-oriented ideology which originally underpinned the postwar world economy.[46] This disciplinary power has the effect of prioritising the interests

---

[41] World Trade Organization, *Trading into the Future*, 2nd edn. (Geneva: WTO, 1998); Lori Wallach and Michelle Sforza (1999), *Whose Trade Organization?* (Washington: Public Citizen/Global Trade Watch, 1999).

[42] Peter Dicken, *Global Shift* (New York: Guilford, 1992); John Agnew and Stuart Corbridge, *Mastering Space* (London: Routledge, 1995); D. Held, A. McGrew, D. Goldblatt, and J. Perraton, *Global Transformations* (Cambridge: Polity, 1999); Robinson and Harris, 'Global Ruling Class'.

[43] Kate Bronfenbrenner, 'We'll Close!: Plant Closings, Plant-Closing Threats, Union Organizing and NAFTA', *Multinational Monitor* (March, 1997), pp. 8–13; and 'Raw Power: Plant-Closing Threats and the Threat to Union Organizing', *Multinational Monitor* (December, 2000), online at: <http://www.essential.org/monitor/mm2000/00december/power.html>

[44] See, for example, Andrew Ross (ed.), *No Sweat* (London: Verso, 1997); R. Kamel and A. Hoffman (eds.), *The Maquiladora Reader* (Philadelphia, PA: American Friends Service Committee, 1999).

[45] Howard Wachtel, *The Money Mandarins* (Armonk, NY: M.E. Sharpe, 1990); Agnew and Corbridge, *Mastering Space*; Held et al., *Global Transformations*.

[46] Stephen Gill and David Law, 'Global Hegemony and the Structural Power of Capital', *International Studies Quarterly*, 33 (1989), pp. 475–99; Gill, *American Hegemony*, ch. 5, and 'Disciplinary Neoliberalism'; Wachtel, *Money Mandarins*; Agnew and Corbridge, *Mastering Space*, ch. 7; Walden Bello, *Dark Victory: The United States, Structural Adjustment, and Global Poverty* (San Francisco, CA: Food First, 1994); Arthur MacEwan, *Neoliberalism or Democracy?* (London: Zed Books, 1999).

of investors, who are as a class effectively able to hold entire states/societies hostage. Moreover, the particular interests of the owning class are represented as if they were the general interests of all: 'since profit is the necessary condition of universal expansion, capitalists appear within capitalist societies as bearers of a universal interest'.[47] In this ideological construction, the social and moral claims of working people and the poor are reduced to the pleadings of 'special interests' which must be resisted in order to secure the conditions of stable accumulation. Indeed this is a central part of the ideological justification for the package of austerity policies which the IMF typically imposes on developing countries experiencing financial crisis – the latter itself being largely a result of systemic forces, especially the globalisation of finance and its attendant exchange rate instabilities.[48]

Perhaps ironically, then, neoliberalism's resurrection of market fundamentalism has been attendant upon the increasing extensity and intensity of transnational relations. Even as people in locations around the globe are increasingly integrated into transnational social relations, neoliberalism seeks to remove these relations from the public sphere – where they might be subjected to norms of democratic governance – and instead subject them to the power of capital as expressed through the discipline of the market.[49] In van der Pijl's apt summary, 'The core of the new concept of control which expressed the restored discipline of capital, neoliberalism, resides in raising micro-economic rationality to the validating criterion for all aspects of social life.'[50]

In general, the neoliberal agenda of integrating and depoliticising the global economy fosters a 'race to the bottom' which enhances capitalist power through intensified market competition and the dull compulsion of the economic. Such an implicit class bias is evident in the WTO's governance of the global trading system. The WTO has refused to link human rights or labour rights protections to participation in the global trading system; its rules forbid discrimination against traded goods based upon how they were produced – outwardly similar goods must be treated similarly regardless of whether they were produced by processes abusive to workers or environment; and the WTO's trade-related investment measures (TRIMs) proscribe performance requirements placed upon foreign direct investment (FDI) and shield transnational corporations (TNCs) from potentially important kinds of host government regulation, such as those requiring linkages with local economy, and thus higher levels of employment, developmental spinoffs, and so on.[51] Taken together, these aspects of WTO governance promote nodes of uneven development linked into globalising production systems. And, in combination with the draconian austerity programmes, public sector retrenchment, openness to foreign investment and export orientation enforced by the IMF upon many of the world's

[47] Adam Przeworski, quoted in Thomas, *Alien Politics*, p. 153.
[48] Bello, *Dark Victory*; Robin Hahnel, *Panic Rules* (Boston, MA: South End, 1999); William Tabb, *The Amoral Elephant: Globalization and the Struggle for Social Justice in the Twenty-First Century* (New York: Monthly Review, 2001).
[49] Gill, 'Disciplinary Neoliberalism'; Rupert, *Ideologies of Globalization*, ch. 3; Steger, *Globalism*, pp. 43–80.
[50] Van der Pijl, *Transnational Classes*, p. 129.
[51] Compare: WTO, *Trading*, p. 51 with Wallach and Sforza, *Whose Trade Organization*, ch. 7; WTO, p. 49 with Wallach and Sforza, pp. 15, 22–6; and WTO, p. 35 with Wallach and Sforza, pp. 133, 152.

developing countries, all of this facilitates capital's intensified exploitation of labour and environment through transnational commodity chains.[52]

It is important analytically and politically to note that the world of cheap labour and 'under-pollution' (to paraphrase Lawrence Summers) in which transnational production is organised is a world which is neither race- nor gender-neutral. The great bulk of workers in export processing zones (EPZs) – the most labour-intensive nodes of global production chains – are young women.[53] Their labour may be culturally constructed as cheap insofar as they are presumed to be under the social umbrella of a male (either father or husband) and therefore not requiring a self-sufficiency wage, and insofar as the gender division of labour marks off 'women's work' as 'something that girls and women do "naturally" or "traditionally"' rather than the expression of hard-won, and more highly rewarded, skill – this latter presumptively an attribute of more masculine employments.[54] Further, the austerity programmes of neoliberalism heavily impact women, intensifying the double burden of gendered work as retrenchment of public services puts greater burdens upon households – and therefore feminised domestic labour – for the care of children, the elderly, the sick; even as those same cutbacks impact areas of the gender division of labour, such as education and health care, in which women are concentrated.[55] Economic austerity and a narrowing of options may then channel women toward employment in export industries and EPZs, or into the informal sector. Moreover, Eurocentrism and racism have generated representations of naturalised poverty among peoples of colour in the developing world, attributed to a lack of those things which are presumed to distinguish the more developed (and white) countries – capital, technology, managerial expertise, effective and honest governance, skilled labour, and so forth.[56] Liberalisation of trade with, and investment in, the developing world may then appear as the twenty-first century version of the 'white man's burden'. Bound up with capitalist globalisation, then, are ideologies and relations of gender and race-based domination. Capitalism may not have created these dominance relations, but it has effectively internalised them within the historical structures of capitalist globalisation.

The structures of globalising capitalism generate not only possibilities for domination and exploitation, but also new forms of potential solidarity in resistance to these.[57] These forms of solidarity have in recent decades taken on an increasingly transnational character. For twenty years or more, there has been resistance to the imposition of IMF-mandated neoliberal austerity measures in a number of developing countries, with masses of people protesting against privatisation, dramatically increased costs for basic services, curtailment of subsidies for staple foods, and so

[52] Bello, *Dark Victory*; Joshua Karliner, *The Corporate Planet* (San Francisco, CA: Sierra Club Books, 1997); Hahnel, *Panic Rules*; Tabb, *Amoral Elephant*.

[53] Dicken, *Global Shift*, p. 186; Kamel and Hoffman, *Maquiladora Reader*, pp. 18, 21–2.

[54] Cynthia Enloe, *Bananas, Beaches and Bases* (Berkeley, CA: University of California Press 1989), p. 162; see also Jan Pettman, *Worlding Women* (London: Routledge, 1996), pp. 167–8.

[55] Pettman, *Worlding Women*, p. 168.

[56] Arturo Escobar, *Encountering Development* (Princeton, NJ: Princeton University Press, 1995); Stuart Hall, 'The West and the Rest: Discourse and Power', in S. Hall, D. Held, D. Hubert, and K. Thompson (eds.), *Modernity* (Oxford: Blackwell, 1996), pp. 184–227.

[57] Rupert, *Ideologies of Globalization*, 'Class Powers and the Politics of Global Governance', and 'Anti-Capitalist Convergence?'.

on.[58] Articulating the identities of indigenous peoples, Mexican peasants, and global resistors, Subcommandante Marcos has clearly linked the Zapatista struggle against neoliberalism – inaugurated on the very day the North American Free Trade Agreement (NAFTA) went into effect (1 January 1994) – to the 500 year-long history of European colonialism and North American imperialism. The Zapatistas denounced neoliberalism as the vehicle for commodification of social life and the imposition of a universal model of development which would result in destruction of alternative ways of life – including their own. Eschewing the conquest of state power, the Zapatistas practiced a complex multi-level politics which involved organising self-determining base communities, resisting the military and ideological power of the Mexican state, coordinating with social movements and civil society groups across Mexico, and transnational networking among autonomous but related nodes of resistance.

Inspired by the diverse and dialogical networks of resistance imagined by the Zapatistas, a variety of social movements and activist-oriented non-governmental organisations (NGOs) – perhaps predominantly but by no means exclusively from the global North[59] – have in recent years coalesced into 'a movement of movements' resistant to neoliberal globalisation. Among them may be found a wide variety of groups with overlapping emphases: critics of the International Monetary Fund and World Bank, and advocates of debt relief for developing countries; groups focused upon global inequality and development; advocates of re-regulation and taxation of global finance capital; groups critical of the heightened power of multinational firms; environmental protection advocates; those critical of the WTO and its agenda of global liberalisation; movements of and for small farmers and landless peasants; women's groups and lesbian activists; radical and not-so-radical labour advocates; and anti-capitalist groups motivated by articulations of anarchist and socialist ideologies.[60]

Over the last few years, highly visible mass protests involving tens or hundreds of thousands and explicitly targeting capitalist globalisation and neoliberalism have occurred in numerous locations around the world. The World Social Forum of Porto Alegre, Brazil – conceived as a grassroots-oriented and democratic alternative coinciding with the annual meetings of the World Economic Forum – drew ten thousand participants to its inaugural meeting in 2001 and perhaps as many as 70,000 in 2002 and up to 100,000 in 2003. Highlighting the most important factor bringing these various movements and agendas into (at least partial) alignment, Michael Hardt and Antonio Negri wrote:

---

[58] Bello, *Dark Victory*; George Katsiaficas, 'Seattle was not the Beginning', in E. Yuen, G. Katsiaficas, and D. Rose (eds.), *The Battle of Seattle* (New York: Soft Skull Press, 2001).

[59] For example, People's Global Action – a transnational network coordinating localised nodes of resistance to neoliberal globalisation since 1998 – includes many of the best known direct action groups around the world: the Direct Action Network and the Anti-Capitalist Convergence in North America, the KRRS peasant farmers' movement in India, in Europe Ya Basta (Italy) and Reclaim the Streets (UK), the MST landless peasants' movement of Brazil, and a broad and variegated network of associated groups on every populated continent: see Rupert, 'Anti-Capitalist Convergence?'. For further evidence of the broadly transnational scope of this movement of movements, see E. Bircham and J. Charlton (eds.), *Anti-Capitalism: A Guide to the Movement* (London: Bookmarks, 2001), pp. 149–267.

[60] On Anarchism and the global justice movement, see Rupert, 'Anti-Capitalist Convergence?'

The protests themselves have become global movements, and one of their clearest objectives is the democratization of globalizing processes. This should not be called an anti-globalization movement. It is pro-globalization, or rather, it is an alternative globalization movement – one that seeks to eliminate inequalities between rich and poor and between the powerful and the powerless, and to expand the possibilities of self-determination.[61]

Influential Canadian author-activist Naomi Klein suggests that the movement coalesces around 'a radical reclaiming of the commons' – slowing, halting or reversing tendencies toward privatisation and commodification which effectively colonise and consume public space, thereby displacing grassroots processes of democratic deliberation. 'There is an emerging consensus', she writes, 'that building community-based decision-making power – whether through unions, neighborhoods, farms, villages, anarchist collectives or aboriginal self-government – is essential to countering the might of multinational corporations'.[62] Similarly Maude Barlow and Tony Clarke underscore this common thread woven through what they call the New Democracy Movement: 'the most persistent theme underlying the mobilisation of popular resistance to corporate globalisation is opposition to the systematic assault on democracy and the commons' which they name as 'a form of global class warfare'. 'Developing a new democracy along these lines at local, national and international levels is the only possible antidote to corporate globalisation'.[63] On the broad terrain of formulations such as these – all of which presuppose a view of the world economy as a sphere of social power relations which can and should be reconstructed in more democratic forms – anarchists, socialists, autonomist radicals and activist communities of various kinds have found sufficient common ground to converge for collective acts of resistance. A new kind of social movement was emerging and seemed to be constructing a new political culture, forms of political organisation and activity, which were premised upon transnational solidarity and emergent norms of collective responsibility and reciprocity. This resistance, and the alternative possible worlds which it imagined, were the source of much hope and optimism around the turn of the century.[64]

Governance and resistance in the neo-imperial moment

While the market-oriented liberal vision continues to animate US world-order policy, it is no longer represented by chief US policymakers to be presumptively natural or spontaneous – that is, voluntary, cooperative and multilateral – but is now

---

[61] M. Hardt and A. Negri, *New York Times*, 20 July 2001.

[62] Naomi Klein, 'Reclaiming the Commons', *New Left Review*, 9 (2001), p. 82; 'The Vision Thing', in Yuen, Katsiaficas, and Rose (eds.), *Battle of Seattle*, p. 312; see also *No Logo* (New York: Picador, 1999).

[63] Maude Barlow and Tony Clarke, *Global Showdown* (Toronto: Stoddart Publishing, 2002), pp. 125, 26, 208.

[64] Documents such as *The People's Hemispheric Agreement* (1998) reflect iterative dialogues among transnational coalitions of NGOs and social movement groups seeking to produce preliminary strategies for reconstruction of transnational economic relations and institutions in more democratic, egalitarian and socially responsible forms: see Rupert, *Ideologies of Globalization*, pp. 83–5; also Barlow and Clarke, *Global Showdown*, chs. 6–10.

portrayed more explicitly as the product of the global assertion of unilateral US power, especially military force. Coercion was never absent from neoliberal capitalism, of course, but to the greatest extent possible the exercise of power underlying this system was hidden or disguised. During recent decades the most significant coercive mechanisms prying open the global South for neoliberal capitalism and (re-)subjecting working people to the discipline of capital were the structural adjustment programmes administered by multilateral international financial institutions as part of a generalised, worldwide roll-back of public sector programmes, regulations and protections – a brutal exercise of power simultaneously mystified and legitimated by the scientificity of neoclassical economics. Now, however, there has been a shift in the balance of coercion/consent at the core of US global policy, with the unilateral and directly coercive elements officially foregrounded in ways which they have not been in recent years. The most hawkish and hard-line elements in the Bush administration (the Cheney-Rumsfeld-Wolfowitz axis) have exploited the atmosphere of jingoism and fear in the US following the terrorist attacks of 11 September 2001 to put into effect their long-cherished vision of US global military supremacy, unilateral action, and the pre-emptive use of military force deployed to create a world in which the American model of capitalist democracy is unquestioned.[65] Made public in September 2002, Bush's *National Security Strategy for the United States* clearly and explicitly outlines a long-term vision of US global predominance based upon military power, a world in which the US would face no serious military competitors and tolerate no challenges to its interests and its authority, and in which the US government would feel free to use pre-emptive military strikes against those perceived to be potential emergent challengers or who deviate from the administration's putatively universal model of 'freedom, democracy, and free enterprise'.[66] The Bush administration's rush to war in Iraq may be understood as an expression of this doctrine. And, insofar as the Bush strategy clearly envisions an ongoing series of struggles which are global in their scope, the attack on Iraq may be but the first instance of a policy of self-righteous aggression which is likely to produce serial confrontations with other nations perceived in the White House and the Pentagon as potential 'rogue' states or as possible threats to US interests or 'American values'.

The administration has not, of course, abandoned the longstanding US commitment to the deepening of neoliberal capitalist relations on a global basis. Indeed the Bush doctrine explicitly elevates free trade to the status of 'a moral principle', handed down to us along with liberty and democracy as part of the heritage of Western civilisation, presumed to be universally valid and generally applicable as aspects of 'a single sustainable model for national success: freedom, democracy, and free enterprise'.[67] The institutional forms associated with neoliberal capitalism are explicitly integrated into US national security strategy: 'pro-growth legal and regulatory policies to encourage business investment'; 'lower marginal tax rates'; conservative fiscal policies (no small irony here); free trade and international capital

---

[65] For a fuller account of the Cheney-Rumsfeld-Wolfowitz axis and their influence on the neo-imperial turn in US foreign policy, see Rupert, 'The Global Justice Movement in a Neo-Imperial Moment'.

[66] White House, *National Security Strategy for the United States* (Washington, DC, 2002), <www.whitehouse.gov/nsc/print/nssall.html>

[67] *National Security Strategy*, pp. 13, 1.

flows.[68] Whereas for much of the preceding decade, the core rationale of neoliberalism had been to use (primarily if not exclusively) multilateral and cooperative means in order to separate politics from economics to the greatest extent possible and thus to mystify the workings of power within the global capitalist economy, the new national security strategy directly and explicitly links neoliberal capitalism with American global military dominance. The new strategy thus shifts the balance of coercion and consent significantly toward the more coercive side of power. It is in this sense, I think, that the present conjuncture represents a 'neo-imperial moment' within the historical development of US-led global capitalism. As we are already seeing, this re-emphasis on coercive power may have the effect of rendering the power relations of neoliberal world order (or some of them at any rate) more transparent and more difficult effectively to legitimate.

Anticipating the immanent US attack upon Iraq, in early 2003 political activists around the world planned demonstrations of popular opposition. The most spectacular result was a series of nearly simultaneous protests on 15 February 2003, involving around 6–11 million persons in several hundred cities worldwide.[69] Demonstrators around the world were joined by hundreds of thousands of Americans demonstrating in New York, San Francisco, Philadelphia, Chicago, Seattle, Miami, Detroit and many other US cities. In a number of locations around the world the magnitude of the demonstrations was historically unprecedented, but in their totality they were a breathtaking show of the scope and intensity of popular opposition not just to the war in Iraq, but to the imperial pretensions of American power.

For 2003, 'fighting militarism and promoting peace' was designated as a central theme of the World Social Forum, the annual grassroots activist extravaganza which has become central to the emergent Global Justice Movement. After the Porto Alegre WSF, author-activist George Monbiot suggested a genetic connection between the GJM and the nascent global peace movement:

the anti-war campaign has, in large part, grown out of the global justice movement. This movement has never recognized a distinction between the power of the rich world's governments and their appointed institutions (the IMF, the World Bank, the World Trade Organization) to wage economic warfare and the power of the same governments, working through a different set of institutions (the UN security council, NATO) to send in the Bombers. . . . the impending war has reinforced our determination to tackle the grotesque maldistribution of power which permits a few national governments to assert a global mandate.[70]

As one Indian delegate told the WSF, 'If we are going to struggle for a better world, then our struggle cannot be separated from a struggle against the hegemony of the United States of America'. The distinguished Egyptian scholar Samir Amin was less clinical in tone: 'As long as the aggressive, fascist strategy of the United States is not defeated, an alternative globalization will not be possible'.[71]

To the extent that building relations of solidarity across national boundaries is the *sine qua non* of the Global Justice Movement, the reassertion of American power in

---

[68] Ibid., p. 12.
[69] As reported, for example, by Reuters, 15 February 2003 and Agence France Presse, 16 February 2003.
[70] George Monbiot, 'Stronger than Ever', *The Guardian* (28 January 2003).
[71] Both quotations are from B. Ehrenreich, 'Another World is Possible', *In These Times* (31 January 2003).

the service of US global privilege, the mobilisation of popular jingoism in support of this (re-)militarised imperialism, and the suppression of alternative voices within the US is likely to weaken the GJM in strategically significant ways. If the GJM does in fact need American social movements to democratise the USA as an integral part of the project of global democratisation – the reciprocal responsibility inherent in transnational solidarity – the onset of a neoimperial moment and the powerful reactivation of longstanding and deeply-rooted cultural tendencies toward American exceptionalism and privilege cannot but damage the culture of transnational solidarity which the movement has struggled to construct.

Conclusion

A Gramscian-inflected historical materialism enables an understanding of globalising capitalism, its relations of power and structures of governance, as the product of struggles – at once material and ideological – among concretely situated social agents. As the emergent neoliberal historic bloc has sought to (re)produce its social powers on an increasingly global scale, they have encountered recurrent bouts of more-or-less explicitly political resistance from a variety of social agents (some explicitly class-identified but many others not) who have challenged neoliberal representations and called into question not just the agenda of the neoliberal globalisation, but the legitimacy of the implicitly capitalist social powers underlying it. In the neo-imperial moment, such challenges have readily broadened to encompass opposition to military expansionism by the US and its (relatively few) imperial partners. However, this refocusing of the Global Justice Movement brings with it an important source of tension, for the ideological cement which bound the movement together and enabled it to begin to envision alternative possible worlds was a culture of solidarity, mutual respect and reciprocity which transcended national boundaries and formal citizenship. The GJM had begun, in short, to (re-)construct a transnational common sense and corresponding forms of political organisation and activity. Although it may not have been their explicit intent, the architects of the newest imperialism may have reinvigorated nationalisms – in the form of US popular jingoism and its global mirror-image, anti-Americanism – within transnational common sense, and thereby placed a roadblock directly in the path of the Global Justice Movement and its potentially transformative project. The future meanings of the global justice movement will be determined in large part by struggles over popular common sense in various locales around the world, and whether activists and 'organic intellectuals' embedded within those sites are able to articulate globalisation/solidarity in opposition to strong currents of globalisation/nationalism.

Whose knowledge for what politics?

KARENA SHAW*

Introduction

We find ourselves amidst an explosion of literature about how our worlds are being fundamentally changed (or not) through processes that have come to be clumped under the vague title of 'globalisation'. As we wander our way through this literature, we might find ourselves – with others – feeling perplexed and anxious about the loss of a clear sense of what politics is, where it happens, what it is about, and what we need to know to understand and engage in it. This in turn leads many of us to contribute to a slightly smaller literature, such as this Special Issue, seeking to theorise how the space and character of politics might be changing, and how we might adapt our research strategies to accommodate these changes and maintain the confidence that we, and the disciplines we contribute to, still have relevant things to say about international politics. While this is not a difficult thing to claim, and it is not difficult to find others to reassure us that it is true, I want to suggest here that it is worth lingering a little longer in our anxiety than might be comfortable. I suggest this because it seems to me that there is, or at least should be, more on the table than we're yet grappling with. In particular, I argue here that any attempt to theorise the political today needs to take into account not only that the character and space of politics are changing, but that the way we study or theorise it – not only the subjects of our study but the very kind of knowledge we produce, and for whom – may need to change as well. As many others have argued, the project of progressive politics these days is not especially clear.[1] It no longer seems safe to assume, for example, that the capture of the state or the establishment of benign forms of global governance should be our primary object. However, just as the project of progressive politics is in question, so is the role of knowledge, and knowledge production, under contemporary circumstances. I think there are possibilities embedded in explicitly engaging these questions together that are far from realisation. There are also serious dangers in trying to separate them, or assume the one while engaging the other, however 'obvious' the answers to one or the other may appear to be. Simultaneous with theorising the political 'out there' in the international must be an engagement with the politics of theorising 'in here,' in academic contexts. My project here is to explore how this challenge might be taken up in the contemporary study of

---

* Many thanks to those who provided me with critical perspectives on the argument developed here, in particular Jef Huysmans, Bice Maiguashca, Naimh Moore, Rob Walker, and Darrell Whitman.
[1] There are many possible reference points here, of course, not least: Judith Butler, Ernesto Laclau and Slavoj Zizek, *Contingency, Hegemony, Universality: Contemporary Dialogues on the Left* (London and New York: Verso, 2000), or Michael Hardt and Antonio Negri, *Empire* (Cambridge, MA and London: Harvard University Press, 2000).

politics, particularly in relation to emerging forms of political practice, such as those developed by activists in a variety of contexts.[2] My argument is for an approach to theorising the political that shifts the disciplinary assumptions about for what purpose and for whom we should we produce knowledge in contemporary times, through an emphasis on the strategic knowledges produced through political practice. Such an approach would potentially provide us with understandings of contemporary political institutions and practices that are both more incisive and more enabling than can be produced through more familiarly disciplined approaches.

The argument proceeds in four parts. I begin with a parable of sorts about the discipline of Anthropology and its knowledge politics, developing this as a reference point that might help us to better understand the terrains of knowledge politics at play in the discipline of International Relations (IR). The second part of the argument considers three efforts to develop the study of activism in the international, exploring the political terrains they explicitly intervene in, as well as those they might contribute to more unintentionally. I then move on to consider one way of shifting these political terrains through a different approach to the study of political practice in general, and activism more specifically, one that might provide a more satisfying answer to whom and for what political project we think we are writing, that might help us to think politically. The article concludes with a brief survey of some of the possibilities and limitations of this approach.

A reference point: the ambivalence of anthropological knowledge

The discipline of Anthropology developed as and through the study of 'culture,' in particular the cultures of distant or exotic – and often colonised – others. This brief led anthropologists into communities to observe the rituals and daily lives of these others, to speculate about their broader import, meaning and significance, and to record this for posterity. What this practice of knowledge production eventually led to at many sites is a rather antagonistic response from some of their subjects. Indigenous peoples in North America, for example, began to experience their relationship to anthropologists as one of frustration, betrayal and anger about the ways in which anthropologists appeared in their communities, observed their daily lives and cultural practices from the mundane to the sacred, gathered information, and disappeared, leaving no apparent reciprocal contribution to their communities.[3] Many indigenous peoples were yet more angered when they began to read what had been written about them, and to realise how it had been used to frame and justify particular social, cultural and political understandings of and policies towards them.

For their part, when they studied indigenous peoples, anthropologists believed they were contributing to an important and valuable intellectual project: not only

---

[2] Although I am interested in the study of political practice more generally, in this article I focus particularly on the study of activism and activist knowledge as this is the focus of those texts I engage. However, the approach I develop here is one that could be applied more generally.

[3] One well-known example of this kind of critique can be found in Vine Deloria, 'Anthropologists and Other Friends', in *Custer Died for Your Sins: An Indian Manifesto* (New York: Macmillan, 1969), pp. 78–100. A more recent version is expressed in Linda Tuhiwai Smith, *Decolonizing Methodologies: Research and Indigenous Peoples* (London and New York: Zed Books, 1999).

were they contributing to the font of knowledge for all humankind,[4] in some cases they were the only ones who were seeking to understand, protect and preserve peoples, cultures and practices that were under threat, in many cases in danger of disappearing or being destroyed altogether either through violence, neglect, or 'the inevitable advance of civilisation'. Both of these projects, but the latter in particular, required that anthropologists write to communities other than those they studied. However, they did of course write to and for a community: a community of their perceived peers, and also a broader community of potential users, be they colonial administrators, museum curators, policymakers, or benevolent organisations campaigning for the protection of indigenous groups. Thus although they didn't necessarily write to indigenous peoples, they did feel they wrote for them, on their behalf, to other audiences.

In retrospect, and through rigorous and extensive critique (both from 'within' and 'outside' the discipline[5]), a darker side to their activity, as identified by indigenous peoples, has been exposed and struggled with, most seriously and extensively within the discipline of anthropology itself. These struggles unearthed and politicised knowledge/power dynamics within disciplinary methodologies and subjectivities, dynamics that were embedded in the colonial contexts from which the discipline emerged. As some argued, however benevolent or helpful anthropologists sought to be, their project itself contributed to a broader set of assumptions and practices that potentially reinforced the apparent inevitability and assimilative effects of 'civilization': the very force indigenous peoples were struggling to resist. Insofar as anthropological work was focused on the documentation of the 'cultures' of those who lived outside of 'modern' civilisation, it reinscribed their difference in ways that seemed to provide them with only two options: to live (irrationally) out of time or to become properly 'modern'. These were of course the options indigenous peoples had been resisting, as they fought instead for the possibility of being both different and modern, capable of managing their own affairs.

As welcome as a recognition of their participation in the colonial project was from the perspective of indigenous peoples, as the critical conversations within the discipline of anthropology continued, even this began to backfire on indigenous peoples. Insofar as anthropologists began to question the foundational assumptions of their own discipline, they also ran the risk of undermining their own authority to

---

[4] Including scholars of IR, who, along with other scholars of the modern social sciences, relied upon anthropologists to document the history of society while they got on with arranging the future of it. See, for example, my discussion of Hedley Bull in Karena Shaw, 'Indigeneity and the International', *Millennium: Journal of International Studies*, 31:1 (2002), pp. 55–82.

[5] This is a large literature, but some influential critiques from within the discipline would include Johannes Fabian, *Time and The Other: How Anthropology Makes Its Object* (New York: Columbia University Press, 1983); Stanley Diamond, 'Anthropology in Question', in Dell Hymes (ed.), *Reinventing Anthropology* (New York: Pentheon Books, 1972), pp. 401–29; James Clifford, 'On Ethnographic Authority', *Representations*, 1 (1983), pp. 118–46; Thomas Weaver (ed.), *To See Ourselves: Anthropology and Modern Social Issues* (Glenview: Scott, Foresman, 1973); James Clifford and George Marcus (eds.), *Writing Culture: The Poetics and Politics of Ethnography* (Berkeley, CA:University of California, 1986); George Marcus and Michael Fischer, *Anthropology as Cultural Critique: An Experimental Moment in the Human Sciences* (Chicago, IL: University of Chicago Press, 1986); Renato Rosaldo, *Culture and Truth: The Remaking of Social Analysis* (Boston, MA: Beacon Press, 1989). After these relatively early interventions, this debate blossomed not least in journals such as *Critical Anthropology* and *Critique of Anthropology*.

speak as anthropologists, thus denying some indigenous groups of key defenders. This was particularly poignant in land claims cases which rested on indigenous groups needing to 'prove' the 'authenticity' of their culture in order to have their claims to their land recognised and acknowledged.[6] As more general anthropological debate brewed about the problems embedded in the concept of 'culture', exposed particularly by any cultural claim to 'authenticity', this ground for indigenous claims began to appear precarious. Suddenly, colonial as it may have been, 'bad old' Anthropology didn't look so bad, as it turned out that the evidence from this kind of Anthropology was necessary to 'authenticate' indigenous peoples' claims, to prove their difference, the coherence and consistency of their cultures, and thus the violences done to them by the failure to recognise their authority. The politics of knowledge is never straightforward, and anthropologists were in a bit of a bind: by confronting their colonial past, they ran the considerable risk of facilitating the advance of the colonial project.

What has emerged from this delicate political terrain is a highly charged and deeply engaged conversation about authority and disciplinarity, methodology and subjectivity, power and knowledge. What has also emerged is a series of careful attempts to negotiate the terrain, its pitfalls mapped at both the abstract and very immediate levels, as struggles continue about the viability of different anthropological authority in legal and political contexts. Anthropologists are not off the hook, from indigenous peoples' perspectives, but nor can indigenous peoples do without them: they are locked together in a complex attempt to decolonise the knowledge practices through which indigenous peoples have been known, have articulated their claims and produced their political subjectivities.

This has involved, among other things, indigenous peoples becoming anthropologists, anthropologists reconsidering what their discipline can and should do, and an extended conversation focused on who the knowledge anthropologists produce should be for, and what it means – how it affects the practices of research and the assessment of the quality and character of the knowledge produced – to shift the assumption of who knowledge is for from a community of intellectual peers, or a contribution to disciplinary conversations, and towards, for example, those who are studied. One consequence of these struggles has been a less coherent discipline, one less clearly identified with a single project, methodology or subject matter. Another consequence has been a more politically engaged set of practices and research communities. Thus although the relationship between indigenous peoples and anthropologists remains politically fraught, it is one that expresses the complexity and difficulty of thinking seriously about the politics of knowledge in changing global circumstances.[7]

[6] See, for example, James Clifford, 'Identity in Mashpee', in *The Predicament of Culture: Twentieth-Century Ethnography, Literature, and Art* (Cambridge, MA and London: Harvard University Press, 1988), pp. 277–346. For more recent examples, see Dara Culhane, *The Pleasure of the Crown: Anthropology, Law and First Nations* (Vancouver: Talonbooks, 1998); Frank Cassidy (ed.), *Aboriginal Title in British Columbia: Delgamuukw v. the Queen* (Lantzville, BC: Oolichan Books & the Institute for Research on Public Policy, 1992) , or Noel Dyck and James B. Waldram (eds.), *Anthropology, Public Policy and Native Peoples in Canada* (Montreal: McGill-Queen's University Press, 1993).
[7] For analyses of contemporary relationships, see Thomas Biolsi and Larry J. Zimmerman (eds.), *Indians and Anthropologists: Vine Deloria, Jr. and the Critique of Anthropology* (Tucson, AZ: University of Arizona Press, 1997).

I've focused on the specific relationship between indigenous peoples and Anthropology; however, the struggle within the discipline has not been about a single issue or problematic. It has been about the complex rethinking of the practice of knowledge production in a changing world, in particular, in a world in which the political implications of the kind of knowledge produced had become increasingly obvious and increasingly unacceptable to both the producers of the knowledge and its 'objects' or subject matter. We can attribute the changes to the brave and clever anthropologists and/or to the obstreperous indigenous peoples who developed the critique, but the changes should also be situated within the context of changing patterns of power and knowledge at other sites in the world, expressed 'globally' through anti-colonial struggles and the emergence of post-colonial states, and 'domestically' though rearticulations of power relations through anti-war movements, the civil rights movement in the US, feminism, struggles for indigenous sovereignty at a variety of sites, struggles to create post-colonial political structures, and so on. These changing patterns of power have also provided the context for the discipline of IR for the past decades, of course, and the discipline has responded to them, adapted in relation to them, and continues to do so, as the brief of this Special Issue suggests. Given this, and given the important differences in disciplinary subject matter and subjectivity, what relevance might the narrative above have in relation to IR as a discipline, if any?

One might presume, from how I've proceeded thus far, that I intend to argue that the discipline needs to 'do the same thing' as anthropology in some way: to decolonise its knowledge practices. But it's not quite so straightforward. Although it shares contexts with Anthropology, IR has played a different role in relation to those contexts and has its own (although not unrelated) politics of knowledge. The story above suggests how interplay between contexts of knowledge and disciplinary structures shapes knowledge and its uses and usefulness, shapes relationships between researcher and researched, and in the end does this in ways that have unintended consequences. Most anthropologists did not seek to produce knowledge that reinscribed colonial relationships, in fact thought they were doing quite the opposite. With hindsight it is easy enough to be critical, but I'm not sure that the kind of knowledge produced through the disciplinary structures of IR provides an innocent ground for such critique. Of course, part of the lesson of the story above is that we simply cannot know with any certainty what effects our research will have – as it turns out much of the 'bad, old' Anthropology remains crucial to indigenous peoples' legal and political struggles, or is helping them to reinvent their societies in ways that they desire. However in order to contribute productively to indigenous peoples' struggles, to change the relationship between the discipline and its subjects in ways that enabled a more defensible or satisfying power/knowledge terrain to emerge, the very core of the discipline – its self-definition, subjectivity, method-ologies, and aspirations – had to be thrown into question. One of the key questions that had to be posed (and answered in many different ways) in this process was the question of for what purpose, and for whom, anthropological knowledge should be produced, as this in turn was the prerequisite for conceptualising research programmes, for selecting sites and methodologies of study. As it turned out, and this is perhaps the most hopeful part of the story, this has considerably enriched and enlivened the discipline, enabling it to extend its relevance as well as opening possibilities for more politically engaged or relevant research.[8]

Activism and the politics of disciplinary knowledge?

Like Anthropology, the discipline of IR has struggled with the question of how changing global relations might require a shift in its subject matter and methodologies. This has been expressed not least in the exploding literature on 'globalisation'. One subset of this literature has focused on emerging forms of activism in international politics, exploring the forms this activity has taken, and what its causes, trajectories and broader implications might be, both for the study of IR and more generally. Thus we have seen the rise of debates about such concepts as 'global civil society', 'epistemic regimes', and 'transnational advocacy networks', as we struggle to integrate the study of these forms of activism into the discipline of IR. These emerging literatures provide an important site in which to examine the political terrains of knowledge: not only the explicit and intended effects of knowledge practices, but their broader unintended effects. The story above about the contribution of anthropology to the colonial project reveals the potential political potency of these unintended consequences. The enrichment of the discipline that has resulted from critical interrogation of these knowledge terrains also reveals the potential embedded in such interrogation. In order to respond to the challenges we face in conceptualising a progressive political agenda today, those of us interested in international politics may well need to continue to explore these questions, not least in relation to those seeking to enact such a political agenda in activist practice. Should we allow their activity to be 'colonised' by IR, allowing the discipline to essentially frame what is important about them, or do we need to consider whether they pose a more fundamental challenge to disciplinary and disciplining practices, and hold out possibilities for other ways of understanding their activity? An answer to this question requires an exploration of the broader terrain of knowledge at play here, a serious consideration of what purpose we think our knowledge is for, and for whom we are producing it.

When perusing this emerging research into activist practices within the discipline of IR, there are some immediately obvious responses to my questions above, about the purpose and intended audience of the knowledge we produce. I'll draw on three recent works to illustrate this: Paul Wapner's *Environmental Activism and World*

---

[8] This research has not least begun to make a substantial contribution to our understanding of contemporary global processes. See, for example: Johantan Xavier Inda and Renato Rosaldo (eds.), *The Anthropology of Globalisation* (Malden, MA and Oxford: Blackwell, 2002); Thomas Blom Hansen and Finn Stepputat (eds.), *States of Imagination: Ethnographic Explorations of the Postcolonial State* (Durham, NC and London: Duke University Press, 2001); Michael Burawoy, Joseph A. Blum, Sheba George, Zsuzsa Gille, Teresa Gowan, Lynne Haney, Maren Klawiter, Steven H. Lopez, Sean O Riain, and Millie Thayer, *Global Ethnography: Forces, Connections, and Imaginations in a Postmodern World* (Berkeley, CA: University of California Press, 2000); Roxann Prazniak and Arif Dirlik (ed.), *Places and Politics in an Age of Globalization* (Lanham, MD: Rowman & Littlefield, 2001).

Civic Politics, Margaret E. Keck and Kathryn Sikkink's *Activists Beyond Borders* and Robert O'Brien, Anne Marie Goetz, Jan Aart Scholte and Marc Williams' *Contesting Global Governance: Multilateral Economic Institutions and Global Social Movements.*[9] All three books develop arguments about the significance of activist practices to the study of international relations. Wapner's focus is on the contribution three environmental non-governmental organisations' strategies and campaigns have made to the development of 'world civic society'. By examining not only the immediate strategies of these groups, but also their broader implications in relation to the development of political cultures outside or beyond domestic civil society, Wapner develops an argument that these groups' activities are not only having an impact in relation to their immediate goals, but are having a wider-ranging effect on the development of international political institutions and practices.

> Transnational environmental groups not only lobby states but also directly shape the activities of other institutions, collectivities, and individuals. They do so by manipulating mechanisms of power that exist outside the realm of state-to-state relations. These include economic, social, and cultural practices that traverse countries and have an impact on public life.[10]

He argues that this, in turn, indicates the need to expand the study of international politics to incorporate a focus on world civic society in order to improve the ability of the discipline to understand and explain the functioning of international politics. 'My hope is that an appreciation for this dimension of global experience will sensitize people to the limitations of the traditional understanding of *world politics*'.[11] By extension, he also hopes to legitimise and encourage world civic politics as a crucial site for the development of global environmental governance.[12]

O'Brien *et al.*'s book also seeks to assess the effects of global social movements on international politics, this time more specifically in relation to the structure and functioning of multilateral economic institutions. Drawing on interviews with activists and with officials from relevant institutions, and observations of interactions between activist groups and these institutions as well as textual research, the book addresses questions such as whether multilateral economic institutions have

---

[9] Paul Wapner, *Environmental Activism and World Civic Politics* (Albany, NY: State University of New York Press, 1996); Margaret E. Keck and Katheryn Sikkink, *Activists Beyond Borders* (Ithaca, NY and London: Cornell University Press, 1998); Robert O'Brien, Ann Marie Goetz, Jan Aart Scholte, Marc Williams, *Contesting Global Governance: Multilateral Economic Institutions and Global Social Movements* (Cambridge: Cambridge University Press, 2000). Many other works might have been chosen; as mentioned above, there has been a veritable explosion of works on activism and international politics. See, for example: Jonathan A. Fox and David L. Brown (eds.), *The Struggle for Accountability: The World Bank, NGOs and Grassroots Movements* (Cambridge, MA: The MIT Press, 1998); Barry K. Gills (ed.), *Globalization and the Politics of Resistance* (Basingstoke: Palgrave, 2000); Alejandro Colas, *International Civil Society: Social Movements in World Politics* (Cambridge: Polity Press, 2001); Ronnie D. Lipschutz, 'Reconstructing World Politics: The Emergence of Global Civil Society', *Millennium*, 21:3 (Winter, 1992), pp. 389–420; M.J. Peterson, 'Transnational Activity, International Society and World Politics', *Millennium*, 21:3 (Winter, 1992), pp. 371–89; Jackie Smith, Charles Chatfield and Ron Pangucco, *Transnational Social Movements and Global Politics: Solidarity Beyond the State* (Syracuse, NY: Syracuse University Press, 1997); Leslie Paul Thiele, 'Making Democracy Safe for the World: Social Movements and Global Politics, *Alternatives*, 18:3 (Summer, 1993), pp. 273–305.

[10] Wapner, *Environmental Activism and World Civic Politics*, p. 153.

[11] Ibid., p. 162.

[12] Ibid., p. 164.

modified their behaviour as a consequence of social movement activism, what their motivations are in engaging with these movements, and what the broader significance of the relationship between these institutions and global social movements might be. 'We argue that there is a transformation in the nature of governance conducted by MEIs [multilateral economic institutions] as a result of their encounter with GSMs [global social movements]. This transformation is labelled "complex multilateralism" in recognition of its movement away from an exclusively state based structure.'[13] As with Wapner's book, then, their explicit aspiration is to make a contribution to broader disciplinary conversations about the significance of these movements and their political practices, and thus to contribute to a better understanding of international politics in and through the discipline. '[O]ur goal is not to account for state behaviour, but to better understand processes of global governance. Our argument is that some attention must be focused upon the interaction of multilateral institutions and civil society groups to understand the form and content of global governance.'[14] In their case, they hope to advance the understanding of multilateralism in the space of the international by developing the idea of complex multilateralism, a hybrid form of multilateralism which they argue provides a better way of understanding how political institutions and practices are functioning in the space of the international. Also like Wapner, however, their efforts are motivated by a desire to promote particular forms of global governance: 'Finally, our inspiration for this study derives ... in concern to understand the ways in which non-elites can participate in the process of governing.'[15]

Keck and Sikkink's is in some ways less tightly focused on the disciplinary problematic than the other two, although it is primarily framed in relation to disciplinary struggles and arguments:

> Reconceptualizing international society does not require abandoning a focus on actors and institutions to seek underlying forces that make states and other forms of association epiphenomenal. We do find, however, that enough evidence of change in the relationships among actors, institutions, norms, and ideas exists to make the world political system rather than an international society of states the appropriate level of analysis. We also believe that studying networks is extraordinarily valuable for tracking and ultimately theorizing about these evolving relationships.[16]

Their research focuses on the structure of activist activity, describing the functioning of what they call 'transnational advocacy networks' and arguing for the importance of these networks in international politics.

> Advocacy networks are significant transnationally and domestically. By building new links among actors in civil societies, states, and international organizations, they multiply the channels of access to the international system. In such issue areas as the environment and human rights, they also make international resources available to new actors in domestic political and social struggles. By thus blurring the boundaries between a state's relations with its own nationals and the recourse both citizens and states have to the international system, advocacy networks are helping to transform the practice of national sovereignty.[17]

---

[13] O'Brien et al., *Contesting Global Governance*, p. 206.
[14] Ibid., p. 207.
[15] Ibid., p. 207.
[16] Keck and Sikkink, *Activists Beyond Borders*, p. 212.
[17] Ibid., p. 1–2.

Their work is grounded in a wealth of research, particularly interviews with activists, observation of and participation in activist practices at a wide variety of sites. The book documents the emergence of activist networks, their strategies and effects, and their potential broader implications and develops this into an argument for the contribution of these networks to the formation of international society and to the practice of contemporary international politics.

The concept of a transnational advocacy network is an important element in conceptualizing the changing nature of the international polity and particularly in understanding the interaction between societies and states in the formulation of international policies. It suggests a view of multiple pathways into the international arena, a view that attributes to domestic actors a degree of agency that a more state-centric approach would not admit. . . . This approach suggests answers to some of the questions about how issues get on the international agenda, how they are framed as they are, and why certain kinds of international campaigns or pressures are effective in some cases but not in others.[18]

All three works thus share this aspiration to advance the understanding of international or world politics. They each develop arguments for why we must take activist activity into account in order to have a sufficient understanding of world politics. They each contribute to the opening up of new areas of study in the discipline, not only by acknowledging and representing the experiences of a range of international actors, but also by enabling issues and practices previously excluded from study into the discipline to become part of its conversations. In this way, then, they share their primary audience – who the knowledge they produce is for – and their primary or explicit political terrain, or sense of the project to which their work is meant to contribute. Like the anthropologists, they write most immediately and explicitly to a disciplinary community, a community of their institutional peers. This is most evident in the tight disciplinary framing each book sets out in its introduction.[19] And the political terrain they intervene in most explicitly is also a disciplinary terrain: each seeks to improve the understanding of the functioning of international politics, to enable the discipline to better explain and understand the structures and functioning of politics in the space of the international. They seek to contribute to a better representation of the world through the discipline, while at the same time sharing a more implicit aspiration to shape the practices of global governance in particular ways.

This is a significant political terrain, and their interventions are likely to have a range of effects, some obvious and others less so; some intended and others less so. Perhaps the most immediate and obvious is that each book seeks to open up space for new kinds of research, to enable and inspire researchers to spend more time exploring actors in the international that have previously been generally ignored. In so doing they contribute to a pluralisation of the discipline, the development of new research programmes and conversations and a much improved representation of

---

[18] Ibid., p. 217.
[19] Keck and Sikkink might protest that their framing is trans-disciplinary, in that it explicitly draws from several disciplines and resists reducing its relevance to IR. However, the work is no less framed in relation to disciplinary concerns because of this: its significance remains articulated in relation to disciplinary conventions of knowledge production, if those of more than one discipline.

politics in the international. Insofar as the discipline itself plays a broader role in reflecting, representing and legitimating changes in how international politics functions, this may have a wider-ranging effect as well. Disciplinary knowledge has played an important role in legitimating forms of international order, particular institutions and practices. The representations, legitimations and contestations effected by the discipline circulate not only amongst the immediate academic community, but into larger contexts, through practices such as international law, policymaking, the constitution, recognition and legitimation of political subjectivities, and so on. They express and reframe globalised efforts to establish grounds upon which differences can be resolved. So, for example, these literatures are not only documenting or reflecting changes in the structure and character of international governance, they also seek to develop arguments for the dangers and possibilities inherent in these changes and for how these dangers and possibilities might or should be acted upon. Their contributions are thus important especially insofar as global institutions are being restructured, and the principles by which they are being restructured and the question of what groups should participate in such a restructuring are far from agreed. Literatures of this kind may thus provide languages, logics and perspectives which might inform these restructurings, or persuade relevant actors that representatives of social movements, for example, have a role to play in such restructurings. These are important political terrains indeed.

So what of my earlier concern about unintended consequences of such forms of knowledge production – is there any reason to push our exploration beyond the obvious contributions such works offer to the development of more progressive disciplinary understandings and thus perhaps to more progressive structures and institutions in international politics? I want to suggest there is. Building on the understanding above of the primary audience for the work and the disciplinary knowledge politics it seeks to intervene in, as well as how this terrain might be useful or relevant to activist struggles, I move now to develop a reading of the potential limits to this framing of research into contemporary activism, to an exploration of some of the broader terrains of knowledge politics that might be foreclosed by foregrounding disciplinary struggles in this way. My broader purpose is not to discount the relevance of the explicit terrains discussed above, but rather to unearth other terrains we might seek to engage through the study of activist activity.

First, then, and perhaps most obviously, the choice of IR scholars as the most explicit audience has certain limitations, some of them quite obvious: it is a small, largely but not entirely Anglo-American, well educated community which shares a very distinct and reified understanding of its intellectual turf (thus the necessity of engaging in disciplinary and disciplining conversations). The authors of all three works suggest that they intend their readership to stretch far beyond this audience, perhaps to include the activists who they studied or others interested in the future shape of the international, and it well may. However, such readers are often put off by books that are so heavily shaped by disciplinary conversations, finding their relevance primarily embedded in the discipline and thus unclear to them. One of the reasons for this is that few potential readers, such as international activists, actually approach their activity from the abstract 'outside', from which our research usually begins. Activists are much more likely to be working from a particular context, with specific aims, objectives, resources, and limitations. From that particular context, our representations of the international might not only be of limited use, they may appear to be quite alien, bearing little resemblance to the world politics they see or participate in. But is this a problem? After all, it is a critique relevant to a large percentage of academic work, and as suggested above, the same actors who find the work to be of limited use in understanding the international may seize upon it to help articulate, formulate or justify their actions. In this way the books might provide legitimacy for the aims of such actors, for example, their methods or their articulations of possible broader contexts for interpreting and responding to their activities. Here, though, we should be careful of attributing too much one-way causality to the discipline. I made the argument above that the discipline has played a role in legitimating international practices. This is a plausible claim, but it's much less certain how much of a role this is, whether the discipline primarily reflects international events back to it, or actually helps to set discursive boundaries or norms that shape its structure. This isn't a question that can be easily resolved, but any resolution of it suggests important limitations to considering the discipline as a primary tool in a struggle towards progressive political institutions. As others have documented, there have been normative discourses in IR from the beginning of the discipline, just as there have been 'realist' or power politics discourses.[20] Although we might wish to put our faith in the eventual triumph of the former, as we can see from contemporary events around Iraq, such faith should not substitute for effective political analysis. So my first hesitation about the ways in which the works above frame their audience and political project in the study of activism would reside in my scepticism about whether the discipline provides the most effective of political terrains, either because of its causal strength or its broader role and effects in representing world politics.

Perhaps more troubling, to reinforce the authority of the discipline as a legitimator of such activity maintains a certain idea of whose agency should shape the international: to what extent should we reinscribe the authority of our disciplinary conversations in this way, particularly when we own up to the relatively narrow intellectual and historic framing of the discipline? Here again we might reflect on the dilemma of the anthropologists: they sought to use their disciplinary authority to support the cause of people who they believed had little voice, but the unintended consequences of their actions played a role in maintaining certain forms of colonial relationships. Eventually, many recognised that it was as problematic to maintain the discipline in its inherited form as to relinquish responsibility entirely, thus posing them with the delicate political terrain they have since been struggling with, balanced between an effort to critically reinvent the discipline's authority and yet simultaneously maintain their commitment to support indigenous peoples in their complex political struggles. As suggested above, IR as a discipline is hardly innocent on these grounds. Similar critiques have been made of the extent to which the history and structure of the disciplinary conversations in IR have inscribed power relations in ways that have very real

---

[20] See, for example, Franke Wilmer's analysis in *The Indigenous Voice in World Politics* (Newbury Park, CA: Sage Publications, 1993) of the interplay between these discourses in relation to indigenous politics in IR, and my analysis of some of the dangers embedded in relying on the development of normative discourses: Karena Shaw, 'Indigeneity and the International'.

political ramifications.[21] We may wish to dismiss these critiques, but to do so is to wander into the possibility not only of reinscribing unintended political effects, but also of rendering the discipline less and less relevant in a world where much political activity is focused on contesting these kinds of power relations. Even if we believe these critics, however, there is no simple way forward, as Anthropology's struggles can attest. Political terrains overlap, and to focus on one to the exclusion of others is to run significant risks. My second hesitation, then, involves the dangers of strengthening the legitimacy of the discipline, given the limits of its project and purpose under contemporary circumstances.

This leads to my third concern, which has to do with how the framing of research specifically in relation to the discipline of IR shapes its effects in particular ways. The creation of common reference points and understandings, of course, is what all conversation is about, and is not necessarily a bad thing. In the case of IR, this tends to work in ways that reify a particular 'subject': international or world politics, and a particular 'space' in which it happens. This 'space' may no longer be an assumed space 'between' sovereign states – the discipline has developed much more complex ways of delineating itself – but it continues to delineate itself nonetheless. In the books above this is indicated in part by the very choice of subject matter: *world* civic society, *multilateral* economic institutions, *global* social movements, and *trans*-national advocacy networks. Interestingly, in the Keck and Sikkink book, the imposition of these boundaries is explicitly resisted, not least as it becomes clear in several places that to measure the effects of transnational advocacy networks one must consider a spatial structure that ranges from the very local or particular right up to the international. The authors often seem uncomfortable with the task of assessing these networks' effects strictly by the criteria of their participation in the international, and in fact read them to be not only crossing the international-domestic-local divide constantly, but in this process also reframing the meaning of sovereignty itself. At the same time, however, the book concludes with an assessment of the contribution of these networks to *international* society, implicitly reinscribing a particular spatial, and disciplinary, framing. My concern is over what constraints we place on our subject matter, and its contribution to the development of diverse political terrains, in order to argue for its inclusion in a disciplinary conversation. We can certainly see and trace the activities of transnational advocacy networks at the international level, but does it make sense to primarily bound, measure, explain and understand their activity in this way? Or are these activists operating with very different concepts of political space, ones that are done a certain kind of violence by framing them into the international? The question here is whether it makes sense to stretch the boundaries of IR in our efforts to render it more inclusive, representative, or interesting, or whether we need to more rigorously reveal its limitations in order to enable a more substantial reconsideration of the political terrains effected by the contemporary disciplining of knowledge. On one reading, one that I don't think

[21] See, for example, R.B.J. Walker, *Inside/Outside: International Relations as Political Theory* (Cambridge: Cambridge University Press, 1993); Richard K. Ashley and R.B.J. Walker (eds.), 'Speaking the Language of Exile: Dissidence in International Studies', Special Issue of *International Studies Quarterly*, 34:3 (1990).

goes entirely against the intention of the authors, Keck and Sikkink's book provides ample evidence for the latter approach, even though it concludes with and is framed by the former. My third hesitation, then, is about how the framing of activist activity necessary to intervene in disciplinary knowledge politics disciplines our understanding of it in ways that might be problematic, or at least renders such activity less challenging or enabling than it could be.

In all cases, the books make clearly delineated interventions into disciplinary conversations, ones that are aimed at enhancing the engagement of activist work within the discipline by detailing not only its immediate and intended effects, but its contributions to the broader development of international politics. From a disciplinary perspective, their 'knowledge politics' are clearly towards the recognition of these activities, their legitimation and refinement. None of the works, however, read the activist activities to substantially reveal the limitations of the ways of knowing the international that are reified through the discipline in ways that *should* require more than an extension of the boundaries of the discipline: in the end each forwards a revised framework which reinforces disciplinary adequacy. None of them argues for more than an adaptation of the boundaries, an act of greater flexibility or inclusion. Nor is there much explicit concern about the limits the disciplining places on the understanding of or relationship to the subjects of study. Is this a problem? The answer depends on whether one believes it makes sense to think the political through the limitations imposed by these disciplinary histories and constraints. My concern with these limitations leads to my three hesitations, about whether the discipline has enough causal authority to make it an effective site for knowledge politics; about whether we want to enhance its authority and legitimacy, given the relative narrowness of the discipline and its structural role in the social sciences, and about whether this framing actually makes sense as a way of understanding the radical potential of these practices. Although each of the texts discussed above, to my mind, significantly adds to our understanding of international or world politics, and does so in ways that highlight the activities of progressive political agents, I'm not sure they help us as much in our efforts to theorise the political, or indeed to think politically, under contemporary circumstances. I want to continue here to suggest a different way of understanding these activist practices, a different model through which to analyse the political through their activities, one that I think might enhance the political terrains enacted by the works above.

Strategic knowledge and/of the political

Now we arrive at a challenge: what other kinds of projects are there to be pursued, what other possibilities are there for studying activism, and what do they offer to us? The analysis above is driven by a sense that there are other possible knowledge terrains we might seek to activate, other ways we might seek to study activism or frame our intellectual work in order to respond differently to the question of what and whom knowledge is for under contemporary political circumstances. There are of course many kinds of knowledge being produced about activism other than those produced in relation to the discipline of IR. Perhaps most obviously, there is the material produced by activists themselves, which often seeks to articulate logics and justifications for their projects, to make sense of their own activities, convince others to participate, or set out possible strategies or trajectories for change.[22] These texts tend to combine research and analysis with polemic. They, too, are geared to particular audiences and participate in terrains of knowledge politics. While they provide an important 'snapshot' on movements and are probably the best material to read to get a sense of the varying goals of activists, their self-representations, assumptions, aims, objectives and political discourses, they tend towards the manifesto rather than the sustained analysis and provide a very partial view of the terrain of struggle. In fact, they generally don't even provide a very good idea of the underlying political analysis that guides and shapes the strategies pursued by campaigners, and they certainly don't provide a basis upon which to evaluate their broader effects. There are also approaches which seek to bridge the gap between activist and academic literatures, insofar as they combine analyses of particular movements or activist projects, and indeed are sometimes written by activists, with more recognisably 'academic' research and often quite explicitly political as well as intellectual projects.[23] They tend to be aimed at a broader audience than the IR literature above, and to contain more breadth of analysis and research than the activist manifestos. There are also libraries of work focusing on social movements more generally, often emerging from other disciplinary contexts. All of these contribute in different ways to our understanding of activism, and they each inform in different ways my approach below, but I would also seek to distance my project somewhat from them. This is primarily because I'm less interested in activism as a phenomenon in and of itself, but more in what we can learn from activism and activists to help us think politically today. My interest in this latter question emerges from the two questions that are driving my analysis: my concern with the challenge of conceptualising a progressive political project under contemporary circumstances, and with the role that knowledge production might play in this process. I begin by briefly revisiting my first reference point: the ambivalence of anthropological knowledge.

Interestingly, the study of activism by IR scholars relies upon the development of a relationship between researcher and researched (scholar and activist) that bears some similarity to the relationship between anthropologists and indigenous peoples. It is not, in contrast to the anthropologist/indigenous relationship, shaped by colonial relationships; this is a very important difference. However, it is similar in

---

[22] Book-length examples specifically focused on anti-globalisation activism include: Emma Bircham and John Charlton (eds), *Anti-Capitalism: A Guide to the Movement*, 2nd edn. (London: Bookmarks Publications, 2001); Kevin Danaher and Roger Burbach (eds.), *Globalize This! The Battle Against the World Trade Organization and Corporate Rule* (Monroe, ME: Common Courage Press, 2000); Naomi Klein, *Fences and Windows: Dispatches from the Front Lines of the Globalization Debate* (London: Flamingo, 2002); Colin Hines, *Localization: A Global Manifesto* (London: Earthscan Publications, 2000); Waldon Bello, *Deglobalization: Ideas for a New World Economy* (London: Zed Books, 2002); Veronika Bennholdt-Thomsen, Nicholas Faraclas and Claudia Von Werlof (eds.), *There is an Alternative: Subsistence and Worldwide Resistance to Corporate Globalization* (London and New York: Zed Books, 2001). Of course, much more of this material is available in other formats, particularly on the Internet.

[23] Relevant examples of this kind of literature would be Gills (ed.), *Globalization and the Politics of Resistance*; Michael Edwards and John Gaventa (eds.), *Global Citizen Action* (London: Earthscan Publications, 2001); Joshua Karliner, *The Corporate Planet* (Sierra Club Books, 1997); Robin Broad (ed.), *Global Backlash* (Lanham, MD: Rowman & Littlefield, 2002).

that both sets of researchers seek to understand and represent the meanings created by their subjects: the ideas that shape their actions, the strategies they use to achieve their goals, the networks and structures they create, their effects in the world, their imaginaries of the future. Anthropologists sought such knowledge from indigenous peoples in order to contribute to our understanding of 'culture'; IR scholars might seek knowledge from activists in order to contribute to a broader understanding of 'world politics'. In each case it is a relatively abstracted object constructed through the knowledge process – 'culture' or 'world politics' – that is being 'known'; the assumption is that the process of knowing and the knowledge produced are essentially neutral (or objective), and the beneficiaries of this knowledge are also essentially abstract: humanity in general. This is presumably knowledge that is valid from any perspective, in any context, to any reader. This is not to say that these constructions have no correspondence with or impact on the immediate lives of those studied; quite the contrary. It is to point out the particular dynamic of knowing that has been set up: in both cases the subjects are being studied in order to extract knowledge about something abstracted from them, something bigger than them, other than them. Their insights, practices, or knowledge are being objectified in a particular way. The similarity between the relationships in both cases can be extended in that both kinds of research require observation and engagement, involvement with and participation of the 'subjects' of their research, thus setting up an interesting question about reciprocity. This is highlighted by the fact that in both cases, researchers and researched have essentially different projects: indigenous peoples' cultural practices – and the knowledge of them and embedded in them – were performed for reasons quite unrelated to anthropologists' desires to know about and preserve them. Activists have their own political ambitions, and although they might find the discipline of IR relevant to them at some point, their primary concern is not the development of the discipline. In both cases, then, the activity of the researcher is in some way parasitic on the activity of the researched. However, the effects of parasites are not always negative for the hosts, as we saw in the reference point above; even 'bad old' anthropology has proved to be important to indigenous peoples.

So how might this similarity in the relationship between researcher and researched be relevant to my project here? Part of my answer is already perhaps obvious: at the same time as this kind of research produces a more sophisticated picture of world politics (or culture) in some ways, it also potentially reifies it in ways that render the knowledge useful primarily in reproducing a disciplinary conversation, a shared set of terms and assumptions that frame the subject matter. This keeps the knowledge one step distant from political terrains other than those discussed above. It keeps the knowledge one step distant from the immediate political terrains of the researched, for example. Further, although the research relies upon the generosity of its subjects, it often provides its subjects little agency in the way of shaping the research project to be mutually beneficial, leaving the subject at the mercy of the researcher, and the well-intentioned researcher to hope that the subject might at some point find some value in the research. But should we care? Surely, after all, the broader power relations are different – the projects of researchers in both cases, the projects of the researched, and the power relationships between researcher and researched are importantly very different. Activists haven't complained about this use of their knowledge, and are no doubt happy to have their work recognised and valued.

However, one of the interesting developments in the anthropologist-indigenous relationship might suggest a different possibility inherent in the knowledge of activists, and the knowledge produced through the researcher-subject relationship. Over the last decade, there has been a wide-ranging recognition of the potential value of indigenous knowledge about the world on its own terms. There has also been a recognition of the distinct character of the kind of knowledge they hold, or the terms themselves. This is expressed not only in the scramble to document indigenous knowledge about particular flora and fauna – not least as guides to future pharmaceutical research – but also their knowledge about the ecosystems they live in and how they can be managed to be both productive and ecologically sustainable. This scramble has been characterised both by a recognition of the inherent value of this knowledge, but also an effort to ensure that it is protected, that it is not separated or abstracted from its holders, ostensibly for the benefit of all mankind, but more pragmatically, for the benefit of a relatively few investors. Indigenous peoples themselves appear happy enough to share their knowledge, but only under conditions which ensure that their communities benefit from it in some way.[24] Some anthropologists, particularly ethnobotanists, have assisted them in their efforts to ensure this by coordinating research projects, and structuring these research projects in ways that ensure the communities providing the knowledge see the benefit of their contributions, both through ensuring the results are reproduced in formats that the communities have access to, and by assisting indigenous peoples in securing patent protection of their knowledge, based in part on its uniqueness and potential value. This role contrasts with the earlier role of anthropologists in relation to indigenous peoples, not least in the kind of knowledge sought from indigenous peoples, and the relationship between these knowledges and indigenous peoples themselves. As indigenous peoples have become more aware of the value of their knowledge, and of the kinds of models available to protect it, they have become much more protective of it, frequently demanding a role not only in the distribution of benefits from the knowledge, but in the actual research projects. The politicisation of indigenous knowledge has produced a more constrained research environment for the researcher, and has produced very different kinds of research. Some researchers bemoan the constraints, others are distinctly aware that the research they produce – even as it may not be controlled by them in the way we might expect as academics – is being used by their subjects themselves for their own purposes, contributing to a more general empowerment of these communities in a variety of ways.

What relevance might this have for the study of activist knowledges? One hint emerges from an argument developed by William Chaloupka in relation to environmental social theory.[25] Drawing on the work of Foucault, Chaloupka argues

---

[24] See, for example, Marie Battiste and James (Sa'ke'j) Youngblood Henderson, *Protecting Indigenous Knowledge and Heritage: A Global Challenge* (Saskatoon, Saskatchewan: Purich Publishing, 2000), or Vandana Shiva, *Biopiracy: The Plunder of Nature and Knowledge* (Totnes, Devon: Green Books, in association with The Gaia Foundation, 1998). For a more wide-ranging consideration of the relationship between contemporary researchers and indigenous peoples, see Linda Tuhiwai Smith, *Decolonizing Methodologies*.

[25] William Chaloupka, 'There must be some way out of here: strategy, ethics and environmental politics', in Warren Magnusson and Karena Shaw (eds.), *A Political Space: Reading the Global through Clayoquot Sound* (Minneapolis, MN: University of Minnesota Press, 2003), pp. 67–90.

that to theorise the political today requires that we think strategically, that we not only think about the ethical or structural characteristics of politics, but that we are attentive to its strategic character. On Chaloupka's reading, this requires attentiveness to relations of power, to their particular configurations at specific sites, and that we attune our analyses to these particularities, resisting the impulse towards more 'global' forms of analysis. It is this kind of strategic analysis which is likely to be effective in practice, not only the practice of activists, but also that of intellectuals seeking to understand contemporary relations of power. Chaloupka's analysis is directed towards both activists and environmental social theorists, as he feels that both are too likely to assume the strategic and focus on the ethical, on developing arguments for how society *should* organise its relationships with nature or with each other. He argues that this provides only a very limited approach to take if we wish to think politically today. His context is thus rather precise, but in some ways not that different from my own, in that the terrain I've set out thus far is very much about thinking between the disciplinary practices of IR and the political practices of activists. I want to explore here what it might mean to think and write about the strategic element of politics, and what opportunities this might offer as a model for thinking politically, for producing knowledge that responds to some of the concerns I've raised above.

In Chaloupka's chapter, he uses the example of specific activists' strategic thinking as a way of illustrating more generally what it means to think strategically about politics, and thus to think politically today. Crucially, then, he is not arguing that activists know the way forward, particularly, or even that we need to think like activists, but he is using the strategic knowledge of activists as a model for what it might mean to think politically today, or how the practice of the intellectual might need to change under contemporary circumstances. This intrigues me not least because it resonates with my reading of some of the potential embedded in activist knowledges as a way of knowing the world, and, in turn, of making an issue known to the world through campaigning. However, this kind of knowledge isn't easy to access: it doesn't often emerge in public, where activists are focused on the mobilisation of public opinion or the justification of their activities, and thus tend to rely more on ethical absolutes than strategic analysis. It is more often evident in informal conversations, or behind the scenes planning of campaigns. It is often knowledge that isn't explicitly valued by the holders of it themselves, or is downplayed in conversation: strategising tends to happen behind closed doors; it isn't the kind of knowledge activists like to present publicly. As such it isn't often studied or understood, is rarely taken seriously by academics and generally is kept behind the scenes by activists.[26] While this immediately suggests some challenges in writing directly about the strategic knowledge of activists, this doesn't necessarily imply that it isn't a model or kind of knowledge worth exploring further.

What are the characteristics of this kind of knowledge, though, that might make it worth pursuing further? Here my analysis builds on and extends Chaloupka's

---

[26] Interestingly, this isn't true of Keck and Sikkink's work, which uses activist campaigns precisely as a focal point for understanding activist networks. It is partly because of this that I find their book to be the most rich and provocative of those above, as it is capable of a counter-reading that situates it on a broader political terrain than the one it explicitly frames for itself.

insights, drawing on my own experience of a particular set of activist campaigns.[27] Some of the most obvious, but I think less distinctive, characteristics of this kind of knowledge are its very current, mobile, contingent and creative qualities. In order for activist campaigns to be successful, they must be built on some understanding of issues at stake that is persuasive to their intended audiences, which can be very diverse. This requires that activists have access to up to date research and are able to adapt that research to relevant audiences and contexts: perhaps a lay audience with no understanding of the issues one day, a debate with relevant experts in front of an audience with immediate familiarity with the issues another, policymakers with invested interests and yet a different set of concerns on a third.[28] Each of these contexts requires a set of strategic judgements about not only the background and understanding of the audience, but also its political salience: what kind of understanding of the issues they need in order to be able to act in ways that will enhance the campaign. These judgements rely on a broader reading of political terrains faced by the campaign, and the ability to produce relevant information and adapt it appropriately. The skills to do this are impressive, but the underlying reading of the political terrain – the strategic terrain – is what I think we can learn a great deal from.

In order to plan effective campaigns, activists have to have a complex mapping of the political terrain they face, beginning from where they perceive themselves to be in relation to the issue or problem they seek to address, and moving on to an analysis of how this terrain can be shaped or manipulated: what needs to change – policy, public opinion, political institutions, economic relations – in what combinations; what forces are likely to effect such change; what institutions or people can be pressured, and in what ways. One of the most important characteristics of this kind of knowledge is thus precisely that it is usually quite explicitly situated: it is grounded in a reading of a particular site or condition. It then moves out from this site to a consideration of how relations of power are arrayed, what the world looks like from there, in relation to particular problematics, campaigns, or issues. It thus seeks to negotiate from the particular and into a universal (not *the* universal). Why a universal? Because it seeks to mobilise forces, to produce agreement, to establish universals of particular kinds: definitions of human rights, practices of ecological management, enactments of equality or justice, and so on. Although there is a general tendency in both IR and Politics as disciplines to devalue situated, specific knowledges of this kind in favour of the 'objective', or distanced understanding of

---

[27] I have described one such set of campaigns in 'Encountering Clayoquot: Reading the Political', in Magnusson and Shaw (eds.), *A Political Space*, pp. 25–66. It is probably worth clarifying here that I am referring to specific activist campaigns rather than to general social movements – thus my choice of language throughout the article. Although there has been terrific work produced on social movements, in the context of the argument I am presenting here, a 'social movement' is no less an abstraction than 'international politics', and work that assumes and reproduces these abstractions potentially suffers from the same problematics identified in the previous section. Nonetheless, as suggested by the previous footnote, significant resources for studying activist practices are embedded in this kind of research.

[28] Sometimes they rely on academic research, but often they require research quite different from that produced by academics. Partly as a consequence, over the past few years, entire NGO operations have come to focus almost exclusively on producing this kind of research. Examples include Corporate Watch (http://www.corporatewatch.org). See also the kinds of research reports produced by Greenpeace (http://www.greenpeace.org/international_en/reports/).

the political triumphed in social scientific literatures, significant arguments have been developed by theorists and others that this kind of knowledge has the potential to provide a kind of objectivity that not only addresses some of the major criticisms of the form of objectivity often pursued in the disciplines of Politics and IR, but also provides a more politically engaged and enabling form of knowledge. This argument, made perhaps most famously by Donna Haraway,[29] but in different forms in other literatures, emphasises the ways in which knowledge is always already situated – no knowledge is unmediated – and when the knowledge is explicit about its situation this enables a consideration of its situatedness to inform its interpretation. In the case of the strategic knowledge of activists, for example, this would open the question – and provide a basis upon which to evaluate – of what institutions were relevant to the particular campaign, and why. This in turn raises questions of what political institutions are for, what practices constitute them, what can they effect, and how they work. Thus, for example, if a campaign to change forestry regulations evades the body primarily responsible for making forestry relations – say, the sovereign authority, what does this reveal about the scope and character of the sovereign authority? Embedded in the strategic decision is a political evaluation, an assessment of how the institution does or doesn't work in relation to the issue in question. If we trace the campaign through, we can evaluate the judgement, assess not only whether it was an astute one, but what its broader implications are for understanding the processes and structures of politics, the relations of power that constitute the strategic field of politics. While the situated character of the assessment of the institution or site would obviously not be adequate as an assessment of that institution's political role or possibility – another activist campaign may find it to be crucial in its struggle because of the difference in the political terrain it faces – it does potentially provide us with a way to understand better in practice the relations of power that constitute and frame that institution.

This leads to a second characteristic of strategic knowledge that is important. In Haraway's development of the idea of situated knowledges, she emphasises that it is not only the situatedness that contributes to the form of the objectivity, but the ways in which that situatedness is revealed through encounters with other situated knowledges. In other words, no subject, or situation, is adequate as a site through which to know the world. It is in the encounter with other knowledges that one's vision, or objectivity, is honed, because the 'truth' of any subject can only be revealed from a wide variety of perspectives. So how does this relate to the strategic knowledge of activists? In its situatedness, its movement from the particular to universals, a campaign of course has to encounter and negotiate other particulars, other situated knowledges. Coalitions must be built amongst groups or individuals whose situation may coincide but differ in important ways. Strategies must be planned that maintain unities while respecting the diversities that result from different situations. Compromises must be struck that acknowledge not only shared distant goals, but differential resources, contexts, or abilities to work towards those

---

[29] Donna Haraway, 'Situated Knowledges: The Science Question in Feminism and the Privilege of Partial Perspective', in *Simians, Cyborgs, and Women: The Reinvention of Nature* (New York and London: Routledge, 1991), pp. 183–203.

goals. So, for example, although a particular site or institution may be problematic from the perspective of one group or campaign, the same site or institution might be crucial for another, thus creating a tension over how that institution should be dealt with: should it be strengthened, and if so, how? Can it contribute to both projects? If not, what does this indicate about the compatibility of the projects, or about the adequacy of the institution? In the longer run – and here we begin to get a glimpse of the wealth that this kind of 'objective' evaluation of a political institution might give us – what tensions must an institution negotiate, what forces is it vulnerable to, what kinds of authorities might be produced through it and how would they be constituted? To 'know' a contemporary political institution or site – such as the Forest Stewardship Council, a sovereign state, the World Trade Organisation, a corporation – through a variety of strategic situated knowledges, such as those produced in and through campaigns, would be a valuable thing, providing us not only with a sense of the potentially diverse effects of that institution in the world, but precisely of the relations of power that constitute, enable and are deployed through it. This would be different from assessing, as some of the literatures above seek to, the extent to which these campaigns affect the institution, and in fact it would not necessarily provide a very satisfying answer to that question. It would be a very different kind of knowledge, a knowledge of relations of power, a knowledge that I want to suggest is vital to thinking politically today.

In addition to the insight provided by its situatedness and the interaction with other situated knowledges, there is another characteristic of strategic knowledge that I think potentially renders it valuable. It is a knowledge grounded in both research and experience, experience gained through multiple campaigns – successful and not – and through the campaigning itself, through interactions with others, collective strategising and decision-making, capacity-building. It is also a knowledge that comes to be expressed in the world through a campaign: an effective campaign enacts and changes relations of power; it restructures terrains of power. Campaigns thus constantly seek to, and frequently succeed in, politicising events, actions, institutions, practices; changing how they are perceived, authorised, and enabled, and what their effects are in the world. They create new nodal points or sites of power and authority. They change peoples' perceptions of their worlds and their material circumstances. As such they not only strategise across diverse contexts, spanning the local and the global, but they rearticulate relationships between local and global, creating new political spaces and sites. They link the local and global not only conceptually, but practically; they construct relationships that effectively reorder relations of power. This is by no means to say this is always effective, let alone 'progressive'. It is to say that they are one of the many sites through which the space and time of the political is being reshaped, and they thus express the logics and relations of power through which these reshapings are being effected.[30] Embedded in these kinds of knowledges, then, are perspectives about how relationships between universals and particulars are being rearticulated through contemporary practices.

---

[30] This latter set of effects – the ways in which these practices are reshaping world politics – is what most interests the authors of the texts discussed above. My approach would seek to extend this interest towards an engagement with the strategic reading of the political that shapes activist practice in this regard.

The above is a quick survey of complex promise, admittedly, but I hope it begins to suggest some of the potential insight contained within of the kind of knowledge produced in and through the strategic thinking activists develop in order to forward their campaigns, and how that might contribute to the question of how to think politically today. I don't seek to suggest here that it is a sufficient understanding of the political, but I do think it expresses a kind of understanding of the political today that is importantly lacking in, say, the efforts of many of us to consider how processes of 'globalisation' are reframing political possibility, or to consider how to theorise the political. But my claim here is based on a sense of its promise, of how it can help us to think politically. The final section of the article explores this promise further, both in terms of the broader implications and challenges posed by the development of such approaches to theorising the political.

What knowledge for whom?

The article thus far has focused on illuminating a particular political terrain that I think could productively be engaged as we seek to explore the challenges posed by theorising the political today, and on gesturing towards one way this engagement might proceed. I began with the complex politics of knowledge production enacted in relationships between anthropologists and indigenous peoples, seeking to provide a reference point through which to consider the political relevance of terrains of knowledge production. It may seem to be a story far removed from the 'realities' of research in IR, but it suggests both the necessity and potential of interrogating the consequences – intentional and unintentional – of knowledge production, as well as the tensions embedded in any effort to do so. The texts I engaged in the second section indicate the extent to which the discipline of IR has likewise responded to some of the challenges posed by contemporary developments, revealing the limitations of inherited assumptions about the political inherent in the discipline, and effectively expanding this assumption through documenting a much richer set of political practices. My own work is parasitic upon this: they have opened the discipline in particular ways, but these openings still resist an explicit engagement with the questions of for whom and for what political purpose their knowledge is produced, even as the research is clearly motivated by explicit concerns in this regard. My efforts in the third section are towards identifying a different kind of knowledge, and practice of knowledge production, we might pursue in order to theorise the political, one that may enable us to respond more effectively to the dual challenges I identified at the beginning of the article, about the project of progressive politics and the role of knowledge and knowledge production under contemporary circumstances.

I've argued that there may be considerable potential embedded in the kinds of knowledges produced by activists in their strategising, that these knowledges can help us to think politically, or theorise the political today. Some of the potential embedded in this kind of knowledge is suggested above. In particular, insofar as institutions which in the past have 'bounded' our understanding of politics, such as the sovereign state, no longer provide the same kind of frame for this understanding, we need to open the question more rigorously of where and how we should look in order to understand the political. In other words, rather than looking in familiar places and documenting how changes in political practice are happening in them, beginning from the strategic maps produced by political actors might draw our attention to political practices and institutions where we wouldn't otherwise have looked. They might also help us to understand the relations of power as they are expressed at different sites in ways other than we are used to. Each of these would contribute to an understanding of the political today that might not only be more accurate, but more enabling, providing a better basis for understanding the relations of power through which political possibilities are being constituted.

Much as in Anthropology, those of us who seek to think politically today need to establish emerging conversations that are geared to different audiences in order to respond to changing knowledge/power terrains. Insofar as this kind of knowledge requires confrontation and engagement with other situated knowledges, it might also provide an important ground through which to constitute conversations in ways that could effectively disrupt the eurocentric character of the discipline of IR, or indeed, the political terrain enacted by the modern disciplining of knowledge. If an understanding of a particular institution or site of politics required engagement with a variety of perspectives, with the meaning of that institution in a variety of strategic political contexts, this would reveal the limitations embedded in the relatively narrow perspectives provided by the discipline. In order to understand the emerging practices and forms of international politics, we need to create conversations that will enable us to see the international from and through the particular, without assuming that any particular is necessarily representative of the whole. This kind of knowledge could be contributed to by some kinds of activists, who might be well placed to contribute to an understanding of the respatialisation of the international, to understand how politics is working, and what relations of power are being constituted through it. This in turn has the potential to enable conversations across different understandings and experiences of the international, conversations through which differences might be mediated rather than resolved.

Perhaps the most interesting potential embedded in this model resides in this question of who the knowledge we produce is for. If we pursue collaborative projects with activists, we may find our research practices and questions being significantly shaped by their concerns. I am not, however, recommending that we become 'hired guns' for activist research. As I suggested above, the kinds of research activists need differs in important ways from the kinds of questions we are used to posing, and this is not entirely a bad thing. As we saw in relation to indigenous peoples, it is not always obvious to us what kinds of knowledge we need. One of the interesting things about this approach is that it opens collaborative possibilities with others as well, not least students. In the complex and changing environments of university education today, we are often pulled in very different directions: should we be teaching skills or knowledge? What kinds of knowledge will be useful to our students? As we face agendas of widening participation, or the increased participation of groups previously marginalised from university education, we struggle at times to explain the relevance of the knowledge to which we seek to introduce them. The abstractions of IR, for example, have appeared to former indigenous students of mine to have about as much relevance to them as life on Mars. They were interested in how to help their communities to achieve self-determination; what relevance did regime theory have to this? One of the most effective ways I have found to enable them to find relevance in these debates is precisely to assist them to map strategic terrains of possibility for their aspirations. How? By tracing the routes taken by other communities in struggles they came to see as simultaneously similar to and different from their own; by confronting them with other situated knowledges and helping them to develop their own. Through such a pedagogical exercise, their own sense of the political terrains of possibility expanded. Suddenly they not only saw the relevance of institutions and sites of politics which had previously seemed distant and irrelevant to them, such as the United Nations, the Internet, major environmental groups, or international trade regimes, but also the value of understanding their contexts, functions and impacts. However, the resources to which one has access in order to develop such an understanding are relatively limited, and the interpretative work necessary to set this up as a project and to develop the analysis of the strategic terrain is significant. More research that is attentive to this way of thinking politically would significantly enhance teaching possibilities, potentially enabling the teaching of politics to involve a kind of politicisation and capacity building, to enable students not only to see their situation in the world more clearly, but in a more politically engaged way.

All of this is not to suggest that there aren't significant challenges and dangers posed by this model of knowledge, of course, or that we can be certain of the consequences of the terrains of power it might constitute. There is always a danger in triumphing a partiality of perspective; partial perspectives run the risk of myopia. Further, situated knowledges might challenge and enhance partial perspectives in ways that are enabling, but the reverse can happen as well: engagement with other situated knowledges can produce knowledge that continues to be partial and misleading in important ways. Understanding political institutions and practices in this way could disempower as well as empower, not least as relations of power are rarely neutral, never simple to untangle, and always ambivalent. The rigorous development of this idea of objectivity is thus crucial, not least beginning with the insistence that objectivity requires a broad range of engagement with other situated knowledges. As a criterion through which to evaluate knowledge claims it is no less workable than existing practices of epistemological evaluation; as a teaching practice it poses challenges of comprehensiveness and adequacy.

I began with the story about relationships between anthropologists and indigenous peoples not only as a cautionary tale, or indeed as a guide to a way forward, but as a reference point to consider as we try to think through not only how we produce our knowledge, but who we produce it for, and in what kind of responsibility or political terrain it is embedded. I emphasise the strategic character of activist knowledge not as a 'way out' or 'way forward', but as another reference point to consider as we try to perceive what the characteristics of the knowledge we produce are or should be. I think there are kinds of knowledge produced through these practices that have the potential not only to enhance our understanding of contemporary politics, but to help us think, act and teach politically under contemporary circumstances.

Index